CLASSICS AND CONTEMPORARY THOUGHT

Thomas Habinek, editor

Reading Sappho

Reading Sappho

Contemporary Approaches

 EDITED BY

Ellen Greene

 UNIVERSITY OF CALIFORNIA PRESS

Berkeley   Los Angeles   London

This book is a print-on-demand volume. It is manufactured
using toner in place of ink. Type and images may be less
sharp than the same material seen in traditionally printed
University of California Press editions.

University of California Press
Berkeley and Los Angeles, California

University of California Press, Ltd.
London, England

Library of Congress Cataloging-in-Publication Data

Reading Sappho : contemporary approaches / edited by Ellen Greene.
    p.   cm. — (Classics and contemporary thought : 2)
    Includes bibliographical references and index.
    ISBN 978-0-520-20601-4 (pbk. : alk. paper)
    1. Sappho—Criticism and interpretation. 2. Love poetry, Greek—History
and criticism. 3. Women and literature—Greece. I. Greene, Ellen, 1950–
II. Series.
PA4409.R474 1996
884′.01–dc20   96-13702
                                                              CIP

Printed in the United States of America

The paper used in this publication meets the minimum requirements of
ANSI/NISO Z39.48-1992 (R 1997) (*Permanence of Paper*).

To my father and to the memory of my mother

CONTENTS

ACKNOWLEDGMENTS

I wish to thank Tom Habinek, the series editor, and Mary Lamprech, the Classics editor at the University of California Press, for their enthusiastic support of this project. I am grateful to the friends and colleagues who generously offered advice and support, especially Harriette Andreadis, André Lardinois, Yopie Prins, and my colleagues in the Classics Department at the University of Oklahoma, especially my ever supportive chair, Jack Catlin. I also want to thank Mary Lefkowitz for introducing me to the beauty of Sappho's fragments in a seminar at Berkeley. Finally, I thank Jim Hawthorne for his counsel, for computer expertise, and for his love and friendship.

SERIES EDITOR'S FOREWORD

Thomas Habinek

The series *Classics and Contemporary Thought* seeks to encourage dialogue between classical studies and other fields in the arts, humanities, and social sciences. It is based upon the recognition that each generation puts its own questions to the raw material of the past and is grounded in the conviction that the classical past still has much to say to the contemporary world. In contrast to much conventional classical scholarship which seeks ever more sophisticated or detailed answers to questions inherited from earlier scholarship, works selected for publication in this series use the skills of the classicist to address new issues or pose new questions. Because the literature and art of ancient Greece and Rome are distant from our own experience, their interpretation requires the mediation of specialists. But the obligation of such specialists is to the present as much as to the past. It is, in essence, to make the past available to the present.

The essays collected by Ellen Greene in two volumes entitled *Reading Sappho: Contemporary Approaches* and *Re-Reading Sappho: Reception and Transmission* seek to make the poetry of Sappho more readily available to contemporary readers in a variety of disciplines and from a variety of backgrounds. They do not pretend to represent the totality of modern responses to Sappho. Rather, the essays in *Reading Sappho: Contemporary Approaches* focus on the leading interpretations of Sappho, her context, and her achievement advanced by scholars in the field of classical studies in recent years, while the essays in volume two, *Re-Reading Sappho: Reception and Transmission*, examine reactions to Sappho at different stages of history from antiquity to the twentieth century. The juxtaposition of the two volumes provides a useful contrast between contemporary and earlier approaches to the poetry of Sappho, while illustrating the more general claim that each generation makes of the past what it will. Our encounter with the poetry of Sappho today is shaped both by our own experiences and concerns as inhabitants of a late twentieth century post-industrial society and the interests, attitudes, and preconceptions of previous generations of readers, translators, and scholars. By exploring both we can arrive at a richer understanding of Sappho and perhaps even of ourselves.

The essays in the first volume, *Contemporary Approaches*, reflect some of the broader social and intellectual developments that have characterized the last three decades and provide insight into the reconfiguration of classical studies that has accompanied those changes. The increasing empowerment of women, with the resultant interest in women's history, women's writing, and women's "ways of knowing," has accounted for the focus on Sappho as the first female writer in the Western tradition whose works have survived in any quantity. Sappho has become a test case for both the constructivist and the essentialist views of culture and gender, with scholars placing corresponding emphasis on discontinuities and continuities between her era and our own. As proto-queer, Sappho raises comparable issues with respect to sexual orientation: is she the recovered voice of a long-suppressed lesbian consciousness, or does she instead invite us to consider alternative ways of categorizing human sexual behaviors and emotions? Also running through the volume are conflicting views of the importance of institutions and their impact on the creativity of the individual artist. The earlier of the essays, in particular, advocate a direct experience of Sappho's poetry and emphasize the texture of her language and the specificity of her imagery. While later essays never fully abandon such approaches, they pay more attention to Sappho's poetry as a cultural phenomenon, one shaped by and shaping in turn the myths and rituals of the ancient Greek peoples. In this respect, Sappho studies of the past thirty years have followed the trajectory of literary studies more generally, moving toward more deeply historicized and contexualized interpretations.

Underlying the essays in the second volume, *Reception and Transmission*, is a different set of questions concerning the relationship between past and present. For some of the contributors, the vagaries in accounts of Sappho from antiquity through the twentieth century testify to the unrecoverability of past experience or past literature in any but the most attenuated form. In their versions of the reception of Sappho, each generation is seen to create its own Sappho on the basis of its own needs and interests. For other contributors, exploring past versions of Sappho becomes a way of moving closer to a true account of the poet in her original context—like excavating layers of earth at an archaeological site or unwrapping a mummy. For still others, earlier generations' encounters with Sappho become models for our own potentially fruitful relationship with the past. These conflicting views of the task of the critic or historian are not easily reconciled. What unites them, however, is a sense of Sappho as a figure of potential. While the indeterminacy of certain aspects of Sappho's poetry may, as Glenn Most argues, be due to cultural constraints on the expression of female desire in archaic Greece, it is an uindeniable source of the interest she continually attracts from disparate readers. Indeed, the fragmentary nature of the surviving texts has only increased their value for succeeding generations. For some, it has meant the opportunity to create whatever Sappho they need. For others, the historical irony implicit in the fragmentary preservation of poems of yearning and separation serves as a reminder of the inevitable incompleteness of human knowledge and affection.

One year before the publication of the earliest of the essays contained in these volumes, Sylvia Plath's poem "Lesbos" appeared in her posthumous collection *Ariel*. While Plath's poem mimics the dialogue style, the temporal compression, and the natural imagery that characterizes Sappho's writing, its speaker places herself, rather than the unnamed addressee, in the position of departing lover. Plath's suicide makes it tempting to associate her with Sappho, whom legend describes as leaping to her death in despair over a failed love relationship, but the testimony of Plath's poetry suggests that she belongs instead to a long line of female writers who have found it necessary to reject the authoritative example of Sappho in order to get on with their creative lives. In her case, the rejection of Sappho marks a more widespread generational resistance to the hegemony of the elite classical tradition, a refusal, in Muriel Rukeyser's words, to enter "the populated cold of drawing rooms." In a sense, Plath (along with Rukeyser and others), by denying Sappho's authority, closed the door on one generation's reading of her poems and their significance. What we have before us, in the two volumes compiled by Ellen Greene, is a report in progress on the present generation's encounter with Sappho—through direct experience of her texts, through contextualized interpretations, and through reflection on her meaning for past readers and re-readers.

INTRODUCTION

Ellen Greene

μνάσασθαί τινά φαιμ' ἔτι κἄτερον ἀμμέων
Someone, I say, will remember us in the future.
SAPPHO (FR. 147 L.-P.)

As the earliest surviving woman writer in the West, Sappho stands at the beginning of Western literary history. Despite a reputation that "has been battered more often than it has been burnished,"[1] Sappho has exerted an intense and lasting presence in the Western imagination. Aristotle's comment, however, that Sappho was honored "although she was a woman" speaks to the fact that Sappho's reputation owes at least as much to her gender as to her talent as a love poet.[2] Interest in Sappho, particularly in the scholarly tradition, has often reflected a voyeuristic fascination with the "queerness" of a woman writing poetry in which men are "relegated to a peripheral, of not an intrusive, role."[3] Curiosity about Sappho over the centuries has been fueled by the fragmentary condition of her poems, the lack of any concrete information about her life, and the implications of homoeroticism in her work.

Much of the scholarship on Sappho, until relatively recently, has focused either on textual reconstruction and analysis or on Sappho's sensationalized "biography." In the past thirty years, however, with the feminist wave of the 1960s and 1970s, Sappho's poetry has begun to be reevaluated. Like so many other women writers who have been gradually brought out of their literary closets, Sappho has resurfaced—not as the hysteric or "schoolmistress" of previous generations, but as a powerful and influential voice in the Western cultural tradition. With Giuliana Lanata's article, "Sappho's Amatory Language," originally published in 1966 and appearing here in English for the first time, Sappho scholarship turns decidedly away

---

1. Catherine Stimpson, series editor's foreword to *Fictions of Sappho*, by DeJean.
2. Arist. *Rh.* 1389b12.
3. DeJean, "Fictions of Sappho" 790.

1

from the obsession to reconstruct Sappho's biography and to rationalize away the homoerotic aspects of her poetry.

Edgar Lobel and Denys Page's 1955 commentary on Sappho marked a turning point in Sappho scholarship. Their book, *Poetarum Lesbiorum Fragmenta*, with a complete text and commentary on Sappho's fragments, became the definitive edition of Sappho's poems and, to a large extent, resolved the philological issues of textual reconstruction. Within a decade or so of their commentary, in the late 1960s and early 1970s, an efflorescence of literary and contextual criticism emerged in which scholars began to read Sappho's poetry for its literary content and its relation to literary and mythical tradition. Changes in Sappho criticism, moreover, coincided with general changes in classical scholarship; in the 1970s efforts to assimilate methodologies from other branches of literary and cultural studies began to appear. In addition, feminist scholarship and, more recently, gender theory and criticism have provoked discussion about how Sappho's gender has both shaped her poetic discourse and influenced the social context of her poetry.

This book is the first anthology devoted to scholarly studies of Sappho's work. Significantly, it represents the fruit of two and a half decades of a burgeoning corpus of Sappho scholarship—due largely to the serious study of women in antiquity and to inquiries into Greek and Roman sexual attitudes and practices.[4] The aim of this collection is to draw well-deserved attention to Sappho's importance as a poet *and* to present the diverse and often contradictory critical approaches toward Sappho that have become the hallmark of Sappho scholarship. The book divides into four section: "Language and Literary Context," "Homer and Oral Tradition," "Ritual and Social Context," and "Women's Erotics." These categories represent a simplified organization of a range of positions that often overlap and are more diverse than such categorization might suggest. They are meant to guide the reader through the major strands in Sappho scholarship and to provide a sense of the lively debate and competing critical positions within Sappho studies that have continued to engage scholars over the last several decades.

The opening section of the collection, "Language and Literary Context," illustrates the first wave of essays (after Page and Lobel) that focus on literary content in Sappho's poetry: that is, Sappho's use of literary conventions

---

4. See especially Cantarella, *Bisexuality in the Ancient World;* Foley, ed., *Reflections of Women in Antiquity;* Foucault, *The History of Sexuality,* vol. 2, *The Use of Pleasure;* Foucault, *The History of Sexuality,* vol. 3, *The Care of the Self;* Halperin, Winkler, and Zeitlin, eds., *Before Sexuality;* Peradotto and Sullivan, eds., *Women in the Ancient World;* Richlin, ed., *Pornography and Representation in Greece and Rome;* and Snyder, *The Woman and the Lyre.*

(topoi) and poetic devices, including elements of ritual language, the assimi-
lation of oral modes of discourse, and the relationship of Sappho's poetry to a
literary and cultural tradition. The first essay by Lanata is one of the earliest
articles to focus closely on Sappho's erotic language within the context of
both the epic and lyric traditions.

In a similar vein, Mary Lefkowitz's 1973 article, "Critical Stereotypes
and the Poetry of Sappho," shows how traditional biographical approaches
to Sappho fail to do justice to her poetry. Lefkowitz objects to early<-
>particularly Victorian—views of Sappho's work as the product of an "ab-
normal" female psychology. Lefkowitz's article takes issue with the tendency
of male critics to assume that the art of women writers is merely an emotional
outpouring indicative of psychological disturbance or "deviance." She argues that Sappho's poetry is not, as Denys Page avers, "without artifice,"
but rather that Sappho's poetry shows a sophisticated and ingenious use of
traditional poetic figures and literary topoi.

While Lanata and Lefkowitz locate Sappho within an archaic literary
tradition, Gregory Nagy's essay focuses on the mythical tradition as a way
of contextualizing her poetry. Nagy's essay "Phaethon, Sappho's Phaon,
and the White Rock of Leukas: 'Reading' the Symbols of Greek Lyric"
examines the origins of the Greek myths of Phaethon and Phaon that led
to the famous Sappho-Phaon story. Nagy looks for mythological parallels
in the various accounts of the story primarily in archaic Greek lyric, Homer,
and a fourth-century Greek play, *The Leukadia*, by Menander. Nagy analyzes
the symbolism of the White Rock and its complex relationship to both the
mythical figure of Phaon and to Sappho—as both mythical figure and poet.

Charles Segal explores yet another facet of Sappho's use of literary
convention. His article, "Eros and Incantation: Sappho and Oral Poetry,"
investigates the ways Sappho's poetic language embodies modes of discourse
used in oral poetry. Segal examines the "ritualizing, incantatory" qualities
of Sappho's language and investigates the extent to which Sappho's poems
reflect personal experience expressed within a social and ritual context.
Segal articulates the problem that we, as modern readers, often encounter
when we try to draw the line between the personal and the conventional
in Sappho's poetry:[5]

> The total aesthetic experience produced by [Sappho's poems] results from a
> coming together of the two levels of communication, the ritual and the private.
> It is here, at these points of juncture between the social, outward-facing, public

5. See Page duBois's new book, *Sappho Is Burning*, which discusses how Sappho is an
important figure in the development of the history of subjectivity in the West. DuBois sees
Sappho's fragments as offering "aesthetic, philosophical, and ideological alternatives to the
Eurocentric notions that Western humanism has so long revered" (26–27).

dimension and techniques of her art and their private, more personal, less ritualistic aspect, that Sappho especially exemplifies her originality and artistry. It is also where she is most difficult for the modern sensibility to grasp.

Indeed, the relationship between a "private" voice and a "public" discourse in Sappho's poetry is extremely vexed, since archaic Greek culture is thought to be far more communal and certainly more reliant on oral forms of communication than is our own culture.

An important dimension in investigating the oral qualities of Sappho's verse is the interrogation of Sappho's use of Homer. The second section, "Homer and the Oral Tradition," includes Page duBois's essay "Sappho and Helen" and John Winkler's essay "Gardens of Nymphs: Public and Private in Sappho's Lyrics"—essays that focus specifically on Sappho's use of Homeric myths and formulas. DuBois argues that Sappho's reinterpretation of the Homeric Helen overturns many of the male assumptions embedded in Homeric narrative, and that Sappho's "reading" of the Helen myth reflects a *feminine* consciousness that emphasizes Helen as a *subject* of her own desires, rather than as an object of male desire.

Winkler's essay also looks at Sappho's use of Homer as a way of "allowing us, even encouraging us, to approach her consciousness as a woman and poet reading Homer." Winkler explores the tension between the "public" and "private" character of Sappho's poems by investigating how Sappho's use of Homeric material reflects the encounter between her private, woman-centered world and male public culture. Through an examination of fragments 1, 2, 16, and 31, Winkler explores Sappho's revision of Homeric myth and argues that in Sappho's appropriation of the "alien" text of Homer, she reveals the implicit inadequacy of the exclusion and denigration of women in Homer and thus, in a sense, revises traditional "male" readings of Homer.

A related area of inquiry in recent Sappho criticism focuses on the performative and cultural context of Sappho's poetry. The section "Ritual and Social Context" includes essays that investigate the ritual and social purposes Sappho's erotic poems might have served in her community on Lesbos. This area of scholarship invites the most speculation about Sappho since we have little or no conclusive evidence for the social conditions on Lesbos at the time Sappho composed her poems. The scholarly debate about Sappho's audience and the performative context of her poems focuses on questions concerning the relationship between Sappho's expression of personal passions and the public, social function of her art, and how participation in a communal cultural discourse may be reconciled with Sappho's distinct, highly individuated voice—a voice that seems to articulate "private" feelings so compellingly.

An aspect of the debate about Sappho's audience centers on the traditional dichotomy between choral and monodic poetry. Gordon Kirkwood's 1974 study, *Early Greek Monody*, assumes that Sappho's voice is primarily monodic, that is, spoken as a solo voice expressing emotions of an exclusively personal and intimate nature. Similarly the eminent scholars Bruno Snell and C. M. Bowra assume that "the distinction between choral lyric and monody is fundamental." Thus, Bowra writes of Sappho's "remarkable intimacy and candour," and Snell refers to Sappho's "deeply emotional confessions."[6] Many recent scholars have contested the strict division between choral lyric and monody, arguing that although Sappho speaks in the first person, the "I" cannot possibly denote merely private consciousness, but rather suggests an embodiment of the shared or communal.

Claude Calame's article, "Sappho's Group: An Initiation into Woman-hood," the first essay in the section, "Ritual and Social Context," addresses the debate in Sappho criticism about the modern construction of a *thiasos*, a group of woman with ritual and cultic functions to which Sappho has often been linked as a sort of leader. Calame looks at Sappho's own fragments as well as other archaic Greek fragments for evidence of the existence of a Lesbian "circle" or group whose female members may have been affiliated with one another through the bonds of friendship and erotic love. Further, Calame examines the ways in which such a "circle" may have functioned. He argues that there is evidence to suggest that Sappho gathered groups of young woman around her as both students and companions. Musical and erotic instruction in the Lesbian "circle," Calame maintains, were crucial elements in preparing young girls for their roles as adult, married women. However, Calame argues against the view of Sappho as a "schoolmistress"; his article emphasizes that the education imparted to the young women of Sappho's group, through the performance of song and cult acts, was entirely ritualized in both form and content.

Judith Hallett's article, "Sappho and Her Social Context: Sense and Sensuality," continues the debate raised by Segal about the relationship between Sappho's expression of personal passions and the public, social function of her art. Hallett's discussion of Sappho's social context, however, raises the question about what the social purpose and public function Sappho's poetry may have been in the context of a community of women operating in a socially segregated society. Hallett's essay is one of the earliest to consider Sappho's gender as a crucial factor in the "public" dimension of her poetry. Hallett argues that Sappho's erotic verses may be viewed as an institutional force, a social vehicle *for women* designed to impart sensual

---

6. Bowra, *Greek Melic Poetry* 178; Snell, *The Discovery of the Mind* 52–59.

awareness and confidence in young females "on the threshold of marriage and maturity."

In responding to Hallett's article, Eva Stehle's essay, "Romantic Sensuality, Poetic Sense: A Response to Hallett on Sappho," fuels the debate over the public and private in Sappho by taking issue with Hallett's (and other's) views about the dominance of a social function for Sappho's poetry. Stehle argues that the private emotional reality in Sappho's poems is paramount, superseding any function Sappho's poetry might have as an "institutional force." Moreover, she maintains that Sappho's "strong personal focus and introspective quality" would be subversive to a public celebratory setting. Taking fragment 94 as her example, Stehle argues that Sappho's poetic expressions of desire in an atmosphere "of segregation in sensuous surroundings" suggest an alternate female world quite apart from the assumptions of male public culture—assumptions associated with competition and domination.

In contrast to Eva Stehle's view, in a new essay entitled "Who Sang Sappho's Songs?" André Lardinois suggests the possibility that all Sappho's poems were chorally performed. Lardinois questions the traditional distinctions between choral and monodic poetry and argues that Sappho's poems ought to be regarded chiefly as choral in nature rather than as personal or autobiographical forms of expression. Lardinois specifically addresses the question of *how* Sappho's songs were sung. Although he acknowledges that we have very little information about the actual performance of Sappho's poems, Lardinois examines a number of the major fragments and shows how they can be interpreted as being performed "with the help of choruses." His analysis focuses primarily on the pluralistic voice in Sappho (the use of "we"), references and allusions in the poems that suggest a communal atmosphere, and the use of poetic topoi common in choral songs. Although Lardinois points out the many ways in which Sappho's poetry is similar to that of her male counterparts, at the end of his essay he acknowledges the possibility of differences in tone and subject matter between Sappho and male poets. He sees the difference, as he says, not "as a difference between a public (male) and a private (female) world (Stehle, Winkler, Snyder)," but as a "difference between two distinct public voices."

The next section in the collection, "Women's Erotics," explicitly takes up the issue of gender difference. Feminist approaches in recent Sappho criticism question the extent to which Sappho's poems present a woman specific discourse that secures a female perspective within male-dominated discursive systems. A number of essays in this volume argue that Sappho assimilates conventional social and literary formulas to a woman's consciousness. Stehle, Williamson, Skinner, and I argue that although Sappho utilizes many conventional formulas of archaic Greek poetry, her poems, nonetheless, speak a different language than that of her male counterparts and produce a significantly different version of desire—one that is markedly nonhierarchical or, as Marilyn Skinner puts it, is "conspicuously nonphallic."

Skinner's essay "Woman and Language in Archaic Greece, or, Why Is Sappho a Woman?" investigates the degree to which Sappho's poetry represents a distinct creative tradition that transcends the "androcentric cultural categories" that dominate the patriarchal discourses of ancient Greece. Sappho's poems, Skinner argues, offer a woman-centered perspective that not only perpetuates women's culture but also reflects a "nonnormative" subject position for women that "defiantly locates itself against patriarchy." Moreover, Skinner theorizes that the nonhierarchical, nonphallic model of desire represented in Sappho's fragments provided an alternative cultural norm to both men and women, an alternative that allowed women to claim an authentic subject position and men to "escape from the strict constraints of masculinity."

Eva Stehle suggests, in "Sappho's Gaze: Fantasies of a Goddess and Young Man," that Sappho's poems can be read as implied criticism of a patriarchal value system. Stehle makes use of recent work in feminist theory on how the erotic gaze promotes gender hierarchies and preserves women's object status. She argues that in describing "the effect of the gaze on the gazer," Sappho departs from the erotic poetry of her male counterparts by breaking down "the opposition between viewer and viewed that is created by the gaze." In other words, Sappho uses the gaze not to objectify the one desired, but to "dissolve hierarchy." In my essay, "Apostrophe and Women's Erotics in the Poetry of Sappho," through readings of Fragments 1 and 94, I extend Stehle's argument in order to focus on how Sappho's use of apostrophe creates a model of eroticism that is both intersubjective and nonhierarchical.

Anne Carson, in her essay "The Justice of Aphrodite in Sappho Fr. 1," interprets fragment 1 (the "Hymn to Aphrodite") in a way that demonstrates how the poem reiterates the traditions of Greek erotic poetry. In particular, Carson argues that Sappho presents a version of desire in accord with the hierarchical mode of eroticism prevalent in male homoerotic relations. Further, Carson's effort to integrate Sappho's poem not only with the conventions of archaic lyric but also with "archaic currents of thought" militates against the view (taken by Stehle, Williamson, and myself) that Sappho's mode of discourse represents female homoerotic desire with its own symbolic systems and conventions.

In her essay, "Sappho and the Other Woman," Margaret Williamson contends in contrast that Sappho's fragments produce a version of erotic experience that defies cultural norms. Through an examination of the subject positions mapped out in Sappho's poetry, she, like Stehle, argues that Sappho's erotic discourse differs considerably from that of male writers for whom "the only form self–other relationships seem to take is that of struggle that will end in the mastery of one over the other."

As these essays show, the last several decades of Sappho studies have been enormously productive. It is my hope that this volume will *further* stimulate the growing field of scholarship on Sappho, and help to situate Sappho as an important voice in the Western literary tradition. Moreover, this collection will, I hope, contribute to the ever-expanding project of recovering women writers and attending to their roles in literary and cultural history. It is my belief that as this project goes forward, Sappho will remain an authorizing and enduring presence. As the first female literary voice in the Western tradition, Sappho's poetry can lay claim to a special, originary status within that tradition. Despite the vastly diverse responses to and interpretations of Sappho's poems, readers of Sappho throughout the ages have, nonetheless, recognized in her eloquent expressions of desire the paradoxical conjuncture of pain and pleasure, bitterness and sweetness that lies at the heart of erotic experience. As Anne Carson puts it, "It was Sappho who first called eros 'bittersweet.' No one who has been in love disputes her."[7]

7. See Carson, *Eros the Bittersweet* 3.

PART I

Language and Literary Context

ONE

Sappho's Amatory Language

Giuliana Lanata

Translated by William Robins

At times, Sapphic poetry—most particularly the amatory lyric of Sappho—has been injured by its own extensive success. It has come about, in other words, that, confronted by such an imposing phenomenon, ancient as well as modern criticism has abdicated its proper nature as an interpreter in order to surrender itself to the "ardent" and "ineffable" tones of dithyrambic exaltation, of mawkish sentimentality, of decadent *sensiblerie*. A patient (and petulant) excerptor of the vast specialist literature on the topic could compile without too much difficulty a small anthology of bad taste within the field of so-called imitative criticism. Even a critic as sober, moderate, and cautious as D. L. Page let himself take part at one point, introducing in two pages of his *Sappho and Alcaeus* a description of the "society" of Lesbos fit for the pen of J. A. Symonds, which seems directed less by any kind of critical necessity than by the "Mediterranean" myths of a nineteenth-century Englishman: "exquisite gardens, where the rose and hyacinth spread perfume; pine-tree-shadowed coves, when they might bathe in the calm of a tideless sea."[1] Welcome, then, are the calls for methodical sobriety put forward by Max Treu at the beginning of the brief interpretive essay included in his edition of Sappho,[2] and according to which Page's book is, in fact, to such a great degree informed.

From another angle, due to an incomprehension already current in antiquity about the historicosocial context within which to place Sappho's poetry for a correct evaluation of its contents, criticism took the road of

This essay was originally published as "Sul linguaggio amoroso di Saffo," *Quaderni urbinati di cultura classica*, no. 2 (1966) 63–79.

1. Page, *Sappho and Alcaeus* 140–41.
2. Treu, ed., *Sappho* 137–38.

11

a more or less sensitive or fervent or scandalized denunciation, or more often a hazy and evasive psychologism of a kind that strove (and strives, for this is not a closed chapter) to illustrate "amorous fullness," to reconstruct the interior history of a "beautiful soul." In this choir there is no lack of voices, animated by chivalric indignation, that in response to any "calumny" point to the "skilled housewife"[3] in Sappho, the "madame landlady" for some pensioned Edwardian, a second Madame de Maintenon, the "lady professor" of literature and belles-artes. Nor does it seem that any better service has been rendered to the interpretation of Sappho's poetry by those modern critics who have made a great display of the latest Freudianisms.

Thus whoever today would reconsider in its complexity what is usually improperly called *Sapphofrage* is tempted to repeat, albeit with amused irony and with different motivation, some words that Gunther Zuntz wrote in his tastefully disdainful Latin: "Philologorum in mores inquisituro luculentam sane hae interpretandi rationes praebent materiam: ad Sappho nihil pertinet."[4] If, among other things, it is true that "the eternal feminine" is exalted more willingly in criticism written, for example, in Italian, in criticism written in German hints of *südliche Glut* (southern passion) frequently appear.

Naturally, there have been many espousals of positions that were supposed to "de-dramatize" the question and bring it back to more appropriate terms. So, for example, Erich Bethe in an article that remains fundamental[5] (but also Beloch, DeSanctis, and Marrou, to mention some names) has clarified very lucidly the place that homosexual love occupied in archaic Greek society—in Sparta as well as in Chalcis, in Lesbos as well as in Crete, within both male and female communities or associations—where it constituted one of the bonds and at the same time established itself as an important pedagogic instrument. Typical of this historical moment in Greek civilization is the tendency to consider the learning process as the work of a careful and overshadowing vigilance exercised on the ἐρώμενος by the ἐραστής, who for his own sake is pledged to make himself worthy of his role as a guide. However, the idealization of this picture as wrought by the idyllic or "prude" moralism of various later sources should not blind our eyes to the reality of the amorous relations to which archaic lyric attests with complete naturalness.

As far as regards Sappho in particular, the question has been restudied recently by Reinhold Merkelbach, who in a long article, "Sappho und ihr Kreis," reexamined the internal and external evidence that enable a reconstruction, around the poetess, of a *Mädchenbund*, a circle held together by communal life and by sacral bonds, within which they could (no, indeed, they had

---

3. See *POxy.* 2506.48.III.42–43, and Treu, "Neues über Sappho" 10–11.
4. Zuntz, "De Sapphus carminibus" 88–89.
5. Bethe, "Die dorische Knabenliebe."

to) establish those particular erotic tensions that the poetry of Sappho reveals. Unfortunately, behind this *Mädchenbund* the still-unexorcised specter of the *Mädchenpensionat* rises again in some way, even if *cum grano salis*, and Merkelbach avoids a direct engagement through comparisons with the nature of Sapphic eros, to which he quickly nods in a note that proves sybilline to me.[6]

On the other hand it is to say the least curiously indiscrete, and not generally justified by language parallel to ephebic poetry, for Page to presume to find in the fragments of Sappho any "evidence for practice" beyond evidence "for inclination" for homosexual love.[7] For if, for example, Solon or Anacreon can be very explicit,[8] yet in the ephebic collection that closes the compilation of Theognis (and where Sapphic imitation is widely evident, as I will discuss more thoroughly below) one finds rather rare "evidence for practice" in the sense intended by Page. Moreover, and just to ironize a little in such a "compromising" situation, Sappho certainly did not mean to provide a kind of sociological documentation on the sentimental and sexual initiation of the girls on Lesbos in the manner of Margaret Mead, or like that furnished so prolixly by Mary McCarthy concerning the girls at Vassar College.

And, it might be said in parentheses, one needs to proceed cautiously here as in any analogous case of using fragments to reconstruct a "biography" that might otherwise run the risk of being "romanticized." For example, in fragment 121[9] it is certain, it seems to me, that the lady speaking in the first person, rejecting love or marriage with a younger man, is not Sappho. K. J. Dover has recently urged a salutary caution in interpreting the fragments of archaic lyric where the poet seems to speak *in propria persona*, citing rather conveniently fragment 10.1 of Alcaeus, ἔμε δείλαν, ἔμε παίσαν κακοτάτων πεδέχοισαν, where the feminine form shows that the person who speaks is not Alcaeus.[10] The problem of the right age for marriage appears in a typical Hesiodic sequence (*Op.* 695 ff.) and recurs with frequency in Greek poetry, as is shown by, among others, the τμῆμα of Stobaeus who cites the Sapphic fragment (4.22.5; IV pp. 542 ff. Hense). Likewise in the case of Sappho, who gives a joking variation of it in her famous fragment 105, one ought to think rather of an epithalamic motif.

I therefore would not like to investigate here the "amorous life" of Sappho or the "life" of the *thiasos*, but would rather like to attempt a reconstruction,

6. Merkelbach, "Sappho und ihr Kreis" 3 n. 2.

7. Page, *Sappho and Alcaeus* 144.

8. Respectively fr. 12.2 D. and fr. 407 P. (43 Gent.)

9. Unless indicated otherwise, Sappho and Alcaeus are cited according to the edition of Lobel and Page.

10. Dover, "The Poetry of Archilochus" 206 ff.

which will be based above all on data provided by the language (given that others have already clarified the historicosocial assumptions) of the environment and conditions in which a very specific poetic experience, though by no means unique in the archaic Greek world, matured. The problem of the name with which to define the Sapphic circle does not seem truly essential. It could be called θίασος, it could perhaps be called ἑταιρεία; ἑταίρα recurs three times in Sappho (frs. 126, 142, 169), and there is also the masculine συνέταιρος in the fragment on the marriage of Hector and Andromache (44.5) with which she to a certain degree can make available some "concrete experience"[11] of her own time even in the description of a mythic past. Fragment 160, "I shall now sing for my ἔταιραι this beautiful song of joy"[12] —τάδε νῦν ἑταίραις ταῖς ἔμαις τέρπνα κάλως ἀείσω—is a precious testimony of the precise audience to whom Sapphic poetry was originally addressed. Nor do I know if it is simply a coincidence that the feminine συνεταιρίς, attested only once in Greek, appears in Corinna,[13] a woman poet in whom the influence of Sappho is evident in various aspects.

In another Sapphic fragment (150) the expression μοισοπόλων οἰκία (ο δόμος) occurs: "It is not right that there should be a lament in a house of μοισοπόλοι," οὐ γὰρ θέμις ἐν μοισοπόλων †οἰκίαι / θρῆνον ἔμμεν'. Our source, Maximus of Tyre, affirms that Sappho here speaks to her daughter Cleis, so there would be no reason to think of other "boarders" of the οἰκία. But, by speaking of herself as μοισοπόλος, I do not think Sappho is using simply some generic term for designating herself as a "poetess,"[14] but shows herself belonging within a cultic association whose members count among their bonds that of the cult of the Muse; μοισοπόλος occurs with precise cultic significance in an epigraphic document described by Franz Poland.[15] But the divinity that appears with typical prominence in the fragments of Sappho is, as is well known, Aphrodite, who was also, for example, worshiped at Athens and at Ephesus with the appellation ἑταίρα; for ἑταῖροι and ἑταῖραι, or as Athenaeus attests, συνήθεις καὶ φίλαι of noble lineage, were joined together in her name.[16] If the constant copresence in Sappho's poetry of

11. Mazzarino, "Per la storia" 41.

12. If ἑταίραις ταῖς ἔμαις is in fact dative. Even if the conjectural τέρποισα of Sitzler, for example, is accepted, the testimony remains fundamentally the same.

13. *AP* 7.7 = fr. 5.7 D.

14. The term occurs with its meaning now faded in Eur. *Alc.* 445 and *Phoen.* 149, and a pair of times in the *AP*.

15. Poland, *Geschichte des griechischen Vereinswesens* 206–7; *IG* 7.2484 (second century B.C.E.).

16. For Athens, see Ath. 17.571c = Apollod. fr. 244 B 112 *FGrH*. For Ephesus, Ath. 13.573a = Eualc. fr. 418.2 *FGrH*. See also Hesych. Phot., s.v. Ἑταίρας (Ἀφρ.) ἱερόν; and Dümmler, s.v. "Aphrodite," *PW* 1.2:2734.

the Charites and the Muses (whose ties with Aphrodite are attested ever since the Homeric hymn to Apollo)[17] shows that Sapphic eroticism, however intense and "ineluctable,"[18] is nevertheless free from the mysterious and relentless frenzy that, for example, Eros connotes in the verses of Ibycus,[19] and if in ode 1 Aphrodite appears in order to temper rather than to stir up the "aches of the heart," then the choice of Aphrodite as the divinity typically appropriate and almost unique among the Sapphic circle could not have been fortuitous. Page's anxiousness to deny that Sappho might have had an official role as a "priestess"[20] hinders him from then giving a positive evaluation of the place occupied by this divinity in her poetry.

Now, except for a fragment where she is invoked as goddess of the sea (fr. 5), Aphrodite is, in Sappho's poetry as in Homer or in the *Hymns*, the goddess who *subdues* with the torment and passion of love.[21] And if ode 1 could make us think of a particular and personal type of Sapphic religion, the fragment from the Florentine ostracon (2) brings us back to a precise cultic environment, as is guaranteed by phrases such as the ἔναυλον ἄγνον of lines 1–2, and so also to a precise occasion or circumstance in which Sappho and the ἔταιραι of her circle celebrated the divinity to whom their existence was most closely linked, in the space sacred to her and in the fullness of her attributes.[22]

Merkelbach has underlined some coincidences, in elements improperly called "descriptive," between the fragment from the ostracon and fragment 5 of Ibycus, where the description of an "untouched garden," where Cidonian apples blossom irrigated by flowing waters, serves as a backdrop to the frenzy of Eros.[23] Yet rather than to the "gardens of the nymphs" of which Merkelbach thinks, I believe that fragment 2 of Sappho refers

17. Ll. 189–96. For Muses, Graces, and Aphrodite within the sphere of ephebic eros, see e.g. Plut. *Amat.* 758c.

18. Fr. 130: Ἔρος ... ἀμάχανον.

19. Fr. 5.10 P.: αἴσσων παρὰ Κύπριδος ἀζαλέαις μανίαισιν ἐρεμνὸς ἀθαμβής.

20. Page, *Sappho and Alcaeus* 126–28.

21. Δάμνα, fr. 1.3; δάμεισα ... δι' Ἀφροδίταν, fr. 102.2. For δαμνάω in this sense, cf. Hom. *Il.* 14.199, 316; Hes. *Theog.* 122.

22. At this point I ought to insert a retraction of what I wrote in "L'ostracon fiorentino" 87. I still believe that there are good probabilities for maintaining that the ode of the ostracon ended with l. 16, and that in the text of Ath. 463e the τούτοις τοῖς ἑταίροις ἐμοῖς τε καὶ σοῖς following the Sapphic citation should be referred to the συνιοῦσι καὶ ἡμῖν of 463c, and does not constitute a free citation from a succeeding strophe of Sappho. But it does now seem to me likely that when Athenaeus introduced the mention of ἑταῖροι he might have had present the earlier part of the ode, which is unknown to us, and reproduced its situation freely; and what I then said in haste concerning the "intimate and personal" character of the religion of Sappho now seems to me entirely unsatisfactory.

23. Merkelbach, "Sappho und ihr Kreis" 26–27.

to a clearly Aphrodisian environment, where elements that in other contexts and other periods would be "landscapist" have a cultic meaning that has already been emphasized by Bruno Gentili with particular reference to the amatory language in Anacreon's poetry and archaic lyric, where the mention of apples or roses always alludes to the presence or power of Aphrodite.[24]

Besides fragments 4 and 5 K of the *Cypria*, already cited by Gentili, where the "spring flowers"—crocuses hyacinths violets roses narcissi lilies—embellish the clothes and form the crowns that adorn the φιλομμειδὴς Ἀφροδίτη and her ἀμφίπολοι, Nymphs and Charites, I would like to recall the passage of the Διὸς ἀπάτη[25] where, to conceal the embrace of Hera and Zeus, the earth miraculously makes fresh grass and flowers of lotus and crocus and hyacinth shoot up under them. And also in Hesiod's *Theogony* (l. 279), Poseidon possesses one of the Hesperides "on a soft field and in the middle of spring flowers," ἐν μαλακῶι λειμῶνι καὶ ἄνθεσι εἰαρινοῖσιν, a passage to which lines 9–10 in fragment 2 of Sappho bear comparison: "there a field where the horses graze blossoms with spring flowers," ἐν δὲ λείμων ἱππόβοτος τέθαλε / ἠρίνοισιν ἄνθεσιν.[26] That, besides the apples and roses of line 6, the "field where the horses graze," λείμων ἱππόβοτος, ought also to be linked to a sacral Aphrodisian environment, and gains confirmation not only from the image of the "horses of Aphrodite" of the girls ready for love in a new fragment of Anacreon,[27] but also from a quatrain of the ephebic collection of Theognis (ll. 124 ff.), where the commentators generally refer to Anacreon, although here, as is often the case, the most notable similarities are with Sappho:

Παῖ, σὺ μὲν αὕτως ἵππος, ἐπεὶ κριθῶν ἐκορέσθης,
αὖθις ἐπὶ σταθμοὺς ἤλυθες ἡμετέρους
ἡνίοχόν τε ποθῶν ἀγαθὸν λειμῶνά τε καλόν
κρήνην τε ψυχρὴν ἄλσεά τε σκιερά.

O youth, like a horse, since you are sated with fodder, turn again to my stables, desiring a good rider and a beautiful field and a fresh spring and shady woods.

Here, besides the coincidences of κρήνην ψυχρήν / ὕδωρ ψῦχρον (Sappho 2.5) and ἄλσεα σκιερά / ἐσκίαστ' (Sappho 2.7), we can observe λειμῶνα τε

---

24. Gentili, ed., *Anacreon* 184 ff. Besides the passages cited there, compare also Bacchyl. 17.114–16; Hesych. s.v. Ἄνθεια· Ἀφροδίτη, παρὰ Κνωσίοις.

25. *Il.* 14.347 ff.

26. The conjecture ἠρίνοισιν, which, a few years ago in "L'ostracon fiorentino," I accepted only with some reluctance given the hopeless paleographic situation of the text, now seems less unlikely to me.

27. 346.8–9 P. = 60 Gent.; see also Gentili's commentary on pp. 183–87.

καλόν / ἐν δὲ λείμων κτλ. (Sappho 2.9). The αὖθις will also be noted, which corresponds to the typical δηὖτε with which Sappho indicates with a nearly formulaic insistence the recurrence of a well-known situation. And I would also like to note that a word so rarely attested in Greek outside of medical literature as κῶμα, which is in line of the ostracon fragment to indicate the drowsiness that falls from the rustling leaves, appears significantly in the above-cited section of the Διὸς ἀπάτη (l. 359)[28] to indicate the drowsiness that welcomes Zeus after his embrace with Hera.

Fragment 2, where all the elements allow us to reconstruct a precise sacral environment where everything defines Aphrodite as the goddess who bestows love (and already Page, referring to fr. 96.26 ff., Ἀφροδίτα / καμ[ ]νέκταρ ἔχευ ἀπὺ / χρυσίας, underlined the recurrence and typicality of the situations that prescribe poems of this kind in the Sapphic environment),[29] can open our understanding for all those fragments, which it is not necessary to cite here in their entirety, where Sappho represents herself and the girls of her circle who adorn themselves and enjoy the flowers sacred to the goddess. In particular in line 11 of fragment 94, to which I will turn again later, Sappho recalls for a girl who is leaving part of the κάλα of their past life, the crowns of violets and roses, the garlands of flowers, and immediately afterward also the "satisfaction of love's longing" (ll. 21–23); and here Page has clearly shown that the ἐξίης πόθο[ν of line 23 can mean nothing but "you freed yourself from your desire by giving it satisfaction," as the analogy with the Homeric ἐξ ἔρον εἶναι reveals.[30] That πόθος in Sappho takes on a specifically erotic meaning is made clear above all from fragments 48.2 and 102.2, where it is associated with the typical δάμναμι (I am overcome). So also fragment 126, "sleeping (you would sleep?) on the breast of a tender friend," δαύοισ' (δαύοις?) ἀπάλας ἐτάρας ἐν στήθεσιν, seems able to be interpreted in the sense of a tender amorous yielding, at least if, in our ignorance of the context (which in the fact of the matter renders every interpretation conjectural), some light is shed for us by its repetition by Theocritus in the *Epithalamium of Helen*, so rich in Sapphic reminiscences: "Sleep breathing love and passion, one on the chest of the other," εὖδετ' ἐς ἀλλάλων στέρνον φιλότατα πνέοντες / καὶ πόθον (ll. 54–55).[31]

Thus, the μοισοπόλος Sappho addresses herself above all to the ἔταιραι united to her both by the ties of the cult of Aphrodite and also sometimes

28. As well as in a rather significant passage of the *Odyssey*, 18.201.
29. Page, *Sappho and Alcaeus* 44.
30. Page, *Sappho and Alcaeus* 79–80; cf. also Fränkel, *Dichtung und Philosophie* 31 n. 8.
31. The Sapphic fragment should not, however, be attributed to an epithalamium, because there is no instance of ἐταίρα = νύμφη in Sappho. Cf. Treu, *Sappho* ad loc. For πόθος with an amatory meaning in Archilochus, see Broccia, *Πόθος e ψόγος* 20–21.

by ties of a love that cannot in any way be identified with a "maternal tenderness,"[32] and who were part of the very life of the ἑταιρεία. And once these amorous ties, like those of the cult, became an object of poetry, this ought to have provided an adequate expressive instrument, a language that could respond to the needs of an experience of a new and particular situation. Merkelbach suggests a comparison between the love poetry of Sappho and troubadour or *stilnuovo* lyric:[33] one might be confronted here with an analogous escape into an "impossible love" in environments where, at moments historically, culturally, and socially entirely different, amorous passion did not find satisfying the answer to be had in a relation with a beloved man or beloved woman destined to then become spouse and companion for life. Apart from all the necessary cautions in comparing completely different cultural situations, apart from the "sublimation" of Sapphic eroticism, which Merkelbach starts to introduce in this way but which I cannot share, I believe that this suggestion might be partly used in a different sense. Just as troubadour and *stilnuovo* lyric develop particular languages typical of these schools and constituting one of the elements distinguishing them from other "styles" of amorous lyric, so in Sapphic lyric one can isolate the elements of a series of amatory representations articulated in a language in which Homeric, Hesiodic, and Archilochean precedents are yoked together to characterize a new situation. In this situation they acquire a new resonance by the unusual frequency with which they are employed to function as thematic words, by the new meanings with which they are invested, and also by the copresence of newer terms dictated by the needs of a changed situation.

A language of this kind naturally finds significant correspondences in Anacreon and in the ephebic lyric of Pindar and Theognis, which accordingly ensure which meanings are to be read in the amorous lyric of Sappho. On the other hand, the "imitations" and later applications of this language, for example by Alexandrian poets, should be examined with greater caution, because in the literary game of allusion, embedding, and citation a twist away from the meaning of the original might always be at work. An analysis of this language should be linked both to the environmental considerations mentioned above and also to a series of researches such as those of Turyn, Treu, Kazik-Zawadzka, and Marzullo, which, even in the diversity of methodological bases and of results, have contributed to defining the historical position of Aeolic poetry, and of Sapphic poetry in particular, in its relations to the epic tradition.[34]

32. Latte, review of Fränkel 37.
33. Merkelbach, "Sappho und ihr Kreis" 16.
34. Turyn, *Studia Sapphica*; Treu, *Von Homer zur Lyrik*; Kazik-Zawadzka, *De Sapphicae Alcaicaeque elocutionis colore epico*; Marzullo, *Studi di poesia eolica*.

It is still necessary to warn, in relation to our specific problem, that vague appeals to "universal laws of the human heart," as well as gleanings of *loci similes* such as those contained in the *Studia Sapphica* of Turyn, which illustrate the persistence of several topoi up to late Latinity with parallels in the Romance literatures, are insufficient for the aims of a precise evaluation of the amatory lyric of Sappho. Just to present a macroscopic example, one might try to pair the φώναι / σ' οὐδ' ἔν εἴχει of Sappho's fragment 31.7–8 with the "ogne lingua deven tremando muta" (every tongue becomes mute in trembling) of the *Vita Nova*. It will be seen that what might perhaps be thought of as a mere physiological response valid in every case, or in the case of every "sensitive soul," in Dante expresses his reverential inhibition before the terrestrial image of Paradise, while in Sappho it is integrated into a very different framework of "signs" as will be analyzed below.

Likewise, nothing is more frequent in amatory lyric than the topos of "love and death," and even in Sappho it recurs with particular insistence. Yet if the "it seems to me I am almost dead," τεθνάκην δ' ὀλίγω 'πιδεύης / φαίνομ', of the ode handed down by Longinus (fr. 31.15–16) used to appear as the unrepeatable impulse of desperation of a "solitary soul," the Berlin papyrus has since reinstituted two "variations" on the same theme: in fragment 94.1, "truly I wish I were dead," τεθνάκην δ' ἀδόλως θέλω, and in fragment 95.11–13, "a longing to die holds me, and to see the dewy banks of Acheron flowering with lotus," κατθάνην δ' ἴμερός τις [ἔχει με καὶ / λωτίνοις δροσόεντας [ὄ/χ[θ]οις ἴδην Ἀχερ[. But the characteristic expressive "conventionality" with which the motif is handled by Sappho reveals that the relative fixity of its formulation expresses a moment typical of the Sapphic experience of eros, destined to repeat itself more times in analogous situations: to be precise, the ἀμαχανία (helplessness; fr. 130) when faced with the necessity of separation, institutionally germane to the Sapphic circle, or when faced with the impossibility of possession, which thus suggests as a solution the desire for death.[35] The motif is taken up again, as is well known, by Anacreon, who, perhaps because he uses it outside of a situation or context immediately clear to his listeners, introduces with γάρ a clarification that Sappho does not find necessary: "Might I die, for I can find no other release from these sufferings," ἀπό μοι θανεῖν γένοιτ'· οὐ γὰρ ἄν ἄλλη / λύσις ἐκ πόνων γένοιτ' οὐδαμὰ τῶνδε (fr. 411a P. = 29 Gent.). Similarly, the young girl of the new parthenium of Alcman (3 P.), which even more clearly than the previous example attests to an interlacing of impassioned amorous relations among the instigators,

---

35. On this see also Page, *Sappho and Alcaeus* 83, who has called attention to the frequency of the motif; but in my point of view he excessively "de-dramatizes" Sappho's text.

is gazed at "more consumingly than sleep or than death," τακερώτερα / δ' ὕπνω καὶ σανάτω (ll. 61–62).[36]

As is the case with a large part or with all the rest of erotic Greek poetry, the amatory language of Sappho has in common with the Homeric-Hesiodic tradition some terms such as δάμναμι, ἔρος, ἵμερος, πόθος, and φιλότης, or for example an adjective such as λυσιμέλης (limb-relaxing) to characterize Eros (an epithet attested in this sense beginning with Hes. *Theog.* 121, 911). These terms were so diffuse that it is superfluous to cite parallel passages; it is more interesting to try to note how they recur with typical frequency in texts that mention analogous situations to those described in Sappho's poetry, as in the already-cited parthenium 3 P. of Alcman (ll. 61–62): "she gazes at me with passion that loosens my limbs," λυσιμελεῖ πόσωι[37] ποτιδέρκεται, and in the Chalcidian popular song (fr. 873 P.), where love for the παῖδες who lack neither nobility of origin nor the favor of the Charites[38] is likewise called λυσιμελής. One could also note, with all the caution demanded by the fragmentary state of the testimonies, that in the Sapphic lexicon (in which, to the degree it is known to us, the greater part of the terms are attested to only once) words such as δάμναμι, ἔραμαι, ἔρατος, Ἔρος/ἔρος, πόθος, ποθήω recur with a significant frequency,[39] equal only to the frequency of appearance of terms that connote other characteristic aspects of Sapphic sensuality such as ἄβρος, ἆδυς, ἄπαλος, γλύκυς, and, naturally, κάλος. And it might perhaps be a coincidence ascribable to the tastes and the particular criteria of choice of the later sources, but Sapphic neoformations such as δολόπλοκος[40] (weaver of wiles) to denote Aphrodite, or γλυκύπικρος

---

36. On this see Gentili, "Aspetti del rapporto poeta" 78 n. 18.

37. λυσιμέλης πόθος is already in Archilochus, fr. 118: ἀλλά μ' ὁ λυσιμέλης, ὦ 'ταῖρε, δάμναται πόθος.

38. So also ephebic love, like Sapphic eros, is tied to *charis*, and thus represents, differently from heterosexual love, an element of moderation dear to an aristocratic environment such as one can reconstruct around Sappho, just as at Chalcis (873.1 P.: πατέρων λάχετ' ἐσθλῶν), at Sparta (see among others Plut. *Lyc.* 18d: ὥστε καὶ τῶν παρθένων ἐρᾶν τὰς καλὰς καὶ ἀγαθὰς γυναῖκας), in the Megara of Theognis, etc.

39. Two instances for δάμναμι: 1.3 and 102.2; five cases for ἔραμαι, ἔραννος, ἔρατος: 16.4, 49.1, 132.3, 16.17, 81b.1; twelve instances for Ἔρος/ἔρος: 15b.12, 23.1, 47.1, 54 test., 58.26, 73a.4 (prob.), 112.4, 130.1, 159, 195, 198; seven instances for πόθος, ποθήω, πόθεννος: 15b.11, 22.11, 36, 48, 74b.2, 94.23, 102.2; eight instances for ἱμερόεις, ἵμερος, ἵμερρω, ἵμερτος: 1.27, 17.10 (prob.), 31.5, 78.3, 95.11, 96.16, 112.4, 137.3 (though in 137.6 the term has a strong ethical coloring, in 78.3 the context is unknown, in 17.10 the integration is uncertain, and in 95.11 ἵμερον does not have an erotic meaning).

40. Fr. 1.2. The term reappears in Simon. fr. 541.9 P., in the *Adesp.* 919.7 (prob.) and 949 P., and in a passage from the second book of Theognis, who as always reshuffles the Homeric inheritance with Sapphic innovations: Κυπρογενὲς Κυθέρεια δολοπλόκε ... δαμνᾶις ... ἀνθρώπων πυκινὰς φρένας (ll. 1386–88).

(bittersweet; fr. 130.2),⁴¹ ἀλγεσίδωρος (paingiver; fr. 172), or μυθόπλοκος (weaver of tales; fr. 188) to connote Eros, are also always dictated by this same need to express a particular experience without precise literary precedents.

Moreover, according to the historical process, already amply illustrated by others, that enables words from epic language to assume meanings partly or entirely new in the age of lyric, some terms from epic assume in Sappho a new amatory meaning. δονέω, which in Homer for example can be said of the wind that shakes or stirs the trees, of the pestering that puts heifers to flight, and so on, appears in Sappho 130.1 in its first attestation for the love that "stirs, shakes, upsets the soul"; the meaning recurs in Pindar (*Pyth.* 4.218–19), where the ποθεινὰ Ἑλλάς (desired Hellas), and so the passion for Jason, upsets (δονέοι) Medea "burned in the heart," ἐν φρασὶ καιομέναν, and in the *Ecclesiazusae* of Aristophanes (l. 954),⁴² where a young lady, vainly awaiting a man, softly sings a love song in which she invokes her beloved to spend the night with her, "for a love upsets me with trembling," πάνυ γὰρ δεινός τις ἔρως με δονεῖ. K. J. Dover thinks the disposition of this Aristophanic love song, "δεῦρο δή, δεῦρο δή" (ll. 952, 960), to be typical of popular song,⁴³ but it is also clear that in this case the popular song was reelaborated by Aristophanes with an intent of literary parody (Μοῦσαι, δεῦρ' ἴτ' ἐπὶ τοὐμὸν, / μελύδριον εὑροῦσαί τι τῶν ἰωνικῶν, ll. 882–83; "Muses, come here to me, find an Ionian ditty"). This is shown by the interlacing of reminiscences and citations: line 956, "an extraordinary passion is (lies) in me," ἄτοπος δ' ἔγκειταί μοί τις πόθος, is to be compared with Archilochus, fragment 104 D.: "he lay miserable from the passion," δύστηνος ἔγκειμαι πόθωι. And the response of the youth, lines 973–74: "Oh my care, covered with gold, offspring of the Cyprian, bee of the Muse, raised by the Charites," ὦ χρυσοδαίδαλτον ἐμὸν μέλημα, Κύπριδος ἔρνος, / μέλιττα Μούσης, Χαρίτων θρέμμα, is to be compared, as van Leeuwen has already done, with fragment 7 P. of Ibycus: "O Euryalus, offspring of the blue-eyed Graces, care of the [8] of the beautiful locks, the Cyprian and Peitho with the soft gaze raised you among flowers of roses," Εὐρύαλε γλαυκέων Χαρίτων θάλος 〈 〉 / καλλικόμων μελέδημα, σὲ μὲν Κύπρις / ἅ τ' ἀγανοβλέφαρος Πει- / θὼ ῥοδέοισιν ἐν ἄνθεσι θρέψαν. And if line 954 cited above truly contains, as I believe, a Sapphic reminiscence, this would make it equally believable that also in lines 877 ff. and 911 ff. Aristophanes freely echoes the famous δέδυκε μὲν ἀ σελάννα (the moon has

---

41. Compare Theog. 1353–54: πικρὸς καὶ γλυκύς ἐστι . . . ἔρως, and then *AP* 12.109.3 (Meleager); 5.134.4 (Posidippus).

42. And then in Theoc. 13.65, where it is perhaps more Sapphic than Homeric, as Gow, ed., *Theocritus* ad loc., would hold.

43. Dover, "The Poetry of Archilochus" 221.

set; 94 D.), as well as assisting the argument of the supporters of the infinitely contested authenticity of the fragment.[44]

A significant convergence of terms and expressive modules that characterize in no uncertain way the passion of unreciprocated love is naturally found again in the famous ode cited in *On the Sublime* (31), although I would like to say that, as far as concerns the overall interpretation of this ode, I cannot persuade myself that we are in fact dealing with an epithalamium, even of some less traditional type. For it seems to me that at line 16 the refrain φαίνομ' ἔμ' αὔται (it seems to me), now fortunately restored by the new Florentine fragment,[45] excludes for the φαίνομαι of the first verse any such meaning as "appear, present oneself as" ("in die Erscheinung treten") that would entail interpreting the arrangement of the ode as a variation of the motif of the *makarismos* of the spouse, according to the interpretation maintained by Bruno Snell especially.[46]

The nature of the eros described by Sappho in this fragment should not be identified simply on the basis of the concretely physical or physiological aspect of the well-known sequence of the "signs" of amorous turmoil. The representation of an emotional state or of a cognitive act by means of its ensuing eruption in a concrete physical attitude is normal enough for the Greeks of the archaic age;[47] and for this reason, as Hermann Fränkel has aptly noted, a passion that is assessed on the plane of its realization does not then have to add anything such as "so much do I love you."[48] Such an addition is even less necessary since all the language of the ode, it seems to me, sets up a precise kind of reading, which later seems to have been that of the ancients generally—such as that of Theocritus in the second *Idyll*, just to cite from among many possibilities the example of a poet whom we have seen was influenced often by the amatory language of Sappho.

The ὡς γὰρ ἔς σ' ἴδω (for when I look at you) of line 7 has a precedent in a section of the epic that has already been shown to be important for the interpretation of fragment 2, in the Διὸς ἀπάτη, where Zeus, facing Hera clothed in all of her seductiveness, is said to "hardly see her, love enwraps his prudent soul," ὡς δ' ἴδεν, ὥς μιν ἔρως πυκινὰς φρένας ἀμφεκάλυψεν (*Il.* 14.294).[49] It also finds a significant correspondence in the encomium for Theoxenus, in which the old Pindar confesses his melting passion for

44. See Marzullo, *Studi di poesia eolica* 53 ff.

45. Istituto papirologico G. Vitelli, *Dai papiri della Società Italiana* 16–17.

46. Snell, "Sapphos Gedicht" 71 ff.

47. Onians, *Origins of European Thought* 3, 17–18.

48. Fränkel, *Dichtung und Philosophie* 199–200.

49. See also, e.g., *h. Hom. Ven.* 56–57.

the ephebic beauty: "But because of Aphrodite I melt like the wax of the sacred bees beneath the sun, when I see the young limbs of the boys," ἀλλ' ἐγὼ τᾶς ἔκατι κηρὸς ὡς δαχθεὶς ἔλαι / ἰρᾶν μελισσᾶν τάκομαι, εὖτ' ἂν ἴδω / παίδων νεόγυιον ἐς ἤβαν (fr. 123.10–13). This, in Sappho as in Pindar,[50] is not the motif of "love at first sight," as one will find it later in its Theocritan reuse,[51] but rather the express registration in a nearly formulaic manner of the power of erotic seduction that the "bright" spectacle of beauty exercises on the senses and through the senses. However, "the bright love of the sun and beauty," τὸ λά[μπρον ἔρος τὠελίω καὶ τὸ κά]λον (fr. 58.26) in Sappho are not simply aesthetic longings; the "bright dazzling," ἀμάρυχμα λάμπρον (fr. 16.18)[52] of the face of Anactoria even in memory summons love again, as the "rays that dazzle," ἀκτῖνας μαρμαρυζοίσας (Pind. fr. 123.2–3)[53] from the eyes of Theoxenus immediately overwhelm in the waves of passion anyone who does not have a heart of iron. In Sappho it is not the image of the wave but that of the "bewilderment of the heart," expressed by a verb such as πτόαμι of "already ancient erotic specificity,"[54] the particular meaning of which has found confirmations in new fragments of Alcaeus and Anacreon,[55] but which was already attested earlier by a collage of the collection of Theognis where the turmoil from confronting ephebic beauty is expressed with linguistic elements drawn from Homer, Hesiod,[56] and especially Sappho: "Suddenly sweat runs unstoppably under my skin, and I am bewildered by the sight of the flower of youth, pleasant and beautiful together," αὐτίκα μοι κατὰ μὲν χροιὴν ῥέει ἄσπετος

---

50. And, perhaps, yet again in Sappho fr. 6.8 L.-P., ὠσιδω[, and in Alcman, fr. 3.79 P.,]α ἴδοιμ' αἴ πως μὲ.. ον φιλοι.

51. Theoc. Id. 2.82, χὠς ἴδον, ὡς ἐμάνην, ὥς μοι πυρὶ θυμὸς ἰάφθη.

52. This particular experience of beauty must also have had a nearly formulaic expression in Sappho; cf. fr. 4.6–7,]σαντιλάμπην,]λον πρόσωπον.

53. The reference to the ἀμάρυχμα of Sappho is already, for example, in Bowra, Pindar 276. The term is attested for the first time in Hes. frs. 21, 94.6: Χαρίτων ἀμαρύγματ' ἔχουσα. The "bright" beauty that excites longing is also, for example, in h. Hom. Ven. 89–91: ὡς δὲ σελήνη / στήθεσιν ἀμφ' ἀπαλοῖσιν ἐλάμπετο, θαῦμα ἰδέσθαι. / Ἀγχίσην δ' ἔρος εἷλεν κτλ.

54. Cf. Setti, "Nota" 534 n. 2; and also Broccia, "Per l'esegesi" 8 ff., which I was able to see only after the draft of my article was completed, and which already insisted on the parallel with Theog. 1018. This "specialization," pertinent to the domain of homosexual love, can be found down to late antiquity; cf. for example Ath. 13.601e: Κρῆτες γοῦν, ὥς ἔφην, καὶ οἱ ἐν Εὐβοίαι Χαλκιδεῖς περὶ τὰ παιδικὰ δαιμονίως ἐπτόηνται; and Harp., s.v. τοὺς σφόδρα ἐπτοήμενους περὶ τὰ παιδικά.

55. Alc. fr. 283.3, κἀλένας ἐν στήθ[ε]σιν [ἐ]πτ[όαισ-; Anac. fr. 346.1, 11–12 P. = 60 Gent., πολλοὶ πολ]ιητέων φρένας ἐπτοέαται. Cf. also Gentili, ed., Anacreon 191 and n. 1. For Sappho, cf. again fr. 22.14.

56. Cf. Hes. Op. 447, κουρότερος γὰρ ἀνὴρ μεθ' ὁμήλικας ἐπτοίηται.

ἱδρώς, / πτοιῶμαι δ᾽ ἐσορῶν ἄνθος ὁμηλικίης / τερπνὸν ὁμῶς καὶ καλόν (ll. 1017–19).

The "sweat" that floods the limbs (Sappho 31.13) is, for example, already in the *Homeric Hymn* to Pan: "The soft desire to unite himself with the love of the nymph of the beautiful braids, daughter of Driope, flowered in him and assailed him," θάλε γὰρ πόθος ὑγρὸς ἐπελθὼν / νύμφηι ἐϋπλοκάμωι Δρύοπος φιλότητι μιγῆναι (ll. 33–34), while the particular use of πῦρ (fire) at line 10 is entirely unique in archaic Greek[57] and might have, I believe, a meaning somewhat close to its meaning of "fever" as attested in the medical literature. And this matching with an entirely different technical language need not seem strange; even in ode 1.3, the term ἄσα, "agony" (also rather rare, and taken up later with an analogous meaning by Anac. fr. 347.8 P. = 71 Gent.) ought in part to be close to the physiological meaning of "nausea" attested in the medical literature, and ought to indicate something more than a "mental discomfort" since, as Page has already noted,[58] it recurs, tied as in Sappho to ἀνία, in a medical text that speaks of a man who is prey to "torments and agonies," ἀνιᾶται καὶ ἀσᾶται, through an alteration that exhibits itself in his physical equilibrium.[59] Here then is love as a partial "malady,"[60] not in the romantic sense of the term but in the concrete sense of a disturbance that invades the senses. In this sense certain expressions are still loaded with all of the expressive violence of their literal meaning, and at the same time are innovators with respect to preceding use even within the ambit of archaic lyric: expressions such as "my soul burned with passion," ἔμαν φρέναν καιομέναν πόθωι (fr. 48.2,[61] where the "soul," φρήν, that can be "devoured," βόρηται [fr. 96.17], or "tossed about," τινάσσει [fr. 47], by Eros as by a wind, is still obviously to be understood in a very concrete sense);[62] or the "cooking" of passion, ὄπταις ἄμμε of fragment 38, which will later be taken up frequently in Alexandrian literature[63] —for example, by Meleager, who plays with a rather baroque *pointe* upon the image of Eros as

---

57. And in Greek in general, where the term in this sense reappears in the Alexandrian age; see Theoc. *Il.* 2.82, 11.51; Callim. *Epigr.* 25.5 (ἀρσενικῶι θέρεται πυρί) and *Aet.* fr. 75.17, where πῦρ is the flame of the mysterious malady that burns Cydippe.

58. Page, *Sappho and Alcaeus* 6.

59. Hippocr. *De morbo sacro*, vol. 6, p. 388, ll. 21–22 Littré. Hippocrates might also have used as technical terms expressions from poetic language, according to the process signaled by Leumann, *Homerische Wörter* 303 ff. (for a specific case see Janni, "Due note omeriche"); this does not however exclude the reverse possibility, of the poetic use of prosaic technical terms.

60. For analogies in Theocritus, see the commentary to *Id.* 2.84 and 30.2 in Gow, *Theocritus*.

61. Καίεσθαι in this sense is in Pindar in the passage from *Pyth.* 4.219 cited above.

62. On this see also Onians, *Origins of European Thought* 32–33, 54–55, although the latter pages do not seem at all acceptable to me.

63. Theoc. *Id.* 7.55, 23.34; Callim. *Epigr.* 43.5. In Ar. *Lys.* 839 the sense is highly ironic.

"cook" of the soul,[64] or employs, in a by then highly stylized manner, the contrast "to burn with love—to find relief in coolness."[65] This contrast is attested for the very first time in fragment 48 of Sappho: "You came, and it was a good thing; I was longing for you, and you gave coolness to my soul burned by passion," ἦλθες, εὖ δ' ἐπόησας, ἔγω δὲ σ' ἐμαιόμαν, / ὂν δ' ἔψυξας ἔμαν φρένα καιομέναν πόθωι, where it seems to me that the conjecture ὀνέψυξας[66] finds confirmation in a passage of the second book of Theognis (l. 1273), where he laments that the παῖς (boy) that has destroyed his νόον ἐσθλόν (good mind) later "gave coolness for a short while," ἄμμε δ' ἀνέψυξας μιχρὸν χρόνον. And in the context of fragment 48, μαίομαι, which in Homer or in Hesiod (as in the rest of Greek poetry) indicates a rather general "going in search, pursuing," assumes, along the lines shown above for δονέω, the specifically erotic meaning of "to long for."[67]   This meaning is guaranteed by its pairing with ποθήω in fragment 36, καὶ ποθήω καὶ μάομαι, which is known to us through the *Etymologicum Magnum* but is also found inscribed on one of the wellknown vases with ephebic inscriptions, the one attributed to Euphronius:[68] Λέαγρος καλὸς · μαμε καὶ ποτέω; and notwithstanding the poor accuracy of the transcription, it does not seem doubtful that here we find ourselves in front of a Sapphic citation, and that the author or the commissioner of the vase thus read in the text of Sappho a precise message of love.

Sapphic poetry could thus speak to the common reader who did not close himself to the comprehension of its contents with the same clearness with which it spoke to Pindar or to Theognis. And the selections that Sappho performed within the lexical patrimony of the epic, as the new linguistic means with which she gave expression to a world different from the epic world, were destined in their turn to be "leader of a school" and to become traditional. I have sought to isolate a few elements of this language and, by placing them in the tradition to which even a "marvel" like Sappho has to be associated, to characterize through them some aspects of Sapphic eros, the chorality and the concreteness of a particular erotic experience. I like to hope that the data of this study will also be of use to those who wish to study the poetry of Sappho with different methods.

64. *AP* 12.92.7–8, ὀπτᾶσθ' ἐν κάλλει, τύφεσθ' ὑποκαόμενοι νῦν / ἄκρος ἐπεὶ ψυχῆς ἔστι μάγειρος Ἔρως.

65. *AP* 12.132.7–8 ἃ ψυχὲ βαρύμοχθε, σὺ δ' ἄρτι μὲν ἐκ πυρὸς αἴθηι, ἄρτι δ' ἀναψύχεις πνεῦμ' ἀναλεξαμένη.

66. Which pleases neither Pfeiffer, review of Diehl and Lobel 317, nor Treu, *Sappho* ad loc.

67. The same could probably be said for the πεδήπομεν of fr. 94.8, which finds no parallel in the current uses of μεθέπω.

68. Cf. Robinson and Fluck, *Greek Love-Names* 33.

TWO

Critical Stereotypes and
the Poetry of Sappho

Mary R. Lefkowitz

Criticism of creative art seems curiously dependent on biography.[1] It appears difficult to separate an artist's life from his work, or to regard literature or music or paintings primarily as public statements. Since the act of creation is assumed fundamentally to be an emotional response, the artist is viewed as an active participant in the world he has created. In the case of male writers, the assumption seems always to be that the artist, whether Catullus, Brahms, or Goya, uses the full range of his intellectual powers to come to terms with his problems. It is understood that the methods and the problems vary considerably from artist to artist. But in the case of female artists, the assumptions on which criticism is based tend to be narrowly defined: (1) *Any creative woman is a "deviant," that is, women who have a satisfactory emotional life (home, family, and husband) do not need additional creative outlets.* The assumption behind this assumption is that "deviance" in the case of women results from being deprived of men—in other words, women artists tend to be (a) old maids or (b) lesbians, either overt female homosexuals or somehow "masculine." (2) *Because women poets are emotionally disturbed, their poems are psychological outpourings, that is, not intellectual but ingenuous, artless, concerned with their inner emotional lives.* As a result, criticism of two such different poets as Sappho and Emily Dickinson can sound remarkably alike.

Dr. John Cody's recent analysis of Emily Dickinson's poem "I had been hungry, all the Years" provides a vivid illustration of the special criticism

This essay is based on a paper presented at the 1972 meeting of the American Philological Association. I am grateful to Professor William M. Calder III, Professor Katherine A. Geffcken, Jennifer Wheat, and James E. G. Zetzel for corrections and criticism. This essay was originally published in slightly different form as "Critical Stereotypes and the Poetry of Sappho," *Greek, Roman, and Byzantine Studies* 14 (1974) 113–23.
    1. See esp. Cherniss, "The Biographical Fashion."

applied to female artists. I prefer to begin with Emily Dickinson rather than with Sappho, because Dickinson wrote in English (which I understand better than I do Greek) and because the facts of her life are relatively well documented: she was a recluse, unmarried, wore white, wrote in the bedroom of her house in Amherst poems on little pieces of paper, some of which were published in her lifetime.

> I had been hungry, all the Years—
> My Noon had Come—to dine—
> I trembling drew the Table near—
> And touched the Curious Wine—
>
> 'Twas this on Tables I had seen—
> When turning, hungry, Home
> I looked in Windows, for the Wealth
> I could not hope—for Mine—
>
> I did not know the ample Bread—
> 'Twas so unlike the Crumb
> The Birds and I, had often shared
> In Nature's—Dining Room—
>
> The Plenty hurt me—'twas so new—
> Myself felt ill—and odd—
> As Berry—of a Mountain Bush—
> Transplanted—to the Road—
>
> Nor was I hungry—so I found
> That Hunger—was a way
> Of Persons outside Windows—
> The Entering—takes away—
>   (579 Johnson, ca. 1862)

My own impression of this poem is that its primary concern is disappointment: something long-awaited comes; once you have it, it disappears; thus in retrospect the anticipation seems more rewarding than the thing itself. The central thought is expressed in the terminology of food: the narrator of the poem is "hungry"; then "noon" (the dinner hour) has come like a guest, to dinner; there is a table with "Curious Wine" (the narrator doesn't know what it is). The narrator had been like the birds, eating what was left; now he/she leaves the wilds, and his/her exclusion, and enters the house. The hunger then goes away and there is nothing. The bread and wine in the poem may take on additional significance if we think of them as elements in the Christian sacrament of the Eucharist: Dickinson was raised by devout churchgoers and drew much of her subject matter and metrical structure from the hymns she heard as a child.[2]

2. On Dickinson's use of hymn meters and form, see T. Johnson, *Emily Dickinson*.

Then the poem might also say: after receiving Communion, what does one have?

To our impressions we can compare what Dr. Cody says in *After Great Pain: The Inner Life of Emily Dickinson.* He reads the poem as an analyst would interpret dreams, along canonical Freudian lines: hunger connotes sexual experience, and Emily Dickinson's

> imbibing of physical affection quickly becomes a glut and overwhelms her painfully. The experience is novel in an uncongenial way and causes her to sicken and feel strange. She feels that sexuality is too common a territory for her (a "Road") because she is acclimated to an unfrequented and lofty habitat. (She comes of a "Mountain Bush" and feels out of place, perhaps degraded, in the "Road"; one senses in this word unpleasant connotations of too easy accessibility, prosaic purposes, dustiness, and commercial transactions.

Once we accept the premise that the poem primarily concerns sex, it is possible to interpret its imagery more specifically:

> It is a commonplace that a woman's introduction to sexual intimacies may be frightening and disappointing. The bruising of delicate membranes may draw blood. Thus, the line "The Plenty hurt me—'twas so new" may refer not only to the overpowering emotion generated by her own and another's passion but also to the overwhelming and painful effects of physical force. The transplanted berry may be the hymeneal blood (the first color commonly associated with berries is red); the "Mountain Bush," the mons veneris; and the "Road," the vagina. We cannot imagine that Emily Dickinson was unaware of these anatomical facts.)[3]

Whether or not she was more than "dimly aware" of these "unconscious sexual preoccupations" is not the issue: Cody's analysis enables us to see that Emily Dickinson, who "has for so long been thought of as an ethereal other world creature" was in fact "a living flesh-and-blood woman who, Victorian Age notwithstanding, was well aware that whether she liked it or not she had no choice but to share in the physiological reactions of the rest of humanity."[4]

If we in turn analyze Cody's analysis, we find that it rests on several questionable assumptions: (1) That poems are like dreams, that is, are individual expressions of emotional problems, rather than public statements meant to be understood by and communicated to a large audience who had not read Freud on roads, berries, etc. But Emily Dickinson, as her correspondence shows, was most interested in getting into print and being recognized. (2) That Dickinson's problem is sexual deprivation, specifically, inability to accept or to enjoy men, an interpretation read in from her biography.

---

3. Cody, *After Great Pain.*
4. Ibid., 142.

The same basic assumptions tend to be made about Sappho's famous poem, φαίνεταί μοι (31 Lobel-Page [L.-P.]), though in less vividly stated forms. Compared to Emily Dickinson's, we know virtually nothing about Sappho's life. We can glean from biographies and passing references written long after her death the names of her family, that she lived in Mytilene at the end of the seventh century, that she wrote nine books of lyric poetry, that she was a female homosexual, short, dark, and ugly, and that she died by throwing herself off the White Rock in west Greece because of her unrequited love for a ferryman named Phaon ("shining"). Much of this information seems to have been derived from interpretations by ancient scholars (all male) of her poetry, some also from caricatures of her in comedy; the story of her death is obviously based on myth.[5] Again a portrait emerges of an emotional deviant: deprived because of her ugliness of male attention (like the ferryman's) which she craves.

Thus biography, itself derived from interpretation of the poems, is in turn reapplied to the poems and affects our interpretation of them. In the case of φαίνεταί μοι, especially, much influential criticism has tended to center on the "facts" of Sappho's life:

φαίνεταί μοι κῆνος ἴσος θέοισιν
ἔμμεν' ὤνηρ, ὅττις ἐνάντιός τοι
ἰσδάνει καὶ πλάσιον ἆδυ φωνει-
4 σας ὑπακούει

καὶ γελαίσας ἰμέροεν, τό μ' ἦ μὰν
καρδίαν ἐν στήθεσιν ἐπτόαισεν
ὡς γὰρ ἔς σ' ἴδω βρόχέ, ὥς με φώναι-
8 σ' οὐδ' ἒν ἔτ' εἴκει,

ἀλλ' ἄκαν μὲν γλῶσσα †ἔαγε†, λέπτον
δ' αὔτικα χρῶι πῦρ ὑπαδεδρόμηκεν,
ὀππάτεσσι δ' οὐδ' ἒν ὄρημμ' ἐπιρρόμ-
12 βεισι δ' ἄκουαι,

†ἔκαδε μ' ἴδρως ψῦχρος κακχέεται†, τρόμος δὲ
παῖσαν ἄγρει, χλωροτέρα δὲ ποίας
ἔμμι, τεθνάκην δ' ὀλίγω 'πιδεύης
16 φαίνομ' ἔμ' αὔται

ἀλλὰ πὰν τόλματον ἐπεὶ †καὶ† πένητά
(ed. Page)

Wilamowitz saw "that man" in the poem's first stanza as the husband of the girl. The girl is one of Sappho's students, and the poem concerns the man

5. On the evidence for Sappho's life, see esp. McEvilley, "Imagination and Reality" 259–63. On the significance of the myth of Sappho's death, see Nagy, "Symbols of Greek Lyric."

and schoolmistress Sappho's jealousy of him.[6] This interpretation transposes the poem to the realm of sexual normality: there is no evidence at all in the text that "that man" is a husband, or the girl Sappho's pupil, or that Sappho ran a girl's school.[7] Page, in what is recognized as the authoritative English commentary on Sappho, is aware of the limitations of Wilamowitz's criticism but still retains the same basic assumptions about the poem. In his analysis, he realizes that the man only appears in the first stanza, but at the same time he is reluctant to take his attention off of him.

> But we must not forget that the *man* was the principal subject of the whole first stanza; and we shall not be content with any explanation of the poem which gives no satisfactory account of his presence and his prominence in it. If Sappho wishes to describe nothing more than the symptoms of her passion for the girl, what motive could she have for connecting that description thus closely with an occasion when the girl is engaged in merry conversation with a man? Surely that occasion is not devoid of all significance: and then it appears impossible to exclude the element of jealousy from Sappho's emotional response to the scene. Sappho loves the girl: and it is clearly suggested that the girl is not, at least at this moment, particularly interested in Sappho. Sappho is present in the company: but it is the man, not Sappho, who is sitting close by the girl, rejoicing in her laughter and converse. To maintain that Sappho feels no jealousy of the man would be to ignore the certain response of human nature to a situation of the type described, and to deprive the introduction of the man, and his relation to the girl, of all significance. On this point, at least, there is little room for doubt.[8]

The girl is talking to him, and not to Sappho; the physical symptoms that Sappho describes in such detail result specifically from jealousy. In addition, Page tends to see the poem as a direct outpouring of emotion, in much the same way that Cody read Dickinson. Sappho's language

> is realistic, severely plain and candid, unadorned by literary artifice. First, very quietly, "I have no longer any power to speak." Then she says something—we do not know exactly what—about her tongue. Then in simple words, "a subtle fire has stolen beneath my flesh," and still more simply "with my eyes I see nothing." Then a homely metaphor, "my ears are humming": and the next phrase could not be more bleak and unadorned, whether the words meant "sweat pours down me" or "a cold sweat covers me." Then, without artifice, "a trembling seizes me all over"; thereafter an image which owes nothing to literary tradition, and surely

6. Wilamowitz, *Sappho und Simonides* 58. Wilamowitz, in his interpretation, was attempting to restore objectivity to the criticism of Sappho's poetry: "when the name Sappho is mentioned today, more people will think of sexual perversion than of a great poetess" (17).

7. The authority of Wilamowitz continues to make scholars uneasy about abandoning the girls' school hypothesis; see, e.g., Merkelbach, "Sappho and ihr Kreis." Two school texts treat it as a live possibility: Campbell, *Greek Lyric Poetry*, and Gerber, *Euterpe*.

8. Page, *Sappho and Alcaeus* 28.

reflects her own manner of thought and speech, "paler than grass am I"; and finally the homeliest phrase of all, "I seem to fall a little short of being dead." Rarely, if anywhere, in archaic or classical poetry shall we find language so far independent of literary tradition, apparently so close to the speech of every day. Style is in harmony with dialect; both products of nature, not artifice.[9]

His translation supports his interpretation. Sappho's verbs are attenuated into nouns, "terrifies" (ἐπτόαισεν)[10] becomes the conventional love-song term "a-flutter"; "runs under" (ὐπαδεδρόμηκεν) has become "has stolen" (as in "has stolen my heart away"?); "whirrs," like a spinning *rhombos* (ἐπιρρόμβεισι) has become "is humming"; pours down (κακχέεται), "covers"; "hunts" (ἄγρει) merely "seizes"; the violent "greener" than grass (χλωροτέρα ποίας) merely "paler." Missing also is a sense of the military terminology in the opening stanza: the Homeric "equal to the gods" has become somehow "fortunate." "Sits opposite" only represents part of the meaning of ἐνάντιος, "in opposition," as in battle. In the last stanza, the reassurance "all can be endured" (τόλματον) has become a frustrated "all *must* be endured."

George Devereux, the anthropologist, sees the poem rather as an emotional outpouring of "envy" of "that man," as opposed to simple "jealousy":

> The core of the problem can best be stated in somewhat colloquial terms: "What does this man—and indeed any man—have that Sappho does *not* have?" "What can a man offer to a girl that Sappho cannot offer?" The answer, I think, is obvious (*Od.* 11.249 ff. [This is the passage where Poseidon says to Tyro: "rejoice lady, in my love, and as the year goes by you shall bear glorious children, etc."]) and leads to a clinically highly documentable and crucial finding: few women are as obsessed with a (neurotic) feeling of incompleteness<->with the clinically commonplace "female castration complex"—as the masculine lesbian. Moreover, the latter experiences her "defect" with violent and crushing intensity particularly when her girl-friend is taken away from her not by another lesbian, but by a *man*, who has what she does not have and which she would give her life to have.[11]

---

9. Ibid., 30. It is interesting to note that early critics of *Wuthering Heights*, which was first published under the pseudonym Ellis Bell, found the novel "forceful." When it was revealed that the author was in fact Miss Emily Brontë, critics were quick to discover that both characterization and description in the novel had been adversely affected by the necessary experiential limitations of a woman's life: see Carol Ohmann, "Emily Brontë in the Hands of Male Critics," paper read at MLA Women's Forum, December 1970. On the tendency to read contemporary values into ancient texts, see my article "Cultural Conventions."

10. On the meaning of πτοέω see H. Frisk, *Griechisches*. The secondary definition "flutter" given in LSJ does not represent the root meaning of the verb, which is cognate to πτήσσω and πτώσσω, "crouch in fear" (not to πέτομαι, "fly"). In *Od.* 22.298–99 πτοέω is used to describe the suitors' reaction to Athene holding her aegis above them from the rafters: "Their hearts were terrified (φρένες ἐπτοίηθεν); they fled in panic (ἐφέβοντο) along the hall like a herd of cattle."

11. Devereux, "The Nature of Sappho's Seizure" 22.

According to Devereux, Sappho in the poem is describing the sort of anxiety attack that Devereux has frequently witnessed in homosexual patients.

If Sappho's poem had just been dug out of the sand and if we had never heard of Wilamowitz or looked in Page or read Devereux's article, our interpretation of the poem might be very different. Perhaps it is impossible for any of us to approach Sappho with the same objectivity that we can maintain in reading Emily Dickinson, because we always seem to come to ancient texts with dictionary in hand. But to look at the text itself, without any preconceptions about the identity of the narrator, the poem says: "That man seems to me like the gods (ἴσος θέοισιν, a designation that in Homer connotes unusual strength) who sits opposite (or in opposition), who hears you (female) speaking sweetly and laughing passionately.[12] This (i.e., hearing you) terrifies my heart in my breast (i.e., the effect of you on me, the narrator, is very different from your effect on 'that man'). For whenever I look at you then I can speak nothing still, but in silence my tongue is broken (ἔαγε, a verb used to describe broken bones), and immediately a light fire runs under my skin, and with my eyes I see nothing, and my ears whirr, and a cold sweat holds me down, and a shuddering hunts all of me, and I am greener than grass, and from dying little lacking I seem to myself to be (repetition 'to myself' signifies a conclusion, and reference to the narrator, a transition to a new subject).[13] But all is endurable, since even a poor man"—does the poem go on to say that god makes even a poor man rich (as in the introduction to the *Works and Days*), that is, that there is some hope for change, or eventual triumph?[14]

Looking at the text, it seems fair to say that quantitatively at least the main emphasis in the poem falls on the narrator's feelings. It is important to remember that what she is describing is an illusion: "he seems to me" (φαίνεταί μοι), "I seem to myself" (φαίνομ' ἔμ' αὔται). The time is indefinite, the illusion happens over and over: "whenever I look at you" (ὥς with subjunctive ἴδω). The man has no specific identity; he is "whoever (ὄττις) sits opposite." The exaggerated terms in which the narrator's reactions are described add to the sense of illusion: the broken tongue, the sweat that grasps, the shuddering that hunts, and being greener than grass do not portray the condition of the narrator in real life. The phrase "greener than grass" at the end of the list of symptoms has particular impact. It translates the Homeric "green fear" for one's life in battle into the context of daily existence. In the same way, the man like the gods in the first stanza is not a

---

12. On the meaning of ἴσος θέοισιν, see Wills, "Sappho 31 and Catullus 51," and Marcovich, "Sappho Fr. 31" 26.

13. On ἔαγε as "is crippled," see West, "Burning Sappho" 311; Marcovich, "Sappho Fr. 31" 27–29. On the structure of the poem, see Saake, *Sapphostudien* 53–54.

14. On the contents and translation of the fifth stanza, see West, "Burning Sappho."

Homeric hero but someone sitting opposite a girl. It is as if Sappho were saying that what happens in a woman's life also partakes of the significance of the man's world of war. When she writes a long narrative poem about Hector and Andromache it is to describe their wedding.[15] When she speaks in her poem to "Aphrodite on intricate throne, immortal" of pursuing and fleeing, it is describing not the grim chase of Hector by Achilles, "as in a dream one cannot pursue someone who flees" (*Il.* 22.200), but the conquest of an unwilling lover, "if she flees now, soon she'll pursue you."[16] Her victory is achieved by the intervention of Aphrodite, not through her own powers. In φαίνεταί μοι also, any change that is to come about must take place through endurance. As a woman, she must rely on the special weapons of the oppressed, miracles and patience.

This interpretation may not tell us everything we want to know about the poem, but I think at least it reveals what the poem is *not* about. There is nothing specifically stated in the poem about jealousy of a rival. What the man has that she (the narrator) doesn't have (*malgré* Devereux) is not male generative capacity but physical strength: he seems "like the gods" while she is faint and powerless.[17] What she (the narrator) feels is not jealousy but the response of lovers to beauty in their beloved: when the suitors see Penelope in *Odyssey* 18 "their knees were loosened, and their hearts were beguiled with passion" (212). As for Sappho's style, if being untraditional is artless, then we can agree (in Page's words) that she is "without artifice." But it might be fairer to comment on the dramatic personification "trembling hunts me down" or her conversion of Homeric formulae, e.g., taking "like the gods" from the context of war to the struggles of emotion, and turning the conventional "green fear" into the startling, entertaining "greener than grass am I."[18] The sense of illusion that she creates in the opening "he seems" and its echo "I seem to myself" in the fourth stanza is one of the first expressions of what will later become one of the primary concerns of poetry and philosophy: the effects of the imagination.[19] The deliberate generality of the poem, the absence of proper names and specific references to time and place, indicate that this poem is meant to bring to mind no particular

15. This point was suggested to me by Marilyn Skinner.

16. John Marry made these observations about the use of Homeric vocabulary in fr. 1 L.-P. in a panel discussion on Sappho in November 1972 at the University of Massachusetts, Amherst.

17. On the contrast implied between mortal and immortal, see McEvilley, "Imagination and Reality"; Privitera, "Ambiguità antitesi" 37–80.

18. On Sappho's use of Homeric vocabulary and unusual metaphor, see Marcovich, "Sappho Fr. 31" 26–32.

19. On imagination and reality in this poem, see also McEvilley, "Imagination and Reality" 171; and on the connotations of φαίνεσθαι, see Saake, *Zur Kunst Sapphos* 20.

place or occasion. It tells of "that man—whoever" and of the narrator's reactions "whenever I look at you."[20] It is no more directly representative of the historical Sappho's feeling at any given moment in history than the sonnet "Th' Expense of Spirit" is a transcript of a day in the life of William Shakespeare.[21]

To recapitulate: biographical criticism, in the case of the women poets Dickinson and Sappho, may keep us from seeing what the poets say. Dickinson's dignified, remote poem about disappointment becomes an outcry of sexual frustration, Sappho's song about the weakness of a woman in love a jealous admission of penis envy. Applying assumptions our society makes about "normal" female psychology to the work of women poets can do little to advance our understanding of their poems. This is not to say that their poems are not different because they are by women; I think perhaps they are. Dickinson writes about her "inner life" and Sappho about her love for her female friends and the pleasures of singing and being together because these activities, not war or games or government, were the experiences that her society and times permitted to women. Those who are secluded in some way from the concerns of the larger society are by necessity thrown onto themselves and thus have time and scope to express what others, in more diffracted contexts, do not have time to articulate or to understand. Such enforced withdrawal has made women's poetry distinctive and influential.

20. But cf. for example Bowra's appealing re-creation of the circumstances from his own imagination; see *Greek Lyric Poetry* 184–87. Wilamowitz, of course, read Ἄγαλλι, which helped to particularize the occasion.

21. Peterson, "A Probable Source," shows that "Th' Expense of Spirit" is based on a handbook description of the consequences of lust.

THREE

Phaethon, Sappho's Phaon, and the White Rock of Leukas: "Reading" the Symbols of Greek Lyric

Gregory Nagy

In the arcane Greek myths of Phaethon and Phaon there are latent themes that help resolve three problems of interpretation in Greek poetry. The first of these problems is to be found in the *Partheneion* of Alcman (*PMG* 1). It concerns a wondrous horse conjured up in a simile describing the beauty of the maiden Hagesikhora, center of attention in the song-and-dance ensemble:

δοκεῖ γὰρ ἤμεν αὔτα
ἐκπρεπὴς τὼς ὥπερ αἴτις
ἐν βοτοῖς στάσειεν ἵππον
παγὸν ἀεθλοφόρον καναχάποδα
τῶν ὑποπετριδίων ὀνείρων
(Alcman *PMG* 1.45–49)

For she appears
outstanding, as when someone
sets among grazing beasts a horse,
well-built, a prizewinner, with thundering hooves,
from out of those dreams underneath the rock.

So the problem is, what is the meaning of ὑποπετριδίων? I translate it as "underneath the rock" following the scholia of the Louvre Papyrus, which connect this adjective with πέτρα *pétra*, "rock," and quote the following passage from the *Odyssey*:

πὰρ δ' ἴσαν 'Ωκεανοῦ τε ῥοὰς καὶ Λευκάδα πέτρην
ἠδὲ παρ' 'Ηελίοιο πύλας καὶ δῆμον ὀνείρων
(*Od.* 24.11–12)

This essay was originally published in slightly different form as "Phaethon, Sappho's Phaon, and the White Rock of Leukas," *Harvard Studies in Classical Philology* 77 (1973) 137–77.

And they passed by the streams of Okeanos and the White Rock [*Leukàs pétra*]
and past the Gates of the Sun and the District of Dreams.

This interpretation has been rejected by Denys Page, who argues: "The
reference to [*Odyssey*] xxiv 11f. is irrelevant; nothing is said there about dreams
living under rocks."[1] Instead, Page follows the *Etymologicum Magnum* 783.20,
where we read ὑποπτεριδίων, "sustained by wings," so that the wondrous
horse being described would be something "out of winged dreams"; in
support of this interpretation, Page adduces passages where dreams are
represented as winged beings (e.g., Eur. *Hec.* 70).[2] All the same, Page
retains the reading ὑποπετριδίων in his edited text, so that we are left to
assume some sort of ad hoc metathesis of ὑποπετριδίων to ὑποπτεριδίων,
as if the local Laconian dialectal pronunciation of the word for "wing"
were *petr-* rather than *pter.* Other experts, though hesitantly, go along
with the interpretation "under rocks," allowing for some vague notion of
dreams abiding underneath some mysterious rock in the Laconian poetic
imagination.[3] In the most accessible chrestomathy of Greek lyric, the editor
chooses to take ὑποπετριδίων at face value: "the dreams are those of siestas
taken underneath a shady rock."[4]

The second problem of interpretation, then, is the significance of the
White Rock, *Leukàs pétra*, in *Odyssey* 24.11. This mysterious place has to be
viewed in the overall context of *Odyssey* 24.1–14, describing the passage of the
spirits of the suitors of Penelope, who have just been killed by Odysseus, into
the realm of the dead. This description, known as the Introduction to the
Second Nekyia, represents a distinct subgenre of Greek epic. It is replete with
idiosyncrasies in both theme and diction,[5] and its contents afford a precious
glimpse into early Greek concepts of afterlife. Nowhere else in Homeric
diction do we find the puzzling expressions Ἠελίοιο πύλας, "Gates (*púlai*) of
the Sun"; δῆμον ὀνείρων "District (*dēmos*) of Dreams"; and Λευκάδα πέτρην,
"White Rock (*Leukàs pétra*)." On the level of content, however, there do exist
Homeric parallels to the first two of the three expressions.

---

1. Page, *Alcman* 87.

2. Ibid., 87.

3. Wilamowitz, "Der Chor" 252 n. 2.

4. Campbell, *Greek Lyric Poetry* 203. I infer that the editor had in mind passages like Hes.
Op. 588–89.

5. For a survey, see Page, *The Homeric Odyssey* 116–19. For some, including Page, such
idiosyncrasies mean that the passage is an insertion and does not intrinsically belong where
it is found in the text. I disagree, believing that the epic genre consists of several subgenres and
that each subgenre has its idiosyncrasies in theme and diction. For a survey of the principle
that each epic subgenre (such as that of similes) has its own distinctive archaisms as well as
innovations, see Householder and Nagy, *Greek* 22–23.

In the instance of Ἡελίοιο πύλας, "Gates (púlai) of the Sun," there is
a thematic parallelism between *púlai*, "gates," and Homeric *Púlos*, "Pylos."
As Douglas Frame has demonstrated, the royal name *Néstōr* and the place
name of King Nestor's realm, *Púlos*, are based on mythological models.[6]
I should stress that Frames arguments are used not to negate a historical
Nestor and the historical Pylos, but rather to show that the kernel of the
epic tradition about Nestor and Pylos was based on local myths linked with
local cults. The clearest example is a story, represented as Nestor's own tale
within the *Iliad*, that tells of the hero's retrieving the cattle of Pylos from the
Epeians (*Il.* 11.671–761). Frame argues convincingly that the retrieved cattle
are a thematic analogue to the Cattle of the Sun.[7] The etymology of *Néstōr*,
explained by Frame as "he who brings back to light and life," is relevant.[8] We
may note the association of words built out of the root *nes-*, most prominently
nóos (mind) and *nóstos* (homecoming), with the theme of sunrise.[9] In fact, the
entire plot of Odysseus's travels is interlaced with diction that otherwise
connotes the theme of sunset followed by sunrise. To put it more bluntly,
the epic plot of Odysseus's travels operates on an extended solar metaphor,
as Frame argues in adducing the internal evidence of Homeric theme and
diction.[10] Likewise, when Nestor returns the cattle to Pylos, it is implicit that
Pylos is the Gate of the Sun and an entrance to the underworld.[11] There
are survivals of this hieratic connotation in the local Pylian lore of classical
times (Paus. 4.36.2–3).[12] In a Homeric allusion to the myth about Herakles'
descent into the underworld and his wounding of Hades (*Il.* 5.395–404) the
name Pylos actually serves to connote the realm of the otherworld rather
than any realm of this world: ἐν Πύλῳ ἐν νεκύεσσι (in Pylos, among the
dead; *Il.* 5.397). Hades himself is the *pulártēs*, "gate closer" (*Il.* 8.367, etc.). In
short, the thematic associations of *Púlos* imply that the Gate of the Sun is also
the Gate of the Underworld, and thus we have a parallel to the context of
Ἡελίοιο πύλας, "Gates (púlai) of the Sun," in *Odyssey* 24.12. Accordingly, a

6. Frame, *The Myth of Return* 81–115.

7. Ibid., 87–90, 92. Just as Nestor brings his cattle back to Pylos, so also another figure,
Melampous, on whose solar significance see 91–92.

8. See Nagy, *Greek Mythology* 218.

9. See ibid., 218. Cf. also 92 ff., with reference to Frame's demonstration of the traditional
theme that represents sunrise as symbolically parallel with a return to "consciousness," the
Greek word for which is *nóos*.

10. Note esp. Frame, *The Myth of Return* 75–76, 78, on *Od.* 13.79–95, where the "return" of
Odysseus coincides with sunrise, at which point the hero can finally awaken from the deathlike
sleep that had held him for the duration of his nighttime sea voyage homeward. Cf. Nagy,
Greek Mythology 218, and also Segal, "The Phaeacians."

11. Frame, *The Myth of Return* 92–93.

12. For details, see ibid., 90–91.

Homeric expression like πύλας Ἀίδαο περήσειν, "pass by the gates of Hades" (*Il.* 5.646; cf. 23.71) implies that the *psukhaí* (spirits) of the dead traverse to the underworld through the same passage traveled by the sun when it sets.

In the instance of δῆμον ὀνείρων, "District *dēmos* of Dreams" (*Od.* 24.12), the concept of a community of dreams situated past the Gates of Hades is thematically consistent with other Homeric expressions involving dreams. After a person dies, his *psukhē* (spirit) flies off ἠΰτ' ὄνειρος, "like a dream" (11.222). Hermes, who is conducting the *psukhaí* of the dead suitors (24.1), is also the conductor of dreams, ἡγήτορ ὀνείρων (*h. Hom. Merc.* 14). Since it is Hermes who leads the *psukhaí* of the suitors past the Gates of the Sun (24.11), it is significant that another of his inherited epithets is *pulēdókos* (*h. Hom. Merc.* 15), to be interpreted as "he who receives [the *psukhaí*] at the Gates."[13] These are the Gates of Hades, or we may call them the Gates of the Sun. But there is also another name available. Since Hermes conducts dreams as well as the ghosts of the dead, and since dreams move like ghosts, it is not surprising that dreams, too, have gates (*Od.* 19.562; cf. 4.809).[14] Since the Ἡελίοιο πύλας, "Gates (*púlai*) of the Sun," are already mentioned in 24.12, we may expect δῆμον ὀνείρων, "District (*dēmos*) of Dreams," in the same line to be a periphrastic substitute for a redundant concept, "Gates of Dreams."

In the instance of Λευκάδα πέτρην, "White Rock" (*Od.* 24.11), we find no parallel in Homeric theme and diction. All we can say about the White Rock at this point is that its collocation with δῆμον ὀνείρων, "District (*dēmos*) of Dreams" (24.12), seems parallel to the expression ὑποπετριδίων ὀνείρων, "from dreams underneath a rock," in Alcman's *Partheneion* (PMG 1.49).

As we begin to examine the attestations of *Leukàs pétra*, "White Rock," beyond Homer, we come upon the third problem of interpretation, concerning the White Rock and a figure called Phaon:

> οὗ δὴ λέγεται πρώτη Σαπφὼ
> τὸν ὑπέρκομπον θηρῶσα Φάον
> οἰστρῶντι πόθῳ ῥῖψαι πέτρας
> ἀπὸ <u>τηλεφανοῦς</u>. ἀλλὰ κατ' εὐχὴν
> σήν, δέσποτ' ἄναξ, εὐφημείσθω
> τέμενος πέρι <u>Λευκάδος</u> ἀκτῆς
> (Men. F 258 Koerte)[15]

---

13. This epithet serves as a counterexample to the argument of Page, *The Homeric Odyssey* 117, that in Homeric poetry Hermes functions as psychopomp only in *Od.* 24. Cf. also Whitman, *Homer and the Heroic Tradition* 217–18, on *Il.* 24.

14. As for the epithet ἀμενηνῶν (without vital force [*ménos*]) applied to ὀνείρων (dreams) here at *Od.* 19.562, we may note that it is applied in the *Odyssey* exclusively to the dead throughout its other attestations (νεκύων ἀμενηνὰ κάρηνα at 10.521, 536; 11.29, 49).

15. This passage must have belonged to the introductory anapests of the play (scholia A to Hephaestion 6.3).

where they say that Sappho was the first,
hunting down the proud Phaon,
to <u>throw</u> herself, in her goading desire, from the <u>rock</u>
<u>that shines from afar</u>. But now, in accordance with your sacred utterance,
lord king, let there be silence throughout the sacred precinct of the headland
of <u>Leukas</u>.

This fragment, alluding to a story about Sappho's jumping into the sea for
love of Phaon, is from a play of Menander's entitled *The Leukadia*. We infer
from Menander's lines that Sappho leaped off the White Rock of Leukas in
pursuit of Phaon. It is to Strabo that we owe the preservation of these verses
(10.2.9 C452). He is in the process of describing Cape Leukas, a prominent
white rock jutting out from Leukas into the sea and toward Kephallenia.[16]
From this rock Sappho is supposed to have jumped into the sea after Phaon.
Strabo goes on to describe a shrine of Apollo Leukatas situated on Cape
Leukas and an ancestral cult practice connected with it. Every year, he
reports, some criminal was cast down from the white rock into the sea below
for the sake of averting evil, ἀποτροπῆς χάριν. Wings and even birds would
be fastened to him, and men in fishing boats would be stationed below the
rock in order to retrieve the victim after his plunge.

As Wilamowitz has convincingly argued,[17] Menander chose for his play a
setting that was known for its exotic cult practice involving a white rock and
conflated it in the quoted passage with a literary theme likewise involving
a white rock. There are two surviving attestations of this theme. The first
is from lyric:

ἀρθεὶς δηῦτ' ἀπὸ <u>Λευκάδος</u>
<u>πέτρης</u> ἐς πολιὸν κῦμα κολυμβῶ <u>μεθύων</u> ἔρωτι
(Anac. *PMG* 376ob)

One more time taking off in the air, down from the <u>White</u>
<u>Rock</u> into the dark waves do I dive, <u>intoxicated</u> with lust.

The second is from satyr drama:

ὡς ἐκπιεῖν γ' ἂν κύλικα μαινοίμην μίαν
πάντων Κυκλώπων μὴ ἀντιδοὺς βοσκήματα[18]
ῥῖψαί τ' ἐς ἅλμην <u>Λευκάδος</u> πέτρας ἄπο
ἅπαξ μεθυσθεὶς καταβαλών τε τὰς ὄφρυς.
ὡς ὅς γε πίνων μὴ γέγηθε μαίνεται
(Eur. *Cyc.* 163–68)

---

16. Corinthian settlers called the entire territory Leukas, after Cape Leukas; cf. Strabo
10.2.8 C452.

17. Wilamowitz, *Sappho und Simonides* 25–40.

18. For a discussion of the restoration μὴ, see ibid., 30–31 n. 2; following Wilamowitz,
Dieterich, *Nekyia* vii, retracts his earlier reading without μὴ.

> I would be crazy not to give all the herds of the Cyclopes
> in return for drinking one cup of that wine
> and <u>throwing myself</u> from the <u>white rock</u> into the brine,
> once I am <u>intoxicated</u>, with eyebrows relaxed.
> Whoever is not happy when he drinks is crazy.

In both instances, falling from the white rock is parallel to falling into a swoon—be it from intoxication or from making love. As for Menander's allusion to Sappho's plunge from a *Leukás* (white rock), Wilamowitz reasonably infers that there must have existed a similar theme, which does not survive, in the poetry of Sappho. Within the framework of this theme, the female speaker must have pictured herself as driven by love for a certain Phaon, or at least so it was understood by the time New Comedy flourished.[19] So the third and the last of the three problems is, why should Sappho seem to be in love with a mythical figure?

About Phaon himself we have no reports beyond the meager fragments gathered in Sappho fragment 211 Voight (V.). It appears that he was an old *porthmeús* (ferryman) who was transformed into a beautiful youth by Aphrodite herself; also, the goddess fell in love with this beautiful Phaon and hid him in a head of lettuce. Besides specifically attesting the latter myth in Cratinus (fr. 330 Kock), Athenaeus (69d–e) also cites striking parallels in Eubulus (fr. 14 Kock) and Callimachus (fr. 478 Pfeiffer), where we see that Adonis, too, was hidden in a head of lettuce by Aphrodite. This thematic parallelism of Aphrodite and Phaon with Aphrodite and Adonis becomes more important as we come to another myth about the second pair.

According to the account in book 7 of the mythographer Ptolemaios Chennos (ca. C.E. 100; by way of Phot. *Bibl.* 152–53 Bekker),[20] the first to dive off the heights of Cape Leukas was none other than Aphrodite herself, out of love for a dead Adonis. After Adonis died (how it happened is not said), the mourning Aphrodite went off searching for him and finally found him at "Cypriote Argos," in the shrine of Apollo *Eríthios*. She consults Apollo, who instructs her to seek relief from her love by jumping off the white rock of Leukas, where Zeus sits whenever he wants relief from his passion for Hera. Then Ptolemaios launches into a veritable catalogue of other figures who followed Aphrodite's precedent and took a ritual plunge as a cure for love. For example, Queen Artemisia I is reputed to have leaped off the white rock out of love for one Dardanos, succeeding only in getting herself killed. Several others are mentioned who died from the leap, including a certain iambographer Charinos, who expired only after being fished out of

---

19. Wilamowitz, *Sappho und Simonides* 33–37.
20. Westermann, *Scriptores* 197–99.

the water with a broken leg, but not before blurting out his four last iambic trimeters, painfully preserved for us with the compliments of Ptolemaios and Photius as well. Someone called Makes was more fortunate: having succeeded in escaping from four love affairs after four corresponding leaps from the white rock, he earned the epithet *Leukopetras*. We may follow the lead of Wilamowitz in questioning the degree of historicity in such accounts.[21] There is, however, a more important concern. In the lengthy and detailed account of Ptolemaios, Sappho is not mentioned at all, let alone Phaon. From this silence I infer that the source of this myth about Aphrodite and Adonis is independent of Sappho's own poetry or of later distortions based on it.[22] Accordingly, the ancient cult practice at Cape Leukas, as described by Strabo (10.2.9 C452), may well contain some intrinsic element that inspired lovers' leaps, a practice also noted by Strabo. The second practice seems to be derived from the first, as we might expect from a priestly institution that becomes independent of the social context that had engendered it. Abstracted from their inherited tribal functions, religious institutions have a way of becoming mystical organizations.[23]

Another reason for doubting that Sappho's poetry had been the inspiration for the lovers' leaps at Cape Leukas is the attitude of Strabo himself. He specifically disclaims Menander's version about Sappho being the first to take the plunge at Leukas. Instead, he offers a version of the *arkhaiologikóteroi*, "those more versed in the ancient lore," according to which Kephalos son of Deioneus was the very first to have leaped, impelled by love for Pterelas (Strabo 10.2.9 C452). Again, I see no reason to take it for granted that this myth concerning historical *Leukás* had resulted from some distortion of the cults features because of Sappho's literary influence.[24] The myth of Kephalos and his dive may be as old as the concept of *Leukás*, the White Rock. I say "concept" because the ritual practice of casting victims from a white rock such as that of Leukas may be in inheritance parallel to the epic tradition about a mythical White Rock on the shores of the Okeanos (as in *Od.* 24.11) and the related literary theme of diving from an imaginary White Rock (as in the poetry of Anacreon and Euripides). In other words, it is needless to assume that the ritual preceded the myth or the other way around.

Actually, there are other historical places besides Cape Leukas that are associated with myths about diving. For example, Charon of Lampsakos

---

21. Wilamowitz, *Sappho und Simonides* 28.

22. Ibid., 28.

23. For an articulate discussion of this general tendency, see Jeanmaire, *Couroï et Courètes*, esp. 310 on the Mysteries.

24. Wilamowitz, *Sappho und Simonides* 27.

(fifth century B.C.E., *FGrH* 262 F 7)[25] reports that Phobos, of the lineage Kodridai, founder of Lampsakos, was the first to leap ἀπὸ τῶν Λευκάδων πετρῶν, "from the White Rocks," located apparently on the north shore of the Smyrnaean Gulf, not far from Phokaia.[26] We may compare, too, the myth about the death of Theseus. He was pushed by Lykomedes and fell into the sea from the high rocks of the island *Skûros* (Heraclides by way of Paus. 1.17.6; scholia to Ar. *Plut.* 627). The island derives its name *Skûros* from its white rocks (LSJ, s.vv. *skûros* and *skîros/skírros*).[27] In fact, the entire Theseus myth is replete with themes involving names derived from *skûros/skîros*. Even the "grandfather" of Theseus is *Skurios* (Apollod. 3.15.5), while Theseus himself casts *Skírōn* off the *Skirōnídes pétrai* (Strabo 9.1.4 C391; Plut. *Thes.* 10; Paus. 1.33.8).[28] For the moment, I merely note in passing the ritual nature of the various plunges associated with Theseus and his "father" Aigeus,[29] and the implications of agonistic death and mystical rebirth in both ritual and myth.[30]

25. By way of Plutarch *De mul. vir.* 255a–e.

26. See the commentary of Jacoby, *Die Fragmente* 262 F2, 16.

27. Gruppe, *Griechische Mythologie* 585. The basic meaning of *skíros*, "hard rock" (whence "chalk, gypsum"), survives in the variant reading for *Il.* 23.332–33, preserved by Aristarchus (scholia Townley). Nestor is telling about a landmark, an old tree trunk (23.326–28), with this added detail: λᾶε δὲ τοῦ ἑκάτερθεν ἐρηρέδαται δύο λευκώ (and two white rocks are propped up on either side; *Il.* 23.329). In the vulgate, at *Il.* 23.331–33, this image of two white rocks propped up on a tree trunk is described as either a *sēma* (tomb) or a *nússa* (turning post) belonging to a past generation (see Nagy, *Greek Mythology* 215). Instead of the two verses 332–33, describing the alternative of a turning post, Aristarchus reads the following single verse: ἠὲ σκῖρος ἔην, νῦν αὖ θέτο τέρματ' Ἀχιλλεύς (or it was a *skíros*, but now Achilles set it up as a turning point). In the *Tabulae Heracleenses* (*DGE* no. 62.19, 144), *skíros* designates a rocky area unfit for planting, on which trees grow wild. For a useful discussion of words formed with *skir-*, see Robert, "Athena Skiras."

28. Pausanias tells us (1.33.8) that the specific name of Skiron's white rock was Molouris, and that it was sacred to Leukothea, the White Goddess (on whom see Nagy, "Theognis" 79–81). It is from the Molouris that Leukothea flung herself into the sea with her "son" Melikertes (Paus. 1.44.7). At the top of Molouris was a shrine of Zeus Aphesios, the "Releaser" (Paus. 1.44.8).

29. As for the agency of *Lykomedes* (*Lukomédēs*) in the plunge of Theseus (Heraclides by way of Paus. 1.17.6; scholia to Ar. *Plut.* 627), we may compare the agency of *Lykourgos* (*Lukoûrgos*) in the plunge of Dionysus (*Il.* 6.130–41). We may note, too, the words describing what happened to Dionysus after he dove into the sea: Θέτις δ' ὑπεδέξατο κόλπῳ (and Thetis received him in her bosom; 6.136). For the ritual significance of the wolf theme, see Jeanmaire, *Couroï et Courètes* 581.

30. For a detailed discussion, see Jeanmaire, *Couroï et Courètes* 324–37. We may note in general the parallelism between the procedure of initiation (ritual) and the story of death (myth). Cf. Nagy, "Pindar's *Olympian* 1." For a pathfinding work on the theme of rebirth in the *Odyssey*, see Newton, "The Rebirth of Odysseus."

A more immediate concern is that the mythological examples I have
cited so far do not attest the lovelorn theme as a feature of the plunges
from white rocks. There is, however, a more basic sexual theme associated
with the *Thoríkios pétros*, "Leap Rock," of Attic Kolonos (Soph. *OC* 1595).
Kolonos itself, meaning "summit," is proverbially white or shining bright
(ἀργὴς κολωνός; Soph. *OC* 670). As for the name *Thoríkios*, it is formally
derivable from the noun *thorós*, "semen" (e.g., Hdt. 2.93.1), by way of the
adjective *thorikós*; the noun *thorós* is in turn built on the aorist *thoreîn* of the
verb *thrôiskō*, "leap."[31] Even the verb can have the side meaning "mount,
fecundate" (Aes. *Eum.* 660). From the form *Thoríkios* itself, it is difficult to
ascertain whether the name may connote leaping as well as fecundating. And
yet, thematic associations of the formally related name *Thórikos* suggest that
leaping is indeed involved. The provenience of Kephalos, son of Deioneus,
the figure who leaped from the white rock of Leukas (Strabo 10.2.9 C452),
is actually this very Thorikos, a town and deme on the southeast coast of
Attica (Apollod. 2.4.7).[32]

The sexual element inherent in the theme of a white rock recurs in a myth
about Kolonos. Poseidon fell asleep in this area and had an emission of
semen, from which issued the horse *Skirōnítēs*:

ἄλλοι δέ φασιν ὅτι περὶ τοὺς πέτρους τοῦ ἐν Ἀθήναις Κολωνοῦ καθευδήσας
ἀπεσπέρμηνε καὶ ἵππος Σκύφιος ἐξῆλθεν, ὁ καὶ Σκιρωνίτης[33] λεγόμενος.
(scholia to Lycoph. 766)

Others say that, in the vicinity of the rocks at Athenian Kolonos, he Poseidon,
falling asleep, had an emission of semen, and a horse *Skúphios* came out, who is
also called *Skirōnítēs*.

The name Skironites again conjures up the theme of Theseus, son of
Poseidon, and his plunge from the white rocks of Skyros.[34] This Attic myth is
parallel to the Thessalian myth of *Skúphios* Skyphios:

Πετραῖος τιμᾶται Ποσειδῶν παρὰ Θεσσαλοῖς ... ὅτι ἐπί τινος πέτρας κοιμη-
θεὶς ἀπεσπερμάτισε, καὶ τὸν θορὸν δεξαμένη ἡ γῆ ἀνέδωκεν ἵππον πρῶτον,
ὃν ἐπεκάλεσαν Σκύφιον. (scholia to Pind. *Pyth.* 4.246)

31. *DELG* 444.
32. The leap of Kephalos into the sea was at first probably localized in Thorikos and only
later transposed to Cape Leukas. For a discussion of the political motivations for such a
mythological transposition, see Gruppe, "Die eherne Schwelle" 373.
33. The reading Σκιρωνίτης is preferable to Σκειρωνίτης, as we know from the evidence
of vase inscriptions; see Kretschmer, *Die griechischen Vaseninschriften* 131 ff.
34. Gruppe, "Die eherne Schelle" 372, argues that Kolonos marks one of the places claimed
to be the spot where Theseus descended into the underworld.

Poseidon *Petraîos* [of the rocks] has a cult among the Thessalians ... because he, having fallen asleep at some rock, had an emission of semen; and the earth, receiving the semen, produced the first horse, whom they called *Skúphios*.

There is a further report about this first horse ever:

φασὶ δὲ καὶ ἀγῶνα διατίθεσθαι τῷ Πετραίῳ Ποσειδῶνι, ὅπου ἀπὸ τῆς πέτρας ἐξεπήδησεν ὁ πρῶτος ἵππος. (scholia to Pind. *Pyth.* 4.246)

And they say that there was a festival established in worship of Poseidon *Petraîos* at the spot where the first horse leaped forth.[35]

The myth of Skironites/Skyphios, featuring the themes of leaping, sexual relief, and the state of unconsciousness, may help us understand better the puzzling verses of Anacreon already quoted:

ἀρθεὶς δηὖτ' ἀπὸ Λευκάδος
πέτρης ἐς πολιὸν κῦμα κολυμβῶ μεθύων ἔρωτι
(Anac. *PMG* 376)

One more time[36]
taking off in the air, down from the White
Rock into the dark waves do I dive, intoxicated with lust.

The theme of jumping is overt and the theme of sexual relief is latent in the poetry,[37] while the situation is reversed in the myth. In the poem the unconsciousness comes from what is likened to a drunken stupor; in the myth it comes from sleep.[38] As for the additional theme of a horse in the myth, we consider again the emblem of Hagesikhora's charms, that wondrous horse

35. The rock associated with Skyphios is the *Pétrē Haimoniē* (A.R. 3.1244 and scholia). Note, too, the Argive custom of sacrificing horses by throwing them into the sea (Paus. 8.7.2); see Nilsson, *Griechische Feste* 71–72.

36. For an appreciation of the contextual nuances in δηὖτε (one more time), I recommend as an exercise in associative esthetics the consecutive reading of the passages cited by Campbell, *Greek Lyric Poetry* 266, with reference to the triple deployment of δηὖτε at Sappho frs. 1.15, 16, 18 V. Cf. Nagy, "Copies and Models" 418–20.

37. If plunging is symbolic of sexual relief, it follows that the opposite is symbolic of sexual frustration:

ἀναπέτομαι δὴ πρὸς Ὄλυμπον πτερύγεσσι κούφης
διὰ τὸν Ἔρωτ'. οὐ γὰρ ἐμοὶ ... θέλει συνηβᾶν.
(Anac. *PMG* 378)

I flutter up toward Olympus on light wings
on account of Eros. For he ... refuses to join me in youthful sport.

38. Note the association of wine with the shade from a rock in the following words of Hesiod: εἴη πετραίη τε σκιὴ καὶ βίβλινος οἶνος, "let there be a shade under the rock and wine from Biblos" (*Op.* 589; see further at 592–96).

of Alcman's Laconian fantasy, who is "from those dreams under the Rock," τῶν ὑποπετριδίων ὀνείρων (*PMG* 1.49).

We may note that, just as Poseidon obtains sexual relief through the unconsciousness of sleeping at the white rocks of Kolonos, so also Zeus is cured of his passion for Hera by sitting on the white rock of Apollos Leukas (Ptolemaios Chennos by way of Phot. *Bibl.* 152–53 Bekker). At Magnesia, those who were *hieroí* (sacred) to Apollo would leap from precipitous rocks into the river *Lēthaîos* (Paus. 10.32.6). This name is clearly derivable from *lēthē* forgetfulness. In the underworld, Theseus and Peirithoos sat on the θρόνος τῆς Λήθης, "throne of *Lēthē*" (Apollod. *Epit.* 1.24; Paus. 10.29.9). I have already quoted the passage from the *Cyclops* of Euripides (163–68) where getting drunk is equated with leaping from a proverbial white rock. We may note the wording of the verses that immediately follow that equation, describing how it feels to be in the realm of a drunken stupor:

ἵν' ἔστι τουτί τ' ὀρθὸν ἐξανιστάναι
μαστοῦ τε δραγμὸς καὶ παρεσκευασμένου
ψαῦσαι χεροῖν λειμῶνος, ὀρχηστύς θ' ἅμα
κακῶν τε λῆστις.

(Eur. *Cyc.* 169–72)

where it is allowed to make this thing stand up erect,
to grab the breast and touch with both hands
the meadow[39] that is made all ready. And there is dancing
and forgetting *[lēstis]* of bad things.

Again, we see the theme of sexual relief and the key concept *lēstis*, "forgetting."

In short, the White Rock is the boundary delimiting the conscious and the unconscious—be it a trance, stupor, sleep, or even death. Accordingly, when the suitors are led past the White Rock (*Od.* 24.11), they reach the *dēmos oneirōn*, "District of Dreams" (24.12), beyond which is the realm of the dead (24.14).

Even with the accumulation of this much evidence about the symbolism of the White Rock, it is still difficult to see how it relates to the mythical figure Phaon and how he relates to Sappho. One approach that might yield more information is to study the mythical figure Phaethon, who shares several characteristics with Adonis and Phaon. For now, I postpone the details and citations, offering only the essentials. Like Adonis and Phaon, Phaethon is loved by Aphrodite, and like them, he is hidden by her. Like Adonis, Phaethon dies. Like Phaon, Phaethon means "bright" (for the morphology of *Pháōn/Phaéthōn*, we may compare

39. Euphemism for female genitalia.

Homeric *phlégō/phlegéthō*, "burn").[40] Unlike Phaon, however, about whom
we have only meager details, the Phaethon figure confronts us with a
wealth of testimony, much of it unwieldy and conflicting; we now turn to
this testimony.

In the commentary to his edition of the Hesiodic *Theogony*, Martin West
observes that *Phaéthōn* (l. 987), like *Huperíōn*, is a hypostasis of the sun-god
Hélios.[41] The thematic equation of *Hélios* with *Huperíōn* and *Phaéthōn* isoo
apparent in epic diction, where *huperíōn*, "the one who goes above" (*Od.* 1.8,
etc.) and *phaéthōn*, "the one who shines" (*Il.* 11.735, etc.) are ornamental epithets of *Hélios*. The mythological differentiation of identities is symbolized in
genealogical terms: in one case, *Huperíōn* is the father of *Hélios* (*Od.* 12.176;
Hes. *Theog.* 371–74), while in the other, *Phaéthōn* is the son of *Hélios*. The
latter relationship is a basic feature of the myth treated by Euripides in the
tragedy *Phaethon*.[42] What follows is an outline of the myth as found in the
Euripidean version.

Phaethon, the story goes, was raised as the son of Merops and Klymene.
His real father, however, is not the mortal Merops but the sun-god Helios.
At his mother's behest, Phaethon travels to Aithiopia, the abode of Helios, in
a quest to prove that the Sun is truly his father. He borrows the chariot
of Helios for a day; driving too near the earth, he sets it afire. Zeus then
strikes him dead with his thunderbolt, and Phaethon falls from the sky.[43]

A cross-cultural perspective reveals many myths, indigenous to a wide
variety of societies, that are analogous to this Greek myth. There are
parallels, for example, in the myths of the Kwakiutl and Bella Coola Indians
in British Columbia. From the traditions collected by the anthropologist
Franz Boas,[44] the following outline emerges. The Sun impregnates a woman
who bears him a son (called Born-to-be-the-Sun in the Kwakiutl version).
When the boy goes to visit his father, he is permitted to take the Suns place.
Exceeding his limits, the boy sets the earth on fire, whereupon he is cast
down from the sky.[45]

It does not necessarily follow, however, that the Phaethon myth merely
represents the sunset. I sympathize with those who are reluctant to accept
the theory that "Phaethon's fall attempts to explain in mythical terms why
the sun sinks blazing in the west as if crashing to earth in flames and yet

40. Cf. Nagy, *Greek Mythology* 153.

41. West, ed., *Hesiod* ad loc.

42. Fragments edited by Diggle *Euripides: Phaethon.*

43. For attestations of the same myth beyond Euripides, cf. ibid., 3–32.

44. Boas, *Kwakiutl Tales* 123, 125, 126; also Boas, *The Mythology of the Bella Coola Indians*
100–103.

45. For detailed comparisons with the Greek myth, see Frazer, *Apollodorus* 388–94, app. xi:
"Phaethon and the Chariot of the Sun."

returns to its task unimpaired the following day."[46] One counterexplanation runs as follows: "Phaethon's crash is an event out of the ordinary, a sudden and unexpected calamity, occurring once and not daily."[47] In such matters, however, I would heed the intuitively appealing approach of Lévi-Strauss. A myth, he concedes, "always refers to events alleged to have taken place long ago." Nevertheless, "what gives the myth an operational value is that the specific pattern described is timeless; it explains the present and the past as well as the future."[48] Accordingly, I find it unnecessary to entertain the proposal, based only on naturalistic intuition, that the Phaethon myth represents the fall of a meteorite.[49] The meteorite explanation, as also the sunset explanation, operates on the assumption that the message of the Phaethon myth is simply a metaphorical expression of some phenomenon that occurs in the sky. I disagree. The Phaethon myth presents a problem, not a solution. Furthermore, this problem addresses the human condition, not just celestial dynamics.

There is another Phaethon myth, preserved in Hesiodic poetry, which is preoccupied with both aspects of the solar cycle, not only with death but also rebirth. In this myth Phaethon is the son not of Helios but of Eos the dawn goddess (*Theog.* 986–87). In the same context we hear that Eos first mates with Tithonos, bearing Memnon, king of the Aithiopes, and Emathion (984–85); then she mates with Kephalos, bearing Phaethon (986–87); then Aphrodite mates with Phaethon (988–91), having abducted him (990).[50] The parallelism between the mating of Eos with Kephalos and the mating of Aphrodite with their son, Phaethon, is reinforced in the *Hymn to Aphrodite*: when Aphrodite seduces Anchises, the goddess herself cites the abduction of Tithonos by Eos as precedent 218. There are also other parallels, as when a hero called Kleitos is abducted by Eos (*Od.* 15.250–51). Or again, the nymph Kalypso cites the abduction of the hero Orion by Eos as a precedent for her abduction of Odysseus (5.121–24).[51]

Let us focus on the association of Phaethon with Aphrodite in *Theogony* 988–91. It arises, I propose, from a sexual theme implicit in a solar transition from death to rebirth. In the logic of the myth, it appears that the setting sun mates with the goddess of regeneration so that the rising sun may be

---

46. Diggle, *Euripides: Phaethon* 10 n. 3, paraphrasing and rejecting the formulation of Robert, "Die Phaethonsage" 440.

47. Ibid.

48. Lévi-Strauss, *Structural Anthropology* 205.

49. Diggle, *Euripides: Phaethon* 10 n. 3.

50. For a more detailed discussion of Hes. *Theog.* 986–91, see Nagy, *The Best of the Achaeans* 191.

51. It is pertinent to note here the argument that Kalypso is a hypostasis of Aphrodite herself, in the aspect *Melainís* (the black one): see Güntert, *Kalypso,* esp. 189. For a definitive treatment of Kalypso figure, see Crane, *Backgrounds and Conventions.*

reborn. If the setting sun is the same as the rising sun, then the goddess of regeneration may be viewed as both mate and mother.

Such an ambivalent relationship actually survives in the hymns of the *Rig-Veda*, where the goddess of solar regeneration, the dawn Uṣas, is the wife or bride of the sun-god Sūrya (1.115.1, 7.75.5, etc.) as well as his mother (7.63.3, 7.78.3).[52] In the latter instance, the incestuous implications are attenuated by putting Uṣas in the plural, representing the succession of dawns; similarly, Uṣas in the plural can designate the wives of Sūrya (4.5.13). Yet even if each succeeding dawn is wife of the preceding dawn's son, the husband and son are always one and the same Sūrya, and the basic theme of incest remains intact.

This comparative evidence from the *Rig-Veda* is important for understanding the Greek evidence, because Indic *Sūrya* (Sun) and *Uṣás-* (Dawn) are formally cognate with Greek *Hélios* (Sun) and *Ēós* (Dawn);[53] furthermore, the epithets of Uṣas in the *Rig-Veda*, *divá(s) duhitár-* and *duhitár- divás*, both meaning "Daughter of the Sky," are exact formal cognates of the Homeric epithets *Diòs thugátēr* and *thugátēr Diós*, meaning "Daughter of Zeus."[54] The Homeric hexameter preserves these epithets only in the following patterns:

A. — ⏑⏑ — ⏑⏑ — |θυγάτηρ Διός| — ⏑ ⏑ — ⏕ six times
B. — ⏑ Διὸς θυγάτηρ | ⏑⏑ — ⏑⏑ — ⏑ ⏑ — ⏕ eight times
C. — ⏑⏑ — ⏑⏑ — ⏑ | Διὸς θυγάτηρ ⏑ ⏑ — ⏕ eighteen times

We see from this scheme that it is cumbersome for the meter to accommodate the name of Eos, 'Ηώς, in a position contiguous with these epithets. Thus it is not surprising that Eos is not combined with these epithets anywhere in attested Greek epic, despite the comparative evidence that such a combination had once existed, as we see from the survival of the Indic cognates *divá(s) duhitár-* and *duhitár-divás* in the *Rig-Veda*.

Within the framework of the Greek hexameter, we may have expected at least one position, however, where the name of Eos could possibly have been combined with *thugátēr Diós*, "Daughter of Zeus":

D. *— ⏑⏑ — ⏑⏑ — |θυγάτηρ Διὸς 'Ηώς

And yet, when 'Ηώς (Dawn) occupies the final portion of the hexameter and when it is preceded by an epithet with the metrical shape ⏑ ⏑ — ⏑ ⏑ this epithet is regularly ῥοδοδάκτυλος, "rosy-fingered" (or "rosy-toed"), not θυγάτηρ Διός *thugátēr Diós*, "Daughter of Zeus." I infer that the epithet

52. For more on Indic sun-gods, see Nagy, *Greek Mythology* 93 ff.
53. Schmitt, *Dichtung und Dichtersprache* chap. 4.
54. Ibid., 169–73.

θυγάτηρ Διός *thugatḗr Diós*, "Daughter of Zeus," in position D must have been ousted by the fixed epithet ῥοδοδάκτυλος, "rosyfingered," as in the familiar verse ἦμος δ ἠριγένεια φάνη ῥοδοδάκτυλος Ἠώς (when early-born rosy-fingered Dawn appeared . . .; *Il.* 1.477, etc.).

In short, for both metrical and formulaic reasons, Greek epic fails to preserve the combination of *Ēṓs* (Dawn) with *thugátēr Diós*, meaning "Daughter of Zeus."[55] By contrast, when the name *Aphrodite* occupies the final position of the hexameter, her fixed epithet is *Diòs thugátēr*: — ⏑⏑ — ⏑⏑ — ⏑ | Διὸς θυγάτηρ, Ἀφροδίτη (. . . Daughter of Zeus, Aphrodite; *Il.* 3.374, etc.). From the standpoint of comparative analysis, then, Aphrodite is a parallel of Eos in epic diction. Furthermore, from the standpoint of internal analysis, Aphrodite is a parallel of Eos in epic theme. Just as Eos abducts Tithonos (*h. Hom. Ven.* 218), Kleitos (*Od.* 15.250), Orion (*Od.* 5.121), and Kephalos (Eur. *Hipp.* 455), so also Aphrodite abducts Phaethon (*Theog.* 990). When Aphrodite seduces Anchises, she herself cites the abduction of Tithonos by Eos for an actual precedent (*h. Hom. Ven.* 218–38), as we have already seen. Throughout the seduction episode, Aphrodite is called *Diòs thugátēr*, "Daughter of Zeus" (*h. Hom. Ven.* 81, 107, 191).

The archaic parallelism of Eos and Aphrodite suggests that Aphrodite became a rival of Eos in such functions as that of *Diòs thugátēr*, "Daughter of Zeus." From the comparative evidence of the *Rig-Veda*, we would expect Eos to be not only mother but also consort of the Sun. There is no such evidence in Greek epic for either Helios or any hypostasis such as the Phaethon figure. Instead, the Hesiodic tradition assigns Aphrodite as consort of Phaethon, while Eos is only his mother (*Theog.* 986–91). In other words, the Hesiodic tradition seems to have split the earlier fused roles of mother and consort and divided them between Eos and Aphrodite respectively. This way, the theme of incest could be neatly obviated.

Although the epithet *Diòs thugátēr/thugátēr Diós* does not survive in combination with Eos, the goddess herself is in fact likewise ambivalent. Homeric diction features her snatching up youths as if she were some Harpy, and yet she gives them immortality. To review this point, the example of Kleitos will suffice (*Od.* 15.250–51).[56] Such an ambivalence inherent in the Eos figure

55. I disagree with Schmitt's statement that Eos is Daughter of Helios (*Dichtung und Dichtersprache* 172–73). Technically, she does appear as Daughter of the Sun in *Theog.* 371–74, but here the name of her "father" is Hyperion; as for Helios, he is her "brother." For the image of Eos as Daughter of the Sun, we may compare the special image of Uṣas as Daughter of the Sun-God Sūrya in the *Rig-Veda* (2.23.2), as distinct from the usual image of Uṣas as Daughter of the Sky-God Dyaus, *divá(s) duhitár-* (*Rig-Veda*, passim); the noun *dyáus*, "sky," personified as the Sky-God Dyaus, is cognate of Greek Ζεύς.

56. See Nagy, *Greek Mythology* 242.

is so uncomfortable that it tends to be attenuated in the diction. For instance, the verb used to describe the abduction of Orion by Eos is not the concretely violent *hḗrpasen*, "snatched," but the more abstract *héleto*, "seized" (*Od.* 5.121).[57] Once the wording *hḗrpasen* snatched is removed, the connotation of death from Harpies disappears and a new theme is introduced, death from Artemis *Od.* 5.121–24.

The alternative to a death from Artemis is a violent abduction by a *thúella*, "gust of wind" (*Od.* 20.63), the action of which is there described as *anarpáxasa*, "snatching up." As precedent for being abducted by a gust of wind and plunged into the Okeanos, Penelope's words evoke the story of the daughters of Pandareos, abducted by *thúellai*, "gusts of wind" (20.66), the action of which is described as *anélonto*, "seized." This mention of abduction is followed by a description of how the daughters of Pandareos had been preserved by the Olympian goddesses (20.67–72); the preservation of the girls is then interrupted by death, at the very moment that Aphrodite is arranging for them to be married (20.73–74). Death comes in the form of abduction by *hárpuiai*, "snatching winds" (20.77), the action of which is now described as *anēreípsanto*, "snatched up."[58]

In this story about the daughters of Pandareos (*Od.* 20.66–81), we see a sequence of *preservation followed by abduction/death.*[59] In the story about Orion and Eos (5.121–24), by contrast, the pattern is *abduction/preservation followed by death*, in that Eos abducts and preserves the hero while Artemis arranges for his death.[60] Finally, the story about Aphrodite and Phaethon (Hes. *Theog.* 986–91) presents yet another pattern, that of *abduction/death followed by preservation.*[61] In each of these narrative alternatives, we see various patterns of differentiation in the ambivalent function of Eos as the undifferentiated agent of abduction, death, and preservation.

The abduction of Phaethon by Aphrodite is most directly comparable to the abduction of Kleitos by Eos (*Od.* 15.251–52), where again we see the patternt *abduction/death followed by preservation*. The Kleitos figure is represented as son of Mantios 15.249 and grandson of the seer Melampous 15.242. As Frame has shown, the Melampous myth centers on the theme

57. See ibid.

58. For further details on this difficult passage concerning the daughters of Pandareos, *Od.* 20.66–81, see Nagy, *The Best of the Achaeans* 194, 25 n. 2.

59. Further discussion at ibid., 201, 37 n. 3.

60. More detailed discussion at ibid., 201–3.

61. Ibid., 191–92. As for the Tithonos story in the *Hymn to Aphrodite*, the sequence is suspended: *abduction = preservation, with no death ensuing.* Appropriately, Tithonos therefore never rises from the Okeanos, as would a reborn Sun. Whenever Eos rises, she leaves Tithonos behind (*Il.* 19.1–2 vs. *Od.* 5.1–2; *h. Hom. Ven.* 227, 236).

of retrieving the Cattle of the Sun.[62] The solar function of the Melampous figure and his genetic affinity with the Kleitos figure together imply a solar affinity for Kleitos as well. The wording *hḗrpasen* for the abduction of Kleitos at *Odyssey* 15.251 implies that he was taken by a maleficent Harpy and dropped into the Okeanos. This theme of death is parallel to sunset. On the other hand, the subject of *hḗrpasen* is Eos herself, and the theme of sunrise is parallel to rebirth. Since the abductor of Kleitos is represented as the Dawn, it is at least implicit that Kleitos is to be reborn like the Sun and thus preserved.

So long as the Dawn is present, the day waxes. Once the Sun reaches noon, however, the Dawn ceases and the day wanes. This vital role of Eos is explicit in Homeric diction (e.g., *Il.* 20.66–69). Implicitly, the Sun is united with the light of Dawn until noon; afterward, the Sun descends into the Okeanos, only to be reborn the next day. In the story of Eos and Kleitos a parallel death and rebirth are implied. The sequence of events, to repeat, is *abduction/death followed by preservation.*[63] In the Orion story (*Od.* 5.121–24), on the other hand, the sequence is the inverse: *abduction/preservation followed by death.*[64] We may note that Orion's relation to the Dawn is the inverse of the Sun's. Translated into the symbolism of celestial dynamics, Orion's movements are accordingly astral, not solar, and we see an astral representation of the Orion figure already in Homeric poetry (*Od.* 5.174; *Il.* 18.488).[65] Like the Sun, the constellation Orion rises from the Okeanos and sets in it (*Od.* 5.275; *Il.* 8.489), but, unlike the Sun, it rises and sets at nighttime, not daytime. In the summer, at threshing time, Orion starts rising before Dawn (Hes. *Op.* 598–99). In the winter, at ploughing time, Orion starts setting before Dawn (*Op.* 615–16). In summer days the light of Dawn catches up with the rising Orion, and he can be her consort in the daytime.[66] In winter days the light of Dawn arrives too late to keep Orion from setting into the Okeanos. One related star that does not set, however, is Arktos (*Od.* 5.275 *Il.* 18.489). The Arktos Bear watches Orion, *dokeúei* (*Od.* 5.274 *Il.* 18.488), and the verb *dokeúei* implies doom. In Homeric diction it is used when marksmen or savage beasts take aim at their victims (*Il.* 13.545, 16.313, 20.340).[67] As for Arktos as "Bear," the name implies the goddess Artemis.[68] In other

---

62. Frame, *The Myth of Return* 91–92. Suffice it here to note the suggestive verses at *Od.* 15.235–36.

63. See immediately above.

64. See Nagy, *Greek Mythology* 252.

65. More detailed discussion in Nagy, *The Best of the Achaeans* 201–3.

66. This theme is pertinent to the name *Ōríōn (Oaríōn)*, which seems to be connected with *óar* (wife), *óaros* (companionship, keeping company), etc.

67. Further details at Nagy, *The Best of the Achaeans* 190–92.

68. The argument is presented at Nagy, *Greek Mythology* 202.

words, the astral passages of *Odyssey* 5.273–75 and *Iliad* 18.487–89 implicitly repeat the theme of Orion's dying at the hands of Artemis, explicit in *Odyssey* 5.121–24.[69] The latter passage involves two goddesses, a beneficent Eos and a maleficent Artemis.[70] We may contrast the passage about Kleitos, involving an ambivalent Eos who is both maleficent and beneficent (*Od.* 15.251–52).[71] The theme of death is implicit in *hḗrpasen*, "snatched" (251), while the theme of preservation is explicit in ἵν ἀθανάτοισι μετείη, "so that he may be with the immortals" (252).

Similarly, Aphrodite is ambivalent in the Hesiodic passage about Phaethon (*Theog.* 989–91). Again, the theme of death is implied in *anereipsaménē*, "snatching up" (990). The epithet *daímōn*, "supernatural being" (991), on the other hand, implies divine preservation, as we see from the context of *daímōn* in *Works and Days* 109–26.[72]

To sum up: like Eos, Aphrodite is both maleficent and beneficent in the role of abductor, since she confers both death and preservation. When Phaethon's parents are Helios and Klymene, the stage is set for his death, implicit in the Klymene figure. When his parents are Kephalos and Eos, the stage is set for both his death and his preservation, implicit in the Eos figure as well as in her alternate, Aphrodite. Thus, I disagree with the spirit of the claim that "on the evidence available to us the son of Helios and the son of Eos and Cephalus must be pronounced entirely different persons."[73] Such an attitude is overly prosopographical. We are dealing not with different persons but with different myths, cognate variants, centering on the inherited personification of a solar child and consort.

Since the epithet *múkhios* (secreted) as applied to Phaethon in *Theogony* 991 implies that he was hidden by Aphrodite, we see here an important parallelism with Phaon and Adonis, who were also hidden by Aphrodite.[74] Just as Phaethon implicitly attains preservation in the cult of Aphrodite, so also Adonis in the cult of Apollo *Erithios*.[75] As for Phaon, he explicitly attains preservation in the myth where he is turned into a beautiful young man by Aphrodite (Sappho fr. 211 V.). From the myths of Phaethon, we see that the themes of concealment and preservation are symbolic of solar behavior, and

69. On the implications of the Orion myth for the fate of Odysseus in the *Odyssey*, see ibid., 202–3; see also 207 n. 15.

70. See ibid., 251.

71. See ibid., 242.

72. Further details at Nagy, *The Best of the Achaeans* 190–92.

73. Diggle, *Euripides: Phaethon* 15 n. 3.

74. See Nagy, *Greek Mythology* 228–29.

75. See ibid., 229–30.

we may begin to suspect that the parallel myths of Phaon and Adonis are based on like symbolism.

The very name *Pháōn*, just like *Phaéthōn*, suggests a solar theme.[76] His occupation too, that of ferryman (Sappho fr. 211 V.), is a solar theme, as we see from the studies of Hermann Güntert on other mythological ferrymen.[77] As an interesting parallel to Phaon, I single out a solar deity in the *Rig-Veda*, Puṣan,[78] who regularly functions as a psychopomp and who is at least once featured as traveling in golden boats (6.58.3); he is the wooer of his mother (6.55.5) and the lover of his sister (6.55.4, 5). A frequent and exclusive epithet of Puṣan is *āghṛnī-*, "glowing, bright," comparable in meaning to *Pháōn* and *Phaéthōn*.

Let us pursue our current center of attention, the solar figure Phaon, in the poetics of Sappho: another solar theme associated with Phaon is his plunge from a white rock, an act that is parallel to the solar plunge of Phaethon into the Eridanos. The Eridanos is an analogue of the Okeanos, the boundary delimiting light and darkness, life and death, wakefulness and sleep, consciousness and unconsciousness.[79] We have also seen that the White Rock is another mythical landmark delimiting the same opposites and that these two landmarks are mystical coefficients in Homeric diction (*Od.* 24.11). Even the Phaethon figure is connected with the White Rock, in that his "father" Kephalos is supposed to have jumped off Cape Leukas (Strabo 10.2.9 C452) and is connected with the place name *Thórikos* (Apollodorus 2.4.7).[80] The theme of plunging is itself overtly solar, as we see from Homeric diction: ἐν δ᾽ ἔπες Ὠκεανῷ λαμπρὸν φάος Ἡελίοιο (and the bright light of Helios plunged into the Okeanos; *Il.* 8.485). In the Epic Cycle the lover of Klymene is not Helios but "Kephalos son of Deion" (Κεφάλῳ τῷ Δηίονος; *Nostoi* fr. 4 Allen),[81] a figure whose name matches that of Kephalos son of Deioneus, the one who leaped from the white rock of Leukas (Strabo 10.2.9 C452) and who hails from Thorikos (Apollod. 2.4.7).[82]

If indeed the Phaon and Adonis myths operate on solar themes, it remains to ask about the relevance of Aphrodite. Most important of all, how do we interpret Aphrodite's plunge from the White Rock? We hear of her doing so out of love for Adonis Ptolemaios Chennos by way of Phot. *Bibl.* 152–53

---

76. See ibid., 235.
77. See esp. Güntert, *Kalypso* and *Der arische Weltkönig* 273. For the problem of the Aśvin-s (on whom see also *Der arische Weltkönig* 112–13), see immediately below.
78. On whom see Nagy, *Greek Mythology* 97 ff.
79. See the longer version in ibid., 236–39.
80. See ibid., 230, 232.
81. The son of Klymene and Kephalos is named Iphiklos (*Nostoi* fr. 4 Allen).
82. See ibid., 232.

Bekker,[83] and the act itself may be connected with her known function as substitute for the Indo-European dawn-goddess of the Greeks, Eos. As we have seen, Aphrodite has even usurped the epithet of Eos, *Diòs thugátēr*, "Daughter of the Sky," as well as the roles that go with the epithet. From the Homeric standpoint, Aphrodite is actually the *Diòs thugátēr* par excellence, in that even her "mother's" name is *Diōnḗ* (*Il.* 5.370, 381). It still remains, however, to explain Aphrodite's plunge, from the White Rock as a feature characteristic of a surrogate Indo-European dawn-goddess.

Here we may do well to look toward Aphrodite's older, Near Eastern, heritage. As the Greek heiress to the functions of the Semitic fertility goddess Ištar, Aphrodite has as her astral symbol the planet of Ištar, better known to us as Venus.[84] The planet Venus is of course the same as *Hésperos* the Evening Star and *Heōsphóros* "dawn-bearer," "*Ēṓs* bearer" the Morning Star. In the evening Hesperos sets after sunset; in the morning Heosphoros rises before sunrise. We have the testimony of Sappho's near contemporary, Ibycus (*PMG* 331), that Hesperos and Heosphoros were by this time known to be one and the same. From the Indo-European standpoint, on the other hand, Hesperos and Heosphoros must be Divine Twins, as represented by the Dioskouroi, the Greek "Sons of Zeus" who are cognates of the Indic Aśvin-s.[85] At the battle of Aigospotamoi, there is supposed to have been an epiphany of the Dioskouroi in the form of stars, on either side of Lysander's admiral ship; after their victory the Spartans dedicated to the Dioskouroi two stars of gold at Delphi (Plut. *Lys.* 12, 18).

In the poetics of Sappho, the Indo-European model of the Morning Star and Evening Star merges with the Near Eastern model of the Planet Aphrodite. Sappho's Hesperos is a nuptial star, as we know directly from the fragment 104 V. and indirectly from the celebrated *hymenaeus* (wedding song) of Catullus 62, *Vesper adest*. Since Hesperos is the evening aspect of the astral Aphrodite, its setting into the horizon, beyond which is Okeanos, could have inspired the image of a plunging Aphrodite. If we imagine Aphrodite diving into the Okeanos after the sun, it follows that she will rise in the morning, bringing after her the sun of a new day. This image is precisely what the Hesiodic scholia preserve to explain the myth of Aphrodite and Phaethon: ὁ ἠῷος ἀστήρ, ὁ ἀνάγων τὴν ἡμέραν καὶ τὸν Φαέθοντα, ἡ Ἀφροδίτη (the star of Eos, the one that brings back to light and life [verb *an-ágo*] the day and Phaethon, Aphrodite;[86] scholia to Hes. *Theog.* 990). For the mystical

83. See ibid., 229.
84. Scherer, *Gestirnnamen* 78–84, 90, 92, 94.
85. Güntert, *Der arische Weltkönig* 266–67. See Nagy, *Greek Mythology* 255 ff.
86. Both Wilamowitz, *Sappho und Simonides* 37 n. 3, and Diggle, *Euripides: Phaethon* 15 n. 1, find this statement incomprehensible.

meaning of *an-ágō* as "bring back the light and life from the dead," I cite the contexts of this verb in Hesiod *Theogony* 626 (εἰς φάος, "into the light"), Plato *Republic* 521c (εἰς φῶς, "to light"), Aeschylus *Agamemnon* 1023 (τῶν φθιμένων, "from the realm of the dead"), and so on.[87]

From Menander fragment 258 K., we infer that Sappho spoke of herself as diving from the White Rock, crazed with love for Phaon. The implications of this image are cosmic. The "I" of Sappho's poetry is vicariously projecting her identity into the goddess Aphrodite, who loves the native Lesbian hypostasis of the Sun-God himself. By diving from the White Rock, the "I" of Sappho does what Aphrodite does in the form of Evening Star, diving after the sunken Sun in order to retrieve him, another morning, in the form of Morning Star. If we imagine her pursuing the Sun the night before, she will be pursued in turn the morning after. There is a potential here for *amor versus*, a theme that haunts the poetry of Sappho elsewhere:

καὶ γὰρ αἰ φεύγει, ταχέως διώξει
(Sappho fr. 1.21 V.)

for even if she now flees, soon she will pursue.

Sappho's special association with Aphrodite is apparent throughout her poetry. The very first poem of the Sapphic corpus is, after all, an intense prayer to Aphrodite, where the goddess is implored to be the *súmmakhos* battle ally of the poetess fr. 1.28 V.. The "I" of Sappho pictures herself and Aphrodite as parallel rather than reciprocal agents:

ὄσσα δέ μοι <u>τέλεσσαι</u> θῦμος ἰμέρρει, <u>τέλεσον</u>
(Sappho fr. 1.26–27 V.)

and however many things my <u>spirit</u> [*thūmós*] yearns to
<u>accomplish</u> [verb *teléō*, active], I pray that you [Aphrodite] <u>accomplish</u> [verb *teléō*, active]

I draw attention to the wording τέλεσσαι, "to accomplish," an active infinitive instead of the expected passive τελέσθην, "to be accomplished."[88] If someone else needs something done by Aphrodite, Sappho's poetry opts for the passive infinitive τελέσθην, not active τέλεσσαι:

[Κύπρι καὶ] Νηρήιδες ἀβλάβη[ν μοι
τὸν κασί]γνητον δ[ό]τε τυίδ' ἴκεσθα[ι

---

87. See again Frame, *The Myth of Return* 150–62, on the epithet of the Aśvin-s *Násatyau*, which he interprets as "they who bring back to life and light"; for the Aśvin-s as Evening/Morning Star, see Nagy, *Greek Mythology* 255–56.

88. For a similar effect, we may compare the opposition of active *faciam*, "that I do," and passive *fieri*, "to be done," both referring to the verbs *odi et amo* in Catull. 85.

κὤσσα ϝ]οι θύμῳ κε θέλη γένεσθαι
πάντα τε]λέσθην

(Sappho fr. 5.1–4 V.)

Aphrodite and Nereids, grant that my brother
come back here unharmed,
and that however many things he wishes in his spirit *[thumon]* to happen for him
may all be accomplished [verb *teléō*, passive]

The figure of Sappho projects mortal identity onto the divine explicitly as
well as implicitly. I cite the following examples from one poem:

πόλ]λακι τυίδε [ν]ῶν ἔχοισα
σε θέᾳ σ' ἰκέλαν ἀρι-
γνώτᾳ σᾷ δὲ μάλιστ' ἔχαιρε μόλπᾳ
ε]ΰμαρ[ες μ]ὲν οὐ[κ] ἄ[μ]μι θέαισι μόρ-
φαν ἐπή[ρατ]ον ἐξίσω-
σθαι

(Sappho fr. 96.2–5, 21–23 V.)

Many times turning your attention [*nóon*] in this direction

you, a likeness of the well-known goddess.
And it is in your song and dance that she delighted especially.

It is not easy for us
to become equal in lovely shape
to the goddesses.

An even more significant example is Sappho fragment 58.25–26 V., two
verses quoted by Athenaeus 687b. Sappho is cited as a woman who professes
not to separate *tò kalón* (what is beautiful) from *habrótēs* luxuriance:

ἐγὼ δὲ φίλημμ' ἀβροσύναν ... τοῦτο, καί μοι
τὸ λά[μπρον ἔρως⁸⁹ ἀελίω καὶ τὸ κά]λον λέ[λ]ογχε

(Sappho fr. 58.25–26 V.)

But I love luxuriance [*(h)abrosúna*] ... this,
and lust for the sun has won me brightness and beauty.⁹⁰

From *Oxyrhynchus Papyri* 1787 we can see that these two lines come at the end
of a poem alluding to mythical topics. According to Lobel and Page, lines 19
and following refer to Tithonos fr. 58 L.-P.. Be that as it may, we do see images
about growing old, with hair turning white and the knees losing their strength

___

89. Cf. Hamm, *Grammatik* 241.

90. This interpretation differs from that of, e.g., Campbell, *Greek Lyric* 1:100, who reads
τὠελίω (τὸ ἀελίω), agreeing with τὸ λάμπρον. Even if we were to accept the reading
τὠελίω, we could theoretically interpret the crasis along the lines of τῶ ἀελίω = τὠελίω
(cf., e.g., πω ἔσλον = πῶσλον at Alc. 69.5 V.; cf. Hamm, *Grammatik* 91e).

(Sappho fr. 58.13–15 V.). The fragmentary nature of the papyrus prevents certainty about the speaker and the speaker's predicament, but somebody is feeling helpless, asking rhetorically what can be done, and bemoaning some impossibility (58.17–18). Also, the Lesbian Eos is mentioned: βροδόπαχυν Αὔων, "rosy-armed Dawn" (58.19).

As a coda to this poem, the last two verses, which I interpret as proclaiming Sappho's "lust for the sun," amount to a personal and artistic manifesto. The (h)abrosúna (luxuriance) of Sappho transcends the banal discussion of Athenaeus, who quotes these two verses. For Sappho, (h)ábros (luxuriant) is the epithet of Adonis (fr. 140 V.), as also of the Kharites, "Graces" (128 V.), on whose chariot Aphrodite rides (194 V.). At Sappho fragment 2.13–16 V., (h)ábrōs (14) is the adverb describing the scene as Aphrodite is asked to pour nectar. The use of (h)ábros (luxuriant) and (h)abrosúna (luxuriance) in Sappho reminds us of the Roman neoterics and their allusive use of lepidus/lepos in expressing their artistic identity. As for Sappho's "lust for the sun" and "love of (h)abrosúna (luxuriance)," these themes combine profound personal and artistic ideals. In verses preceding the coda, the words of Sappho perhaps alluded to Phaon as an old man, compared with Tithonos. Or perhaps Phaon was son of Tithonos. We do hear a myth where Phaethon is son of Tithonos (Apollod. 3.14.3); just as Phaethon was son of Ēós (Dawn), perhaps Phaon was son of the Lesbian cognate, Aúōs (Dawn) mentioned in the same poem, Sappho fragment 58.19. The expression ἔσχατα γᾶς φέροισα, "[she], taking to the ends of the earth," in line 20 of this poem, along with ἔμαρψε, "snatched," in the following line 21, remind us of Okeanos/Eridanos and Harpies.

In any case, the fact remains that there is a Lesbian myth about Phaon as an old man (Sappho fr. 211 V.); significantly, in this same myth Aphrodite herself assumes the form of an old woman, whom the old Phaon generously ferries across a strait (ibid.) I suspect that the figure of Sappho identifies herself with this figure of an old woman. Similarly, we may compare the myth of the mourning Aphrodite's plunge from the White Rock out of love for the dead Adonis (Ptolemaios Chennos by way of Phot. Bibl. 152–53 Bekker) as pertinent to the poetics of Sappho, where the explicit theme of mourning for Adonis (fr. 168 V.) may be connected with the latent theme of Sappho's self-identification with Aphrodite.[91]

In short, there is a mythical precedent for an aging lady to love Phaon. The implicit hope is retrieved youth. After Aphrodite crossed the strait, she, became a beautiful goddess again, conferring youth and beauty on Phaon, too (again, Sappho fr. 211 V.). For all these reasons, perhaps, Sappho loves Phaon.

---

91. See Nagy, Greek Mythology 229 ff.

FOUR

Eros and Incantation:
Sappho and Oral Poetry

Charles Segal

I

For Sappho and her audience poetry is public communication. It is not fully separated from gesture, for it retains close associations with dance and with music. It is, in some sense, magic. It is also a necessary and basic form of handing down and communicating knowledge about the gods, society, the nature of human life.

Our growing awareness of the implications of oral composition and oral performance in early Greek poetry has opened new perspectives on the archaic lyric. We shall try to extend these perspectives to Sappho, taking her most famous and most familiar poem, *phainetai moi* (fr. 31 L.-P.), as our focal point.[1] In so remote and so fragmentary a poet much must remain pure speculation. With this caveat in mind, we may still be able to gain some fresh insight into these scanty but beautiful texts.

"Longinus" quotes *phainetai moi* in order to illustrate the effect of conjoining the signs of intense passion. Given the formalistic bias and rhetorical approach of ancient literary criticism, Longinus's point of view is natural enough. Yet the rapid sequence of the symptoms which the poem lists point in quite another direction. It conveys a ritualizing, incantatory quality.

---

1. All citations of the text of Sappho are from Edgar Lobel and Denys Page, *Poetarum Lesbiorum Fragmenta,* referred to as L.-P. A version of this paper was delivered as a public lecture at Haverford College in April 1973. I am indebted to Professors Jenny Clay, Richard Hamilton, and Joseph Russo for helpful comments. I thank Professor Mary Lefkowitz for allowing me to see a paper on *phainetai moi* in advance of publication and Professor Charles Beye for friendly and sympathetic criticism.

This incantatory quality has a special relevance for early love poetry. Such poetry seeks to create a verbal equivalent to the magnetic, quasi-magical compulsion which the ancient poets called *thelxis*, "enchantment," or *peithō*, "persuasion." The repetitions and recurrent rhythms of the poetic language evoke the magical effect of eros itself; and this "magic" is also the mysterious *peithō* or *thelxis* which the archaic poetess undergoes when gripped by the beauty of a young girl. He is like an elemental power of nature, a violent wind or an "overpowering creature" that "looses her limbs":

Ἔρος δ᾽ ἐτίναξέ μοι
φρένας, ὡς ἄνεμος κὰτ ὄρος δρύσιν ἐμπέτων.

(47 L.-P.)

Eros has shaken my wits, like a wind from the mountain falling on oaks.

Ἔρος δηὖτέ μ᾽ ὁ λυσιμέλης δόνει,
γλυκύπικρον ἀμάχανον ὄρπετον.

(130 L.-P.)

Eros, looser of limbs, tosses me about, bittersweet, overmastering creature.

We have to translate such verses into our own psychology and explain this anthropomorphic Eros as a force or a psychic power. But for Sappho the "power" of love is a god, as power often is for the ancient Greeks, and as such is to be summoned before her by the incantatory power and the quasi-magical *thelxis* of her poetry. Her poetry both portrays *thelxis* and, in a sense, *is* *thelxis*.

The need to deal with complex emotions by projecting them into situations of personal confrontation or vivid exchanges of words and gestures may reflect not some innate flair for drama in Mediterranean peoples or the inadequate psychology of a supposedly primitive stage in the history of Greek thought, but rather the mental habit of a people whose cultural life—values, history, basic lore about nature and the arts—is encoded in an oral tradition and expressed and affirmed in contexts of oral recitation. In such a culture the act of using language to achieve a coherent picture of reality and to transmit it to future generations takes place in a situation of oral interchange. As Russo and Simon have suggested in a stimulating essay,[2] the personified encounter between a god and mortal in Homer's scenes of decision or doubt may be a function of the mentality which shaped, and was shaped by, oral composition and performance. It is a question of a deeply rooted cast of mind, not of an inadequate psychological vocabulary or deficient powers of abstraction, as the exponents of the genetic and evolutionary interpretation of Greek culture maintain.

2. Russo and Simon, "Homeric Psychology," esp. 495–98.

Sappho is fond of these situations of personal encounter. In a number of poems she calls forth the love-goddess, Aphrodite, and brings the divinity of love into the speaker's presence.[3] Now this evocation of the goddess can be regarded as a form of *thelxis*: by this technique Sappho practices, in a highly sophisticated form, the magic of love. What more appropriate love charm than to bring Aphrodite herself before you?

The fact that some of these love poems are themselves cast into ritual form invites speculation about their social function. A number of scholars have suggested as context some sort of *thiasos*, an association of girls and women who felt themselves joined by a bond that they could celebrate religiously.[4] "Religion" is a vague word, and one must be careful to distinguish between its functions in archaic and modern societies. One must be especially careful, in a discussion of archaic Lesbos, to banish any notions of Pre-Raphaelite spiritualism or mystical communion. In archaic Greece one venerates the gods at least as much for their elemental power as for their moral purity. The fragments on Eros cited above will serve as illustration. In the early sixth century B.C.E. the division between sacred and secular is likely to have been slight. Nearly all human activity has a sacred dimension, as the last part of Hesiod's *Works and Days* suggests. The forms of association that united Sappho and her friends would naturally involve the veneration of a deity; and, on the evidence of the fragments, Aphrodite is the likeliest candidate, though we hear also of the Muses, the Graces, and once of Hera. This divinity presides over and solemnizes their shared activities. Needless to say, the presence of Aphrodite would not inhibit the physical expression of love among the members of this community.

Early Greek society, like many holistic societies, seems to have dealt with erotic emotion and experience in far more public and stylized forms than modern industrial societies. Examples are the conventionalized banter exchanged by choruses in the epithalamia or the ritualized competition, centering often on the question of physical beauty, in Alcman's *Partheneion*. Some tantalizing lines of Alcaeus indicate that female beauty on Sappho's Lesbos played an important role in cult and had a formalized, agonistic setting (Alc. 130.32–37 L.-P.).[5]

---

3. See frs. 1, 5, 15.9–12 L.-P.

4. For some interesting speculation along these lines see Gentili, "La veneranda Saffo," esp. 47 ff.; Merkelbach, "Sappho und ihr Kreis" 1–4. It is unfortunate that Merkelbach has still not been able to free himself from Wilamowitz's fantasies of Sappho the schoolmistress running some sort of "Mädchenpensionat" (4 with n. 1, 6).

5. Gentili has some suggestive aperçus on the cultic and ritual context of Sappho's poetry and possible connections between these ritual elements and their poetic expression. See his "La veneranda Saffo"; see also "L'interpretazione dei lirici greci" 20, and "Lirica greca arcaica," esp. 67.

Not only did much of the choral poetry of early Greece have a ritual and sacral context, but epic too probably has its roots in ritual and incantation as well. We may draw here upon the work done on oral epic by Milman Parry and Albert Lord. Parry long ago observed (but did not explore) the affinity between formulaic repetition in Homer and ritual. Commenting on a recurrent formula in Homer, he remarked "how the use with it of other words which are always the same, and which always bring back the phrase with the same rhythm at the same place in the verse, act[s] strongly in making it habitual: Homer's formulaic diction is in this much like the chant of ritual."[6] Lord developed this insight in greater detail: "It could be hypothesized," he suggests, "that when myth became ceremonial, told in chant and verse, epic was born."[7] In works like the Akkadian creation epic known as the *Enuma Elish* the ritual function of the poetry predominates, but it plays a role, albeit submerged, even in the secular forms of Homeric epic. Commenting on the alliterative effects of a passage in the *Iliad,* Lord remarks, "To us the effect is poetic magic, the magic of Homer's hexameters."[8] Lord's expression is not just metaphorical, however, for he goes on to remind us of the similarities between the devices of oral narrative and the "practical magic" of charms and incantation: "Yet the effect which results was surely calculated by the originators of this device, not for poetic, but for practical magic. This is a dynamic method of emphasis used by incantation and inherited by oral epic, if I am not mistaken, from far distant times. Magic spells throughout the world use alliteration and assonance to make the charm effective."[9]

The poets of early Greece, down through the fifth century, were keenly aware of and sensitive to the incantatory effects of ritualized sound. It could hardly be otherwise for men raised in an oral culture. The chantlike, singsong pattern of such sound they called ἐπαοιδή. According to Homer and Pindar it could staunch blood and heal wounds (*Od.* 19.457–58; Pind. *Pyth.* 3.51, 4.217). There is, obviously, a close affinity between this ἐπαοιδή or "incantation" and the ἀοιδή of poetic song, between "la formule magique rhythmisée et la diction chantante" (the rhythmical magic spell and the language of song).[10] At the end of his eighth *Nemean* Pindar makes explicit the link between the "incantatory" magic of medicine and the "incantatory"

6. M. Parry, "The Traditional Metaphor in Homer" 38. See also my remarks on the interaction of ritual and formula in the *Odyssey* in "Transition and Ritual."
7. Lord, "Homer and Other Epic Poetry" 198.
8. Ibid., 201.
9. Ibid., 201–2.
10. See Eitrem, "La magie comme motif littéraire" 40; see also Rudhardt, *Notions fondamentales de la pensée* 177 ff.

magic of poetry (*Nem* . 8.49–50), but the "therapeutic" effects of poetry are already familiar from Hesiod (*Theog.* 98–103).

Homer had also recognized the connection between the magical "enchantment" of herbs and drugs and the magical "charm" or *thelxis* of love. Circe, enchantress of many drugs (Κίρχη πολυφάρμαχος; *Od.* 10.276), is also the poem's most successful and most dangerous practitioner of erotic seduction. Her *thelxis* is simultaneously magical and erotic:

τοὺς αὐτὴ κατέθελξεν, ἐπεὶ κακὰ φάρμαχ' ἔδωχεν.

(*Od.* 10.213)

[Circe] *charmed* them herself, when she gave them baleful drugs.

τεύξει τοι κυχεῶ, βαλέει δ' ἐν φάρμαχα σίτῳ
ἀλλ' οὐδ' ὣς θέλξαι σε δυνήσεται.

(*Od.* 10.290–91)

She will fashion a barley drink and cast drugs upon it,
But not even so will she be able to *charm* you.

The experience of love as a magical power has deep roots in Greek literature. Parallels extend from these *pharmaka* of Circe in the *Odyssey* to the *pharmaka* of Nessus in Sophocles' *Trachiniae*, from the *Helen* of Gorgias to the *iynx* of Simaetha in Theocritus's second *Idyll*.[11] Sappho herself speaks of the beloved as "charming" or "enchanting" the mind (θέλγει νόον; 57 L.-P.), and Alcaeus uses the same verb, speaking, apparently, about love magic (B 13 L.-P.). To create a linguistic equivalent to this magical "charm" or *thelxis* Sappho uses the divine epiphany of poems 1 and 2 L.-P. or the simile of fragment 47 L.-P. The four preserved strophes of fragment 31 are bare of myth or simile, but their incantatory effect of sound and rhythm produces an analogous effect.

Homer uses the verb θέλγειν not only of the "charm" of love or desire (e.g., *Od.* 1.56–57, 3.264) but also of the charm of song or of involving, "spellbinding" narration. He so uses it twice of the Sirens (*Od* . 12.40, 44), where he mentions "song" explicitly in the second passage (12.44): ἀλλά τε Σειρῆνες λιγυρῇ θέλγουσιν ἀοιδῇ, "The Sirens charm with sweet song." The verb θέλγειν also describes the fascination which Odysseus's lies exercise on his hearers (*Od.* 14.387, 17.514). Homer may well be applying to the effects of Odysseus's narratives his own experience of the oral poet's ability to "charm"

---

11. See in general Eitrem, "La magie comme motif littéraire," esp. 29–44. Merkelbach, "Sappho und ihr Kreis" 23–25, suggests that fr. 17 L.-P. has affinities with "Zauberlieder"; and see Page, *Sappho and Alcaeus* 58. See also my remarks in "Circean Temptations," esp. 420–22, 438–39. Further examples may be found in Barrett, ed., on Eur. *Hipp.* 513–15 and Gow, ed., on Theocr. *Id.* 11.2.

or "enchant" his audience: the author of the Homeric *Hymn to (Delian) Apollo* uses the same verb, directly after ἀείδειν, of the chorus's effect upon their audience: ὕμνον ἀείδουσιν, θέλγουσι δὲ φῦλ' ἀνθρώπων (They sing a hymn and *charm* the tribes of men; *h. Hom. Ap.* 161).

The idea of magical enchantment in all these passages must be taken quite literally. The formal, rhythmic, and ritual effects of the song are felt to be capable of working real magic on the body and soul of the hearer, whether for healing or for pleasure. The common vocabulary suggests that the process seemed to the archaic poets akin to the effects of love or erotic fascination. In the "Deception of Zeus" in *Iliad* 14 the sexual "charms" (*thelktēria*) of Aphrodite's magical belt or *kestos* include not only love and desire (*philotēs, himeros*), but also the "enchanting" power of language, the "cozening speech (*parphasis*) which deceives the mind of men, no matter how smart they are" (*Il.* 14.216–17).[12]

II

Sappho, I suggest, draws upon this reciprocal relation between poetry and the physical reactions of the body: poetry as *thelxis*. The magical *thelxis* of her words seeks to create—or recreate—the magical *thelxis* of love. And she thinks and lives in a society where ritualized patterns are the essential means of achieving this *thelxis*. Ceremonial or ritual elements in the *background* of poetic composition (which, of course, are not necessarily conscious to the poet) need not imply the actual ceremonial *function* of such poetry. We are concerned primarily with the former, but the division between the two may not have been very clear in archaic Lesbos.

Ritual not only asserts the unity of the society or the group in the presence of the divine, but can also effect a personal transaction with divine powers. This private function of ritual is perhaps dominant in the ode to Aphrodite (fr. 1 L.-P.), where Sappho has the goddess address her by name. In other poems, however, Sappho clearly depicts the public or communal setting, whether real or imagined, of rituals. The grove and altar of fragment 2 L.-P. may have had a number of celebrants. Fragment 154 L.-P. specifically mentions a number of girls standing "about an altar": "The moon shone full, and as they stood around the altar. . ." (αἰ δ' ὠς περὶ βῶμον ἐστάθησαν).

Even in the Aphrodite ode (fr. 1 L.-P.) the ritualized language and situation of the *hymnos klētikos* may have served to relate Sappho's personal experiences to a social context. Her dexterity and wit in evoking the love-goddess and

12. On the interrelations between *thelxis*, sexuality, and the ambiguity of language, see Détienne, *Les maîtres de vérité* 63–65. He notes also that tradition gave to one of the Sirens the name *thelxiepeia*. See also Soph. *Trach.* 660–62.

in creating a suitably graceful atmosphere for her epiphany themselves attest to her mastery of love's violence. The ritualized structure of the poem makes this mastery available and aesthetically comprehensible to others. Whatever its origins, the experience becomes a social act. It is embodied in language and song. Others can participate in it. Indeed, the mastery of love which the poem implies—whether actual or desiderated—becomes repeatable and accessible to the poetess herself on other occasions.

Even in setting forth her personal, emotional life, Sappho is highly conscious of the language of public discourse and familiar formulaic situations. Between these and her own nonformulaic situation and personal discourse she creates subtle and sophisticated counterpoints. In fragment 16 L.-P., for example, not only is there a sharp antithesis, in the opening priamel, between "what some say" and Sappho's "I"; but there is also an elegant contrast between this "I" (ἐγώ) and the wish to make her observations "understandable to all":

οἰ μὲν ἰππήων στρότον οἰ πέσδων
οἰ δὲ νάων φαῖσ' ἐπὶ γᾶν μέλαιναν
ἔμμεναι κάλλιστον, ἔγω δὲ κῆν' ὄττω τις ἔραται·
πάγχυ δ' εὔμαρες σύνετον πόησαι
πάντι τοῦτ'

(16.1–6)

Some say that the host of horsemen is the loveliest thing on the black earth, others of soldiers, others of ships, but I say that it is whatever anyone loves. And to make this understood to all is very easy.

III

With this framework in mind we may now turn to *phainetai moi* (31 L.-P.). The first lines of fragment 31 set the stage for the power of eros. The adverbial ἰμέροεν in line 5 sounds the first explicitly erotic note: the effect of the girl's voice and laughter is to awaken "desire," ἴμερος. The strong verb ἐπτόαισεν in the next line (6) denotes the violence of this "desire." At this point the rhythmic-ritualizing effects become especially marked. ("Rhythm" as used here is a function not just of the meter but of the interaction of meter with sound patterns, sentence structure, and meaning.) Sappho repeats ὡς . . . σ(ε) . . . ὡς με (7). Then she introduces a rapid succession of short clauses, artfully varied through word order, chiasmus, and enjambment. The recurrence of the conjunction δέ, seven times in eight lines, contributes to the ritualizing, incantatory effect.

The carefully built up patterns of alliteration and assonance reinforce these effects. Unfortunately the state of the text does not allow of equal certainty in all places. I shall confine my remarks to the third and fourth strophes, where these devices seem especially prominent:

φαίνεταί μοι κῆνος ἴσος θέοισιν
ἔμμεν' ὤνηρ, ὄττις ἐνάντιός τοι
ἰσδάνει καὶ πλάσιον ἆδυ φωνει-
σας ὐπακούει

καὶ γελαίσας ἰμέροεν, τό μ' ἦ μὰν   5
καρδίαν ἐν στήθεσιν ἐπτόαισεν
ὠς γὰρ ἔς σ' ἴδω βρόχέ, ὤς με φώναι-
σ' οὐδ' ἒν ἔτ' εἴκει,

ἀλλ' ἄκαν μὲν γλῶσσα †ἔαγε, λέπτον
δ' αὔτικα χρῶι πῦρ ὐπαδεδρόμηκεν,   10
ὀππάτεσσι δ' οὐδ' ἒν ὄρημμ', ἐπιρρόμ-
βεισι δ' ἄκουαι,

κὰδε μ' ἴδρως ψῦχρος ἔχειτ, τρόμος δὲ
παῖσαν ἄγρει, χλωροτέρα δὲ ποίας
ἔμμι, τεθνάκην δ' ὀλίγω 'πιδεύης   15
φαίνομ' ἔμ' αὔτᾳ

ἀλλὰ πὰν τόλματον, ἐπει †καὶ πένητα†

(31)

Fortunate as the gods he seems to me, that man who sits opposite to you, and listens nearby to your sweet voice
And your desirable laughter; that, I vow, has affrighted my heart within my breast.
For when I look at you a moment, then I have no longer power to speak,
But my tongue keeps silence, straightway a subtle flame has run beneath my flesh, with my eyes I see nothing, my ears are humming,
A cold sweat covers me, and a trembling seizes me all over, I am paler than grass, I seem to be not far short of death. . . . But all can be endured, since. . . . . .

(Page's translation, modified)

A strong alliteration of *k* and *g* in line 9 seems fairly probable (the emendations μ' ἔαγε and πέπαγε would both conduce to the same effect). It is strengthened by the *k* alliteration of αὔτικα χρῶι in the next line. The *d* sound at the beginning of that line (δ') continues in the impressive drumming *d*'s of ὐπαδεδρόμηκεν, which follows up the chiasmic *pu/up* pattern in πῦρ ὐπαδεδρόμηκεν. A similar but more complex pattern recurs in the next line (11) in the *or-m-/rom-* sequence of ὄρημμ' ἐπιρρομ. The drumming *d* beat of line 10 is taken up again in line 13, reading Page's emendation: κὰδ δὲ μ' ἴδρως ψῦχρος ἔχει. Here, as also in line 10, the alliteration of *k* sounds accompanies the *d*'s. Vowel patterns also reinforce the repetitive effect, especially the strongly marked sequence of open *o* sounds in line 11 and the *a* sounds of line 14: παῖσαν ἄγρει, χλωροτέρα δὲ ποίας. In all these verses the beat of the meter and the recurrent sound patterns work closely together to produce a rhythmico-ritual or ritual-mimetic equivalent to love's "thelctic" power.

Every verse beginning with line 7 contains at least one conjunction: ὡς, γάρ, οὐδέ, ἀλλά, δέ. This polysyndeton enhances the effect of accumulating intensity; but it also creates a rhythmical tempo of excitement and mounting tension analogous to the ritualizing effects of dance or drum beat. The one line that has no conjunction, namely line 16, follows directly after the climactic point of "death" (τεθνάκην; 15). Now the rhythm slows down, and the poem turns to what seems to have been a more contemplative, quieter mood: ἀλλὰ πὰν τόλματον ἐπεί...... (17).[13] Indeed, line 16 opens upon a new dimension of the experience presented in the poem, a shift away from external, physical actions to something internal and mental: φαίνομ᾽ ἔμ᾽ αὔται. The slowing down of the alliterative and repetitive tempo in 15–16 corresponds to the movement to another plane of experience. Now the closing cadence of the adonic, for the first time in the poem, marks a full stop in sense. Now too for the first time in ten lines a connective is absent.

Catullus was aware of this incantatory effect of Sappho's poem; and he attempted to reproduce it, albeit in a more regular, self-consciously formalized way, through alliteration and repeated sound patterns. His third stanza provides the clearest illustration (51.9–12):

> lingua sed torpet, tenuis sub artus
> flamma demanat, sonitu suopte
> tintinnant aures, gemina teguntur
> lumina nocte.

> But my tongue falters, a thin flame flows through my limbs. My ears ring with their own humming, my eyes are covered in twofold night.

Here we should note the complex pattern of *t* and *s* and *is/us* sounds in the first line; the *m*, *a*, *n*, *u/o*, and *t* patterns in the second line; the verb *tintinnant*, whose onomatopoeia imitates Sappho's ὐπαδεδρόμηκεν as well as her ἐπιρρόμβεισι. Catullus has also exploited rhythmic and assonantal echoes between *gemina* and *lumina* in the last two lines and the sequence of *t, g,* and *c* in *gemina teguntur / nocte*. Sappho's patterns are subtler and less

---

13. For this sense of l. 17 see Fränkel, *Dichtung und Philosophie* 199 n. 16: "Im Text steht τολματον, '*kann* ertragen werden,' und nicht τολματεον, '*muss* ertragen werden' (wie meist übersetzt wird)." And also: "Unser Text bricht an der Stelle ab, wo die Sprecherin begonnen hat aus einem gewissen Abstand auf das Ereignis zu reflektieren" (200). See also Wills, "Sappho 31 and Catullus 51" 190, on this "withdrawal from the specific experience." For similar movements in Sappho cf. frs. 26.11–12, 96 L.-P.

obvious. Closer to a situation of oral and musical performance, she could count on a finer perception of subtle effects. In the case of her poetry, too, the recurrent beat of the musical accompaniment provided in itself a certain measure of incantatory regularity, thus permitting her greater freedom and variation in her sound patterns.

The kind of rhythmical and repetitive pattern noted above is not uncommon in Sappho's verse, despite its fragmentary condition. The fullest parallel occurs in a poem whose chief subject is the *peithō* of eros, namely 1 L.-P.

This poem in fact uses the ritual form of the hymn, albeit for personal and possibly humorous purposes. As Page observes, "This is not a cult-song, an appeal for epiphany recited with ritual accompaniment on a formal occasion in honor of Aphrodite: yet it is constructed in accordance with the principles of cult-song."[14] Page sees humor in the triple recurrence of δηὖτε in lines 15, 16, 18.[15] Yet this repetition is also a prelude (perhaps in a light vein and certainly on a purely private, moral level) to the more solemn, more markedly ritual effect of the love-goddess's own words in the next strophe (21–24):

> καὶ γὰρ αἰ φεύγει, ταχέως διώξει,
> αἰ δὲ δῶρα μὴ δέκετ', ἀλλὰ δώσει.
> αἰ δὲ μὴ φίλει, ταχέως φιλήσει
> κοὐκ ἐθέλοισα.

> For if she runs away, soon will she pursue. If she receives
> not gifts, soon will she receive them, and if she does
> not love, soon will she love, even unwilling.

Aphrodite, appropriately, speaks in language which itself imitates the incantatory, hypnotic effect of love's *thelxis*. That effect depends on the repetition of the simple sentence structure ("If she flees, soon will she pursue; if she doesn't receive gifts, she will give them; if she doesn't love, soon will she love"). The rhythmical echo between the first and third lines, ταχέως διώξει ... ταχέως φιλήσει, almost seems to assure the success of this spell-like promise.[16]

Other repetitions and alliterations contribute to this effect of incantation: the threefold repetition of αἰ, the double repetition of δέ ... δέ and of φίλει ... φιλήσει; the analogous repetition (with an etymological play) of δῶρα ... δώσει (22); the alliteration and rhyme of διώξει ... δώσει (at the end of two successive lines, 22–23); the strong *d* alliteration in διώξει ... δὲ δῶρα ...

14. Page, *Sappho and Alcaeus* 16, with the bibliography in n. 1.

15. Page, *Sappho and Alcaeus* 12 ff.

16. Note also the artful variation in the placement of the caesura. Coming after the fifth syllable in the first and third lines (21, 23), it reinforces the repetition of ταχέως, whereas in the second line of the strophe (22), it comes after the seventh syllable.

δέκετ' ... δώσει ... δέ; the triple rhyme of σει in the first three lines and the brilliant variation upon that in the assonance -λησει / -λοισα (φιλήσει ... ἐθέλοισα) between the last two lines (23–24). Sappho then follows up this ritualizing mimesis of the magic of desire with an actual ritual form, the hymnic invocation to the goddess, ἔλθε μοι καὶ νῦν (come to me now also; 25). The ceremonial effect of this latter phrase is especially prominent because it echoes, in a kind of ring composition, the invocation at the beginning of the poem (5): ἀλλὰ τυίδ' ἔλθ(ε) (but come here).

As the enchantment takes effect, Aphrodite herself becomes gentler. The opening prayer, "Subdue me not with pain and anguish" (3), becomes at the end, "Release me from harsh cares" (25–26). The goddess's power to "conquer" (δάμνα), which is actually exemplified, later, in her promise to make the unwilling girl fall in love (21–24), now shows its benign side, "release" (λῦσον; 25). The goddess who inflicts the anguish of love can also remove it.

These ceremonial effects of rhythm, repetition, and alliteration are more striking, naturally, in poems that are closer to public statement and to social situations. Hence one finds a noticeably high proportion of such effects in the epithalamia. These poems, even apart from repetition and alliteration, have strongly ritualistic qualities, as a paper by Marcovich has emphasized.[17] I list the following examples:

Ἔσπερε πάντα φέρων ὅσα φαίνολις ἐσκέδασ' αὔως
†φέρεις ὄιν, φέρεις αἶγα, φέρεις† μάτερι παῖδα.

(104a)[18]

Evening star who brings all that the bright dawn scattered.
You bring the sheep, you bring the goat, you bring the child to her mother.

οἶον τὸ γλυκύμαλον ἐρεύθεται ἄκρῳ ἐπ' ὔσδῳ,
ἄκρον ἐπ' ἀκροτάτῳ, λελάθοντο δε μαλοδρόπηες
οὐ μὰν ἐκλελάθοντ', ἀλλ' οὐκ ἐδύναντ' ἐπίχεσθαι.

(105a)

As the honey-apple reddens in the topmost bough,
on the top of the topmost bough, and the apple pickers have forgotten it,
No, not forgotten it: they could not reach it.

παρθενία, παρθενία, ποῖ με λίποισ' ἀποίχῃ·
†οὐκέτι ἤξω πρὸς σέ, οὐκέτι ἤξώ

(114)

17. Marcovich, "Sappho Fr. 31" 32, apropos of fr. 111 L.-P. On the ritualistic elements in the epithalamia, see also Page, *Sappho and Alcaeus* 119–23. Treu, *Sappho, griechisch und deutsch* 151–52, 227, observes the continuation of such ritual elements down into the epithalamia of Hellenistic times (cf. *P. Ryl.* 17 = Pack no. 1456). Marcovich offers some Yugoslav examples, as does Bowra, *Greek Lyric Poetry* 222.

18. Demetrius, who cites this fragment, uses it, in fact, to illustrate the effects of repetition (*Eloc.* 141). The repetition is perhaps reinforced by a *figura etymologica* in *Hes-pere ... pheron ... phereis*, an observation that Professors Clay and Hamilton suggested to me independently.

Maidenhood, Maidenhood, where have you gone and left me?
I'll never come back to you, never come back to you.

τίω σ' ὦ φίλε γάμβρε κάλως ἐικάσδω·
ὄρπακι βραδίνῳ σε μάλιστ' ἐικάσδω.

(115)

To what shall I well compare you, bridegroom?
To a slender sapling do I most compare you.

†χαίροις ἀ νύμφα,† χαιρέτω δ' ὁ γάμβρος.

(117)

Hail to the bride, to the groom hail.

Fragment 112 exhibits not only verbal repetition in consecutive lines (more marked if we read Fick's attractive ὡς in the second line), but also a rapid accumulation of the groom's attractions listed in polysyndeton and with a run-on effect analogous to fragment 31 L.-P.:[19]

ὄλβιε γάμβρε, σοὶ μὲν δὴ γάμος ὡς ἄραο
ἐκτετέλεστ', ἔχῃς δὲ πάρθενον †ὰν† ἄραο...
σοὶ χάριεν μὲν εἶδος, ὄππατα δ'...
μέλλιχ', ἔρος δ' ἐπ' ἰμέρτῳ κέχυται προσώπῳ
. . . . τετίμακ' ἔξοχά σ' Ἀφροδίτα.

Happy groom, the marriage, as you prayed, is accomplished,
You hold the girl whom (?) you prayed for . . .
Graceful your figure, sweet your eyes, eros
is poured over your face. Aphrodite holds you in honor.

One other fragment deserves citation in this connection, 140a L.-P.:

καταθνάσκει, Κυθέρη, ἄβρος Ἄδωνις· τί κε θεῖμεν·
καττύπτεσθε, κόραι, καὶ κατερείκεσθε κίθωνας.

"Ripe Adonis, Cytherea, dies. What should we do?"
"Beat your breasts, maidens, your garments rend."

This ritual lament for Adonis, the earliest known in European literature, utilizes a heavy alliteration of *k* and *t* sounds and the repetition of κατ-

19. I do not wish to enter upon the old controversy as to whether fr. 31 L.-P. is a marriage song, although the material here assembled could be used to point in that direction: for the question and its history see Page, *Sappho and Alcaeus* 30–33, with the bibliography cited 30 n. 2. The reply to Page by Merkelbach 6–12 = *Antike Lyrik*, ed. W. Eisenhut, "Ars Interpretandi," 82–89, presents perhaps the most acceptable view of the marriage-song interpretation, i.e., that the ritual context allowed Sappho to express an intensity of emotion that normal discourse and the normal modes of relation in society would render difficult. On the other hand, we know too little of what conventions on archaic Lesbos would or would not have permitted.

in compound verbs at three of the four main rhythmic pauses in the two lines.[20]

IV

This poetry is meant to be recited or sung and certainly heard. It is therefore subject to the conditions of oral performance. Eric Havelock has called attention to the mimetic qualities of that performance, the close rapport and interaction built up between poet and audience in the act of oral recitation or, as Havelock calls it, "the total act of poetic representation."[21] Oral recitation of this type relies upon "the manipulation of verbal, musical and bodily rhythms" and exploits "a set of psychosomatic mechanisms for a very definite purpose."[22] Havelock is speaking of the effect of the continuous recitation of oral poems of some length. Yet something analogous may occur even in shorter poems. Here, of course, the poet has to concentrate and intensify rhythmical patterns which would accumulate more slowly and gradually in the expansive frame of epic.

Correspondingly, the paideutic effect which Havelock thinks results from the audience participation in the recitation of oral epic would not be the same for lyric poetry such as Sappho's. Here too, however, there may be something analogous. The effect of this poetry would be not so much to reinforce social norms as to lift the daimonic power of eros out of the realm of the formless and terrible, bring it into the light of form, make it visible to the individual poet and, by extension, to his or her society. Eros and its

---

20. Fr. 168 may also contain a scrap of an Adonis song, and one should add the Linus-lament of fr. 140b. On possible cult associations see Bowra, *Greek Lyric Poetry* 211–14. Even in poems of an apparently more personal, less public nature the effect of rhythmic repetition can "imitate" what I have called the "thelctic" power of eros. We may observe the effect of the anapests and the diaeresis in fr. 47 L.-P. (cited above, p. 59). Even more striking is the interaction of the lilting ionic rhythms with the sound patterns in fr. 102 L.-P.:

γλυκήα μᾶτερ, οὔτοι δύναμαι κρέκην τὸν ἴστον
πόθῳ δάμεισα παῖδος βράδιναν δι' Ἀφροδίταν.

Sweet mother, no longer can I strike the loom,
By love for a boy(?) subdued
Through slender Aphrodite.

Especially noteworthy here are the repeated *k* and *a* sounds of the first line and the drumming beat of the *t* and *d* sounds, reinforced by the assonance of *a*, in the second line. Instances could be multiplied, but these will serve as representative examples.

21. Havelock, *Preface to Plato* 26. Though I owe a great deal to Havelock's important analysis of the mentality of the oral performance, I do not necessarily accept all the conclusions that he draws for the function of oral poetry in archaic Greece.

22. Ibid., 156.

magical "charm" leave the darkness of the purely private, personal sphere. Its power can be recreated by human verbal means and thus raised to the level of public discourse, shared on a social occasion, in a community of friends or lovers, and, in the case of the epithalamian poetry, enlisted in the service of the social institutions that make for continuity and stability (compare, e.g., fr. 31 L.-P. with 112 L.-P.). Perhaps the desire to control and delimit the uncontrollable and the limitless lay at the origin of the impulses to write such poetry.

Here again we need not necessarily exclude the private and subjective element. By evoking the past, calling up its memories (as in frs. 94 and 96 L.-P.), making present the deities and myths of love, and recreating its magical force through incantatory patterns of sound and sense, Sappho creates a *pharmakon*, a "drug" or "charm," to cure the sufferings of love. Already in Hesiod song can allay pain, and in Theocritus poetry is the surest *pharmakon* for love's agony (*Id.* 11.1–3).

In the case of Sappho, however, we cannot be sure where to draw the line between the personal and the conventional.[23] It is not necessarily the unique but the recurrent and universal features of her experience of love that Sappho seeks to present. The formalized patterns of her language may, in fact, have served to link her own emotional life to situations of frequent and repeated occurrence in the culture or subculture to which she belonged. As Merkelbach and others have suggested, Sappho returns repeatedly to the experience of love and loss not only in order to grasp the nature of her own emotions, but to focus and clarify intensely involving situations which the girls and women of her society would undergo again and again.[24] The roots of Sappho's poetry, in other words, may lie not just in the intensity of her own erotic experiences (and I see no reason to deny their reality) but also in her capacity to intuit, to live imaginatively, and to recreate poetically the emotional experiences that were of greatest concern to the circle to which she belonged. The formalized language of love, then, not only expresses private emotionality, but constitutes a means of generalizing erotic experience and translating the personal and private into a visible and communicable form. Considered in this perspective, the epiphany of Aphrodite in fragment 1 would not stand so very far, *mutatis mutandis*, from her appearance to Helen in *Iliad* 3 or from the epiphany of Athena to Achilles in *Iliad* 1 or to Odysseus in *Odyssey* 13.

In an oral culture, as we have suggested earlier, formalized and ritualized patterns are the natural medium for an exchange of this sort. They cast the private and idiosyncratic into the mold of the universal and the generic.

---

23. See Merkelbach, "Sappho und ihr Kreis," esp. 18; Page, *Sappho and Alcaeus* 83 on fr. 94.
24. See Merkelbach, "Sappho und ihr Kreis" 14–19.

Hence Sappho's reliance upon a fairly stable and well-defined "vocabulary" of erotic motifs and symbols: the wish to die, memory, roses, garlands, perfumes and unguents, the sheltered grove, the moon. What can be dramatically enacted in situations of confrontation can also be shared: it is assimilable to the society's basic form of cultural transmission. In Sappho's own words, one's personal preference for "what one loves" becomes "intelligible to all" (fr. 16).

We need not conceive of Sappho as a group therapist or assume that the therapeutic function of her work played a conscious role in what notion she may have had of her *Dichterberuf.* The fragments speak of commemoration and oblivion, not of help or advice.[25] But there is evidence enough from the fragments to indicate that the desire to understand the emotions of love in herself and in others was, consciously or not, a major aim of her poetry. We may compare, for example, the brief fragment cited by the Stoic Chrysippus, "I know not what to do. Double are my thoughts" (*noēmmata;* fr. 51 L.-P.).

In recreating the brilliance surrounding the great lovers of heroic myth— Helen and Paris, Hector and Andromache, Leda, Adonis, Endymion, Medea[26]—Sappho found another way to grasp the essence of love. The need to relive her and others' erotic experiences and to set them against these paradigms from the mythical past may be inextricably intertwined with the desire to shape patterns of beautiful sounds. In both cases she calls up the reality of eros as vividly as she can. In a fictional or at least aesthetically distanced situation she can more freely and more reflectively contemplate that god's dark and dangerous domain.

The result, as in the case of Homeric epic, is a conquest of daimonic violence, an absorption of what is chaotic and threatening into the radiant forms of art, an extension of speech, of the *logos,* over the unspeakable. The powers of magic and incantation, the *thelxis* of eros, obeying the measured rhythms of the world of art, lose their raw, savage power. In a poem like 1 L.-P. the incantatory element is already a latent metaphor, several stages removed from primitive magic.

The process provides evident relief and release. The elemental force of eros is not in itself diminished, but it now occupies a place in a human world where it loses the edge of its terror. What Havelock says of the paideutic

---

25. See especially frs. 55, 147; also 128, 150, 160 L.-P. For a more personal aspect of memory cf. 94.7–10, 96.16, 129 L.-P. For discussion and bibliography see Lanata, *Poetica pre-platonica* 50–55.

26. The references are as follows: Helen, fr. 44; Andromache, fr. 16; Leda, fr. 166; Adonis, frs. 140, 168, 211; Endymion, fr. 199; Medea, fr. 186. Merkelbach, "Sappho und ihr Kreis" 23 speaks of an "Ineinanderfallen von Mythos und Realität" (conflation of myth and reality).

effect of oral epic poetry can, *mutatis mutandis,* be applied to the effects of oral lyric:

> In performance the co-operation of a whole series of motor reflexes throughout the entire body was enlisted to make memorization and future recall and repetition more effective. These reflexes in turn provided *an emotional release of the unconscious layers of personality* which could then take over and *supply to the conscious mind a great deal of relief from tension and anxiety, fear and the like.* This last constituted the *hypnotic pleasure of the performance.* Pleasure in the final analysis was exploited as the instrument of cultural continuity.[27] (emphasis added).

The personal lyric, of course, does not "exploit" the pleasure of emotional release for the same ends. It sufficed to produce a unique aesthetically and emotionally pleasurable experience, for which the archaic sensitivity to and enjoyment of the ritualistic patterns of word, sound, and rhythm singularly prepared the poet's audience. Havelock calls attention to early Greek culture's

> automatic relish in life and its naturalistic acceptance of life's varied and manifold moral aspects. The Greeks, we feel, were both controlled in their experience and yet also unfettered and free to an extent that we cannot share. They seem to enjoy themselves. They seem to take *natural pleasure in fine shape and sound* which we too sometimes recognize as beautiful not only after we have first pulled ourselves up by our own boot straps to an educated level of perception.[28] (emphasis added).

V

Sappho's artistry lies in her power not only to create and utilize such rhythmico-ritualizing effects but also to move between this public, social form of utterance and quieter, more relaxed, more private moments. The former is rooted in concrete, physical observation and in the mutual participation between poet and hearer in the rapid, tense rhythmical and repetitive tempo; the latter deals in less tangible experiences and the more inward terms of "seeming," imagining, dreaming. Here the staccato rhythm loosens, as in line 16 of fragment 31: φαίνομ' ἔμ' αὔται. One should hardly assume, however, that at such moments the poet has forgotten her audience or is lost to the world in a self-centered revery. Rather, she has merely shifted to another plane of discourse and another mode of communication. The total aesthetic experience produced by such a work as 31 L.-P. results from a coming together of the two levels of communication, the ritual and the private. It is just here, at these points of juncture between the social, outward-facing,

27. Havelock, *Preface to Plato* 157.
28. Ibid., 157–58.

public dimension and techniques of her art and their private, more personal, less ritualistic aspect, that Sappho especially exemplifies her originality and artistry. It is also where she is most difficult for the modern sensibility to grasp.

The very existence of an interplay between one level of style that is close to ritual and public discourse and another that is freer and more private introduces an essential difference between oral epic and oral lyric in the archaic age. This difference, in turn, is analogous to the differences between Homeric and Hesiodic poetry. Hesiod's intrusion of his self-conscious "I" and, like Sappho, of his own name[29] accompanies a nascent critical attitude. He feels a certain distance, be it ever so slight, from total absorption in the "truth" of his art.[30] With this distance there comes a complexity which goes beyond and shatters the unity, continuity, and impersonality of the narrative surface in epic.

Oral epic holds the audience's total involvement and forbids looking away from this absorbing world to the actuality of the poet, as person, standing before his audience. The poet of oral epic becomes transparent to his tradition and his technique. With that transparency he holds his hearers spellbound, literally, to the unbroken flow of his "honey-sweet voice" (*Il.* 1.249; Hes. *Theog.* 39–97). Hence the disturbing effect of Penelope or Odysseus's weeping at Phemius's and Demodocus's songs (*Od.* 1.335 ff., 8.83 ff., 521 ff.): it breaks the all-absorbing spell of the epic world with the intrusion of present reality and present grief. The poet of oral lyric or of oral didactic poetry or even of oral hymnic poetry (cf. *h. Hom. Ap.* 169–73) does not lay claim to this degree of impersonality. Hence he can afford to break the continuity of his narrative surface with more than one type of discourse. Yet the techniques of these latter poets can depend also, at least in part, on the poet-audience relationship of the oral performance; and, as in the case of ritualistic elements in Sappho's love poetry, they draw heavily upon at least one aspect of that relationship—the *thelxis* created by rhythmed beat and sound—for their major effects.

It follows from this line of approach that we need neither accept the notion of a definitive break in mentality between Homeric epic and lyric poetry advocated by Snell and his followers[31] nor deny the lyric poets their radical innovation in search of new forms of personal expression. As a number of recent works have suggested, the situation is more complicated

---

29. Compare *Theog.* 22 and Sappho 1.20, 94.5 L.-P.

30. Contrast *Il.* 2.485 and *Theog.* 26–28. See also Havelock, *Preface to Plato* 99.

31. Snell, *The Discovery of the Mind* chap. 3, "The Rise of the Individual in Early Greek Lyric."

than Snell allowed.[32] The lyric poets did not simply abandon the mentality and the techniques of oral poetry or merely rework the old epic formulas to fit the needs of their pressing drive for personal expression. The new expressiveness of personal emotion interacts with the older public forms and finds its realization *both* through and against the conventions and the poet-audience relationship of oral recitation. The balance shifts even within a single poem. But the habits of the oral tradition, as one would expect, remain deeply ingrained. They reveal themselves externally in the deliberate echoing of epic phraseology and epic situations;[33] but they are reflected, at a deeper level, in the poet's reliance upon the auditory, mimetic reflexes created in oral performance, where insistent rhythm still evokes age-old incantation, where patterned sound, tempo, and ceremonial gesture can still work their magic.

32. See, e.g., Gentili, "Lirica greca arcaica" 89; Russo, *The Meaning of Oral Poetry* 37-39. Lloyd-Jones stresses other aspects of the continuity between Homer and the archaic age in *The Justice of Zeus,* esp. chap. 2.

33. Frs. 16 and 44 are the most celebrated examples in Sappho: see Bowra, *Greek Lyric Poetry* 232-33; Harvey, "Homeric Epithets" 206-23; Damon, "Modes of Analogy" 272-80; Lanata, "Sul linguaggio amoroso," esp. 72-75; and, apropos of fragments in Ionic and Lesbian Greek, M. Parry, "Traces of the Digamma" 402-3, speculated on the Lesbian poets' dependence on an oral tradition.

PART II

Homer and the Oral Tradition

FIVE

Sappho and Helen

Page duBois

Denys Page seems unimpressed with Sappho's fragment 16 Lobel-Page (L.-P). He complains of line 7: "The sequence of thought might have been clearer. . . . It seems inelegant then to begin this parable, the point of which is that Helen found τὸ κάλλιστον in her lover, by stating that she herself surpassed all mortals in this very quality."[1] Of the whole: "The poem opens with a common device[2]. . . In a phrase which rings dull in our doubtful ears, she proceeds to illustrate the truth of her preamble by calling Helen of Troy in evidence. . . . And the thought is simple as the style is artless. The transition back to the principal subject was perhaps not very adroitly managed. . . ."[3] Of the end, "The idea may seem a little fanciful: but this stanza was either a little fanciful or a little dull."[4]

I will argue that the very elements with which Page finds fault—the catalogue, the example of Helen, the return to the catalogue at the poem's end—structure it firmly while permitting its center to open into a moment of radiant presence. In addition, the poem is extraordinary in its rhetorical strategy, its attempt to move from the particularity of narrative discourse to a more general, logical, philosophical language. I see also in this poem, one of the few texts which break the silence of women in antiquity, an instant in which women become more than the objects of man's desire. Sappho's fragment 16 reaches beyond the confines of the lyric structure, looks both

This essay was originally published in slightly different form as "Sappho and Helen," *Arethusa* 11 (1978) 89–99.

1. Page, *Sappho and Alcaeus* 53.
2. Ibid., 55.
3. Ibid., 56.
4. Ibid., 57.

forward and backward in time, expresses the contradictions of its moment in history.

Here is the full, reconstructed text:

ο]ἰ μὲν ἰππήων στρότον οἰ δὲ πέσδων
οἰ δὲ νάων φαῖσ' ἐπ[ὶ] γᾶν μέλαι[ν]αν
ἔ]μμεναι κάλλιστον, ἔγω δὲ κῆν' ὅτ-
τω τις ἔραται·

πά]γχυ δ' εὔμαρες σύνετον πόησαι   5
π]άντι τ[ο]ῦτ', ἀ γὰρ πόλυ περσκέθοισα
κάλλος [ἀνθ]ρώπων 'Ελένα [τὸ]ν ἄνδρα
τὸν [πανάρ]ιστον

καλλ[ίποι]σ' ἔβα 'ς Τροΐαν πλέοι[σα
κωὐδ[ὲ πα]ῖδος οὐδὲ φίλων το[κ]ήων   10
πά[μπαν] ἐμνάσθη, ἀλλὰ παράγαγ' αὔταν
    ]σαν

        ]αμπτον γὰρ [
    ] . . . κούφως τ[   ]οησ[   ]ν
. .]με νῦν 'Ανακτορί[ας ὀ]νέμναι-   15
σ' οὐ] παρεοίσας·

τᾶ]ς κε βολλοίμαν ἔρατόν τε βᾶμα
κἀμάρυχμα λάμπρον ἴδην προσώπω
ἤ τὰ Λύδων ἄρματα καὶ πανόπλοις
πεσδομ[άχεντας.[5]   20

Some say a host of horsemen, others of infantry,
and others of ships, is the most beautiful thing
on the dark earth: but I say, it is what you love.

Full easy it is to make this understood of one and all:
for she that far surpassed all mortals in beauty,
Helen, her most noble husband

Deserted, and went sailing to Troy, with never a
thought for her daughter and dear parents. The
[Cyprian goddess] led her from the path...
... (Which) now has put me in mind of Anactoria far away;

Her lovely way of walking, and the bright radiance
of her changing face, would I rather see than
your Lydian chariots and infantry full-armed.

The poem begins with a brief catalogue, a listing of horsemen, infantry, ships. The ἐπὶ γᾶν μέλαιναν of line 2 is ambiguous in its position; it refers back to the catalogue and forward to the infinitive construction ἔμμεναι κάλλιστον in line 3. The dark earth is the basis for this host of warriors, and

5. Ibid., 52.

warships, perhaps, and recalls the diction of the Homeric poems. Sappho sets ἔγω against this background of choices, against the dark earth, and then she makes the declaration which is the logical heart of the poem, "I say it (τὸ κάλλιστον) is what one loves."

The next stanza overpowers the doubter; she asserts the ease of proof of her statement and moves immediately into an example. The poet's strategy here is rhetorically subtle; at first the reader associates the abstract (τὸ) κάλλιστον above with Helen herself. But the epic heroine has another function within the poem; she is not herself "the most beautiful thing." She moves toward it, drawn by desire.[6] Helen stands at first, set up by πόλυ περσκέθοισα, the hyperbole of which is echoed by τὸν πανάριστον of line 8; her name is surrounded by superlatives, masculine and feminine. In line 7, which begins with κάλλος, the quality for which she is immortal in men's memory, she is surrounded by ἀνθρώπων and ἄνδρα. She surpasses all mankind with respect to beauty. Sappho's proof is for a moment deferred, but the force of her example, the superiority of Helen to all, is stressed.

The third stanza begins with καλλίποισ'; the line ends with πλέοισα. The first letters of the first participle echo the καλλ- of κάλλος, and link the leaving behind, her act of desertion, with her beauty. The line expresses motion: we see Helen leaving, going, sailing; the ἔβα, the aorist, anchors her action in a single past moment. The participles catch her endlessly moving, taking steps, sailing away on a ship which recalls the third element of the catalogue at the poem's beginning. The following line sets her motion against the static force of that which she left behind, all those who should have been dear to her, who ought to have satisfied her. She forgets all; the μνα- of ἐμνάσθη perhaps plays on the root μαν-, μαιν-, suggesting madness. (Alcaeus, in his poem about Helen, calls her ἐκμάνεισα.)[7] The stanza ends with a sentence that is lost; someone, something, leads the heroine astray.

There follows a fragmentary passage that is legible again at με νῦν; we have moved from the world of legend back to the ἔγω of line 3, and to the present, the singer's time. The next word is Ἀνακτορίας. If the logical center of the poem is the generalizing statement of lines 3 and 4, the moment of presence, the phenomenological center, arrives with the name of Anaktoria. We are made aware of her absence only with οὐ παρεοίσας· the participle allows us to imagine her presence as well. Sappho's memory creates her; the act of making poetry becomes the act of making here, now, the absent loved one.

The last stanza completes the process of memory and finally returns the listener to the wider world. The ἐρατόν of line 17 echoes ἔραται of line 4,

---

6. F. Will, "Sappho and Poetic Motion."
7. Page, *Sappho and Alcaeus* 275.

makes whatever is lovely about Anaktoria partake of the general statement at the beginning. The βᾶμα is linked to ἔβα of line 9 and stresses the connection of Helen with all desire, with Anaktoria. Sappho would rather see her way of walking, her shining face, than the Lydian chariots, than the armed foot soldiers. The last two substantives return us to the "prooïmion," to the level of generalizing statement.

The poem works on the tension between desire, love, presence, and absence, and on the threat of war outside, the drama of pursuit in love. In each of the three parts of the lyric Sappho refers to the world of war, the world of men and heroes—in the catalogue of warriors and ships, in the mention of Helen, where the Trojan War is suppressed but present behind the text, in the mention at the end of chariots and foot soldiers. The notion of desire shimmers through the tripartite rhetorical structure, through the allusions to war; Sappho's choice of Anaktoria takes place in the context of a refusal of alternatives.

Lattimore mistranslates this poem in a way which reveals the consequences of its compactness, its far-reaching compression. He translates lines 3 and 4 thus: "but I say she whom one loves best is the loveliest."[8] In fact, the Greek κῆν' ὄτ]τω τις ἔραται does not mean that: κῆν' is neuter; ὄττω also does not show gender. Lattimore's translation, however, brings out an important aspect of the poem, a confusion between things and people which is essential to its logic. Lattimore makes the poem exclusively a love poem, a poem about Anaktoria. Sappho is writing something more, a sketch on the abstract notion of desire. At least as important as Anaktoria is the poet's attempt to universalize her insight, to move toward logical thought. She is defining desire with the vocabulary at hand.

Sappho wants to answer the question: what is τὸ κάλλιστον ἐπὶ γᾶν μέλαιναν? Her answer is a type of definition, a general statement— κάλλιστον is *whatever* one desires. The catalogue which precedes the general statement is not meant to be exhaustive; it is a "doublet" which includes kinds of men and ships, which transcends both these classes. Helen is a particular case, and her action proves the general statement; her beauty and fame are enlisted only to give weight to the general definition. Anaktoria is another particular, for Sappho the most beautiful thing on earth, in the poem another element in a proof. The partial listing at the end of the poem simply closes the "ring."

All the elements of the poem, which establish the opposition love/war, men/women, men/things, work also to create a definition, a logical summary under a heading that subsumes them all. Sappho is concerned to say new

8. Lattimore, *Greek Lyrics* 40.

things with the old vocabulary, as we see if we read the poem juxtaposed with this passage from the *Nicomachean Ethics*, where Aristotle is attempting to define τἀγαθὸν καὶ τὸ ἄριστον, the end at which human actions aim:

τὸ γὰρ ἀγαθὸν καὶ τὴν εὐδαιμονίαν οὐκ ἀλόγως ἐοίκασιν ἐκ τῶν βίων
ὑπολαμβάνειν οἱ μὲν πολλοὶ καὶ φορτικώτατοι τὴν ἡδονήν· διὸ καὶ τὸν βίον
ἀγαπῶσι τὸν ἀπολαυστικόν. (1.5, 1095b14–17)[9]

Bruno Snell says of Sappho's fragment 16, "That one man should contrast his own ideas with those of others is the theme of [this] poem by Sappho."[10] Yet elsewhere I think he comes closer to the real consequences of the type of thinking exemplified in this poem, which is not simply about personal taste. "But both of them [Archilochus and Sappho] are evidently concerned to grasp a piece of genuine reality; to find Being instead of Appearance."[11] Although she might have done so, Sappho is not saying that Anaktoria = τὸ κάλλιστον. Much of the energy of the poem comes from the force of her personal preference, her ability to make Anaktoria walk before us, but Anaktoria's presence is straining to break out of a structure which gives her existence wider meaning.

Helen is an element of the old epic vocabulary, yet she means something new here. Sappho subverts the transitional interpretation of her journey to Troy. And in so doing she speaks of desire in new terms, circling down on a definition of the abstract force. Eros as a term is insufficiently abstract; Eros is a god, Aphrodite a personification. Sappho moves toward the abstract by employing the substitutability of things, people, ships. She achieves a representation of desire by the accumulation of detail, examples, personal testimony.

The problem is very different from that which the Homeric poet sets himself, and Sappho's use of example fits into a more hypotactic structure. Homer's Phoenix tells the Meleager story as an example to persuade Achilles to return to battle. He is not concerned to describe, to define the nature of anger or withdrawal. The story works rhetorically to put Achilles' action in a context, to convince Achilles to act further, to ensure the outcome of his wrath in terms of heroic pattern.

Homer uses this kind of example rarely; he describes more often by means of simile, sets next to some action on the battlefield an event from the pastoral

---

9. "To judge from men's lives, the more or less reasoned conceptions of the good or happiness that seem to prevail among them are the following. On the one hand the generality of men and the most vulgar identify the good with pleasure, and accordingly are content with a life of enjoyment" (Aristotle, *Nichomachean Ethics* 13).

10. Snell, *The Discovery of the Mind* 47.

11. Ibid., 50. See also Wills, "The Sapphic 'Umwertung.' "

world outside the poem's supposed space. The one scene seems equivalent to the other. Sappho is defining an abstraction, and she operates by citing several particulars which are logically subordinate to a whole, working by addition toward that whole.

The move from mythical to rational thought, from religion to philosophy, is caught here in a moment of transition. Sappho is progressing toward analytical language, toward the notion of definition, of logical classes, of subordination and hypotactic structure. Her ability to do so coincides in time with the invention in the eastern Mediterranean, in nearby Lydia, of coined money, a step which Aristotle sees as enabling abstract thought, as permitting the recognition of abstract value. The exchange between persons who are different but equal requires an equalizer:

διὸ πάντα συμβλητὰ δεῖ πως εἶναι, ὧν ἐστὶν ἀλλαγή, ἐφ' ὃ τὸ νόμισμα ἐλήλυθε, καὶ γίνεταί πως μέσον· πάντα γὰρ μετρεῖ, ὥστε καὶ τὴν ὑπεροχήν καὶ τὴν ἔλλειψιν.... (*Eth. Nic.* 5.5, 1133a19–21)[12]

The invention of money allows things, even men, to be measured by a common standard. Sappho measures men and women and things not by setting them in a hierarchy, in a situation of relative value, but against a common standard, that of "the most beautiful thing on the dark earth."

Before the invention of coined money, men exchanged valuable things. The Homeric world is characterized by an exchange of gifts; women too are exchanged, as gifts, as valuable prizes of war. The Trojan War is caused by a violation of proper exchange, since Menelaos, the recipient of Helen, loses possession of her. The *Iliad* begins with the return of Chryseis to her father and Agamemnon's seizure of Briseis. Sappho's Helen is very different from Homer's. In the *Iliad* Helen is caught within the walls of Troy; we see her weaving a web which is like the war, pointing out the Greeks heroes to Priam. She is forced by Aphrodite to go to Paris's bed when the goddess snatches him from danger on the plain below. She mourns for Hektor, and laments her coming with Paris to Troy. Because of Aphrodite's promise to the shepherd, Helen has been traded for the apple of discord; she has become a thing, passively waiting to be reclaimed.

In the *Odyssey*, Helen greets Telemachos along with Menelaos; she is a contented queen, and Homer alludes to her stay in Egypt. According to an alternate version of the story, her εἴδωλον (image) was at Troy; she gives her guest nepenthe, which she received in Egypt. We hear her story of

---

12. "Hence all commodities exchanged must be able to be compared in some way. It is to meet this requirement that men have introduced money; money constitutes in a manner a middle term, for it is a measure of all things, and so of their superior or inferior value" (Aristotle, *Nichomachean Ethics* 282). Cf. E. Will, "De l'aspect éthique."

Odysseus's spying trip within the walls, and she claims to have assisted him. In an ironic juxtaposition, her husband immediately recounts the tale of the wooden horse and Helen's treacherous behavior, when she called to each warrior, imitating the voice of his wife. Only Odysseus kept them from crying out and betraying their mission.

Women in the Homeric world are exchanged, given as prizes, stolen, sold as slaves. The narrative structure of the *Odyssey* works on the passage of Odysseus from one woman to another, from the beautiful Kalypso to his faithful wife Penelope; he moves across the epic landscape defining himself, encountering fixed female creatures and moving beyond them. George Dimock, in a fine example of what Mary Ellmann would call "phallic criticism,"[13] says of the initial situation of the poem: "Leaving Calypso is very like leaving the perfect security of the womb; but, as the Cyclops reminds us, the womb is after all a deadly place. In the womb, one has no identity, no existence worthy of a name. Nonentity and identity are in fact the poles between which the actors in the poem move."[14] Odysseus, the only actor in sight, defines himself by leaving the womb—Kalypso; and the other boundary of his journey, from which he will depart again with his oar, is the bed of Penelope, another fixed, static place on the map of the poem, set like Kalypso's island as a landmark by which the hero marks out his direction, his existence.

The goddesses of the *Odyssey* act, but they too—except for Athena the virgin warrior, not born of woman, half-female—are static figures. In their *Dialectic of Enlightenment*, Horkheimer and Adorno speak of the sirens who tempt Odysseus, and of the circular, mythic creatures like them in the poem, figures which belong to the past which Odysseus is transcending in his *nostos*, in his trajectory through the landscape from Aia to Ithaka:

> The mythic monsters whose sphere of power he enters always represent ossified covenants, claims from pre-history. Thus in the stage of development represented by the patriarchal age, the older folk religion appears in the form of its scattered relics: beneath the Olympian heavens they have become images of abstract fate, or immaterial necessity.... Scylla and Charybdis have a right to whatever comes between them, just as Circe does to bewitch those unprepared with the gods' antidote.... Each of the mythic figures is programmed always to do the same thing. Each is a figure of repetition, and would come to an end should the repetition fail to occur.[15]

Odysseus moves away from Kalypso's island, away from Nausikaa and the Phaeacians, learning from Circe and leaving her, past the Sirens, past Scylla

---

13. See Ellmann, *Thinking about Women.*
14. Dimock, "The Name of Odysseus" 111.
15. Horkheimer and Adorno, *Dialectic of Enlightenment* 57–58.

and Charybdis. The cyclical female forms mark the landscape and cannot themselves move within it; Odysseus returns to Penelope and then moves past her too, deeper inland. Women in the world of the *Odyssey* are trapped in cyclical, mythic time; except for Athena, they belong to an age which Odysseus leaves behind as he makes himself, discovers himself through his journey.

The study of narrative structure, which has been a focus of recent literary criticism, seems unable to see beyond the type of text exemplified by the *Odyssey* . Women appear to have a static, fixed quality in oral literatures, and structuralists generalize from oral texts to describe women as objects, things to be exchanged, markers of places, geographically, textually. Lévi-Strauss discusses women almost as words exchanged in a conversation among men.[16] In the analysis of narrative which Vladimir Propp began with his study of the folktale, woman is a princess, the object of the hero's quest, a prize.[17] A.J. Greimas, in presenting his "actantial model," applies categories appropriate to oral literature to any conceivable love story:

> Par example, dans un récit qui ne serait qu'une banale histoire d'amour, finissant, sans l'intervention des parents, par le mariage, le sujet est à la fois le destinataire, tandis que l'objet est en même temps le destinateur de l'amour:

$$\text{Lui} \quad \underline{\text{Sujet} + \text{Destinataire}}$$
$$\text{Elle} \quad \text{Objet} + \text{Destinateur}^{18}$$

The attempt to universalize models of structure denies the historicity of the models: women may be exchanged like words in some cultures, according to anthropologists, but every love story is *not* accurately represented by the narrative shapes of these cultures. Women are not always objects, sending love. Oral cultures have patterns of exchange and marriage very different from those of literate societies, and the diagram, the insistence on the subject-object duality, fail to take into account the possibility of women's status as subjects in their own right.

Sappho's poem, although not a narrative, in fact reverses the pattern of oral literature, of the Homeric poems—men trading women, men moving past women. She sees Helen as an "actant" in her own life, the subject of

16. Lévi-Strauss, *The Elementary Structures of Kinship* 496.

17. Propp, *Morphology of the Folktale.*

18. Greimas, *Sémantique structurale* 177. Translated in *Structural Semantics* 203: "For instance, in a narrative that is only a common love story ending in marriage without the parents' intervention, the subject is also the receiver, while the object is at the same time the sender of love:

$$\text{He} \quad \underline{\text{Sender} + \text{Receiver}}$$
$$\text{She} \quad \text{Object} + \text{Sender.}$$

a choice, exemplary in her desiring. Sappho's idea of Helen is different even from that of her contemporary Alcaeus; he registers strong disapproval of Helen, in his narration of her story, by comparing her to the more virtuous Thetis.[19] Alcaeus insists on the destructive aspects of Helen's love, her responsibility for the perishing of the Trojans and their city.

Sappho does not judge Helen, and she does not make the epic heroine the victim of madness. Helen is one who acted, pursuing the thing she loved, and for that action Sappho celebrates her. Even the simple reversal of Greimas's model, which would make Helen "subject," is inadequate. Perhaps the failure of women to write narrative poetry, the silence which Sappho did not break, is linked to the invisible pressure of models like this one, patterns which insist on women's receptivity, passivity.

Sappho acts, as did Helen, in loving Anaktoria, in following her in her poem, in attempting to think beyond the terms of the epic vocabulary. Her action is possible because the world of oral culture, of a certain type of exchange, a type of marriage characteristic of such societies, is no longer dominant. The Greek world is, in the seventh century, in a stage of transition.[20] The institutions of the democratic cities have not yet evolved. The lyric age, the age of the tyrants, is a period of confusion, turbulence, and conflict; it is from the moment, this break, that Sappho speaks.

Louis Gernet, in his "mariage des Tyrans," analyzes the anachronistic features of the marriage of the tyrants, the elements of their alliances characteristic more of the legendary past, the age of the magical kinds, than of a society moving toward urbanization.[21] J.-P. Vernant's study of Greek marriage also helps to explain the peculiar situation of women in the seventh and sixth centuries:

> On peut parler d'une coupure entre le mariage archaïque et celui qui s'instaure dans le cadre d'une cité démocratique, à la fin du VIe siècle athénien. Dans l'Athènes post-clisthenienne les unions matrimoniales n'ont plus pour objet d'établir des relations du puissance ou de services mutuels entre de grandes familles souveraines mais de perpetuer les maisons, les foyers domestiques qui constituent la cité. . . .[22]

19. Page, *Sappho and Alcaeus* 278–79.
20. Mossé, *La tyrannie dans la Grèce antique* .
21. Gernet, *Anthropologie de la Grèce antique* 344–59.
22. Vernant, "Le mariage" 62–63. Translated in his *Myth and Society in Ancient Greece* 60: "In this respect one can speak in terms of a break between archaic marriage and marriage as it became established within the framework of a democratic city, in Athens, at the end of the sixth century. In the Athens of the period after Cleisthenes, matrimonial unions no longer have as their object the establishment of relationships of power or of mutual service between great autonomous families; rather, their purpose is to perpetuate the household, that is to say the domestic households that constitute the city. . . ."

The return of the tyrants to incest reveals a need at this time to redefine, to restructure the institution of marriage, so important in the lives of women in such cultures, to make it correspond to the new demands of urban, democratic life.

During the seventh century the old institutions which perpetuated the dominance of the aristocracy, the system of noble *oikoi*, the rural economy, premonetary exchange, were being challenged by growing mercantile, commercial, artisan groups which were clustering around the acropoles.[23] The conflict which Alcaeus documents in his political poems emerged at this time, when new definitions, new loci of power were being established, and as the aristocrats, the families of Sappho and Alcaeus among others, fought for survival.

The transitional nature of Sappho's society, the possible lack of definition for her class, for women, freed her from the rigidity of traditional marriage, or from the identity which arose from that fixed role. They permitted her to make poetry like the Anaktoria poem, a love poem which is at the same time an extension of the possibilities of language, and they enabled her to see Helen as an autonomous subject, the hero of her own life.

23. Arthur, "Early Greece."

SIX

Gardens of Nymphs:
Public and Private in Sappho's Lyrics

Jack Winkler

Monique Wittig and Sande Zeig in their *Lesbian Peoples: Material for a Dictionary* devote a full page to Sappho.[1] The page is blank. Their silence is one quite appropriate response to Sappho's lyrics, particularly refreshing in comparison to the relentless trivialization, the homophobic anxieties, and the sheer misogyny that have infected so many ancient and modern responses to her work.[2] This anxiety itself requires some analysis. Part of the explanation is the fact that her poetry is continually focused on women and sexuality, subjects that provoke many readers to excess.[3] But the centering on women and sexuality is not quite enough to explain the mutilated and violent discourse which keeps cropping up around her. After all Anakreon speaks of the same subjects. A deeper explanation refers to the *subject* more than the object of her lyrics—the fact that it is a *woman* speaking about women and sexuality. To some audiences this would have been a double violation of the ancient rules which dictated that a proper woman was to be silent in the public world (defined as men's sphere) and that a proper woman accepted the

This essay was originally published in slightly different form as "Gardens of Nymphs: Public and Private in Sappho's Lyrics," in *Reflections of Women in Antiquity*, edited by Helene P. Foley, 63–90 (New York: Gordon and Breach, 1981).

    1. English translation of *Brouillon pour un dictionnaire des amantes* (1976). There are some uncritical myths in Wittig's own account of Sappho in her essay "Paradigm."

    2. Lefkowitz, "Critical Stereotypes," and Hallett, "Sappho and Her Social Context," analyze the bias and distortions found in critical comments, ancient and modern, on Sappho.

    3. My statement that this is Sappho's central topic throughout her nine books is based not merely on the few fragments (obviously), but on the ancient testimonies, especially that of Demetrios, who provides my title: "nymphs' gardens, wedding songs, eroticism—in short the whole of Sappho's poetry" (νυμφαῖοι κῆποι, ὑμέναιοι, ἔρωτες, ὅλη ἡ Σαπφοῦς πόησις; περὶ ἑρμηνείας 132). Testimonies are collected in Gallovotti, *Saffo e Alceo*.

administration and definition of her sexuality by her father and her husband. I will set aside for the present the question of how women at various times and places actually conducted their lives in terms of private and public activity, appearance, and authority. If we were in a position to know more of the actual texture of ancient women's lives and not merely the maxims and rules uttered by men, we could fairly expect to find that many women abided by these social rules or were forced to, and that they sometimes enforced obedience on other women; but, since all social codes can be manipulated and subverted as well as obeyed, we would also expect to find that many women had effective strategies of resistance and false compliance by which they attained a working degree of freedom for their lives.[4] Leaving aside all these questions, however, I simply begin my analysis with the fact that there was available a common understanding that proper women ought to be publicly submissive to male definitions, and that a very great pressure of propriety could at any time be invoked to shame a woman who acted on her own sexuality.

This is at least the public ethic and the male norm. It cannot have been entirely absent from the society of Lesbos in Sappho's time. What I want to recover in this paper are the traces of Sappho's own consciousness in the face of these norms, her attitude to the public ethic and her allusions to private reality. My way of "reading what is there"[5] focuses on the politics of space— the role of women as excluded from public male domains and enclosed in private female areas—and on Sappho's consciousness of this ideology.[6] My analysis avowedly begins with an interest in sexual politics—the relations of power between women and men as two groups in the same society. My

4. There was also the category of heroic, exceptional woman, e.g., Herodotos's version of Artemisia, who is used to "prove the rule" every time he mentions her (7.99, 8.68, 8.87 f., 8.101), and the stories collected by Plut. *De mul. vir.* The stated purpose of this collection is to show that *aretē*, "virtue" or "excellence," is the same in men and women, but the stories actually show only that some women in times of crisis have stepped out of their regular anonymity and performed male roles when men were not available (Schaps, "The Women of Greece in Wartime").

5. "A feminist theory of poetry would begin to take into account the context in history of these poems and their political connections and implications. It would deal with the fact that women's poetry conveys . . . a special kind of consciousness. . . . Concentrating on consciousness and the politics of women's poetry, such a theory would evolve new ways of reading what is there" (Bernikow, *The World Split Open* 10–11).

6. Consciousness of course is not a solid object which can be discovered intact like an Easter egg lying somewhere in the garden (as in the Sapphic fr. 166 Leda is said to have found an egg hidden under the hyacinths). Sappho's lyrics are many-layered constructions of melodic words, images, ideas, and arguments in a formulaic system of shared points of view (personas). I take it for granted that the usual distinctions between "the real Sappho" as author and speaker(s) of the poems will apply when I speak here of Sappho's consciousness.

premise is that gender consciousness is at least as fundamental a way of identifying oneself and interpreting the world as any other class membership or category. In some sense the choice of a method will predetermine the kind and range of results that may emerge: a photo camera will not record sounds, a nonpolitical observer will not notice facts of political significance. Thus my readings of Sappho are in principle not meant to displace other readings but add to the store of perceptions of "what is there."

There are various "publics and privates" which might be contrasted. What I have in mind for this paper by "public" is quite specifically the recitation of Homer at civic festivals considered as an expression of common cultural traditions. Samuel Butler notwithstanding, Homer and the singers of his tradition were certainly men and the Homeric epics cannot be conceived as women's songs.[7] Women are integral to the social and poetic structure of both *Iliad* and *Odyssey*, and the *notion* of a woman's consciousness is particularly vital to the *Odyssey*.[8] But Nausikaa and Penelope live in a male-prominent world, coping with problems of honor and enclosure which were differentially assigned to women,[9] and their "subjectivity" in the epic must ultimately be analyzed as an expression of a male consciousness. Insofar as Homer presents a set of conventional social and literary formulas, he inescapably embodies and represents the definition of public culture as male territory.[10]

Archaic lyric, such as that composed by Sappho, was also not composed for private reading but for performance to an audience.[11] Sappho often seems to be searching her soul in a very intimate way, but this intimacy is in some measure formulaic[12] and is certainly shared with some group of listeners. And yet, maintaining this thesis of the public character of lyric, we can still propose three senses in which such song may be "private": first, composed in the person of a woman (whose consciousness was socially defined as

---

7. S. Butler, *The Authoress*.

8. Foley, "'Reverse Similes'"; Domingo, "The Role of the Female" chap. 2.

9. As Kalypso complains, *Od*. 5.118 ff. Perhaps the poet means this to be a short-sighted criticism, illustrating *Od*. 1.32.

10. In this territory and at these recitations women are present—Homer is not a forbidden text to women, not an arcane *arrhēton* of the male mysteries. In the *Odyssey* (1.325–29) Penelope hears and reacts to the epic poetry of a bard singing in her home, but her objections to his theme, the homecoming from Troy, are silenced by Telemakhos. Arete's decision to give more gifts to Odysseus (*Od*. 11.335–41) after he has sung of the women he saw in the Underworld may be an implicit sign of her approval of his poetry. Helen in *Iliad* 6 delights in the fact that she is a theme of epic poetry (357–58) and weaves the stories of the battles fought for her into her web (125–28).

11. Merkelbach, "Sappho und ihr Kreis"; Russo, "Reading the Greek Lyric Poets."

12. Lanata, "Sul linguaggio amoroso."

outside the public world of men); second, shared only with women (that is, other "private" persons; τάδε νῦν ἐταίραις ταῖς ἔμαις τέρπνα κάλως ἀείσω, "and now I shall sing this beautiful song to delight the women who are my companions," fr. 160 L.-P.[13]); and third, sung on informal occasions, what we would simply call poetry readings, rather than on specific ceremonial occasions such as sacrifice, festival, leave-taking, or initiation.[14] The lyric tradition, as Nagy argues,[15] may be older than the epic, and if older perhaps equally honored as an achievement of beauty in its own right. The view of lyric as a subordinate element in celebrations and formal occasions is no more compelling than the view, which I prefer, of song as honored and celebrated at least sometimes in itself. Therefore I doubt that Sappho always needed a sacrifice or dance or wedding *for which* to compose a song; the institution of lyric composition was strong enough to occasion her songs as *songs*. Certainly Sappho speaks of goddesses and religious festivities, but it is by no means certain that her own poems are either for a cult performance or that her circle of women friends (*hetairai*) is identical in extension with the celebrants in a festival she mentions.[16] It is possible that neither of these latter two senses of "private" were historically valid for Sappho's performances. Yet her lyrics, as compositions that had some publicity, bear some quality of being in principle from another world than Homer's, not just from a different tradition, and they embody a consciousness both of her "private," woman-centered world and the other, "public" world. This essay is an experiment in using these categories to unfold some aspects of Sappho's many-sided meaning.

Poem 1 is one of the passages in Sappho that has been best illuminated in recent criticism. Several analyses have developed the idea that Sappho is speaking in an imagined scene which represents that of Diomedes on the battlefield in *Iliad* 5.[17] Sappho uses a traditional prayer formula, of which Diomedes' appeal to Athena at *Iliad* 5.115–17 is an example ("Hear me,

13. The text used in this essay is that of Edgar Lobel and Denys Page, *Poetarum Lesbiorum Fragmenta* (abbreviated L.-P.).

14. Homer seems to include this possibility in the range of performing *klea andrōn* (deeds of men) when he presents Achilles singing to his own *thumos* (spirit), while Patroklos sits in silence, not listening as an audience but waiting for Achilles to stop (*Il.* 9.186–91).

15. Nagy, *Comparative Studies*.

16. Sappho is only one individual, and may have been untypical in her power to achieve a literary life and renown. Claims that society in her time and place allowed greater scope for women in general to attain a measure of public esteem are based almost entirely on Sappho's poems (including probably Plut. *Lyk.* 18.4, *Thes.* 19.3; Philostr. *VA* 1.30). The invention of early women poets is taken to extremes by Tatian in his *adversus Graecos* and by Ptolemy Chennos (chap. 5, pp. 143–44).

17. Cameron, "Sappho's Prayer"; Page, *Sappho and Alcaeus*; Svenbro, "Sappho and Diomedes"; Stanley, "The Role of Aphrodite"; Rissman, *Love as War*.

Atrytone, child of aegis-bearing Zeus; if ever you stood beside my father supporting his cause in bitter battle, now again support me, Athena"), and she models Aphrodite's descent to earth in a chariot on the descent of Athena and Hera (5.719–72), who are coming to help the wounded Diomedes (5.781). Sappho asks Aphrodite to be her ally, literally her companion in battle, *summachos*.

> Intricate, undying Aphrodite, snare-weaver, child of Zeus, I pray thee,
> do not tame my spirit, great lady, with pain and sorrow. But come to me
> now if ever before you heard my voice from afar and leaving your
> father's house, yoked golden chariot and came. Beautiful sparrows swiftly brought
>   you
> to the murky ground with a quick flutter of wings from the sky's height
> through clean air. They were quick in coming. You, blessed goddess,
> a smile on your divine face, asked what did I suffer, this time again,
> and why did I call, this time again, and what did I in my frenzied heart
> most want to happen. Whom am I to persuade, this time again . . .
> to lead to your affection? Who, O Sappho, does you wrong? For one who flees will
> soon pursue, one who rejects gifts will soon be making offers, and one who
> does not love will soon be loving, even against her will. Come to me even
> now, release me from these mean anxieties, and do what my heart wants done,
> you yourself be my ally.[18]

One way of interpreting the correspondences that have been noticed is to say that Sappho presents herself as a kind of Diomedes on the field of love, that she is articulating her own experience in traditional (male) terms and showing that women too have *aretē*.[19] But this view, that the poem is mainly about *erōs* and *aretē* and uses Diomedes merely as a background model, falls short. Sappho's use of Homeric passages is a way of allowing us, even encouraging us, to approach her consciousness as a woman and poet reading Homer. The Homeric hero is not just a starting point for Sappho's discourse about her own love; rather Diomedes as he exists in the *Iliad* is central to what Sappho is saying about the distance between Homer's world and her own. A woman listening to the *Iliad* must cross over a gap that separates her experience from the subject of the poem, a gap which does not exist in quite the same way for male listeners. How can Sappho murmur along with the rhapsody the speeches of Diomedes, uttering and impersonating his appeal for help? Sappho's answer to this aesthetic problem is that she can only do so by substituting her concerns for those of the hero while maintaining the same structure of plight / prayer / intervention. Poem 1 says, among

---

18. Translations of Sappho are my own; ellipses indicate that the Greek is incomplete.
19. Bolling, "Restoration of Sappho"; Marry, "Sappho and the Heroic Ideal."

other things, "This is how I, a woman and poet, become able to appreciate a typical scene from the *Iliad*."

Though the Diomedeia is a typical passage, Sappho's choice of it is not random, for it is a kind of test case for the issue of women's consciousness of themselves as participants without a poetic voice of their own at the public recitations of traditional Greek heroism. In *Iliad* 5, between Diomedes' appeal to the goddess and the descent of Athena and Hera, Aphrodite herself is driven from the battlefield after Diomedes stabs her in the hand. The poet identifies Aphrodite as a "feminine" goddess, weak, *analkis*, unsuited to take part in male warfare (331, 428). Her appropriate sphere, says Diomedes exulting in his victory over her, is to seduce weak women (*analkides*, 348–49). By implication, if "feminine" women (and all mortal women are "feminine" by definition and prescription) try to participate in men's affairs—warfare or war poetry—they will, like Aphrodite, be driven out at spear point.

Poem 1 employs not only a metaphorical use of the *Iliad* (transferring the language for the experience of soldiers to the experience of women in love) and a familiarization of the alien poem (so that it now makes better sense to women readers), but a *multiple identification* with its characters. Sappho is acting out the parts both of Diomedes and of Aphrodite as they are characterized in *Iliad* 5. Aphrodite, like Sappho, suffers pain (ὀδύνῃσι; 354), and is consoled by a powerful goddess who asks "Who has done this to you?" (373). Aphrodite borrows Ares' chariot to escape from the battle and ride to heaven (358–67), the reverse of her action in Sappho's poem.[20] Sappho therefore is in a sense presenting herself both as a desperate Diomedes needing the help of a goddess (Athena/Aphrodite) and as a wounded and expelled female (Aphrodite/Sappho) seeking a goddess's consolation (Dione/Aphrodite).

This multiple identification with several actors in an Iliadic scene represents on another level an admired feature of Sappho's poetics—her adoption of multiple points of view in a single poem. This is especially noteworthy in poem 1 where she sketches a scene of encounter between a victim and a controlling deity. The intensification of pathos and mastery in the encounter is due largely to the ironic *double consciousness* of the poet-Sappho speaking in turn the parts of suffering "Sappho" and impassive goddess. Such many-mindedness is intrinsic to the situation of Greek women understanding men's culture, as it is to any silenced group within a culture that acknowledges its presence but not its authentic voice and right to self-determination. This leads to an interesting reversal of the standard (and oppressive) stricture on women's literature that it represents only a small and limited area of the

20. Di Benedetto, "Il volo di Afrodite"; he refers to the poem as "Aphrodite's revenge" (122).

larger world.[21] Such a view portrays women's consciousness according to the *social* contrast of public/private, as if women's literature occupied but a small circle somewhere inside the larger circle of men's literature, just as women are restricted to a domestic sanctuary. But insofar as men's public culture is truly public, displayed as the governing norm of social interaction "in the streets," it is accessible to women as well as to men. Because men define and exhibit their language and manners as *the* culture and segregate women's language and manners as a subculture, inaccessible to and protected from extrafamilial men, women are in the position of knowing two cultures where men know only one. From the point of view of consciousness, we must diagram the circle of women's literature as a larger one which includes men's literature as one phase or compartment of women's cultural knowledge. Women in a male-prominent society are thus like a linguistic minority in a culture whose public actions are all conducted in the majority language. To participate even passively in the public arena the minority must be bilingual; the majority feels no such need to learn the minority's language. Sappho's consciousness therefore is necessarily a double consciousness, her participation in the public literary tradition always contains an inevitable alienation.

Poem 1 contains a statement of how important it is to have a double consciousness. Aphrodite reminds "Sappho" of the ebb and flow of conflicting emotions, of sorrow succeeded by joy, of apprehensiveness followed by relief, of loss turning into victory. This reminder not to be singlemindedly absorbed in one moment of experience can be related to the pattern of the *Iliad* in general, where the tides of battle flow back and forth, flight alternating with pursuit. This is well illustrated in *Iliad* 5, which is also the Homeric locus for the specific form of alternation in fortunes which consists of wounding and miraculous healing. Two gods (Aphrodite and Ares) and one hero (Aineias) are injured and saved. Recuperative alternation is the theme of poem 1, as it is of *Iliad* 5. But because of Sappho's "private" point of view and double consciousness it becomes not only the theme but the *process* of the poem, in the following sense: Sappho appropriates an alien text, the very one which states the exclusion of "weak" women from men's territory; she implicitly reveals the inadequacy of that denigration; and she restores the fullness of Homer's text by isolating and alienating its very pretense to a justified exclusion of the feminine and the erotic.

Sappho's poetic strategy finally leads to a rereading of *Iliad* 5 in the light of her poem 1. For when we have absorbed Sappho's complex re-impersonation of the Homeric roles (male and female) and learned to see what was marginal

---

21. E.g., J. B. Bury, "while Sappho confined her muse within a narrower circle of feminine interests" (Bury, Cook, and Adcock, *Greek Literature* 494–95), and similarly Jaeger, *Paideia*.

as encompassing, we notice that there is a strain of anxious self-alienation in Diomedes' expulsion of Aphrodite. The overriding need of a battling warrior is to be strong and unyielding; hence the ever-present temptation (which is also a desire) is to be weak. This is most fully expressed at *Iliad* 22.111–30, where Hektor views laying down his weapons to parley with Achilles as effeminate and erotic. Diomedes' hostility to Aphrodite (the effeminate and erotic) is a kind of scapegoating, his affirmation of an ideal of masculine strength against his *own* possible "weakness." For, in other contexts outside the press of battle, the Homeric heroes have intense emotional lives and their vulnerability there is much like Sappho's: they are as deeply committed to friendship networks as Sappho ("He gave the horses to Deipylos, his dear comrade, whom he valued more than all his other age-mates"; 5.325–26); they give and receive gifts as Sappho does; they wrong each other and reestablish friendships with as much feeling as Sappho and her beloved. In a "Sapphic" reading, the emotional isolation of the Iliadic heroes from their domestic happiness stands out more strongly ("no longer will his children run up to his lap and say 'Papa' "; 5.408). We can reverse the thesis that Sappho uses Homer to heroize her world and say that insofar as her poems are a reading of Homer (and so lead us back to read Homer again) they set up a feminine perspective on male activity that shows more clearly the inner structure and motivation of the exclusion of the feminine from male arenas.

I return to the image of the double circle—Sappho's consciousness is a larger circle enclosing the smaller one of Homer. Reading the *Iliad* is for her an experience of double consciousness. The movement thus created is threefold: by temporarily restricting herself to that smaller circle she can understand full well what Homer is saying; when she brings *her* total experience to bear she sees the limitation of his world; by offering her version of this experience in a poem she shows the strengths of her world, the apparent incompleteness of Homer's, and finally the easily overlooked subtlety of Homer's. This threefold movement of appropriation from the "enemy," exposure of his weakness, and recognition of his worth is like the actions of Homeric heroes who vanquish, despoil, and sometimes forgive. Underlying the relations of Sappho's persona to the characters of Diomedes and Aphrodite are the relations of Sappho the author to Homer, a struggle of reader and text (audience and tradition), of woman listening and man reciting. A sense of what we now call the sexual politics of literature seems nearly explicit in poem 16:

> Some assert that a troupe of horsemen, some of foot soldiers, some a
> fleet of ships is the most beautiful thing on the dark earth; but I
> assert that it is whatever anyone desires. It is quite simple to make
> this intelligible to all, for she who was far and away preeminent in
> beauty of all humanity, Helen, abandoning her husband, the ..., went

sailing to Troy and took no thought for child or dear parents, but
beguiled ... herself ... for ... lightly ... reminds me now of Anaktoria absent:
whose lovely step and shining glance of face I would prefer to see than Lydians'
chariots and fighting men in arms ... cannot be ... human ... to wish to share
... unexpectedly.

[This is a poem of eight stanzas, of which the first, second, third, and fifth are
almost intact, the rest lost or very fragmentary.]

It is easy to read this as a comment on the system of values in heroic poetry.
Against the panoply of men's opinions on beauty (all of which focus on
military organizations, regimented masses of anonymous fighters), Sappho
sets herself—"but I"—and a very abstract proposition about desire. The
stanza first opposes one woman to a mass of men and then transcends that
opposition when Sappho announces that "the most beautiful" is "whatever
you or I or anyone may long for." This amounts to a reinterpretation of
the kind of meaning the previous claims had, rather than a mere contest
of claimants for supremacy in a category whose meaning is agreed upon.[22]
According to Sappho, what men mean when they claim that a troupe of
cavalrymen is very beautiful is that they intensely desire such a troupe.
Sappho speaks as a woman opponent entering the lists with men, but her
proposition is not that men value military forces whereas she values desire,
but rather that all valuation is an act of desire. Men are perhaps unwilling
to see their values as erotic in nature, their ambitions for victory and strength
as a kind of choice. But it is clear enough to Sappho that men are in love
with masculinity and that epic poets are in love with military prowess.

Continuing the experiment of reading this poem as about poetry, we might
next try to identify Helen as the Iliadic character. But Homer's Helen cursed
herself for abandoning her husband and coming to Troy; Sappho's Helen,
on the contrary, is held up as proof that it is right to desire one thing above all
others, and to follow the beauty perceived no matter where it leads. There is
a charming parody of logical argumentation in these stanzas; the underlying,
real argument I would reconstruct as follows, speaking for the moment in
Sappho's voice. "Male poets have talked of military beauty in positive terms,
but of women's beauty (especially Helen's) as baneful and destructive. They
will probably never see the lineaments of their own desires as I do, but let
me try to use some of their testimony against them, at least to expose the
paradoxes of their own system. I shall select the woman whom men both
desire and despise in the highest degree. What they have damned her for
was, in one light, an act of the highest courage and commitment, and *their
own poetry* at one point makes grudging admission that she surpasses all the

22. Wills, "The Sapphic 'Umwertung' "; duBois, "Sappho and Helen."

moral censures leveled against her—the Teichoskopia (*Il.* 3.121–244). Helen's abandonment of her husband and child and parents is mentioned there (139, 174), and by a divine manipulation she feels a change of heart, now desiring her former husband and city and parents (139) and calling herself a bitch (180). But these are the poet's sentiments, not hers; he makes her a puppet of his feeling, not a woman with a mind of her own. The real Helen was powerful enough to leave a husband, parents, and child whom she valued less than the one she fell in love with. (I needn't and won't mention her lover's name: the person—male or female—is not relevant to my argument.) Indeed she was so powerful that she *beguiled Troy itself* at that moment when, in the midst of its worst suffering, the senior counselors watched her walk along the city wall and said, in their chirpy old men's voices, 'There is no blame for Trojans or armored Achaians to suffer pains so long a time for such a woman' (156–57)."

So far I have been speaking Sappho's mind as I see it behind this poem. There is an interesting problem in lines 12 ff., where most modern editors of Sappho's text have filled the gaps with anti-Helen sentiments, on the order of "but (Aphrodite) beguiled her ... , for (women are easily manipulated,) light (-minded ...)." We do not know what is missing, but it is more consistent with Sappho's perspective, as I read it, to keep the subject of παράγαγ', "beguiled," the same as in the preceding clause—Helen. "Helen beguiled—itself (or herself)," some feminine noun, such as "city," "blame" (nemesis), or the like. What is easily manipulated and light-minded (*kouphōs*) are the senior staff of Troy, who astonishingly dismiss years of suffering as they breathe a romantic sigh when Helen passes. Perhaps Sappho's most impressive fragment is poem 31:

> The one seems to me to be like the gods, the man whosoever sits facing you and listens nearby to your sweet speech and desirable laughter—which surely terrifies the heart in my chest; for as I look briefly at you, so can I no longer speak at all, my tongue is silent, broken, a silken fire suddenly has spread beneath my skin, with my eyes I see nothing, my hearing hums, a cold sweat grips me, a trembling seizes me entire, more pale than grass am I, I seem to myself to be a little short of dead. But everything is to be endured, since even a pauper. ...

The first stanza is a *makarismos*, a traditional formula of praise and well-wishing, "happy the man who ... ," and is often used to celebrate the prospect of a happy marriage.[23] For instance, "That man is far and away blessed beyond all others who plies you with dowry and leads you to his house; for I have never seen with my eyes a mortal person like you, neither man

23. Snell, "Sapphos Gedicht"; Koniaris, "On Sappho Fr. 31"; Saake, *Zur Kunst Sapphos* 17–38.

nor woman. A holy dread grips me as I gaze at you" (*Od.* 6.158–61). In fact this passage from Odysseus's speech to Nausikaa is so close in structure (*makarismos* followed by a statement of deep personal dread) to poem 31 that I should like to try the experiment of reading the beginning of Sappho's poem as a re-creation of that scene from the *Odyssey*.

If Sappho is speaking to a young woman ("you") as Nausikaa, with herself in the role of an Odysseus, then there are only two persons present in the imagined scene.[24] This is certainly true to the emotional charge of the poem, in which the power and tension flow between Sappho and the woman she sees and speaks to, between "you" and "I." The essential statement of the poem is, like the speech of Odysseus to Nausikaa, a lauding of the addressee and an abasement of the speaker which together have the effect of establishing a working relationship between two people of real power. The rhetoric of praise and of submission are necessary because the poet and the shipwrecked man are in fact very threatening. Most readers feel the paradox of poem 31's eloquent statement of speechlessness, its powerful declaration of helplessness; as in poem 1, the poet is masterfully in control of herself as victim. The underlying relation of power then is the opposite of its superficial form: the addressee is of a delicacy and fragility that would be shattered by the powerful presence of the poet unless she makes elaborate obeisance, designed to disarm and, by a careful planting of hints, to seduce.

The anonymous "that man whosoever" (κῆνος ὤνηρ ὄττις in Sappho, κεῖνος ὅς κε in Homer) is a rhetorical cliché, not an actor in the imagined scene. Interpretations which *focus* on "that someone (male)" as a bridegroom (or suitor or friend) who is actually present and occupying the attention of the addressee miss the strategy of persuasion that informs the poem and in doing so reveal their own androcentric premises. In depicting "the man" as a concrete person central to the scene and godlike in power, such interpretations misread a figure of speech as a literal statement and thus add the weight of their own pro-male values to Sappho's woman-centered consciousness. "That man" in poem 31 is like the military armament in poem 16, an introductory setup to be dismissed: we do not imagine that the speaker of poem 16 is actually watching a fleet or infantry; no more need we think that Sappho is watching a man sitting next to her beloved. To whom, in that case, would Sappho be addressing herself? Such a reading makes poem 31 a modern lyric of totally internal speech, rather than a rhetorically structured public utterance that imitates other well-known occasions for public speaking (prayer, supplication, exhortation, congratulation).

24. Del Grande, "Saffo."

My reading of poem 31 explains why "that man" has assumed a grotesque prominence in discussions of it. Androcentric habits of thought are part of the reason, but even more important is Sappho's intention to hint obliquely at the notion of a bridegroom just as Odysseus does to Nausikaa. Odysseus the stranger designs his speech to the princess around the roles which she and her family will find acceptable—helpless suppliant, valorous adventurer, and potential husband.[25] The ordinary protocols of marital brokerage in ancient society are a system of discreet offers and counteroffers which must maintain at all times the possibility for saving face, for declining with honor and respect to all parties. Odysseus's speech to Nausikaa contains these delicate approaches to the offer of marriage which every reader would appreciate, just as Alkinoos understands Nausikaa's thoughts of marriage in her request to go wash her brothers' dancing clothes: "So she spoke, for she modestly avoided mentioning the word 'marriage' in the presence of her father; but he understood her perfectly" (*Od.* 6.66–67). Such skill at innuendo and respectful obliquity is one of the ordinary-language bases for the refined art of lyric speech. Sappho's hint that "someone" enjoys a certain happiness is, like Odysseus's identical statement, a polite self-reference and an invitation to take the next step. Sappho plays with the role of Odysseus as suitor extraordinary, an unheard-of stranger who might fulfill Nausikaa's dreams of marriage contrary to all the ordinary expectations of her society. She plays too with the humble formalities of self-denigration and obeisance, all an expansion of σέβας μ' ἔχει εἰσορόωντα, "holy dread grips me as I gaze on you" (*Od.* 6.161).

"That man is equal to the gods": this phrase has another meaning too. Sappho as reader of the *Odyssey* participates by turn in all the characters; this alternation of attention is the ordinary experience of every reader of the epic and is the basis for Sappho's multiple identification with both Aphrodite and Diomedes in *Iliad* 5. In reading *Odyssey* 6 Sappho takes on the roles of both Odysseus and Nausikaa, as well as standing outside them both. I suggest that "that man is equal to the gods," among its many meanings, is a reformulation of Homer's description of the sea-beaten Odysseus whom Athena transforms into a godlike man: νῦν δὲ θεοῖσιν ἔοικε τοὶ οὐρανὸν εὐρὺν ἔχουσιν, "but now he is like the gods who control the expanse of heaven" (6.243). This is Nausikaa's comment to her maids as she watches Odysseus sit on the shore after emerging from his bath, and she goes on to wish that her husband might be such.[26] The point of view from which Sappho speaks as one struck to the heart is that of a mortal visited by divine power and beauty, and this

25. Austin, *Archery* 191–200.
26. The comparison to gods runs throughout the Phaiakian scenes: Nausikaa (6.16, 105–9), her maids (18), the Phaiakians (241), Nausikaa's brothers, ἀθανάτοις ἐναλίγκιοι (7.5).

is located in the *Odyssey* in the personas of Odysseus (struck by Nausikaa, or so he says), of Nausikaa (impressed by Odysseus), and of the Homeric audience, for Sappho speaks not only as the strange suitor and the beautiful princess but as the *Odyssey* reader who watches "that man" (Odysseus) face to face with the gently laughing girl.

In performing this experiment of reading Sappho's poems as expressing, in part, her thoughts while reading Homer, her consciousness of men's public world, I think of her being naturally drawn to the character of Nausikaa, whose romantic anticipation (6.27) and delicate sensitivity to the unattainability of the powerful stranger (244 f., 276–84) are among the most successful presentations of a woman's mind in male Greek literature.[27] Sappho sees herself both as Odysseus admiring the nymphlike maiden and as Nausikaa cherishing her own complex emotions. The moment of their separation has what is in hindsight, by the normal process of rereading literature in the light of its own reformulations, a "Sapphic" touch: μνήσηι ἐμεῖ', "Farewell, guest, and when you are in your homeland remember me who saved you—you owe me this." These are at home as Sappho's words in poem 94.6–8: "And I made this reply to her, 'Farewell on your journey, and remember me, for you know how I stood by you.'"[28]

The idyllic beauty of Phaiakia is luxuriously expressed in the rich garden of Alkinoos, whose continuously fertile fruits and blossoms are like the gardens which Sappho describes (esp. frs. 2, 81b, 94, 96), and it reminds us of Demetrios's words, "Virtually the whole of Sappho's poetry deals with nymphs' gardens, wedding songs, eroticism." The other side of the public/private contrast in Sappho is a design hidden in the lush foliage and flower cups of these gardens. There are two sides to double consciousness: Sappho both reenacts scenes from public culture infused with her private perspective as the enclosed woman and she speaks publicly of the most private, woman-centered experiences from which men are strictly excluded. They are not equal projects; the latter is much more delicate and risky. The very formulation of women-only secrets, female *arhēta*, runs the risk not only of impropriety (unveiling the bride) but of betrayal by misstatement. Hence the hesitation in Sappho's most explicit delineation of double consciousness: οὐκ οἶδ' ὄττι θέω· δίχα μοι τὰ νοήμματα, "I am not sure what to set down, my thoughts are double," could mean "I am not sure which things to set down and which to keep among ourselves, my mind is divided" (51).

---

27. Apollonios of Rhodes's Medea is conscious of love in terms drawn from Sappho: see Privitera, "Ambiguità antitesi," and note especially the characteristic presentation of Medea's mental afterimages and imaginings (3.453–58, 811–16, 948–55), which is the technique of Sappho 1, 16, and 96.

28. Schadewalt, "Zu Sappho" 67.

Among the thoughts which Sappho has woven into her poetry, in a way which both conceals and reveals without betraying, are sexual images. These are in part private to women, whose awareness of their own bodies is not shared with men, and in part publicly shared, especially in wedding songs and rites, which are a rich store of symbolic images bespeaking sexuality.[29] The ordinary ancient concern with fertility, health, and bodily function generated a large family of natural metaphors for human sexuality and, conversely, sexual metaphors for plants and body parts. A high degree of personal modesty and decorum is in no way compromised by a daily language which names the world according to genital analogies or by marriage customs whose function is to encourage fertility and harmony in a cooperative sexual relationship. The three words which I will use to illustrate this are *numphē*, *pteruges*, and *mēlon*. The evidence for their usage will be drawn from various centuries and kinds of writing up to a thousand years after Sappho; but the terms in each case seem to be of a semitechnical and traditional nature rather than neologisms. They constitute the scattered fragments of a locally variegated, tenacious symbolic system which was operative in Sappho's time and which is still recognizable in modern Greece.

Numphē has many meanings: at the center of this extended family are a "clitoris" and "bride." *Numphē* names a young woman at the moment of her transition from maiden (*parthenos*) to wife (or "woman," *gunē*); the underlying idea is that just as the house encloses the wife and as veil and carriage keep the bride apart from the wedding celebrants, so the woman herself encloses a sexual secret.[30] "The outer part of the female genital system which is visible has the name 'wings' (*pteruges*), which are, so to speak, the lips of the womb. They are thick and fleshy, stretching away on the lower side to either thigh, as it were parting from each other, and on the upper side terminating in what is called the *numphē*. This is the starting point (*archē*) of the wings (labia), by nature a little fleshy thing and somewhat muscular (or, mouse-like)."[31] The same technical use of *numphē* to mean clitoris is found in other medical writers and lexicographers,[32] and by a natural extension is applied to many

29. Bourdieu, *Algeria* 105; Abbott, *Macedonian Folklore* chap. 11.

30. "One of the men in Chios, apparently a prominent figure of some sort, was taking a wife and, as the bride was being conducted to his home in a chariot, Hippoklos the king, a close friend of the bridegroom, mingling with the rest during the drinking and laughter, jumped up into the chariot, not intending any insult but merely being playful according to the common custom. The friends of the groom killed him" (Plut. *De mul. virt.* 244e).

31. Soranos *Gynaecology* 1.18.

32. Medical writers: Rufinus ap. Oribasios 3.391.1, Galen 2.370e, Aetios 16.103–4 (clitoridectomy), Paulus Aigin. 6.70 (clitoridectomy for lesbians). Lexicographers: Phot. *Lexikon*, s.v.; Pollux 2.174, with the anagram *skairon sarkion*, "throbbing little piece of flesh."

analogous phenomena: the hollow between lip and chin,[33] a depression on the shoulder of horses,[34] a mollusk,[35] a niche,[36] an opening rosebud,[37] the point of a plow[38]—this last an interesting reversal based on the image of the plowshare penetrating the earth. The relation of *numphē*, clitoris, to *pteruges*, wings/labia, is shown by the name of a kind of bracken, the *numphaia pteris*, "nymph's wing," also known as *thelupteris*, "female wing"; by the name of the loose lapels on a seductively opening gown;[39] and by the use of *numphē* as the name for bees in the larva stage just when they begin to open up and sprout wings.[40]

This family of images extends broadly across many levels of Greek culture and serves to reconstruct for us one important aspect of the meaning of "bride," *numphē*, as the ancients felt it.[41] Hence the virtual identity of Demetrios's three terms for Sappho's poetry: nymphs' gardens, wedding songs, eroticism. Several of Sappho's surviving fragments and poems make sense as a woman-centered celebration and revision of this public but discreet vocabulary for women's sexuality. The consciousness of these poems ranges over a wide field of attitudes. The first can be seen as Sappho's version of male genital joking (which she illustrates in 110 and 111),[42] but when applied to the *numphē* Sappho's female ribaldry is pointedly different in tone:

33. Rufus *Onom.* 42; Pollux 2.90; Hesychios.

34. *Hippiatr.* 26

35. Speusippos apud Ath. 3.105b.

36. Kallixinos 2 (*FHG* III 55).

37. Phot. *Lexicon*, s.v. *numphai*: "And they call the middle part of the female genitals the *numphē*; also the barely opened buds of roses are *numphai* and newlywed maidens are *numphai*." The equation of flowers and female genitals is ancient (Krinagoras *AP* 6.345; Achilles Tatius 2.1) and modern (art: Lippard, "Quite Contrary"; Dodson, "Liberating Masturbation"; Chicago, *The Dinner Party* and *Through the Flower*; poetry: Lorde, "Love Poem"). Sappho appears to have made the equation of bride and roses explicit, according to Wirth.

I would not reject the suggestion that Sappho's feelings for Kleis, as imagined in fr. 132, were given a consciously lesbian coloring: "I have a beautiful child, her shape is like that of golden *flowers*, beloved Kleis; in her place I would not ... all Lydia nor lovely. ..." Indeed, taking it a step further, this "child" (*pais*) may be simply another metaphor for clitoris (*Kleis/kleitoris*). The biographical tradition that regards Kleis as the name of Sappho's daughter and mother may be (as so often) based on nothing more than a fact-hungry reading of her poems. (The same name occurs at fr. 98b.1.) On flowers and fruit see Stehle, "Retreat from the Male."

38. Pollux 1.25.2; Proklos ad Hes. *Op.* 425.

39. Pollux 755, 62, 66 (= Ar. *Thesm. Deut.* fr. 325 OCT).

40. Arist. *HA* 551b2–4; Phot. *Lexikon*, s.v. *numphai*; Pliny *NH* 11.48.

41. For the connection of Nymphs to marriage and birth see Ballentine, "Some Phases of the Cult of the Nymphs."

42. See Kirk, "A Fragment of Sappho Reinterpreted"; Killeen, "Sappho Fr. 111"; and Lanata, "Sul linguaggio amoroso," who suggests that fr. 121 may be "una variazione scherzosa nel nota fr. 105" (66).

Like the sweet-apple [*glukumēlon*] ripening to red on the topmost branch,
on the very tip of the topmost branch, and the apple pickers have overlooked it—
no, they haven't overlooked it but they could not reach it.

(105a)

Mēlon, conventionally translated "apple," is really a general word for fleshy
fruit—apricots, peaches, apples, citron, quinces, pomegranates. In wedding
customs it probably most often means quinces and pomegranates, but for
convenience sake I will abide by the traditional translation "apple." Like
numphē and *pteruges*, *mēlon* has a wider extension of meanings, and from this we
can rediscover why "apples" were a prominent symbol in courtship and marriage rites.[43] *Mēlon* signifies various "clitoral" objects: the seed vessel of the
rose,[44] the tonsil or uvula,[45] a bulge or sty on the lower eyelid,[46] and a swelling
on the cornea.[47] The sensitivity of these objects to pressure is one of the bases
for the analogy; I will quote just the last one. "And what is called a *mēlon* is a
form of fleshy bump (*staphulōma*, grapelike or uvular swelling), big enough
to raise the eyelids, and when it is rubbed it bothers the entire lid-surface."

Fragment 105a, spoken of a bride in the course of a wedding song, is a
sexual image. We can gather this sense not only from the general erotic
meaning of "apples" but from the location of the solitary apple high up
on the bare branches of a tree,[48] and from its sweetness and color. The
verb ἐρεύθω, "grow red," and its cognates are used of blood or other red
liquid appearing on the surface of an object that is painted or stained or
when the skin suffuses with blood.[49] The vocabulary and phrasing of this
fragment reveal much more than a sexual metaphor, however; they contain
a delicate and reverential attitude to the exclusive presence-and-absence of
women in the world of men. Demetrios elsewhere (148) speaks of the graceful
naïveté of Sappho's self-correction, as if it were no more than a charming
touch of folk speech when twice in these lines she changes her mind, varying

43. Foster, "Notes on the Symbolism of the Apple"; McCartney, "How the Apple Became
the Token of Love"; Trümpf, "Kydonische Äpfel"; Lugauer, "Untersuchungen zur Symbolik
des Apfels"; Littlewood, "The Symbolism of the Apple"; Kakridis, "Une Pomme Mordue";
POxy. 2637 fr. 25.6; Abbott, *Macedonian Folklore* 147 f., 170, 177.
44. Theophr. *Hist. Pl.* 6.6.6.
45. Rufus *Onom.* 64; Galen *de usu partium* 15.3: "The part called *numpha* gives the same sort of
protection to the uteri that the uvula gives to the pharynx, for it covers the orifice of their
neck by coming down into the female pudendum and keeps it from being chilled." Sappho's
fr. 42, on the warmth afforded by enfolding wings (*ptera*), may be read of labia as well as of
birds.
46. Hesychios, s.v. χύλα.
47. Alexander Tralles περὶ ὀφθαλμῶν, Puschmann, ed., 152.
48. "In other parts (of Macedonia) . . . , especially among the Wallachs, a pole with an apple
on top and a white kerchief streaming from it . . . is carried by a kilted youth in front of the
wedding procession" (Abbott, *Macedonian Folklore* 172).
49. Hippocrates *Epid.* 2.3.1, *Morb. Sacr.* 15, *Morb.* 4.38 (of a blush).

a statement she has already made. But self-correction is Sappho's playful format for saying much more than her simile would otherwise mean. The words are inadequate—how can I say?—not inadequate, but they encircle an area of meaning for which there have not been faithful words in the phallocentric tradition. The real secret of this simile is not the image of the bride's "private" parts but of women's sexuality and consciousness in general, which men do not know as women know. Sappho knows this secret in herself and in other women whom she loves, and she celebrates it in her poetry. Where men's paraphernalia are awkwardly flaunted (bumping into the lintel, fr. 111, inconveniently large like a rustic's feet, fr. 110), women's are protected and secure. The amazing feature of these lines is that the apple is not "ripe for plucking" but unattainable, as if even after marriage the *numphē* would remain secure from the husband's appropriation.[50]

Revision of myth is combined with a sexual image in fragment 166: φαῖσι δή ποτα Λήδαν ὑακίνθωι πεπυκάδμενον, "They do say that once upon a time Leda found an egg hidden in the hyacinth." As the traditional denigration of Helen was revised in poem 16, so the traditional story of Helen's mother is told anew. Leda was not the victim of Zeus's rape who afterward laid Helen in an egg; rather she discovered a mysterious egg hidden inside the frilly blossoms of a hyacinth stem, or (better) in a bed of hyacinths when she parted the petals and looked under the leaves. The egg discovered there is

(1) a clitoris hidden under labia

(2) the supremely beautiful woman, a tiny Helen, and

(3) a story, object, and person hidden from male culture.[51]

The metaphor of feeling one's way through the undergrowth until one discovers a special object of desire is contained in the word μαίομαι, "I feel

---

50. This sense of *numphē* gives further meaning to a fragment of Praxilla, 754 in Page, *Poetae Melici Graeci*. "Looking in beautifully through the windows, your head that of a maiden, but you are a *numphē* underneath," ὦ διὰ τῶν θυρίδων καλὸν ἐμβλέποισα / παρθένε τὰν κεφαλὰν τὰ δ' ἔνερθε νύμφα. Praxilla is, according to Aly's fine interpretation (PW 22:176), addressing the moon shining through her windows (cf. Page 747, σεληναίης τε πρόσωπὸν); its mystery and elusive attraction are expressed by the image of a woman with a youthful, innocent face and a look that bespeaks deeper experience and knowledge. The physical comparison is to a woman whose face alone is visible: wrapped up under all those clothes, says Praxilla, is the body of a sexually mature woman. Page at the opposite extreme envisions a woman peeping into the windows of houses in order to attract other women's husbands ("quae more meretricio vagabunda per fenestras intueri soles, scilicet ut virum foras unde unde elicias"; Page 754 app. crit.). This level of significance may also be relevant to Page 286 (Ibykos) and 929e–g (anonymous).

51. The verb πυκάζω refers not to just any kind of "hiding" but to covering an object with clothes, flower garlands, or hair, either as an adornment or for protection. "Thick" flowers (ὑάκινθον / πυκνὸν καὶ μαλακόν) cover the earth to cushion the lovemaking of Zeus and Hera (*Il.* 14.347–50).

for," "I search out by feeling." It is used of Odysseus feeling the flesh of Polyphemos's stomach for a vital spot to thrust in his sword (*Od.* 9.302), of animals searching through dense thickets for warm hiding places (Hes. *Op.* 529–33), of enemy soldiers searching through the luxurious thicket for the hidden Odysseus (*Od.* 14.356), of Demeter searching high and low for her daughter (*h. Hom. Cer.* 2.44), of people searching for Poseidon's lover Pelops (Pind. *Ol.* 1.46). The contexts of this verb are not just similar by accident: *maiomai* means more than "search for," it means "ferret out," especially in dense thickets where an animal or person might be lurking. In view of the consistency of connotations for this verb there is no reason to posit a shifted usage in Sappho 36, as the lexicon of Liddell, Scott, and Jones does. As these lexicographers read it, Sappho's words καὶ ποθήω μάομαι are redundant— "I desire you and I desire you." Rather they mean "I desire and I search out." I would like to include the physical sense of feeling carefully for hidden things or hiding places.[52] In the poetic verb *maiomai* there is a physical dimension to the expression of mutual passion and exploration. Desire and touching occur together as two aspects of the same experience: touching is touching-with-desire, desire is desire-with-touching.

The same dictionary that decrees a special meaning for *maiomai* when Sappho uses it invents an Aeolic word μάτημι (B) πατέω, "I walk," to reduce the erotic meaning of a Lesbian fragment of uncertain authorship, Incert. 16: "The women of Krete once danced thus—rhythmically with soft feet around the desirable altar, exploring the tender, pliant flower of the lawn." μάτημι is a recognized Aeolic equivalent of ματεύω, akin to μαίομαι. The meanings "ferret out," "search through undergrowth," "beat the thickets looking for game," "feel carefully" seem to me quite in place. Appealing to a long tradition, Sappho (whom I take to be the author) remarks that the sexual dancing of women, the sensuous circling of moving hands and feet around the erotic altar and combing through the tender valleys, is not only current practice but was known long ago in Krete.

I have been able to find no *simple* sexual imagery in Sappho's poems. For her the sexual is always something else as well. Her sacred landscape of the body is at the same time a statement about a more complete consciousness, whether of myth, poetry, ritual, or personal relationships. In the following

---

52. Fr. 48 may be read in a similar sense: ἦλθες καί μ' ἐπόθησας, ἔγω δέ σ' ἐμαιόμαν· / ὂν δ' ἔφλεξας ἔμαν φρένα καιομέναν πόθωι, "You came and you desired me; I searched you carefully; you stirred the fires of my feeling, smoldering with desire." ἔφλεξας is Wesseling's conjecture for φύλαξας; μ' ἐπόθησας is my conjecture for ἐπόησας. I would support this conjecture by reference back to fr. 36, which joins *poth/* and *mai/*, and by the symmetry achieved: you desired me—I felt you—you stirred me—I desired you, which we might call Sapphic reciprocity. Cf. Lanata, "Sul linguaggio amoroso" 79.

fragment, 94, which contains a fairly explicit sexual statement in line 23,[53] we find Sappho correcting her friend's view of their relation.

> ... Without guile I wish to die. She left me weeping copiously and said, "Alas, what fearful things we have undergone, Sappho; truly I leave you against my will." But I replied to her, "Farewell, be happy as you go and remember me, for you know how we have stood by you. Perhaps you don't—so I will remind you ... and we have undergone beautiful things. With many garlands of violets and roses ... together, and ... you put around yourself, at my side, and flowers wreathed around your soft neck with rising fragrance, and ... you stroked the oil distilled from royal cherry blossoms and on tender bedding you reached the end of longing ... of soft ... and there was no ... nor sacred ... from which we held back, nor grove ... sound ...

As usual the full situation is unclear, but we can make out a contrast of Sappho's view with her friend's. The departing woman says δεῖνα πεπόνθαμεν, "fearful things we have suffered," and Sappho corrects her, κάλ' ἐπάσχαμεν, "beautiful things we continuously experienced." Her reminder of these beautiful experiences (which Page calls a "list of girlish pleasures")[54] is a loving progression of intimacy, moving in space—down along the body—and in time—to increasing sexual closeness: from flowers wreathed on the head to flowers wound around the neck to stroking the body with oil to soft bedclothes and the full satisfaction of desire. I would like to read the meager fragments of the succeeding stanza as a further physical landscape: we explored every sacred place of the body. To paraphrase the argument, "When she said we had endured an awful experience, the ending of our love together, I corrected her and said it was a beautiful experience, an undying memory of sensual happiness that knew no limit, luxurious and fully sexual. Her focus on the termination was misplaced; I told her to think instead of our mutual pleasure, which itself had no term, no stopping point, no unexplored grove."

Poem 2 uses sacral language to describe a paradisal place[55] which Aphrodite visits:

> Hither to me from Krete, unto this holy temple, a place where there is a lovely grove of apples and an altar where the incense burns, and where is water which ripples cold through apple branches, and all the place is shadowed with roses, and as the leaves quiver a profound quiet ensues. And here is a meadow where horses graze, spring flowers bloom, the honeyed whisper of winds.... This is the very place where you, Kypris ..., drawing into golden cups the nectar gorgeously blended for our celebration, then pour it forth.

53. West, "Burning Sappho" 322.
54. Page, *Sappho and Alcaeus* 83.
55. Turyn, "The Sapphic Ostracon."

The grove, Page comments, is "lovely," a word used "elsewhere in the Lesbians only of *personal* charm."[56] But this place is, among other things, a personal place, an extended and multiperspectived metaphor for women's sexuality. Virtually every word suggests a sensuous ecstasy in the service of Kyprian Aphrodite (apples, roses, quivering followed by repose, meadow for grazing, spring flowers, honey, nectar flowing). Inasmuch as the language is both religious and erotic, I would say that Sappho is not describing a public ceremony for its own sake but is providing a way to experience such ceremonies, to infuse the celebrants' participation with memories of lesbian sexuality. The twin beauties of burning incense on an altar and of burning sexual passion can be held together in the mind, so that the experience of either is the richer. The accumulation of topographic and sensuous detail leads us to think of the interconnection of all the parts of the body in a long and diffuse act of love, rather than the genital-centered and more relentlessly goal-oriented pattern of lovemaking which men have been known to employ.

I have tried to sketch two areas of Sappho's consciousness as she had registered it in her poetry: her reaction to Homer, emblematic of the male-centered world of public Greek culture, and her complex sexual relations with women in a world apart from men. Sappho seems always to speak in many voices—her friends', Homer's, Aphrodite's—conscious of more than a single perspective and ready to detect the fuller truth of many-sided desire. But she speaks as a woman to women: her eroticism is both subjectively and objectively woman centered. Too often modern critics have tried to restrict Sappho's *erōs* to the straitjacket of spiritual friendship. A good deal of the sexual richness which I detect in Sappho's lyrics is compatible with interpretations such as those of Lasserre and Hallett,[57] but what requires explanation is their insistent denial that the emotional lesbianism of Sappho's work has any physical component. We must distinguish between the physical component as a putative fact about Sappho in her own life and as a meaning central to her poems. Obviously Sappho as poet is not an historian documenting her own life but rather a creative participant in the erotic-lyric tradition.[58] My argument has been that this tradition includes pervasive allusions to physical *erōs* and that in Sappho's poems both subjects and

---

56. Page, *Sappho and Alcaeus* 36.

57. Lasserre, "Ornements érotiques"; Hallett, "Sappho and Her Social Context." "Sarebbe augurabile che nelle allusioni all'amore saffico cadesse in disuso la sgradita definizione di 'turpe amore' inventata da un moralismo se non altro anacronistico" (Gentili, "La veneranda Saffo" 48 n. 55). Stehle, "Romantic Sensuality, Poetic Sense," is excellent.

58. Late Greek rhetoric maintains the tradition of praising a public official at a ceremonial event by a declaration of love. Himerios (48) and Themistios (13) tell their audiences that the honored official is their boyfriend.

object of shared physical love are women. We now call this lesbian.[59] To admit that Sappho's discourse is lesbian but insist that she herself was not seems quixotic. Would anyone take such pains to insist that Anakreon in real life might not have felt any physical attraction to either youths or women? It seems clear to me that Sappho's consciousness included a personal and subjective commitment to the holy, physical contemplation of the body of Woman, as metaphor and reality, in all parts of life. Reading her poems in this way is a challenge to think both in and out of our time, both in and out of a phallocentric framework, a reading which can enhance our own sense of this womanly beauty *as subject and as object* by helping us to unlearn our denials of it.

59. "Women who love women, who choose women to nurture and support and create a living environment in which to work creatively and independently, are lesbians" (B. Cook, " 'Women Alone Stir My Imagination' " 738).

PART III

Ritual and Social Context

SEVEN

Sappho's Group:
An Initiation into Womanhood

Claude Calame

1. THE "CIRCLE" OF SAPPHO AS AN INSTITUTION

With the model of the Hellenistic cult groups in mind, many modern scholars have decided that Sappho possessed a *thiasos* on Lesbos in the traditional sense of the term. Indications of this are very tenuous and the word is never used in connection with Sappho, so it seems more prudent to speak with Merkelbach of the *Kreis* or Lesbian "circle" of Sappho or, in an even more neutral mode, of her group.[1] Nevertheless, it is possible to see through these indications together with some fragments of the poet herself what an association of women at the end of the seventh century could be; the evidence also points to other groups of the same type, of interest as points of comparison with the Spartan educational system for women. The most significant fragment speaks of a *moisopolōn oikia*, a house of women dedicated to the Muses. The term *mousopolos* could have the institutional meaning here that it certainly has in a Boiotian inscription dating perhaps from the second century B.C.E., in which the actors in a theatrical troupe are described.[2]

This essay was originally published in slightly different form in the English translation of *Les chœurs, Choruses of Young Women in Ancient Greece: Their Morphology, Religious and Social Function*, translated by Janice Orion and Derek Collins (Lanham, Md.: Rowman and Littlefield, 1994).

1. See Merkelbach, "Sappho und ihr Kreis" 4 with n. 1, who summarizes the theses of his predecessors, as also West, "Burning Sappho" 324 ff.; Lasserre, *Sappho* 114 ff.; and De Martino, "Appunti" 271. I would like to thank A. Lardinois and B. Zweig for their useful remarks.

2. Sappho fr. 150 Voight (V.); *IG* 7.2484. See Poland, *Geschichte des griechischen Vereinswesens* 206 f., and Lanata, "Sul linguaggio amoroso" 67; in Sappho's fragment, *oikiai*, metrically awkward, is a gloss that has slipped into the line in the place of a probable *domōi*. For other indications that could refer to the existence of the *thiasos* of Sappho, see Treu, "Neues über Sappho" 10 ff., and "Sappho," PW, suppl. 11:1228, 1325 f.

Sappho's "house" or group, like most of the female choruses of the archaic period, was composed of young girls and, beside the epithalamia themselves, were probably composed for wedding ceremonies; her poems mostly speak of *parthenoi, korai,* or *paides.*[3] Indirect testimony defines the bonds linking the girls with the poet with the terms *hetairai (philai)* and *mathētriai.*[4] The first term contains the semantic feature "companionship" and is used not only by the indirect tradition but also by Sappho herself when she speaks of her own companions.[5] Athenaeus cites the fragment in which the term appears and explains that the meaning as used by Sappho is different from the more common one of "hetaira"; in Sappho's meaning, it is employed when women or girls talk of their most intimate friends (*sunētheis kai philas*). Semantic ambiguities of this type have probably led to the tradition that makes of Sappho a *pornē gunē,* a woman of doubtful morals.[6] The second term and its implications will be examined further, emphasizing the pedagogical element in these bonds of friendship and companionship.

There is a probable hint of the institutional base of these relationships in a verse of the famous "Ode to Aphrodite." The use in the same context of the term *adikein,* "to commit an injustice," and *philotēs,* "friendship based on mutual confidence," indicates that the rupture by one of the members of Sappho's circle of the bonds of loving friendship was felt as a juridical violation of the rules. The wrong committed on the person of Sappho at the emotional level was made worse by the injustice committed with regard to the institutional foundation of their relationship. To betray Sappho was not only to betray the intimate and reciprocal relationship of *philia* the poetess was setting up with the girls of her group, but it meant also to break the bonds sanctioned by a contract.[7]

3. *Parthenos*: frs. 17.14, 27.10, 30.2, 153 V., etc.; *korē*: frs. 108, 140 V.; *pais*: frs. 49.2 (Atthis), 58.11 V., etc. See now the detailed study of Lardinois, "Subject and Circumstance" 65 ff. The term *gunē* is used only in frs. 44, 15, 31 (description of the wedding of Hektor and Andromache), and 96.6 f. V. (poem addressed to a young Lydian girl who is no longer in Sappho's circle).

4. *Suda* under *Sapphō* (*S* 107 Adler) = test. 253 V. (see Ael. *VH* 12.19 = test. 256 V.).

5. Sappho fr. 160.1 V. = Ath. 13.571c-d. See frs. 142, 126 V. with Lanata, "Sul linguaggio amoroso" 66 f. The use of the term *hetaira* has led some interpreters to compare Sappho's group with the political hetaireia Alcaeus was animating at the same time at Mytilene (Trümpf, "Über das Trinken" 141 ff.; Burnett, *Three Archaic Poets* 209), and this hypothesis has been now put forward by Parker, "Sappho Schoolmistress" 341 f.; but Sappho's dancing companions are not represented as revelers at the banquet!

6. Sappho test. 261, 262 V.; on this tradition, see below, § 3.

7. Sappho fr. 1.18 V. See Rivier, "Observations sur Sappho" 84 ff.; Carson [Giacomelli], "The Justice of Aphrodite" 226 ff.; and Burnett, *Three Archaic Poets* 254 ff. The bonds of friendship within the Sapphic circle were combined with homoerotic relationships: see below, § 3, and now Calame, *I Greci* 17 f., 72 f.

These indications, to which is added the choreographic and musical activity evidenced in most of Sappho's fragments, show structures in the Lesbos circle analogous to those characteristic of the female lyric chorus: young girls, bound to the one who leads them by ties expressed in the term *hetaira,* perform together dances and songs. This situation is described in the epigram of the *Palatine Anthology* in which young Lesbians, under the leadership of Sappho, form a chorus in honor of Hera.[8] Philostratos also sees a choral image of this type when a picture of young girls (*korai*) singing round the statue of Aphrodite recalls for him the figure of Sappho.[9] These girls, Philostratos explains, are led (*agei*) by a *khorēgos* designated as *didaskalos,* still young, who beats the rhythm while the adolescents (*paides*) sing the praises of the goddess; by marking the beat, the *khorēgos* indicates to the young girls the right moment for beginning the song. It is unnecessary to point out the presence of the typically choral semantic features of "leading" and "beginning" in this scene described by Philostratos.

Sappho was not the only woman in Lesbos at the end of the seventh century to have a circle of young girls about her. She had two rivals in the persons of Andromeda and Gorgo.[10] A fragment of commentary on papyrus tells us that the same relations existed between Gorgo and her companions as between Sappho and her pupils.[11] These relations are referred to by the term *sunzux,* which means, literally, the one who finds himself or herself under the same yoke. The use of this term by the tragedians to refer to the spouse in a matrimonial context has been cited as proof of marriagelike bonds between the members of the group and its leader.[12] The plurality of these bonds within a circle and the frequent use of the term *suzugos* as a synonym for *hetairos,* the companion, suggest that this denomination is the expression of the relationship of "companionship" that, independent of any matrimonial meaning, unites the members with the *khorēgos* in Gorgo's circle as in the

8. *AP* 9.189. The word *choros* appears only once, it is true, in the fragments we have of Sappho: fr. 70.10 V. It is clear that the classical distinction between monodic poetry and choral poetry, which places Sappho's compositions under the category of monodies, does not correspond to reality: on this subject see Calame, *Les chœurs* 1:126 f. with n. 171, and, for Sappho specifically, Lardinois, "Subject and Circumstance" 73 ff., and "Who Sang"; see also Greene, "Apostrophe and Women's Erotics."

9. Philostr. *Imag.* 2.1.1 ff. = Sappho test. 217 V.

10. Max. Tyr. 18.9 = Sappho test. 219 V.; see frs. 57, 131, 144 V. Page, *Sappho and Alcaeus* 133 ff., recognizes the existence of rivals and friends of Sappho, but denies their relations were other than personal, thus denying any official or professional reasons for these bonds; on another rival circle, see perhaps fr. 71 V.

11. Sappho fr. 213 V.

12. Gentili, *Poesia e pubblico* 106 f.; to the parallels cited by Gentili can be added the existence of a Hera Syzygia: see Stob. 2.7.3a. On this subject see Page, *Sappho and Alcaeus* 144 n. 1, and West, "Burning Sappho" 320.

lyric chorus.[13] I shall address later the sexual form which these relationships could take.

A late testimonium by Philostratos, probably not very dependable, reports that a certain Damophyle of Pamphilia had composed for young girls (*parthenous*) love poems (*erōtika*) and also hymns to Artemis Pergaia.[14] Even if Damophyle is difficult to situate historically, it is interesting to note that, again according to Philostratos, this unknown poet passed as a pupil of Sappho, on whose musical activity she modeled herself; consequently the mention is an indirect witness of Sappho's activity, and it is significant that the author used the word "disciple" (*homilētria*) for the girls who sang the compositions of the supposed Damophyle. The term is similar to *mathētria* used in the *Suda* to denote the companions and pupils of Sappho.[15] My list would not be complete without Telesilla, the Argive poet of the beginning of the fifth century. One of her poems is addressed to young girls (*korai*) and tells the story of Artemis fleeing from Alpheios.[16] The adolescent connotations of this myth could point to the fragment as an extract from a partheneion, but no source explicitly says that Telesilla was the leader of a group of girls.

13. The commentary attributed to Gorgo two *suzuges*, namely Gongyla and Pleistodike (probably the girl called by Sappho Arkheanassa; see Treu, *Sappho, griechisch und deutsch* 165); Gongyla is herself named in the *Suda* under *Sapphō* (*S* 107 Adler) = Sappho test. 253 V. as one of the pupils of Sappho; see Sappho fr. 95.4 and possibly fr. 22.10 V. As for Arkheanassa, she reappears in a fragment of Sappho unfortunately very mutilated: fr. 103 Ca, 4 V. It is thus possible that, like Atthis, Pleistodike and Gongyla had left Sappho's confraternity for the rival circle of Gorgo. On the use of *suzugos*, see Eur. *IT* 250 (Orestes *suzugos* of Pylades), *Tro.* 1001 (Pollux *suzugos* of Castor); see also *HF* 673 ff. (*suzugia* of the Muses and the Graces,) Ar. *Plut.* 945.

14. Philostr. *VA* 1.30 = Sappho test. 223 V. See Treu, *Sappho, griechisch und deutsch* 237; see also, for Corinna, fr. 655. Page (P.) 10 ff. 8.

15. It seems to have been a late tradition that made the poet Erinna a companion (*hetaira*) of Sappho. See *Suda* under *Ērinna* (*Ē* 521 Adler) = Sappho test. 257 V. (see also Eust. *Il.* 326.46 ff.); Donado, "Cronologia de Erinna" 349 ff., and Rauk, "Erinna's *Distaff*" 101 ff. See also *AP* 9.190 = Sappho test. 56 Gall., with *AP* 9.26 = Sappho test. 52 Gall., which names nine poetesses, the earthly incarnation of the Muses. Among them are also Telesilla and another supposed companion of Sappho, Nossis (*AP* 7.718) = Sappho test. 51 Gall.; she was actually an Alexandrian poet: see Skinner, "Sapphic Nossis" 5 ff. A women's *thiasos* serving Artemis at Cyzicus is mentioned in the *Suda* under *Dolōn* (*D* 1345 Adler) = Ael. fr. 46 Hercher. On the mention of a relationship of "companionship" in an epigram about Erinna, see *AP* 7.710.7 f. = Erinna fr. 5.7 f. D. (*sunetairis*). The companion of Erinna to whom this funeral epigram is dedicated was a newly married young woman; she had probably left Erinna's circle to be married before death struck: see again *AP* 7.712 = Erinna fr. 4 D. and fr. 1B.47 ff. D.; see Snyder, *The Woman and the Lyre* 86 ff.

16. Telesilla fr. 717 Page (P.); see also fr. 720 P. In "Auf den Spuren" 1 ff., Herzog thinks that the poet headed a *thiasos* dedicated to Apollo, but see Snyder, *The Woman and the Lyre* 59 ff., and Cavallini, "Erinna."

So several women poets, particularly in eastern Greece, gathered around them groups of girls who were both their pupils and their companions; under their direction these adolescents were musically active, often in a cult context, thus making their association into something very similar, if not identical, to the lyric chorus.

2. THE INSTRUCTION GIVEN IN SAPPHO'S GROUP

In Sappho's group, there is no doubt about the didactic relationship between the poet and her companions. For instance, speaking of the famous fragment in which Sappho tells the recipient of the poem that she will disappear and leave no trace in the memory of men if she has not taken part in the "roses of Pieria," in other words in the musical activity of Sappho's circle, Plutarch says that the woman addressed was among those who were *amousai* and *amatheis*, strangers to music and ignorant. It is not only significant that it is Plutarch, with his great interest in pedagogy, who quotes this fragment and who sees that Sappho's circle offered a form of instruction and education by frequenting the Muses. But it has to be pointed out that inside Sappho's group, the memorial function of poetry, current in archaic Greece, takes on a specific role: it is only through poetry itself that the beauty acquired through musical activity will gain a kind of afterlife and that the educated girl will keep it, despite the destructions of time, in the memory of the persons performing the poem that praises her.[17]

Other fragments by the Lesbian poet refer to this pedagogical aspect by characterizing young girls who were not in her circle but in a rival group or were about to join to her circle as ignorant and ungracious.[18] As I mentioned already, the biographical section of the *Suda* itself names three *mathētriai*, three pupils of Sappho, and the *khorēgos* who conducts the young girls as they sing for Aphrodite is called *didaskalos*, the mistress. This relationship between master and pupil is identical to that between the *khorēgos* and the *khoreutai*, according to the lexicographers. Finally a new fragment of commentary on Sappho's poems clearly describes the poet in her role as educator (*paideuousa*); the commentator adds that this education was not only for girls of good family (*tas aristas*) in Lesbos, but also those who came from Ionia.[19] But what was

---

17. Sappho fr. 55 V.; see Plut. *Mor.* 646e–f and Stob. 3.4.12 (*pros apaideuton gunaika*): on this subject see Snell, "Zur Soziologie des archaischen Griechentums" 54 ff. On the memorial function of Sappho's poems, see Burnett, *Three Archaic Poets* 277 ff., and Gentili, *Poesia e pubblico* 116 ff.

18. Sappho frs. 49, 130.3 f., 57 V.

19. *Suda* under *Sapphō* (*S* 107 Adler) = Sappho test. 253 V.; see frs. 16, 15, 95.4 V.; Philostr. *Imag.* 2.11 = Sappho test. 217 V. See above, § 1; P. Colon. 5860 a, b = Sappho fr. S 261A P.; see Gronewald, "Fragmente" 114 ff.

the content of the education given by the poet as instructor to the young aristocratic girls of her group?

If music seems to be the essence of the education Spartan girls received in choruses led by poets such as Alcman, we must remember that neither music nor dance were ends in themselves in Greece; they are the means of communicating by performing and assimilating by *mimēsis* a precise set of contents. By reciting the poems composed by their masters the poets, the *khoreutai* learn and internalize a series of myths and rules of behavior; moreover, archaic choral poetry has to be understood as a performative art, as a set of poems functioning as cult acts in precise ritual contexts. But examining the content of the musical instruction in a cultic context of performance leads to the question of its function, of its pragmatics: what was the aim of the instruction received in the chorus of young girls? For what would this instruction prepare the chorus members?

As far as Sappho's group is concerned, we see with numerous interpreters of this poetry that most descriptions of the poet and her advice bear on the themes of feminine grace and beauty. The life of Sappho's companions unfolded almost completely under the sign of Aphrodite, in an atmosphere and in a setting represented on the mythical level by the famous gardens of the goddess.[20] From a pedagogical point of view, Sappho's circle looks like a sort of school for femininity destined to make the young pupils into accomplished women: through the performance of song, music, and cult act, they had lessons in comportment and elegance, reflected in the many descriptions of feminine adornment and attitudes in the fragments that we have by Sappho.[21]

So Atthis, according to the *Suda* one of Sappho's three dearest companions, was a very young and graceless child (*smikra pais k'akharis*) before joining the group; two sources that cite the fragment specify that "graceless" in this context meant a girl not yet old enough to be married, not yet nubile.[22] Physical grace thus became the mark of nubility; by being in Sappho's chorus the young girl acquires the grace that will make her a beautiful woman, which in turn clears the way for marriage. Consequently, possessing *kharis* signifies gaining the status of adult and the possibility of being a wife, in the same way

20. Sappho fr. 2 V. See Schadewaldt, *Sappho* 25 ff.; Merkelbach, "Sappho und ihr Kreis" 25 ff.; Lanata, "Sul linguaggio amoroso" 68 ff.; Barilier, "La figure d'Aphrodite" 27 ff.; Burnett, *Three Archaic Poets* 217 ff.; Gentili, *Poesia e pubblico* 115 ff.; and, specifically for the signification of the gardens, Calame, *I Greci* 132 ff.

21. Sappho frs. 22.9 ff., 81.4 f., 94.12 ff. V., etc.

22. Sappho fr. 49 V. See Plut. *Mor.* 751d (*tēn oupō gamōn echousan hōran*) and scholia Pind. *Pyth.* 2.42 (II, p. 44 Drachmann).

as "beauty" made the young followers of the cult of Helen at Therapne into women ready for marriage.

And when Andromeda, Sappho's rival, tries to take away young Atthis, the poet attacks her cruelly by describing her dressed as a peasant, a rustic (*agroïōtis*).[23] If "rustic" means simply an exterior lack of elegance, it nevertheless has an impact on the status of the woman described in this way. The status conferred on a girl by Sappho's education is therefore distinguished from the state of ignorance and uncouthness of the child without instruction or the protégée of one of Sappho's rivals, in the same way as "culture" differs from "nature." The education received in Sappho's circle moves the young girl from the uncouthness and lack of culture of early adolescence protected by Artemis to the condition of the educated woman capable of inspiring the love embodied by Aphrodite; it leads her from a state of savagery to civilization. If the companion of Atthis is described by Sappho when she returns to Lydia after her time in the group as shining among the women (*gunaikessin*: no longer among the girls) of her region like the moon among the stars, it is because the education she has undergone on Lesbos has given her divine beauty, and that through the songs and dances (*molpai*) performed by Atthis herself. The reference to Aphrodite, guessed at in the final mutilated verses of the poem, as well as the comparison with the moon with its connotations of bodily liquids and ripeness, suggests that the girl is now an accomplished woman, probably married.[24]

The education of Sappho in her group prepared young girls to be adult, married women by teaching feminine charm and beauty. The poet's connections with marriage are confirmed by the numerous fragments of epithalamia transmitted by quotations, or by a poem such as the one describing the wedding of Hektor and Andromache, which some interpreters would like to be itself an hymenaion.[25] This is apparent again in a passage by Himerius, who paraphrases a poem very certainly by Sappho and shows the poet herself preparing a nuptial chamber for the newly married couple;[26] young girls are arranged there—probably girls from Sappho's circle who form a chorus to celebrate the couple—and a statue of Aphrodite is brought along together

23. Sappho fr. 57 V.; see fr. 131 as well as fr. 81 V.

24. Sappho fr. 96 V., to be compared with fr. 55 V., where the girl who has not had her part of the roses of Pieria, in other words Sappho's education, will die unknown and undistinguished (*aphanēs*); on the connotations of the moon in this poem, see Burnett, *Three Archaic Poets* 304 ff.

25. Sappho frs. 104–17 V.; on the epithalamia of Sappho see Page, *Sappho and Alcaeus* 72 ff., 112 ff.; Calame, *Les chœurs* 1:161 n. 230; and Lasserre, *Sappho* 17 ff. See fr. 44 V., with the interpretations given a. o. by Rösler, "Ein Gedicht" 275 ff., and summarized by Lasserre, *Sappho* 83 ff.

26. Himer. *Or.* 9.4 = Sappho test. 194 V. On this subject see Meerwaldt, "Epithalamia" 19 ff.

with figures representing the Graces and a chorus of *Erōtes*. The preparation of the nuptial chamber was preceded in Himerius's description by a celebration of rites in honor of Aphrodite (*Aphroditēs orgia, agōnas*) during which Sappho herself sang to the sound of the lyre. Even if we cannot know exactly what these rites were, constant reference to the goddess of love shows that the ritual was under the same sign as the values taught by the poet. Thus the acquisition of these same abilities by Sappho's pupils was vindicated in the context of marriage. The education they received aimed at developing in adolescents all the qualities required in women—specifically, young wives. It concerned those aspects of marriage under Aphrodite's protection, namely sensuality and sexuality rather than conjugal fidelity and wife's tasks, which were under the domain of Hera and Demeter. However, this education was not addressed to the same public as the Spartan system of education. Sappho's circle welcomed young adolescents from different parts of Ionia, particularly Lydia, so its character was not strictly Lesbian. The education the girls received, in competition with rival groups such as that of Andromeda, was probably not obligatory. Sappho and her *khoreutai* may have taken part in the official religious life of the island, but the instructional activity of the poet seems not to have been included in the educational system legally subject to the political community of Lesbos. It would be misleading to compare Sappho's group to a real school, not to speak of a "Mädchenpensionat" or a "finishing school." Sappho herself is certainly not to be considered as a "schoolmistress."[27] If she gave through the performance of song and cult acts an education to the girls of her group, this education had an initiatic form and content: it was entirely ritualized. Moreover, Sappho made accomplished women out of her "pupils," but she did not have to make them perfect citizens. She had to initiate them, with the help of Aphrodite, to their gender role as wives of aristocratic families.

3. SAPPHO'S HOMOEROTICISM:
THE INITIATORY FUNCTION

The homoerotic feelings expressed in Sappho's poems have been the object of much debate, which I shall not repeat here. From antiquity on they have been falsified by moralizing resulting from different social attitudes that were

27. Through the notions of *Kreis* or *thiasos*, the qualification of Sappho's group as a "Mädchenpensionat" by U. von Wilamowitz-Moellendorf (in *Die Griechische* 41) had the long fortune that is outlined by Lasserre, *Sappho* 112 ff., and by Parker, "Sappho Schoolmistress" 313 ff. (with the justified criticisms by Lardinois, "Subject and Circumstance" 57 ff.); see also Burnett, *Three Archaic Poets* 211 ff., and Cantarella, *Secondo natura* 107 ff. See P. Colon. 5860 a, b = Sappho fr. S 261A P., and above.

more or less critical toward male and female "homosexuality" and imposed various aesthetic visions on Sappho's poetry.[28] It is difficult to deny, however, that the fragments evoking the power of Eros, to mention only those, refer to a real love that was physically consummated.[29]

It should be noted that the semantic features "companionship," "education," and *homophilia* are all found among the basic elements that make up Sappho's group.[30] The instruction leading to marriage given by Sappho has as its corollary the homoerotic relations between mistress and pupils. In comparison with the male educational system, Sappho's circle, however, offers a new problem in that these homoerotic bonds are not between an older individual and a younger one, but specifically between a woman and her group of young girls. And yet, if Sappho sometimes addresses all her companions (*hetairais tais emais*), the relationships, as expressed in her poems, are nevertheless all individual. Sappho's love pains expressed in several of her poems are provoked by the absence of a single companion, whether Atthis, Anaktoria, or Gongyla; and Sappho asks Aphrodite for a single young girl to entrust her *philotēs* to.[31] There seems to be a contradiction between these singular love protestations and the collective character of the education given to the girls in Sappho's circle. We must presume that only some of the girls had a homoerotic relationship with the poet, while the other adolescents only participated by reciting the passionate poems addressed to the young lover.

28. If Page, *Sappho and Alcaeus* 143 ff., expresses a certain skepticism toward the lacunae in our documentation concerning the reality of "sapphic love," for Marrou, *Histoire de l'éducation* 72; Schadewaldt, *Sappho* 98 ff.; Merkelbach, "Sappho und ihr Kreis" 7 (in spite of 3 n. 2), Lanata, "Sul linguaggio amoroso" 64; West, "Burning Sappho" 320 ff.; Dover, *Greek Homosexuality* 173 ff.; and Gentili, *Poesia e pubblico* 117 ff., the reality of Sapphic *erōs* leaves no doubt. For a history of the image of Sappho's sexuality, see Lardinois, "Lesbian Sappho" 21 ff., and Paradiso, "Saffo" 41 ff.

29. Sappho frs. 47, 130, 48, 49 V.; see also 1.19, 16.4, 94.21 ff. V. For the erotic meaning of the expression *exiēs pothon* in this last poem, see particularly Burnett, *Three Archaic Poets* 298, who points out as well the sexual meaning of the "sleep" in fr. 2.8 V. (pp. 270 ff.).

30. The bonds between *hetairai* were placed under the sign of Aphrodite: Sappho frs. 142, 160, and 126 V., with Ath. 13.571c–d. The connection among education, homosexuality, and an association of companions is found in a gloss of Pollux (4.43 ff.) that makes the terms *agelaioi*, *mathētai*, *hetairoi*, *choreutai*, and *sunerastai* synonymous. See Lardinois, "Subject and Circumstance" 58 ff., against the arguments of Parker, "Sappho Schoolmistress" 341 ff., who makes the *hetairai* of Sappho the participants in a sympotic *hetairia*.

31. Sappho frs. 160, 49, 131, 16.15, 94.4, 1.18 ff. V.; see Max. Tyr. 18.9 = test. 219 V. It is significant that in Sappho's life in the *Suda* under *Sapphō* (S 107 Adler) = test. 253 V., Atthis is described as one of the *hetairai philai*, "the dear companions," while Anaktoria and Gongyla are called *mathētriai*, "pupils." Sappho's poems themselves show that the pupils are also her loved ones: see Marrou, *Histoire de l'éducation* 70 ff. Danielewicz, "Experience" 163, also sees a "didactic purpose" in Sappho's love for the girls in her circle; see as well Cantarella, *Secondo natura* 108 ff.

It was probably the same in Gorgo's circle, in which the homoerotic bond
defined by the term *sunzux* existed, possibly successively, between Gorgo and
two girls, Gongyla and Pleistodike.[32]

The Cretan customs for the boys offer a striking parallel, since the *erōmenos*
is not alone when he goes away from the city with his *erastēs* but is generally
accompanied by his friends who take part in the rite of abducting the
adolescent, go hunting, then celebrate the final banquet at the conclusion
of their expedition into the wilderness with the lover and his beloved; these
same friends share the expenses of the gifts given to the *erōmenos* at the end of
the initiation and join with him in the sacrifice of the ox to Zeus.[33] These
friends of the *erōmenos* have no sexual contact with an *erastēs* but have followed
the same itinerary of initiation as their companion. Their participation in
the sacrifice to Zeus certainly shows that they too have taken the step that
leads to adulthood.

The reality of Sappho's homoerotic feelings and their expression in her
love for a young girl explain how a scholar like Devereux can see in the famous
fragment 31 V. the symptoms of an authentic crisis of "homosexual" anxiety.[34]
He recognizes that the clinical expression of homosexuality is not exclusive
of its sociological aspect. With Sappho, it is true that we seem to have a case
in which homoerotic love has been so internalized that it "short-circuits" any
heterosexual feeling. Hence, maybe, our own awareness when reading the
poems of an internal vibration that goes beyond the expression in traditional
forms of a homoeroticism entirely conforming to its educational function.
This supposed extra dimension does not, however, contradict in any way
the institutional reality of the circle and the pedagogical role of the relations
within it: for Sappho, the ritual and initiatory "pseudo-homosexuality" could
simply become an example of what we call homosexuality. Its educational
and social function stays the same; its expression in poetry is inspired by
a sensibility that finds no balance in a heterosexual life. And even this
conclusion could be modified since Sappho, as she herself says, had a
daughter and, unless her marriage with Cercylas and her love for Phaon

---

32. Sappho fr. 213 V.; see above n. 13.
33. Strabo 10.4.21 = Ephor. *FGrH* 70 F 149.21. See Calame, *Les chœurs* 1:421 ff.
34. Devereux, "The Nature of Sappho's Seizure" 17 ff. Sappho's anxiety attack is not
due to a sudden awareness of a socially sanctioned homosexuality, as Manieri, "Saffo" 44 ff.,
supposes, who in any case is wrong to attribute to Devereux such an interpretation of fr. 31 V.
and who gives no solution to the problem posed by the particular content of this fragment;
Sappho's crisis was probably provoked by seeing her masculine rival for whom she cannot be a
substitute for the girl (cf. Devereux 22). Privitera, "Ambiguità antitesi" 37 ff., is right in saying
that Sappho's symptoms are the sign of her fear when she realizes her love is hopeless and
will never be returned; see also Burnett, *Three Archaic Poets* 229 ff., and Di Benedetto, "Intorno
al linguaggio" 145 ff.

were merely the fantasies of the ancient biographers, she must have crossed the threshold of adult life marked in all Greece by marriage.[35]

I would like to take as proof of the educational and social role of Sappho's homophilia the fact that an adolescent's time in the poet's circle was a transitory step in a process. Most of the fragments of any length that have come down to us contain the memories of girls who returned to their native lands, most often Asia Minor, or left Sappho for a rival school.[36] As I have said, the education in Sappho's circle consisted of preparation for marriage through a series of rites, dances, and songs, mainly dedicated to Aphrodite. We have no definite indication about it. But, independently of any gender distinction, it is probable that some of these rites, as for the boys at Thebes and perhaps at Thera too, consecrated the homoerotic bonds between lover and beloved by means of a sexual initiation appropriate for adolescents with the objective of teaching the girl the values of adult "heterosexuality." The temporary and unreliable character of these bonds may provoke in a homosexually oriented person states of anxiety and depression like those that can probably be traced in almost all Sappho's poems of remembering. This would explain the peculiar and personal feminine tone often felt in the modern reading of Sappho's poetry.

Thus the ability of archaic lyric poetry to express the individual collectively explains how a poem by Sappho can express a personal experience true only for herself and one of her companions but can be accepted, recited, and even reperformed by all the girls in her circle as both a lived and paradigmatic experience. Moreover the language used by Sappho can communicate collectively and can evoke a common system of representations so that all the pupils of the group can have the impression of being participants in the propaedeutic and initiative homoerotic bonds actually experienced by only one of them.

The conventional, formulaic character of the language infuses with life the poem performed by the group, rather than emptying it of meaning. If it seems to readers of Pindar or Ibycus that the homoerotic feelings expressed are a convention for praising the merits of a young man, they may nevertheless have originated in real feelings or in a real experience, feelings and experience that can be repeated through the reperformance of the poem. Moreover it

---

35. Sappho frs. 98b, 132 V. See *POxy.* 1800, fr. 1.14 = test. 252 V., *Suda* under *Sapphō* (S 107 Adler) = test. 253 V.; see also test. 219 V. On the legend of the loves of Sappho and Phaon, see test. 211 V. and Nagy, *Greek Mythology* 223 ff. For the controversy on the nature of Sappho's homoerotic feelings, see Hallett, "Sappho and Her Social Context" ("public, rather personal, statements"), and Stigers, "Romantic Sensuality, Poetic Sense" (a specific feminine form of sensibility); see also Winkler, "Gardens of Nymphs" 89 ff.

36. Sappho frs. 16.15, 94.2 ff., 96, 131 V.; see West, "Burning Sappho" 318 ff.

is surprising to notice that, although the education received by the boys and the girls through the choral performances is differentiated and prepares them for different gender roles, nevertheless the language used to express the homoerotic relationships underlying this ritual formation is basically the same. This kind of reciprocity between the linguistic practice of boys and girls as well as between what an adult can express to an adolescent (Sappho) or a group of girls to an older one (Alcman) is probably typical of a ritual and collective poetry with an educational purpose.

EIGHT

Sappho and Her Social Context:
Sense and Sensuality

Judith P. Hallett

The poetic personality of Sappho and the poetic phenomenon of Sappho have proven difficult for both ancients and moderns to understand. Later generations of ancients—Greeks of the fourth century B.C.E. and thereafter, Romans, and Byzantines—were unaccustomed to supreme lyric talent in a woman who wrote about seemingly private passions. Several ancient sources thus class the late seventh-/early-sixth-century B.C.E. Sappho not among the leading male poets of her time, as the ninth great Greek lyric genius, but as tenth of the female Muses.[1] In so doing, they may have suggested that she had not earned literary stature through toil and competition, as did the men of her field (and, according to some, as had the female poet Corinna). But by calling her a Muse they ranked her an inspired and immortal figure to whom poetic self-expression and success came

An earlier version of this paper was delivered at the American Council on the Teaching of Foreign Languages meeting, Boston, 24 November 1973. The translations that I wrote for that occasion and several of the major points I emphasized in the talk have since been incorporated into Pomeroy, *Goddesses* 53–55. Other earlier versions were delivered at Haverford College, Tufts University, and Boston University. I should also like to thank Dorothea Wender and Sheila Dickison for encouraging this project from the very start; Sir Kenneth Dover for sharing his ideas and providing me with advance access to his book on Greek homosexuality; Norman Austin and Ernst Badian for their invaluable comments and suggestions; and Catherine R. Stimpson, Froma Zeitlin, and Lydia Kirsopp Lake for their helpful criticism. This essay was originally published in slightly different form as "Sappho and Her Social Context: Sense and Sensuality," *Signs* 4 (1979) 447–64.

1. See *AP* 7.14, 9.66, and 9.571: "Sappho is not the ninth of men, but is inscribed as the tenth Muse among the lovely Muses" (by the second-century B.C.E. poet Antipater of Sidon), as well as *AP* 9.506 (by Plato): see also Plut. *Amat.* 18 for the view of Sappho as the tenth Muse. Various, and later, ancient sources do, however, list Sappho among the nine great Greek lyric poets—for example, Gell. *NA* 19.3 and Ath. 14.639e.

naturally.[2] Various works from the fourth century onward also represent Sappho as a mythic heroine, driven by her love for a younger man, Phaon, to a dramatic suicide.[3]

The ancients' belief in Sappho's superiority was so strong that it prevented them from ascribing to her conduct which, by the third century B.C.E., was viewed as disgraceful for a female.[4] Although a number acknowledge the existence of rumors that she participated, physically, in homosexual activity, none lends credence to the charge. Our earliest such source, a biography from the Hellenistic period (third/second centuries B.C.E.), remarks that "she has been accused by a few of being undisciplined and sexually involved with women."[5] In the fifteenth of Ovid's *Heroides*, a fictive epistle from Sappho to Phaon, she is portrayed as discomfited by allegations that she enjoyed erotic attachments with other women; at line 201 she complains that her love for the women of her native Lesbos has made her infamous.[6] A scholiast to Horace (*Ep.* 1.19.28) accounts for the application of the epithet *mascula* to Sappho by asserting that she "is maligned as having been a tribade."[7] And the first biographical entry on Sappho in the tenth-century C.E. lexicon known as the *Suda* simply states that "she was slanderously accused of shameful intimacy with certain of her female pupils."[8]

2. For the Muses' supposed ease at poetic creation, see Hes. *Theog.* 75–103. On the poetic competitions between male artists, see, for example, Hes. *Op.* 654 ff.; on the tradition of Corinna's competition with Pindar, see, e.g., Plut. *De glor. Ath.* 4.347 ff. and Paus. 9.22.3.

3. See, e.g., Men. fr. 258; Ovid *Her.* 15; Ath. 13.596b; the *Suda*, s.v. "Sappho" (β) and "Phaon." Sappho's suicidal leap is also depicted on the apse of the first-century C.E. underground basilica found in 1917 at Rome's Porta Maggiore. On Sappho's image in Greek literature of the fifth and fourth centuries B.C.E., see also Dover, *Greek Homosexuality* 174.

4. See Dover, *Greek Homosexuality* 182. Dover suggests that Hellenistic attitudes toward female sexuality were influenced by those of classical Athens, which regarded the practice as a taboo subject.

5. *POxy.* XV 1800, fr. 1 col. 1.16 ff.; for its date, see Dover, *Greek Homosexuality* 174.

6. Ovid *Tr.* 2.365, "Lesbia quid docuit Sappho nisi amare puellas?" though often cited as evidence for Sappho's homosexuality, probably means that Sappho taught girls to love and belongs to a tradition, discussed by Dover, *Greek Homosexuality* 174–75, of Sappho as an instructor of girls.

7. Hor. *Carm.* 2.13.24–25 "querentem / Sappho puellis de popularibus," cited by Dover, *Greek Homosexuality* 174, as a source for Sappho's homosexuality, merely refers to Sappho's plaintive verses about the girls of her native Lesbos and does not mention her sexual conduct as such.

8. A remark by the fourth-century C.E. Greek rhetorician Themistius (p. xiii; p. 170 D.), to the effect that Sappho lavished praise on her *paidika*, may also deserve mention (this word is a standard Greek term for the youthful beloved in a male homosexual union). Yet as Themistius is only talking about verbal expressions of passion, his statement cannot truly be regarded as testimony to Sappho's sexual habits.

The shamefulness which these writers impute to women's participation in homosexual acts apparently explains their unanimous suspension of belief where Sappho's alleged practices are concerned. Three of these sources— the Hellenistic biography, the first-century B.C.E. Ovidian epistle, and the entry in the *Suda*—concomitantly insist that Sappho's primary erotic allegiances were heterosexual, citing as evidence that she was infatuated with Phaon, was married, and had a daughter.[9] By comparison, the homosexual liaisons attributed to the male poets of Sappho's time do not meet with similar disbelief or disapproval. A number of these same authorities refer to the homosexual involvements of Greek male lyric poets as established facts; like virtually all ancient testimony on the lives of Greek poets, they do not give the impression that male pederasty, at least for the "active" partner, was thought cause for shame.[10] The *Suda* 's comment on Anacreon—"his life was spent on sexual relationships with boys and women, and on poems"—stands in sharp contrast to its words on Sappho. These ancient sources do not even entertain the notion that Sappho was, as they suggest Anacreon may have been, a well-adjusted bisexual. Rather than sanction female homosexual activity they retreat to incredulity.

Modern critics share the ancients' view of Sappho as an extraordinary individual. Yet they do not idealize her as a mythic figure but reckon her a flesh-and-blood human being. Recent scholars even assume that Sappho's homosexuality is an ascertained, or at least ascertainable, fact and try to come to terms with her homoeroticism instead of analyzing and appreciating her poetry. A 1966 essay typifies the customary approach. It claims to focus on the two special difficulties confronting students of Sappho's fragmentary remains: "the moral question" (i.e., involving "the view of Sappho as a homosexual") and the "aesthetic question" ("is Sappho worth reading?").[11] In a 1974 book on Greek lyric poetry, the chapter on Sappho begins by labeling as "crucial" her "relationship to her friends," examines whether the tradition of her homosexuality is a "correct inference," devotes its discussion of her most famous verses, fragment 31 Lobel-Page (L.-P.), to the obvious fact that Sappho is apparently describing her physical response to the attractions of another woman, and finally calls attention to Sappho's "disappointing aspects" while ostensibly summarizing the distinctive features of her poetry.[12]

9. *POxy.* XV, 1800 fr. 1 col. 1.14–16 alleges that she had a daughter; *Her.* 15 depicts Sappho as enraptured with Phaon and hence a converted, if not a diehard, lover of men; the *Suda* speaks of her husband, Cercylus of Andros, as well as her daughter.

10. Passive homosexual behavior by a man no longer a youth was, of course, another matter. See Henderson, *The Maculate Muse* 209 ff., on the abuse of pathics—"evidently the most risible type of homosexual"—in Greek comedy.

11. Davison, "Sappho," in *From Archilochus to Pindar* 287.

12. Kirkwood, *Early Greek Monody* 101 ff.

Fragment 31 L.-P. has, of late, even undergone dissection as a clinical record of acute symptoms suffered by a "masculine lesbian" during an anxiety attack.[13]

Modern criticism of supposedly homosexual, or at least bisexual, Greek male lyric poets, however, does not reflect the same obsession with their sexual preferences to the neglect of their poetry. The same critical study of Greek lyric poetry which accords key importance to the nature of Sappho's relationship with her friends relegates the topic on Anacreon's sexual tastes to a few brief comments, and carefully scrutinizes several of his erotic fragments without agonizing over the gender of their *dramatis personae*.[14] (Interestingly, the one possible reference to homosexuality in the poems of Anacreon which seems to trouble commentators most [fr. 358.5–8 Page (P.)] involves female homosexual behavior: his portrayal of a girl from Lesbos who ignores him to gape *pros allēn tina*, "after another person [or thing] of feminine gender." Several scholars have taken elaborate pains to prove that Anacreon is not characterizing the girl as homosexual in her preferences.)[15] As disturbing as many moderns, nurtured on Judaeo-Christian values, find the idea of male homosexuality, they still seem less disturbed by unmistakable references to male homoeroticism than by possible allusions to its female equivalent. They are also far better able to appreciate works containing male homoeroticism as literary art.

The negative reaction which female homosexuality has aroused from the Hellenistic period onward has, it would seem, caused Sappho to receive different (and increasingly inequitable) treatment from that given Greek male lyric poets. It is my view, however, that the sensual conduct in which the first-person speaker of Sappho's verses often engages with other women may not truly merit the label of "female homosexuality" at all. It is also my thesis that Sappho should not be read merely as a confessional poet who voices private feelings to the female objects of her desire. Rather, I believe that she should be regarded primarily as a poet with an important social purpose and public function: that of instilling sensual awareness and sexual self-esteem and of facilitating role adjustment in young females coming of age in a sexually segregated society. Furthermore, I believe that she should be regarded as an artist voicing sentiments which need not be her own. I should like to establish the validity of this thesis through an examination of Sappho in her social context. For such an examination demonstrates that her concerns were shared by other individuals, and entire institutions, in

13. Devereux, "The Nature of Sappho's Seizure."

14. Kirkwood, *Early Greek Monody* 150 ff.

15. See, for example, in English-language publications alone, Wigodsky, "Anacreon and the Girl from Lesbos" 109; Davison, "Sappho" 247–55; West, "Melica" 205–15. See also Dover, *Greek Homosexuality* 180.

the archaic and classical Greek world, and that these concerns adhere to previously established literary tradition.

◆   ◆   ◆

Revulsion at female homosexuality has, as I have noted, largely inspired past efforts to discredit belief in Sappho's physical homoeroticism.[16] Yet the view that Sappho not merely indulged in, but exhibited an exclusive preference for, homosexual acts has only gained widespread currency in the past few years. Indeed, the modern sense of the words "Sapphic" and "Lesbian" is largely responsible for popularizing the view of Sappho as an exclusive, and physically practicing, homosexual. The terms "Sapphism," "sapphist," and "sapphic" were formally introduced into English only in the last decade of the nineteenth century, when British medical authorities eagerly labeled what they judged to be psychopathological behavior exhibited by the licentious French and accepted the tradition about Sappho's sexual preferences which was accredited in fin de siècle France.[17] The more colloquial word "Lesbian" has a more interesting history. In fifth-century B.C.E. Greek comedy the verb *lesbi[a]zein*, "to act like one from Lesbos," serves to denote fellatio performed by females, probably because of the renown of Sappho's island women for sensual, although apparently heterosexual, expertise.[18] Both the first-century B.C.E. Roman poet Catullus and his first-century C.E. imitator Martial attribute to women whom they call "Lesbia" varied exploits of a sexual, but

16. See, for example, Robinson, *Sappho and Her Influence* 43–44, who denies with fervency that "Sappho is a woman who has given herself up to unnatural and inordinate practices which defy the moral instinct and ... harden and petrify the soul."

17. "Sapphism," according to the *Oxford English Dictionary*, first appears in Billing's *National Medical Dictionary* of 1890; a June 1901 issue of the British medical journal *Lancet* noted that "Sapphism" and other vices have been treated in French but not yet in English novels. The French view of Sappho as a homosexual owes much of its popularity to the 1895 publication of Pierre Loüys's *Songs of Bilitis*. These—closely following upon Loüys's translation of Lucian's *Dialogues of the Courtesans*—purported to be translations of an ancient Greek manuscript, the autobiography of a peasant girl who had belonged to Sappho's homosexual circle and later became a temple prostitute. They were immediately denounced as a forgery by the great scholar U. von Wilamowitz-Moellendorff, who vehemently denied the possibility of Sappho's homosexuality on the grounds that she was "an honorable lady, wife, and mother" (Wilamowitz's 1896 review was also reprinted in his *Sappho und Simonides*). Yet Wilamowitz's crusade does not seem to have convinced Marcel Proust. In *A la recherche du temps perdu*, the narrator's discovery that Albertine and her girl friends are practicing homosexuals coincides with his remark that she would be "like Sappho" if she were to drown by leaping into the sea (see Kostis, "Albertine" 125–35).

18. For *lesbiazein*, see Ar. *Vesp.* 1346, *Ran.* 1308, *Eccl.* 920; cf. also Lucian *Pseudologista* 128. For the sexual image of Lesbian women, see Lucian *Dial. Meret.* 5 and Dover, *Greek Homosexuality* 182–84.

never a homosexual, nature; the former in poem 51, a translation of Sappho fragment 31 L.-P., and the latter at 2.50, a pasquinade on female fellatio. According to standard reference works, the English adjective "Lesbian" denoted intensely erotic, hetero- more than homoerotic, individuals and feelings until only a few decades ago.[19] But its medical and "underground" meaning, first attested in 1890, has gradually taken over as the existence of female homosexual liaisons has become more widely acknowledged among the educated, Anglo-American public.[20]

Whatever the history of the terms may be, the prevalent modern impression that Sappho was a Lesbian, that she herself took part in homosexual practices, is not based on ancient testimony. As we have seen, the ancient sources who as much as mention Sappho's reputation for physical homoerotic involvement (the earliest of which postdates her lifetime by at least 300 years) describe this reputation as nothing more than a wholly disgraceful accusation. This denial is all the more noteworthy when compared with other comments about female homosexual relations in classical antiquity. At 191e of the *Symposium*—a work which precedes Sappho's Hellenistic biography by over a century—Plato's Aristophanes speaks matter-of-factly of women who are attracted to other women, the *hetairistriai*: these, he claims, are halves of an originally all-female whore, and analogous to men who love other males.[21] A poem written over 400 years later by the Roman epigrammatist Martial graphically lampoons a masculine female homosexual. In his *Life of Lycurgus*, the second-century C.E. Greek writer Plutarch ascribed homoerotic liaisons to the women of archaic Sparta, Sappho's

19. Webster's *New International Dictionary*, 3rd ed., still gives "erotic" as the chief nongeographic meaning of "Lesbian," citing "Lesbianism" in the sense of "female homosexuality" as "medical term." The *Oxford English Dictionary* does not even give a sexual meaning for the word "Lesbian." And both Klein, *Comprehensive Etymological Dictionary* 418, and the *Random House Dictionary of the English Language*, s.v. "Lesbian," still list the meaning "erotic" ahead of "Pertaining to female homosexuality."

20. See the 1976 supplement to the *Oxford English Dictionary*, s.v. "Lesbian": it also notes that an 1892 *Dictionary of Psychological Medicine* and James Joyce's 1922 *Ulysses* use the adjective "lesbic" for "female homosexual," no doubt because "Lesbian" carried quite different connotations at that time.

21. As Dover, *Greek Homosexuality* 172, remarks, however, this is the only extant reference to female homosexuality in classic Attic literature; it is also unclear to him whether or not the word *hetairistria* "acquires a derogatory nuance from *laikastria*, 'whore.'" Although Aristophanes' *Lysistrata* (411 B.C.E.) depicts the female title character as complimenting a Spartan woman on her physical charms, and going so far as to touch her breasts (ll. 80 ff.), he does not suggest that these or other sexually deprived women turn to one another for sexual satisfaction (rather, he has them masturbating with phallus substitutes). This would imply—as I argue below—that gestures which moderns would regard as inviting and initiating physical homosexual activity were not so viewed by the Greeks of classical times.

veritable contemporaries.[22]   And Lucian's *Dialogues of the Courtesans*, composed in the late second century C.E., portrays women of Corinth and
Lesbos who shun intercourse with men in favor of relations with other
females.[23]

In addition, the surviving fragments of Sappho's poetry do not provide
any decisive evidence that she participated in homosexual acts. Many of
Sappho's lyrics written in the first person imply an involvement in acts of
heterosexual love. It must not be forgotten, after all, that some of her poems
make reference to a beloved daughter. In fragment 132 L.-P., its first-person
speaker even applies to her daughter, her only child, the adjective *agapetōs*,
a word used in the Homeric epics exclusively for a family's male hope and
heir: "I have a lovely child, whose form is like / gold flowers. My heart's
one pleasure, Cleis, for whom I'd not give all Lydia . . ."[24] Yet her first-person
lyrics never depict the speaker as engaging in acts of homosexual love. To
be sure, a fragmentary lyric ascribed by some to Sappho (fr. 99 L.-P.) has
been interpreted as containing part of a word—*olisbos*—meaning an artificial
phallus. Still, even if one accepts Sappho as the author, and *olisbos* as the
reading, here the poetic context fails to clarify Sappho's relationship to it,
and its to Sappho.[25]

More significantly, there are no references in Sappho's lyrics to any physiological details of female homoerotic involvement—neither when she is
writing in the first person nor when she is describing the actions of other
women.[26] To be sure, this may be nothing more than tasteful reticence,
the literary counterpart of a scene on an archaic vase from Thera dated to
Sappho's time (ca. 620 B.C.E.): the vase depicts two females affectionately
performing the chin-chucking gesture which served as a prelude to heterosexual and homosexual lovemaking among the Greeks, and leaves the rest
to the imagination.[27] It may well be that Sappho wrote more explicitly about

22. Mart. 7.67; Plut. *Lyc.* 18.9, which claims that "highly reputable" Spartan women engaged in love affairs with maidens in order to illustrate the omnipresence and high valuation of
erōs in early Spartan society.

23. Luc. *Dial. Meret.* 5.

24. For *agapētos* in Homer, see *Il.* 6.401 and *Od.* 2.365; 4.727, 817; 5.18. See in this connection
also frs. 121 (to a male lover, and in the first person), 112, 115 L.-P.

25. On this fragment, *POxy.* 2291, see Page, *Sappho and Alcaeus* 144–45, and Kirkwood, *Early
Greek Monody* 269–70. For the use of an *olisbos* in other sexual acts, see Pomeroy, *Goddesses* pl. 12;
Hipponax fr. 92 and Petron. *Sat.* 132; Boardman, *Athenian Red-Figure Vases* pl. 99, view 1.

26. Dover, *Greek Homosexuality* 175–76, would maintain that fr. 94.21–23 L.-P.—"And on soft
beds tender you expelled desire"—refers to the female addressee's satisfying either Sappho's
or her own desire through bodily contact; the expression "to expel desire" is, however, too
vague to permit a definitive interpretation and, in any event, not physiologically explicit.

27. See Dover, *Greek Homosexuality* 173. The vase is also discussed by Pomeroy, *Goddesses*
243, and depicted in Richter, *Kourai* pl. VIIIc. Its scene stands in contrast to that of an Attic

her own, and others', participation in homosexual acts in verses which have been accidentally, or even deliberately, lost. So, too, the surviving lyrics may contain implicit, or euphemistic, allusions to specific homosexual practices which readers today, ignorant of what sexual connotations certain words carried to an ancient Greek audience, have been unable, or unwilling, to perceive.[28] But from the evidence we do have we can only conclude that she did not represent herself in her verses as having expressed homosexual feelings physically.

Nevertheless, when writing in the first person, Sappho does evince a "lover's passion" toward other women and give utterance to strong homosexual feelings. In fragment 31 L.-P., for example, Sappho depicts herself as responding to a female friend's charms with violent physical reactions—"My tongue freezes silent and stiff, light flame trickles under my skin, I no longer see with my eyes, my ears whirring." Later classical authors, moreover, drew on these verses when delineating the symptoms not only of overpowering (heterosexual) passion, but of fear, drunkenness, and epilepsy as well.[29] In other lyrics, too, the speaker, presumably Sappho herself, is portrayed as sensually attracted and aroused by other women. Most notable of these is fragment 49 L.-P., addressing a women named Atthis. Its speaker states: "I adored you, once in the past, when you seemed to me to be a small, graceless child." Fragment 96 L.-P., which avows desire for Atthis, and fragment 1 L.-P., the hymn to Aphrodite, merit note in this context as well.[30]

It is poems of this sort which lead her modern readers to surmise that Sappho must have actually engaged in physical relationships with the women she found sensually appealing, or might as well have done so if she in actuality did not. The psychoanalytical and biographical orientation of recent literary criticism encourages such a conclusion by its tendency to regard the impulses that artists reveal in their work as essentially identical

---

red-figure cup by Apollodorus, dated ca. 500 B.C.E. and pictured in Boardman and La Rocca, *Eros in Greece* 110. This portrays two naked women, one of whom, on her knees, fingers the genital area of her standing companion. These women are, however, thought to be *hetairai* (courtesans) preparing for a celebration with men by anointing one another with perfume; La Rocca finds it unlikely that the scene depicts an erotic relationship between the women (since there are no other examples of this in Attic vase painting) but likely that such relationships existed in a society with such rigid sexual segregation.

28. See Russo's review of Kirkwood, "Reading the Greek Lyric Poets," and Lanata, "Sul linguaggio amoroso" 65–66.

29. For the adaptation of these symptoms to other contexts, by later authors, see Catull. 51 and Lucr. 3.154–56, 476–79, 487–91.

30. Dover, *Greek Homosexuality* 176 n. 10, however, points out that the one phrase in fr. 1 L.-P. indicating the beloved's sex as female is at variance with the usages of Sappho's dialect. Several textual emendations designed to restore linguistic normality would in fact remove the feminine ending.

with their realization in behavior, be they acknowledged by or unknown to the individual.[31] This supposition is also fostered by contemporary notions about male and female sexual behavior. For in our society, we assume that men who express sensual appreciation for women desire (or at least would not object to) physical involvement with them. Furthermore, we are conditioned to view as unfeminine any woman who openly expresses sensual attraction for another human being; she is taking the "sexual initiative" and behaving as only men are supposed to. Indeed, when that object of allure is a woman, as in Sappho's poems, the aggressive female is considered doubly masculine.

Our modern Western social and sexual categories and expectations, however, differ considerably from those of Sappho's milieu. Archaic Greek society was for the most part sexually segregated. A well-born young girl, so far as we can tell, had little contact with males before and after marriage. A bride simply accepted the spouse, often a stranger, her father selected for her.[32] After marriage, a woman in this (as in later periods of Greek) society was excluded from the worldly pursuits which occupied most of her husband's time and life; her sexual charms and needs were, it would seem, neglected and often feared by him.[33] Thus she could hardly have expected her husband's esteem and devotion to sustain her emotionally. Even the union of Hector and Andromache, who were celebrated in early and later Greek literature as the model married couple, is depicted as a highly asymmetrical and rather unaffectionate relationship, in which she is bound to him by dependency more than anything else and chastised for the merest show of independence.[34] The archaic and classical Greeks, however, do not appear to have accorded the state of matrimony or the sexual role of wife much social prestige or respect. Marriage itself was viewed simply

---

31. Many ancient Greeks and Romans seem to have adopted this approach as well. Although Aristophanes' *Thesmophoriazusae* employs in it jest when characterizing the playwrights Euripides and Agathon as misogynist and transvestite, respectively, others—such as St. Jerome (on Lucretius's poisoning by a love philter)—do so seriously. For ancient biography in general, see Fairweather, "Fiction in the Biographies."

32. Consider, for example, Hesiod's account of Helen's wooing (frs. 199 and 200 Merkelbach-West) and the absence of Agariste, daughter of Cleisthenes of Sicyon, from Herodotus's account of her betrothal at 6.126–30.

33. The exclusion of archaic Greek women from men's activities is emphasized by Bowra, *Greek Lyric Poetry* 178; Arthur, "Early Greece" 43; and Lefkowitz, "Critical Stereotypes" 33–34. For the attitudes voiced by men in archaic Greece toward wives' sexuality, see, for example, Semonides' "Essay on Women," esp. ll. 48–49, 53–54, and 90–91, and Hes. *Op.* 373–75, 695–705; see also the discussion in Pomeroy, *Goddesses* 49.

34. Homer *Il.* 6.369–493 is the *locus classicus* on Hector and Andromache. For Sappho's poetic glorification of Hector's and Andromache's nuptials, see fr. 44 L.-P.; for Stesichorus's, see Campbell, *Greek Lyric Poetry* 257; for Euripides' less idealized portrayal of their marriage, see his *Andr.* 222–27.

as a socioeconomic (and sometimes political) institution,[35] necessary for the orderly transfer of property and for the perpetuation and strengthening of family and state; it was not deemed necessary for either partner's emotional well-being. Archaic Greek social institutions attempted to undermine, and archaic Greek poets to disparage, the bonds of marriage.[36] Significantly, the only writer of the archaic and classical periods who delights in the details of marriage rites for their own sake, and who in fact regards the marital union as an important and equal source of pleasure to bridegroom as well as bride, is Sappho. Fragment 115 L.-P., for example, celebrates a bridegroom's sensual beauty: "To what, O beloved bridegroom, should I properly liken you? I should liken you most closely to a slender sapling." Fragment 141b L.-P. describes prayers for "nothing but blessings" to the bridegroom.[37]

Sappho's wedding poems, moreover, indicate that the female members of her milieu were profoundly concerned with their physical desirability as brides and the prospect of losing their maidenhood.[38] The nuptial ceremonies she represents in her lyrics focus on the bride's sexual initiation and its attendant joys. Yet these young women could not have received sexual attentions from their suitors or hoped to find emotional gratification within marriage itself. They could only have turned to other women to become sensually aware, in order to perform adequately in the role to which their society assigned them and to find the sexual validation that could satisfy their needs. Women were the sole individuals with whom they socialized and by whom they were socialized. Other women would also have experienced feelings identical with those of a young woman and been more sensitized to her concerns. In this perspective Sappho's sensually expressive verses may be viewed as an institutional force in and a reflection of her social setting—a social vehicle for imparting sensual awareness, and sexual self-esteem, to

35. On the function of marriage in archaic Greek society, see Lacey, *The Family in Classical Greece* 67–68, 71–72, 197–200, 212–13; and Pomeroy, *Goddesses* 33–42.

36. See Pomeroy's discussion of the epiclerate in Athens, a product of Solon's sixth-century B.C.E. legislation (*Goddesses* 60–62). The Spartans' practice of wife sharing, allowing a wife who has borne children for her husband to produce offspring for another, childless, man as well—described by Plut. *Lyc.* 15 and Xen. *Lac.* 1.4—deserves mention in this context too. For the disparagement of marriage by poets of this period, see, e.g., Archil. fr. 80, Semon. "Essay on Women" 96–114, and Hes. *Theog.* 602–12; for an opposing view, see Hippon. fr. 81.

37. See also frs. 27, 30, 44, 110, 111, 112, 113, 116, 117, 141 L.-P., all formally identified as wedding poems.

38. On maidenhood, see the fragments cited in n. 37 above and frs. 104a, 104c, 197, 114 L.-P.; also Catull. 62.38–44 (another Sapphic echo). Fr. 114 is, in fact, an address to maidenhood: "Maidenhood, maidenhood, where do you go when you leave me? I will never come back to you, no longer come back."

women on the threshold of marriage and maturity.[39] For in the male sector of archaic and classical Greek society, as well as among females in various Greek locales, an array of sociocultural institutions, including the production and performance of highly personalized poetry, appears to have served this precise function.

Admittedly, the behavior and culture of males and females in the sexual apartheid of archaic and classical Greece were very different. The cultural pursuits esteemed by the upper-class Greeks of preclassical and classical times were exclusively male ones: warfare, politics, athletics, worship of the great male deities, art, even the quest for wisdom.[40] These activities, which were formally organized and conducted in accordance with well-defined rules, operated as elaborate and prestigious social institutions. They provided competitive situations for a man to surpass others and achieve the recognition by which he would be known as *agathos*, superior. Along with shrewdness, skill at speaking, strength, and stamina, these institutions put to the test sensual attractiveness, being *kalos*.[41] As virtually all of Greek art from the archaic and classical periods attests, a young man's appearance often determined how other men judged him, whether as an athlete, citizen of his *polis*, artistic inspiration, or intellectual protégé.[42] To be sure, observers or judges may have often complimented a young male on his physical beauty in order to advertise their desire for a physical relationship. Short-lived physical liaisons between older men and youths were a socially sanctioned and much-documented phenomenon in the upper classes, one which thrived to some extent because of women's lowly social state and exclusion from men's affairs. For a young male such a relationship gave emotional satisfaction and the narcissistic gratification of being appreciated as an equal sexual partner.[43] But publicly voiced sensual appreciation of a handsome youth might mean no more than would approbation of his calisthenic or cognitive talents.

39. The argument to follow agrees—in many of its points—with the views of Merkelbach, "Sappho und ihr Kreis." However, I also attempt to consider the psychological purposes served by Sappho's poetry (as well as its "institutional" nature), to delineate the role of physical beauty in her milieu, and to confront the problems of poetic personality and personalism as they relate to her work.

40. For "male institutions" in Greek society, and an analysis of how the Greek "zero-sum game" contest system—in which the rewards had to come from one's competitors—worked in determining athletic, religious, military, political, and artistic success, see Gouldner, *Enter Plato* 12–13, 40–64. See also the discussion of Pomeroy, *Goddesses* 71–74.

41. See the discussion of Licht [Brandt], *Sexual Life in Ancient Greece* 428–30.

42. See, for example, Theog. 933–38; Pind. *Ol.* 8.19, 9.94, 10.99–105; Ar. *Nub.* 972–78; Plato *Chrm.* 157a4 ff. For Greek male physical narcissism, see Gouldner, *Enter Plato* 41–42, and Slater, *The Glory of Hera* 33–35.

43. See Dover, "Eros and Nomos" 31–42, and "Classical Greek Attitudes" 59–73.

Throughout ancient Greece festivals glorified the beauty of boys simply as a religious and aesthetic ideal;[44] the period in which Sappho lived also began to pay artistic homage to the youthful male nude figure.[45] In their victory odes, poets such as Pindar and Bacchylides extol the comeliness of a victorious competitor at the great games as matter-of-factly as they do his lineage or agility; in fragment 108, an encomium to the youth Theoxenus, Pindar claims to react strongly—"melting like bee-stung wax"—to the physical presence of young males.[46] Yet these religious, aesthetic, and poetic tributes cannot be interpreted as "sexual overtures"; rather, they seem to be conventional public gestures intended to enhance the aesthetic appeal of their objects in a culture which placed a high premium on male physical beauty. Greek men of the archaic and classical periods seem to have observed a distinction between sensual appreciation and sexual appetite, as is perhaps best illustrated by Plato's portrayal of Socrates. At 155d3–4 of the *Charmides,* Socrates makes no bones about his immediate response to the physical attractions of this young disciple—"I caught a glimpse of what was inside his clothes, and caught on fire." But, notwithstanding this and other Platonic dialogues in which Socrates enthusiastically remarks upon the beauty of other young men, Plato characterizes Socrates as refusing to succumb to (homo)sexual temptation and as actively dissuading other males from engaging in physical relations with desirable young men.[47]

It only stands to reason, therefore, that Greek society would have similarly institutionalized the sensual education and affirmation of upper-class young women. Since women's social value and contribution were defined mainly in physical, sexual terms, and since daughters were as a rule less educated than sons (their acculturation period terminated upon their marriage and hence considerably earlier than that of men),[48] it also stands to reason that

---

44. Cf. Ath. 13.565f–556a, 609f; Arist. *Eth. Nic.* 1099a; Theophr. fr. 111.

45. For the development of Greek sculpture, see the article by Richter, s.v. "Sculpture, Greek," in the *Oxford Classical Dictionary.*

46. Cf. Bacchyl. 9 Snell 27 ff. and the passages of Pindar cited in n. 42 above. The Athenian vases with *kalos* inscriptions, dating from the mid-sixth century B.C.E. and praising the beauty of a particular boy, also deserve consideration in this context: only rarely is the youth praised known to be a favorite of the vase painter himself. See Robinson and Fluck, *Greek Love-Names* 3, who remark, "that the admiration for a beautiful youth must often have been city-wide and not merely the personal feeling of a single individual is also attested by the multitude of his admirers in many cases, to which the *kalos* inscriptions bear witness."

47. See Alcibiades' testimony to Socrates' self-restraint at *Sym.* 216d–219d and Socrates' own speeches at *Phdr.* 238d–241d, 244a–257b; see also the discussions of Grube, *Plato's Thought* 90–119, and Wender, "Plato, Misogynist" 75–90.

48. That ancient Greek women generally were wed soon after puberty to men of about thirty and that Spartan women's marriage (to men of their own age) when they were in their late teens is anomalous find support in Hes. *Op.* 665 ff.; Xen. *Oec.* 7.5, *Ath.* 56.7; Arist. *Pol.* 1335a28.

Greek female institutions would have focused far more intensively than their male counterparts on fostering sensual consciousness and confidence. The better known and more accessible ancient Greek sources seem more interested in criticizing the "gossiping" networks and domestic associations of married women and express apprehension about women's socializing and sharing sexual knowledge with one another. The seventh-century B.C.E. poet Semonides' "Essay on Women" praises the type of wife who "takes no pleasure in sitting among women when they talk about sexual matters"; a speech delivered by the self-reproachful Hermione in Euripides' *Andromache* castigates other women whose gatherings corrupted her personally, and endanger the domestic tranquility of all husbands, with their "Siren talk"; Aristophanes' *Thesmophoriazusae* and *Ecclesiazusae* caricature women's groups as composed of wives excessively interested in sex and drink, and consequently as threatening to marriage.[49] Yet positive portrayals of other ancient Greek female institutions survive as well—portrayals which provide evidence that these institutions supplied well-born women with the same sort of sensual enlightenment and self-validation which Greek men of their class derived from their associations, and did so without either undermining Greek male society or challenging its view of women's place.

Most prominent among these institutions are, of course, female religious cults. Those which featured the worship of a female divinity often concerned themselves with different aspects of women's experience and its correspondences in nature. Hera, for example, was associated with matrimony, maternity, and the fertility of domestic flora and fauna; Artemis with human childbirth and the fecundity of wild creatures.[50] One of Hera's holy festivals, held on Sappho's native Lesbos, was devoted to a female beauty contest and, like similar celebrations elsewhere, was comparable to the festivals which glorified male beauty.[51] By emphasizing and placing a competitive value on young women's physical appearance, these contests served the

---

See also Plutarch's insistence, at *Lyc.* 15.4, that Spartan brides were "never small and of tender years, but in their full bloom and ripeness," as if to underline their uniqueness among Greek women. On the nature and limitations of women's formal education throughout Greece, see Plato *Leg.* 805d6–806c7.

49. Semon. "Essay on Women" 90–91; Eur. *Andr.* 930 ff. For Aristophanes' portrayal of women's groups, see Pomeroy, *Goddesses* 103–5 (my translation of *Thesm.* 383–413, 497–519), 112–14. On women's groups in archaic Greek society, and their parallelism with men's groups, see also Merkelbach, "Sappho und ihr Kreis" 2–3.

50. On the various cults of Hera and Artemis in archaic and classical Greece, see Roscher, *Ausführliches Lexicon der griechischen und römischen Mythologie* 1:2075–87, 2098–104 (on the *hieros gamos*); 1:559–94.

51. See Alc. fr. 130.32–35 L.-P., as well as a scholiast to *Il.* 9.129; Hesychius, s.v. "*pylaiides*"; Ath. 13.609 ff.; *AP* 9.189; and Theophr. fr. 111 for these contests.

specific purpose of bolstering women's pride in their looks. Furthermore, marriage preparations and ceremonies, which seemed to have prefigured, or reenacted, the nuptials of each female participant, were organized into an institution of their own, one that allowed all to share, vicariously, the attention bestowed upon the bride.[52]

In addition, Greek lyric poetry for and by women also appears to have functioned as a type of institution. Like all ancient Greek lyric verse, monodic (i.e., lyric ostensibly for solo performance) and choral, it directs itself at a public; a recent critic has sensibly questioned the applicability to early Greek monody of "the modern sensibility that understands the 'lyric' poem as the essence of personal expression, the private voice that is meant not so much to be heard as overheard."[53] From what one may determine, archaic Greek "women's poetry" spoke to females committed to the same goals, and conditioned by the same experiences,[54] glorifying both the sensual charms of women and those aspects of their lifestyle which they found sensually gratifying and charming. What remains of Greek "women's" poetry—poems by females such as Sappho and Corinna, poems for females such as Alcman's maiden songs—celebrates, in strikingly affirmative fashion, not only female beauty but also the loveliness of nature and all things divine, the pleasures residing in day-to-day living, the emotional rewards deriving from close companionship.

In this context, the role of Sappho herself as a "sensual consciousness-raiser" falls within a common and culturally important tradition in archaic and classical Greece.[55] Like Sappho, male lyric poets and plastic artists routinely exalt the beauty of the human form, sharing her conception of physical and sensual graces as a reflection of divine favor which contribute to earthly fulfillment. Furthermore, Sappho's subject matter and manner of self-expression in one major respect more closely resemble those of sculptors and vase painters than those of other male poets. Her female subjects are mostly defined by, and limited to, their physical being and states of emotion;

---

52. See Sappho frs. 29, 44.31, 51 L.-P.; Pind. *Pyth.* 3.17 ff.

53. Russo, "Reading the Greek Lyric Poets" 709.

54. See ibid., 720–23. Evidence indicating that Greek female lyric poets directed their work at, and chiefly gained recognition from, female audiences includes Sappho frs. 150 and 160 L.-P., Corinna fr. 655, Pausanias's allegation at 2.20.8 that the female poet Telesilla was "of high repute among women," and the fact that Sappho's poems generally feature women as their addressees.

55. To be sure, "consciousness-raising" is a new concept and coinage, associated primarily with the heightening of political awareness; I would, however, argue that receptiveness to and cultivation of physical beauty were no less valued in and by the males and females of various archaic and classical Greek milieux than is political awareness among educated members of Western society today.

they are not immortalized, as are the subjects of male poetry, for glory achieved by doing. The nature of Sappho's material in fact helps explain her frequent emphasis on visual appearance and human feelings.[56] Nevertheless, to communicate the beauty of what she portrays, especially when writing in the first person, she must verbalize what may be construed as her personal judgment, feelings, and passions, and thereby render herself vulnerable to misconstruction. For such statements may be determined merely, and primarily, by the exigencies of her material. One should not, therefore, assume that Sappho's poems in the first person are autobiographical, even if our ancient authorities on Sappho's life often do just that.[57] A distinction between Sappho and her poetic persona may well often exist, as it so often exists in the verses of her male poetic colleagues.[58]

That Sappho's verses were basically intended as public, rather than personal, statements, that they aimed at instilling sensual awareness and sexual self-esteem in young women, and that even those written in the first person may not express her own feelings seem more obvious if we consider other examples of poetry from a similar social and cultural milieu written in the generation prior to hers. The maiden songs of Alcman, a Spartan male poet of the mid-seventh century B.C.E.,[59] were composed for delivery by a chorus of young unmarried women in a sexually segregated society which, like Sappho's Lesbos, apparently encouraged greater sensual expressiveness for females than did other societies in ancient Greece.[60] One of these maiden songs, fragment 3 P., written in the feminine first-person singular, though

56. Sappho's concern with the visual—expressed through the reiteration of verbs of seeing and an emphasis on the visual aspects of entities—is best illustrated by such fragments as 16 (contrasting what some think *to be* most beautiful with what she would most want to *see*), 17, 23, 31, and 96 L.-P.; concern with other senses is, however, no less prominent (cf. the auditory emphasis of frs. 1.7–12, 44.20 ff.; the emphasis on scent in fr. 2). One might also regard Greek statues of lovely maidens, *korai,* as in certain respects analogous to Sappho's poetic portrayals of comely young women. The first such statue, predating Sappho's poems by half a century, was dedicated to the goddess Artemis by a woman, Nikandrē (most later ones seem to have male dedicators). Unlike similar statues of young men, *korai* are always draped; their charms, moreover, are delineated decorously and subtly (see the discussions of Pomeroy, *Goddesses* 47, and Richter, *Kourai).*

57. See Dover, *Greek Homosexuality* 173, 179; cf. also Lefkowitz, "Critical Stereotypes" 29.

58. On the distinction between poet and persona in archaic Greek lyric, see Dover, "The Poetry of Archilochus" 206, and Lanata, "Sul linguaggio amoroso" 65–66.

59. For Alcman's dates, see Campbell, *Greek Lyric Poetry* 192–93. Dover, *Greek Homosexuality* 181, would follow West's dating of Alcman to Sappho's own time (late seventh and early sixth centuries B.C.E.).

60. Spartan men (according to Plut. *Lyc.* 14 ff.) resided with one another in military barracks until the age of thirty, with the result that not only maidens but women in their first decade of marriage lived apart from their male contemporaries. For Spartan women's (physical) education and sexual image, see Redfield, "The Women of Sparta" 148–49.

clearly recited by a group of young females, appears to have been performed in honor of the goddess Hera; it pays homage to the physical allure, and the responses it evokes, of a woman, Astymeloisa. The speakers compare her to a shooting star, golden sprig, and tender down; they refer to her as "causing longing which loosens the limbs" and casting "glances more melting than sleep and death."[61] A distinguished commentator on these lyrics, which were discovered only in the 1950s, has the distinct impression "that the whole company is in love" with Astymeloisa.[62] Yet critics for two decades have veered away from facing the poem's female "homosexual" sentiments, obviously because the author was a man,[63] and have either dissociated him personally from these lyric statements or maintained that he was voicing his *own* passion for Astymeloisa. Resemblances between this and Sappho's verses largely pass unnoticed, resemblances which include actual, uncommon words. These lyrics call to mind Sappho's "limb-loosening love makes me tremble—bittersweet, irresistible, surreptitious" (fr. 130 L.-P.) and "now she stands out among the Lydian women like the rosy-fingered moon, after the sun has set, surpassing all the stars" (fr. 96.6–9 L.-P.).[64] They suggest that Alcman's maiden songs may have influenced Sappho's "personal" poems and at least belong to the same literary tradition.

Alcman's other, longer and better known, maiden song (fr. 1 P.) is presumably connected with a festival of (Artemis) Orthria, Spartan goddess of fertility and vegetation[65] who, like Hera, was thought to preside over a girl's transition to married life. Here several female chorus members acclaim, in both first-person singular and first-person plural verb forms, one another's outstanding physical qualities graphically and lavishly; here, too, they avow, in sexually charged language, an emotional investment in each other.[66] A recent article has used parallels from Sappho's wedding songs to argue, persuasively, that this poem was also meant as an epithalamium, a marriage

61. Ll. 61–81 of this fragment are translated, and the problems they pose discussed, by Dover, *Greek Homosexuality* 179–80.

62. Bowra, *Greek Lyric Poetry* 32.

63. Lanata, "Sul linguaggio amoroso" 73–74, is a notable exception; she has recently been joined by Griffiths, "Alcman's Partheniaion" 59 ff., which does not deal with fr. 3 P. but with its longer sister, discussed below.

64. *Lusimelēs*, "limb-loosening," found in both Alcman fr. 3 P. and Sappho fr. 130 L.-P., appears but twice in the Homeric epics (*Od.* 20.57, 23.343).

65. Although Bowra, *Greek Lyric Poetry* 51 ff., and Griffiths, "Alcman's Partheniaion" 24 ff., maintain that the song concerns (the Spartan) Helen in her role as goddess of unmarried maidens, and Gentili, "Il partenio" 65–66, argues that Orthria is Aphrodite.

66. On the sexual connotations of the language in this fragment, see, among others, Bowra, *Greek Lyric Poetry* 272; Gentili, "Il partenio" 60 ff.; Dover, *Greek Homosexuality* 180 (on the disputed *teirein* in l. 77); Nagy, "The Symbols of Greek Lyric" 000–00.

hymn, delivered by girls whose own nuptials are imminent to honor the wedding of another "fellow debutante."[67] Should this be the case, these verses
may have even influenced Sappho's renowned choral wedding poems. Its
tone and content at least allow us to infer that many of Sappho's fragments
thought to be personal, autobiographical statements might in fact be part of
public, if not marriage, hymns sung by other females. Fragment 82 L.-P.,
"Mnasidika, of fairer form than soft Gyrinno," and fr. 16 L.-P., which praises
Anactoria's step and face as more desirable than the armaments of Lydia, are
but two examples of such fragments.[68] They recall passages from Alcman's
poem in which the girls receive individual compliments on their attractive
features: "The streaming hair of my kinswoman Hagesichora blooms like
pure gold; her face, like silver—but what can I say openly?" (ll. 51–56), or
"Abundance of purple dye does not suffice as aid, nor the all-golden, many-
hued snake bracelet, nor the Lydian headpiece, glorious divine offering of
softly glancing young girls, nor the hair of Nanno, nor Areta with godlike
beauty, nor Sylakis nor Cleesisera" (ll. 64–72). Furthermore, Sappho's comparisons between beautiful young women in such fragments as 82 and 96
L.-P.—which suggest that the "agonistic" nature of male Greek culture to
some extent permeated women's institutions as well—also have parallels in
this poem by Alcman.[69]

Scholars in the past, both Greek literary critics and ancient social his-
torians, have ignored the similarities between Alcman's maiden songs and
Sappho's lyrics, largely because they regard the former as choral, public
works by a serious male artist, the latter as personal, privately voiced statements by an eccentric female. Even Sappho's verses known to be choral
epithalamia are frequently dismissed as overrepresented among her fragments, as exaggerated in importance for such undistinguished poetry.[70] Yet
recent literary scholarship arguing that even Sappho's apparently monodic

67. Griffiths, "Alcman's Partheniaion" 11 ff., notes, for example, that in lines 64 ff. the
maidens are said to wear purple and gold, which traditionally belonged to a young woman's
dowry. That fr. 3 P. concludes with Astymeloisa's appearance in "male society" ("receiving
honor among the army ... cherished by the populace"; 13–15) suggests that it may have
marked a début, if not a wedding, too. And Plutarch's statement that young men attended the
performance of maiden songs (*Lyc.* 14.4) may imply that they served to introduce marriageable
young women to men.

68. See the discussion of this latter poem, which employs as its paradigm Helen (leaving her
husband and kin at Sparta, and sailing to Troy), by duBois, "Sappho and Helen" 79–82.

69. In fr. 16 L.-P., however, Sappho transcends the question of encouraging competition
among *people* in order to define "the most beautiful *thing* on earth."

70. So Kirkwood, *Early Greek Monody* 102, 104–23, 138; his attitude is criticized by Russo,
"Reading the Greek Lyric Poets" 718–23. Kirkwood, moreover, does not deal with Alcman
in his volume on Greek lyric, judging him a "choral" poet and of no major relevance to
"monodists" such as Sappho.

lyrics were designed to be presented—perhaps by more than one person—at some sort of cultic ceremony, and recent studies in women's social history, which have likened the role of women in archaic Lesbos to that of women in archaic Sparta, provide further reasons for considering the work of Alcman and Sappho together.[71] And the knowledge that Alcman's maiden songs were written by a man who played no part in the actual performance of his lyrics has crucial implications for an understanding of Sappho, a member, and perhaps a follower, of Alcman's literary tradition. For the fact that Alcman's maiden songs, although written in the first person, probably do not express his personal feelings for the girls they portray but merely purport to represent those of their speakers argues for a similar distinction between Sappho and the emotions expressed in her poems. After all, the fact that Alcman's Sparta promoted the display of intimate appreciation for female beauty in public, to the extent that it was "scripted" by artists who did not personally engage in the display, and assigned high value to these testimonials (doubtless because they made women better able to accept their socially and sexually defined role) suggests that Sappho's Lesbos did the same. No evidence indicates that Sappho was any more involved with the women whose charms she praises in her lyrics than was Alcman with Astymeloisa or Hagesichora. No evidence, that is, despite later attempts to make sense of her sensually expressive verses, out of their social and literary context.[72]

Sappho's homosexual image may, of course be an accurate one. The emotional intensity of Sappho's poems, the *erōs*, passionate love, which figures prominently in her verses but barely in Alcman's maiden songs,[73] certainly allows the possibility that Sappho did engage in homosexual acts as a private person. So, too, the women portrayed in Sappho's verses, and in Alcman's maiden songs, may well have expressed their homosexual sentiments physically. But whether or not she or they did so may not be germane to a basic understanding of Sappho as a creative individual, of the literary tradition in which she worked, or of her role in her society.

71. For example, Russo, "Reading the Greek Lyric Poets"; Merkelbach, "Sappho und ihr Kreis"; Segal, "Eros and Incantation" 70–73; Pomeroy, *Goddesses* 55–56.

72. In order to discourage such attempts, in fact, the early-second-century C.E. poet Strato of Sardis concluded his poems, all of which praise the physical allure of young boys, and many of which are written in the first person, with the following disclaimer (*AP* 12.258): "Perhaps in the future, someone, hearing these frivolous verses of mine, will imagine these pains of passion to have been all my own. But I'm forever writing compositions for others who love boys, since some god gave me this gift."

73. For example, at Sappho frs. 15.12, 16.4, 17.47, 49 L.-P.; Alcman fr. 1 P. merely speaks of *erata* Ianthemis at line 76 and uses the verb *eraō*, "to desire passionately," in the context of aiming to please a goddess.

NINE

Romantic Sensuality, Poetic Sense: A Response to Hallett on Sappho

Eva Stehle

Sappho is, as Judith Hallett observes, a difficult poet to write about. Sappho seems straightforward, personal, honest—"confessional," in Hallett's term. But any lyric poet writing in the first person requires a special critical attitude. One must keep in mind that the "I" of a poem is not necessary the "I" of the poet at all. The poet may put into another's mouth words he or she would not speak *in propria persona*. The "I" may be generalized, as in folksong,[1] or a poet may be writing with a specifically personal voice, as Sappho does when she uses her own name in a poem, but describing events that did not necessarily ever take place. The description of events is the poet's setting (like a stage set) for the play of emotions which he or she wishes to expose. The original emotions themselves must have their stimulus in the poet's experience, but the process of clarifying them requires the poet to refine, transform, extrapolate experience imaginatively, perhaps beyond recognition.

This tantalizing paradox—what looks most like a window into the life of the poet may be least true to the events of that life—is enormously complicated in Sappho's case by the fact that she seems to espouse lesbianism. Many react first to this, which they feel compelled to deny, denounce, celebrate, or somehow judge. They then read the poetry accordingly. On the other hand, those who do try first to distinguish poet from persona seem faced with a confused choice of explaining away the eroticism or discussing Sappho's putative "psychopathology." Hallett is absolutely right that the issue of homosexuality intrudes on, if it does not dominate, almost every discussion of Sappho in a way that does not happen with male poets. Hallett's

---

This essay was originally published in slightly different form as "Romantic Sensuality, Poetic Sense: A Response to Hallett on Sappho," *Signs* 4 (1979) 464–71.
1. See Tsagarakis, *Self-Expression in Early Greek Lyric*, for discussion of the problem.

article suggests an approach that, trying to avoid all of these traps, has some good claims to consideration. Her idea of using Greek male treatment of young men and Alcman's two maiden songs as converging context for Sappho is very suggestive. I do have disagreements with her over both her method of argument and her conclusions.

First, I think Hallett underestimates the real complexity of the question of Sappho's poetic persona. If Sappho's purpose was sexual affirmation of young women preparatory to marriage, questions of the interaction of the persona with the public arise. Was Sappho's stance of lover designed to fit with a ritual role played by the actual woman? Or could erotic admiration via poetry be effective if the author dissociated herself from it? If the poetry was treated as coming not from Sappho but from the community, would the strong personal focus and introspective quality not be subversive to the communal solidarity of praise? Would Sappho's reiterated wish to die not appear ill-omened in a public celebratory setting, a rite of passage? In short, Hallett's discussion of the Greek social structure makes the possibility of institutionalized affirmation of girls appear most plausible, but she still must show that Sappho's poetry fits the bill, appearances to the contrary. Detaching the persona from the poet does not make it automatically an impersonal or communal voice, as Hallett seems to assume. Nor does this view of Sappho illuminate the artistry of the poems at all, throw light on, for example, the interconnected themes of beauty and absence, or the tendency to displace the sensuality of the desired woman onto the surroundings.

With respect to evidence for lesbian practice in Sappho's poetry, Hallett argues that Sappho never pictures the speaker as engaging in acts of homosexual love or mentions physiological details, and that "many of Sappho's lyrics written in the first person imply an involvement in acts of heterosexual love" (131). The last line of 94 Lobel-Page (L.-P.) she dismisses as "too vague" to be definite evidence. The point Hallett is making is that the text of Sappho's poems will not support any great insistence that Sappho was a practicing homosexual lover, which is true. Yet Hallett falls into the biographical trap herself with the remark that many lyrics imply heterosexual love. She seems to assume that indications of sexual activity (or lack of them) will be biographical, even if nothing else is, an assumption which leads Hallett to write as though all the fragments were equally good indicators of Sappho's personal sexuality. In fact, the "many" fragments must be mainly the scraps of wedding hymns and bits of "folksong" (e.g., 102 L.-P.), in which the persona, the "I" of the poem, is communal or generalized, as well as the references to Cleis, Sappho's daughter. None of the major fragments, in which the persona is some manifestation of the poet, breathes a hint of sexual interest in a man. The points to be made, it seems to me, are two. First, Sappho's

sexual activity, whatever it was, was integrated with the institution of marriage (which may not have been sexually very demanding).[2] Second, we
must pay attention to the direction of erotic intensity of Sappho's persona, that is, consider the emotional reality of the poems, without trying
to deduce anything about the restriction or range of her enjoyment of sexual activity—and without attributing psychological abnormality or social
maladjustment to her.

I think one implicit purpose of Hallett's whole paper is to combat the
general supposition that Sappho was emotionally abnormal. Certainly the
standard picture of Sappho is of a woman falling unreservedly in love with a
girl, being crushed at the girl's departure, falling unreservedly for the next
girl, who will also depart, becoming ever more exhausted but never more
intelligent in her loving.[3] Hallett's answer is to say that Sappho's poetry has
an institutional erotic function but not private emotional reality. The idea
should, rather, be met head on. Sappho was "abnormal," perhaps, in being
unusually open to romantic impulse, unusually aware of the human urge
for union and the inevitable separateness. When she wished to explore and
clarify these impulses through poetry she chose female homosexual love as the
vehicle because lesbian love offered the most receptive setting for romantic
eros. Escape to a realm of beauty, illusion of perfect union, inevitability
of parting: these could be expressed through union with another woman
because such love was separate from daily domestic life with a husband;
because the other woman could seem to match, reflect, make the emotional
connection far more easily than a man; and because separation, if only by
virtue of the inevitability of marriage, was inevitable. The poems of absence
and longing need not record—each and every one—a parting or failure
in love.[4] By placing her persona in such settings Sappho could explore
the interacting realities of psychological openness to and distance from a
lover. Sappho must have known enough of both the romantic yearning
for transcendent union and the different quality of lesbian intimacy from
heterosexual intimacy to create a romantic, alternate female world.

Before looking at 94 L.-P. in this light, let me say that I disagree with
Hallett over the way in which the Greek disposition to praise young men
should be taken. I think she is right in seeing that the admiration is an

---

2. Plutarch (*Sol.* 20.3) over 700 years later suggests that a man should make love to his wife
three times a month because it eases marital tensions. The passage is cited and discussed
by Pomeroy, *Goddesses* 87.

3. Detailed exposition of this view is given in Schadewaldt, *Sappho*. See also Bagg, "Love,
Ceremony, and Daydream," who suggests that Sappho suffered from guilt.

4. The same reasoning as is typically applied to Sappho would, if applied to Emily
Dickinson, conclude that she had died frequently.

important validation of a youth at puberty and is directed at the whole personality, not just the young man's looks. It makes a good analogy with what Sappho's effect on young women around her may have been. But the praise of young men was undeniably based on sexual attraction.[5] That does not mean that everyone who admired a youth felt the immediate urge to possess him sexually. But it is misleading in emphasis to say, as Hallett does (135), that "sensual appreciation of handsome youth might mean *no more than* approbation of his calisthenic or cognitive talents" (italics mine). For the reason why other qualities could be expressed through language of sexual appreciation is that sexual attractiveness in a young man was highly valued. Desire to possess a young man was socially acceptable. Therefore even those who had no designs on a young man could praise, for example, intellectual capacities via the powerful medium of sexual evaluation.

Likewise, validation of one woman by another in sexual terms must have relied on the social acceptability of one woman as object of sexual interest on the part of another. People in general are, if anything, too little inclined to distinguish between a person's statement of sexual attraction to a forbidden group and that person's likelihood of acting on it. So Sappho's poetic expressions of desire and love would have aroused hostility, not affirmation, if they were directed at a group with whom physical expression of desire was ruled out by the society.

Let us now look at 94 L.-P., the poem which may refer to actual homosexual activity.[6] The poem opens (after a missing line), "Really, I wish to die; weeping she left me." The next three stanzas record a conversation in which Sappho comforts the distraught girl. The comfort turns into a reminiscence of the good things they shared, of which four stanzas are occupied by one occasion: "you adorned yourself with flowers at my side, you put round yourself garlands of flowers, you anointed yourself with oil, on a soft bed you expelled desire" (to paraphrase). The atmosphere is one of segregation in sensuous surroundings. With each stanza the focus is more directly on the body of the other woman. The first contains no mention of it (unless in a lacuna in the text). In the second stanza Sappho refers to her "tender neck." In the third the woman anoints herself (typically done while nude after a bath).[7] And in the fourth she expels longing (someone else's longing,

5. Dover, *Greek Homosexuality*, makes this clear, though, as he also points out (53–54), strict decorum seems to have inhibited public discussion of actual lovemaking. The same would likely be true for Sappho.

6. See Hallett 131 n. 26. For an excellent discussion of the poem see McEvilley, "Sappho, Fragment 94."

7. See *Il.* 14.170–72; *Od.* 6.224–28; *h. Hom. Ven.* 61–63. In the first and third passages lovemaking follows. In the second Nausicaa becomes interested in Odysseus as a potential husband.

according to the verb form). The whole movement of the recollection is toward erotic culmination.

In these four stanzas Sappho's only reference to herself is the "at my side" of line 14, though the detail implies that Sappho pictures herself as present throughout. The concentration is entirely on the sensuousness of the other woman. Its effect could be sexual affirmation of the addressee, and Sappho may have intended, among other things, to create that effect. But there is an artistic reason for focus on the other woman through the four stanzas. Sappho is dramatizing her (or rather her persona's) complete openness to the other woman, her loss of self-consciousness in absorption with the other. Yet this is now memory, and the other woman does not share it. The unity previously so complete is now suddenly, irretrievably dissolved. The persona's (not the poet's) wish to die is a wish to halt the flux, preserve the perfect moment of emotional fusing with another.

Keeping the romantic quality of 94 L.-P. in mind, we can consider Sappho in comparison with Alcman's two maiden songs (1 and 3 Page [P.]). Alcman's tone is similar to Sappho's in some ways, but Hallett's discussion skirted the essential difference that Alcman's poems refer to their own context, a celebration and an appeal to the gods. And the method of praise is different. Alcman draws on the standard imagery of praise found in Homer and applied to both men and women. His picture of human, including erotic, interactions is male. Sappho avoids both. Her imagery and description of personal dynamics differentiate the female from the male.

The most prevalent image in Alcman's first maiden song is of the horse. Four times a girl is compared with a horse, a particular breed of horses, or a trace-horse (ll. 47, 50, 59, 92). In one instance our lack of information about breeds means that we do not catch the point of a comparison: a girl compared in beauty with Agido is a Colaxaean horse running against an Ibenian. There may be a ritual reason for the emphasis on horses; they seem to have figured in the worship of Ortheia.[8] But the references to breeds clearly come from the area of male interest in breeding and racing horses. The image has a tradition in literature also. Paris is compared with a horse in *Iliad* 6.506–11. Ibycus compares himself with a prizewinning racehorse in a love poem (287 P.). Anacreon uses the image for a girl whom he threatens to ride (417 P.). Sappho, in the extant fragments, never uses any such comparison for a woman. When horses do appear in her poetry they are associated with men, implicitly dissociated from women. In the priamel 16 L.-P., for instance, Sappho chooses "what one loves" as most beautiful rather

---

8. See Campbell, *Greek Lyric Poetry* 203, ad l. 48.

than an army of horsemen. In 2 L.-P. a "horse-pasturing meadow" is located within the bounds of a shrine where it will not be open to pasturing animals.[9] A late reference to Sappho's wedding hymns says she compared the grooms to prizewinning horses, the brides to the delicacy of roses (117a L.-P.).

In Alcman's second maiden song Astymeloisa is compared with a "golden shoot" (l. 68). The image of a shoot or sapling is found in the *Iliad* (18.56) of Achilles and in the *Odyssey* (6.163) of Nausicaa. The term is similar to one Sappho herself uses in a wedding hymn to describe the groom (115 L.-P.). But Sappho does not use it of a woman. Instead we find comparisons of women to fruit or flowers. In a wedding hymn a woman is an apple high on a tree (105a L.-P.). Sappho's daughter has an appearance like golden flowers (132 L.-P.).[10]

Again, Alcman compares Agido to the light of the sun in the first maiden song (l. 41). Connection with the ceremony is possible; it took place before sunrise. But there are Homeric parallels: Hera's seductive veil is white like the sun (*Il.* 14.185); Achilles in armor is like the shining sun (*Il.* 19.398). And in both Alcman's songs girls are compared with stars. The image in 3 P. is the more elaborate: Astymeloisa is "like some shining star in flight through the heavens" (ll. 66–67). The star image is used in the *Iliad* of men; Athena is compared with a shooting star (*Il.* 4.75–77).[11] Both sun and star have the masculine gender in Greek. Sappho uses neither image, but twice compares a woman with the moon eclipsing the surrounding stars (34, 96 L.-P.). The moon is female in gender and a goddess in mythology. Sappho, I think, consciously wished to connect women with the mysterious rhythms of the moon as separate from the sharp, bright male world of sun and stars. We owe the preservation of one of these fragments to the commentator who noted the contrast with a passage of the *Iliad*.[12]

But Sappho's images for women's appearance are few, despite her emphasis on vision. Similes are noticeably more frequent in the wedding-hymn fragments, particularly for men. A groom is like Ares or Achilles (105b, 111 L.-P.), or has a honeyed face (112 L.-P.). The disproportion may be accidental, but perhaps Sappho is less concerned to provide praise of the woman

9. See my article, "Retreat from the Male" 92.
10. The comparison of men with flowers was traditional but often as an indication of youth or pathos: see *Il.* 8.306–8; Theog. 1348 West (W.).
11. *Il.* 22.26–31, Achilles; *Il.* 11.62–64, Hector. The point of the comparison is usually visual. But Astyanax is said to be "like a lovely star" (*Il.* 6.40) in a simile called unique. See Scott, *The Oral Nature of the Homeric Simile* 68.
12. Campbell, *Greek Lyric Poetry* 273, ad 34 L-P. The image of moon eclipsing stars is thought to be traditional but does not show up earlier than Sappho. The moon is never used in a comparison with a person in the *Iliad* or *Odyssey*. In *h. Hom. Ven.* 88–90 the effect of a necklace on Aphrodite's breasts is compared with the moon.

on whom she turns her attention than to explore the effect of that woman's presence or absence. Description implies separation between observer and observed. For Sappho another woman's presence rather generates a sensuous environment, figured as flowers, fabric, perfume, sacred precinct, which encloses them both, erasing the separation.

Alcman has the chorus in 1 P. talk of fighting, probably because they are competing with another chorus. Alcman's chorus thinks of it as a battle, one in which they denigrate their own ability to prevail without the aid of the leader, who commands their obedience (ll. 92–95). In 3 P. the chorus describes Astymeloisa, perhaps the leader, in passionate terms but describes her as not answering. Later, as the fragment tails off, the chorus says, "I would become a suppliant of hers" (l. 81). Male assumptions about competition and about dominance and submission have determined the form of erotic expression: love and beauty are contests. Sappho does not picture love relations as domination by one partner over the other. In 94 and 96 L.-P. desire is mutual. In 1 L.-P., the only combative love poem, either Sappho or the other woman is free to initiate the relationship. Dover notices the difference from the style of male homosexual relations but does not pursue the subject.[13]

Finally, Astymeloisa in Alcman 3 P. is known to the army and is a darling of the people (ll. 73–74), while Sappho's encounter with or fantasy of a desired woman is always in an environment isolated from men (except in 31 L.-P.).

Detailed comparison of Alcman with Sappho illuminates Sappho's special romantic quality. Alcman's girls are imagistically and ceremonially integrated with the whole Spartan culture, participating in its values. Sappho used the special conditions of lesbian love to create an alternative world in which male values, those same values which denied Greek women an outlet for erotic fantasy, are not dominant, and within which mutual desire, rapture, and separateness can be explored as female experience.

13. Dover, *Greek Homosexuality* 177. On male competitiveness, see the works cited in Hallett 135 nn. 40, 42.

TEN

Who Sang Sappho's Songs?

André Lardinois

In recent years the traditional division of Greek lyric into exclusively choral or monodic poets has been called into question. The main subject of inquiry has been the choral poets, like Pindar, Stesichorus, and Alcman. It has been argued that some or even most of their poetry was not performed by choruses, but by the poets themselves or other soloists.[1] In this article I want to focus attention on one of the allegedly monodic poets: Sappho. I will argue that there are among her fragments more chorally performed songs than so far has been acknowledged.

Other scholars already have voiced some uneasiness with the traditional picture of Sappho as a monodist. Hermann Fränkel believed that "among the Lesbians too, then, there were songs fairly close to choral lyric," like

I would like to thank Andrew Ford, Richard Martin, Jan Bremmer, Claude Calame, and Dirk Obbink for their valuable suggestions at different stages of this article, which began as a term paper I wrote for Andrew Ford's 1989 Graduate Seminar on Sappho and Alcaeus at Princeton University. A shorter, oral version was delivered at the 1992 APA conference in New Orleans. Some of the arguments are repeated from my article on Sappho, "Subject and Circumstance," which in many ways complements this article by arguing that Sappho was involved in the setting up of young women's choruses.

Fragments and testimonia of all lyric poets, including Sappho, are cited from Campbell's edition in the Loeb Classical Library, *Greek Lyric*, unless noted otherwise. Elegists and iambic poets are cited according to West, *Iambi et Elegi Graeci*.

1. Davies, "Monody"; Heath, "Receiving the κῶμος"; Lefkowitz, "Who Sang Pindar's Victory Odes?"; Heath and Lefkowitz, "Epinician Performance." I mention these scholars without necessarily agreeing with them in every respect (e.g., I still believe, contra Heath and Lefkowitz, that the great majority of Pindar's *epinikia* was sung by choruses). For some critical responses, mainly dealing with Pindar's *epinikia*, see Burnett, "Performing Pindar's Odes"; Carey, "The Performance of the Victory Ode" and "The Victory Ode in Performance"; Bremer, "Pindar's Paradoxical ἐγώ"; and Morgan, "Pindar the Professional."

Sappho fragment 16, "which meditates and argues like choral poetry." More recently, Claude Calame has suggested that Sappho's circle was organized as a young girls' choir which sang or danced to songs composed by Sappho, and Judith Hallett has declared that "many of Sappho's fragments thought to be personal, autobiographical statements might in fact be part of public, if not marriage, hymns sung by other females."[2] Yet, overall the traditional picture has prevailed that Sappho composed songs, essentially about herself (her own emotions), to be performed by herself.

I will first take a look at some of the evidence about Sappho's work. Next I will discuss the applicability to her work of the traditional distinctions between choral and monodic poetry. Special attention will be given to the use of the first-person singular and plural in early Greek poetry, which will also allow us to take a closer look at some of Sappho's fragments (frs. 94 and 96). In a final section I will review the other major fragments and show that they can be interpreted as being performed with the help of choruses.

1. THE ANCIENT EVIDENCE ABOUT SAPPHO'S WORK

It is commonly acknowledged that at least some of Sappho's poetry was choral. One of Sappho's books, probably the ninth, in the Alexandrian edition of her poems consisted wholly of *epithalamia* or wedding songs,[3] at least some of which were meant to be performed by age-mates of the bride.[4]

2. Fränkel, *Early Greek Poetry* 186 nn. 45, 172; Calame, *Les chœurs* 1:127, 368–69; Hallett, "Sappho and Her Social Context," 141.

3. A better term is *hymenaioi*. *Epithalamia* is the name Hellenistic scholars gave to these poems and is not attested before that period. Originally it referred to songs sung in the evening outside the marriage chamber, but Sappho's songs cover a number of occasions on the wedding day, including the wedding procession and the banquet: see Schadewaldt, *Sappho* 32–58; Muth, "Hymenaios" 38–40; Page, *Sappho and Alcaeus* 119–23; Bowra, *Greek Lyric Poetry* 214–23; and Contiades-Tsitsoni, *Hymenaios* 68–109. *Hymenaios*, on the other hand, is an archaic Greek term that was used for all types of song: as Aeschylus suggests, from bridal bath to bridal bed (*PV* 555–56). See Muth on this passage and the two terms in general, and more recently Contiades-Tsitsoni, esp. 30–32.

4. Page, *Sappho and Alcaeus* 112 ff.; Campbell "Sappho" 162. *Hymenaioi* appear to have been primarily choral songs, performed by a chorus of young men and/or young women (Muth, "Hymenaios" 36) and there are clear indications of choral performance in Sappho's wedding songs, for example the dialogue-form of fr. 114 (Page 119 n. 1, 122) and the refrain in fr. 111. Still, Homer (*Od.* 4.17–19) pictures a song performed at a wedding feast that is sung by a soloist and danced to by two tumblers, and Hague has compared Sappho fr. 115 to the *eikasia* games played at symposia, "in which *one person* ridiculed another by making a ludicrous comparison" ("Ancient Greek Wedding Songs" 134; my italics). It is possible that particularly during the banquet there were solo performances of songs related to the bride and groom, with or without the accompaniment of a dancing chorus. Fr. 44, if indeed a wedding song, is a possible candidate for such a performance (Contiades-Tsitsoni, *Hymenaios* 107).

Another type of song that is ascribed to her is religious hymns (test. 21, 47). These need not all have been choral, but some of them appear to have been genuine choral songs, such as fragment 140a, which is composed as a dialogue between a person (or group) impersonating the goddess Aphrodite and a group of young girls.[5]

Page maintained that, apart from these poems, "[t]here is no evidence or indication that any of Sappho's poetry ... was designed for presentation by herself or others (whether individuals or choirs) on a formal or ceremonial occasion, public or private," and that "[t]here is nothing to contradict the natural supposition that, with this one small exception, all or almost all of her poems were recited by herself informally to her companions."[6] One must be wary of relying on "natural suppositions," especially in the case of Sappho, and Page's supposition is actually far from "natural," since generally when scholars find that one or more poems of an archaic Greek poet are choral, they assume that the same holds true for the other poems.[7] Snyder, more carefully, distinguishes between three types of songs: those that are purely public (the wedding songs); those with the conventional form of public poetry (e.g., frs. 1, 2, 16); and those that are purely private (e.g., frs. 31, 94, 96).[8] It is not clear, however, whether she believes that the second group was actually performed in public and/or by others than Sappho herself: "Even though we may not want to go so far as to say that these songs were meant to be performed at some specific occasion, they nevertheless seem in some way connected with familiar rituals of a public character." The question is why we should not go so far as to say that these songs were performed at public occasions, if they indeed follow "the conventional forms of public poetry."[9]

According to the *Suda* (test. 2), Sappho wrote nine books of "lyric songs" (μελῶν λυρικῶν) and also "epigrams, elegiacs, iambics, and solo songs (μονῳδίας)." We know that the epigrams were late Hellenistic forgeries,[10] and of her iambics and elegiacs nothing has survived, but the separate mention of solo songs has caused some surprise: "how did these last differ from

---

5. Parker has recently argued that κόραι in this fragment must be a ritual term, referring to adult women, because "the Adonia was everywhere that we know of a festival of adult women" ("Sappho Schoolmistress" 323). This claim is incorrect and Winkler, to whom Parker refers, does not support it: see my response in Lardinois, "Subject and Circumstance" 65.

6. Page, *Sappho and Alcaeus* 119. He has been followed by most interpreters, most recently Parker, "Sappho Schoolmistress" 331.

7. See Davies, "Monody." Like Davies, I do not favor this approach and therefore will refrain from making such an argument.

8. Snyder, "Public Occasion and Private Passion."

9. Ibid., 3, 10.

10. Campbell, *Greek Lyric* 1:xiii; for their text, 205.

her lyric poetry?" asks Campbell in a footnote to his edition of Sappho's fragments and testimonia.[11] I hope to show that this is more than just a rhetorical question.

As regards the actual performance of Sappho's songs, we have very little information. In later antiquity we hear of performances of her songs both by individuals (a boy; test. 10) and by groups of girls and boys (test. 53), but we do not know how this relates to the original performance context.[12] Some of Sappho's poems seem to have been intended to be recited by herself, like fragment 1, in which she mentions her own name, but such clarity is exceptional: the only other fragments in which Sappho mentions her name are 65, 94, and 133. We cannot be absolutely certain that she sang even these songs herself. Alcman composed several songs (frs. 17, 39, 95b) in which he mentions his own name but which nevertheless may have been performed by a chorus,[13] and both in Pindar's *epinikia* and later in the *parabaseis* of Aristophanes (e.g., *Nub.* 518–62) the chorus or chorus leader can speak in the name of the poet/composer. Sappho further mentions in her poetry that other women sang songs about each other or Aphrodite, and in one case she alludes to a song dance (μολπή) of Atthis.[14] Were these their own compositions or did Sappho compose these songs for them, the same way she composed the wedding songs or the hymns?

The testimonial tradition about Sappho is not uniform either. Horace pictures her as plucking the lyre while singing to herself about her girls (*Carm.* 2.13.24–25 = test. 18), whereas an anonymous poet in the *Anthologia Palatina* describes her as leading a dancing chorus of Lesbian women, "her golden lyre in hand" (*AP* 9.189 = test. 59).[15] Philostratus (*Imag.* 2.1.1–3), finally, is reminded of Sappho when he sees a picture of a female director (διδάσκαλος) leading a band of singing girls (κόραι).[16] We thus have witnesses

11. Ibid., 7.
12. Other references to the performance of Sappho's songs in later times are Plut. *Quaest. conv.* 622c, 711d, but the number of singers is unclear here.
13. Calame, *Alcman* 362 f.
14. Frs. 21, 22, 96.5. In fr. 96.4 the Lydian woman is further said to have compared Atthis to a goddess and it is not unlikely that she did so in a song.
15. The lyre could be used both for choral and monodic performances (Barker, *The Musician and His Art,* see index, s.v. "lyra"). Likewise, the term λυρικός or λυρική (Sappho test. 2, 3, 28), as well as μελοποιός (test. 36, fr. 211a), can refer to a choral or a monodic poet: Färber, *Die Lyrik* 1.7–16. There are a few depictions of female lyre players accompanying choruses on archaic Greek vases (Calame, *Les chœurs* 1:131–32). Sappho is depicted on four Attic vases from the late sixth and fifth century (Snyder, *The Woman and the Lyre* 6). See on these representations of Sappho also Snyder, "Sappho in Attic Vase Painting" (forthcoming), whose analysis suggests that the relevance of these vase paintings for the "real" Sappho is very limited.
16. Himerius (*Or.* 9.4 = Sappho fr. 194) also pictures Sappho as heading a group of young women (παρθένους) in what appears to be a musical performance, but this one is clearly tied

and/or fragments for at least three different types of performances: Sappho sings, with or without her chorus dancing; full choral performances; performances by one of her companions.

Sappho composed songs about young women,[17] and she probably composed her wedding songs for performances by them. The Adonis hymn (fr. 140a), with its reference to κόραι, may represent another type of song Sappho composed for these girls. Both types of song would have been performed in public.[18] It is generally assumed that Sappho sang the other songs herself in the small circle of her companions,[19] but there is really no evidence for this. No one in antiquity says so, not even Horace, who makes Sappho sing to her own lyre in the underworld.[20] This idea seems to have originated in the French salons of the seventeenth and eighteenth century, whose members believed to have found in Sappho a kindred spirit.[21] In the nineteenth century Sappho's "salon" was interpreted as a school for young girls and, more recently, as a female *thiasos*, but, as far as we know, there existed no literary "salons," schools for girls, or private *thiasoi* in archaic Greece.[22]

Modern scholars sometimes make reference to fragment 160 in which the speaker says something like: "I shall now sing these songs beautifully to the delight of my companions" (τάδε νῦν ἐταίραις / ταὶς ἔμαις 'τέρπνα κάλως ἀείσω).[23] We cannot be sure that this is what Sappho actually said

to the marriage ceremony (she leads [?] the girls into the *numpheion*). It is further worth noting that when the third-century B.C.E poet Nossis wants to send a message to Sappho, she sends it to "Mitylene with the beautiful choruses" (χαλλίχορον Μιτυλήναν; *AP* 7.718.1 = Nossis *Epigram* 11.1 Gow and Page).

17. This fact, commonly accepted by Sappho scholars, has recently been disputed by Parker, "Sappho Schoolmistress." I find his arguments unconvincing, however: see Lardinois, "Subject and Circumstance," and Bennett, "Concerning Sappho Schoolmistress." By young women or girls, I mean women between puberty and marriage who in our sources, including Sappho's poetry, are referred to as κόραι, παρθένοι, and sometimes παῖδες.

18. Page, *Sappho and Alcaeus* 119; Campbell, "Sappho" 162.

19. E.g., Page, *Sappho and Alcaeus* 119; van Erp Taalman Kip, "Einige interpretatie-problemen" 340; Stigers [Stehle], "Sappho's Private World" 45; Burnett, *Three Archaic Poets* 209 n. 2.

20. Horace's picture is reminiscent of Achilles playing all by himself on his lyre in *Iliad* 9 (on which, see 170 n. 102) rather than of a performance before a group.

21. Compare Saake, *Sapphostudien* 15–16; DeJean, *Fictions of Sappho* 43 f., 135–36.

22. See Lardinois, "Subject and Circumstance" 63–64, 75–79. See Parker, "Sappho Schoolmistress" 339, for some examples of scholars who interpreted Sappho's "circle" as a *thiasos*. Nineteenth-century scholars: Welcker, *Sappho* 97; Wilamowitz, "Die griechische Literatur" 26.

23. E.g., Lanata, "Sul linguaggio amoroso" 66; Winkler, "Double Consciousness" 165; Burnett, *Three Archaic Poets* 216; Campbell, "Sappho" 162.

(τέρπνα does not fit the meter) or that Sappho herself is the speaker, but even if this were the case, to whom would she address these words? She does not use a second-person plural (as the speaker does in fr. 141) and therefore may be speaking *about* her companions in the presence of a larger audience.   In the Homeric *Hymn to Apollo* the speaker similarly asks his dancing chorus, which consists of young girls (χοῦραι), to remind others how much his singing delighted them (τέρπεσθε; 170). If the *Anthologia Palatina* (test. 59) reflects an authentic tradition and Sappho sometimes performed her songs in public while her chorus danced, fragment 160 may have been part of such a song.[24]

Other possible evidence is fragment 150, in which Sappho calls a house (if δόμῳ is the correct supplement for the unmetrical οἰχίᾳ) that of "the servants of the Muses" (μοισοπόλων).[25] According to Maximus of Tyre, who has preserved the fragment for us, Sappho spoke these words to her daughter, which is probably why most scholars assume that she is speaking here about her own house.[26] Yet, even if this were the case, the fragment does not say that it was in her house, and only in her house, that Sappho and her companions performed their songs. We do not know what she means by the word μουσοπόλος, but we encounter the same term again in a Boeotian inscription where it refers to a theater group.[27] I do not want to deny that Sappho and her companions may have recited songs to each other at her house, but this is by no means evident and, instead, there are good reasons to believe that Sappho composed her songs for public performances.

The closest parallel to Sappho's circle is the groups of Spartan women for whom Alcman composed his songs.[28] These are young girls, at the brink of marriage, who come together to sing in choruses and perform certain rituals. The Spartan evidence strongly suggests that these groups were trained for

---

24. For this type of performance in which a soloist sings while the chorus dances, one may compare Demodocus's song about Ares and Aphrodite, which is sung by Demodocus and danced to by a group of young Phaeacians (*Od.* 8.262–64), the wedding song in *Od.* 4.17–19, or the execution of the Linos song in *Il.* 18.569 f. For some applications of this type of performances to other archaic Greek poets, see Davies, "Monody" 62–63.

25. Page (*Sappho and Alcaeus* 132 n. 1) is probably correct in assuming that οἰχίᾳ ousted another word and originally was a gloss to ἐν μοισιπόλων, meaning by itself "in the abode of the servants of the Muses."

26. E.g., Welcker, *Sappho* 97; Wilamowitz, *Sappho und Simonides* 73; Kranz, *Geschichte der griechischen Literatur* 88; Burnett, *Three Archaic Poets* 211.

27. *IG* VII.2484. See Lanata, "Sul linguaggio amoroso" 67; Calame, *Les chœurs* 1:367.

28. Merkelbach, "Sappho und ihr Kreis" 3; Calame, *Les chœurs* 1:27, 367 f.; Lardinois, "Lesbian Sappho" 26–29.

public performances, not for the privacy of the poet's house. This does not necessarily mean that the girls always had to do both the singing and the dancing. A fresh look at Alcman's poetry might reveal that not all of his "maiden songs" were like fragments 1 and 3, that is, sung by the whole chorus. There is the suggestion of exchanges between the choir and the poet, and of *prooemia* sung by Alcman himself.[29] It is also possible that such a "monodic"-looking fragment as fragment 59a was actually sung by the poet while his maiden chorus danced.[30] I want to argue for such a variety of performances in the case of Sappho's poetry as well.[31]

Finally, we may question whether any archaic Greek poet, male or female, would have composed poetry for something as intimate as a private group of young, adolescent women. Parallels have been drawn between Sappho's circle and the *hetaireia* of the Lesbian poet Alcaeus,[32] but there is quite a difference between a gathering of politically active, adult men and a group of young girls. If Sappho's circle had a counterpart in any male organizations, it was in juvenile bands of boy initiates, not in adult clubs of aristocratic warriors. Such groups were, like Alcman's choruses, trained for performances in public.[33]

2. SAPPHO AND THE DISTINCTIONS BETWEEN CHORAL AND MONODIC POETRY

Critics of the traditional division between choral poetry and monody have pointed out that it is not very old. Plato (*Leg.* 764d–e) is the first to mention it, and he speaks about the *performances* of songs, not about their monodic or choral character.[34] The archaic Greeks themselves do not seem to have been particularly interested in the distinction, for a number of archaic Greek genre names could refer to a poem sung by a soloist or a choral song, such

---

29. On exchanges, see Rosenmeyer, "Alcman's Partheneion I" 338, who points to frs. 26, 38, 39, and 40; on *prooemia*, see Segal, "Alcman" 128.

30. On the monodic character of Alcman fr. 59a, see Davies, "Alcman fr. 59a P.," review of Calame 387–88, and "Monody" 54–55.

31. Besides these different kinds of "maiden songs," Alcman, just as Sappho, also composed marriage songs: for the evidence see Contiades-Tsitsoni, *Hymenaios* 46–67, with Muth's prudent remarks (review of E. Contiades-Tsitsoni 587).

32. Most, "Greek Lyric Poets" 95–96; Burnett, *Three Archaic Poets* 209; Gentili, *Poetry and Its Public* 81.

33. Bremmer, "Adolescents" 138; Buxton, *Imaginary Greece* 23–24. It is is worth noting that other female poets in the classical period were credited with having composed songs for young women's choruses as well: Calame, *Les chœurs* 2:174; Snyder, *The Woman and the Lyre* 40, 50 (Corinna), 54–55 (Praxilla), 60 (Telesilla).

34. Davies, "Monody" 57, Lefkowitz, "Who Sang Pindar's Victory Odes?" 191. Cf. Färber, *Die Lyrik* 1.16, and Harvey, "Classification" 159 n. 3.

as the *skolion*,[35] the *epinikion*,[36] and the *hymenaios*.[37] The differences between choral and monodic poetry that one finds most often cited concern

1. their metrics: the meters of choral songs are said to be more elaborate, the strophic structures longer.
2. their language: monodic poets stay closer to their local dialects, while choral poets make use of a more artificial language, based on Doric and the epic.
3. their contents: choral poets are less intimate and personal than monodic poets.[38]

Note that these differences are all relative: they may be less the result of the number of performers of the song than of the individual poet, the subject of the song, the audience, and so on.

I will now examine how these distinctions relate to Sappho's poetry:

1. There can be no question of any clear, metrical division between Sappho's choral and monodic poetry, since we possess wedding songs (frs. 27, 30), as well as supposedly monodic songs (fr. 1), in the same Sapphic stanza.[39]

35. Harvey, "Classification" 162. Dicaearchus (fr. 88 Wehrli) distinguished three different types of drinking songs: first a song sung by all the guests together, then stanzas sung by each of the guests in turn, and finally songs sung by the experts.

36. Pindar imagines a solo performance of a ὕμνον καλλίνικον in *Nem.* 4.13–16, and Aristophanes in *Nub.* 1355–56 alludes to the (re)performance by a soloist of a Simonides song (fr. 507), which one of the scholiasts ad loc. identifies as a victory ode: see Davies, "Monody" 56–57; Heath, "Receiving the κῶμος" 187 n. 18; and Lefkowitz, "Who Sang Pindar's Victory Odes?" 194–95. It is certainly possible that *some* of Pindar's *epinikia* were composed for solo performances (with or without accompaniment of a dancing chorus); Wilamowitz (*Pindaros* 233, 240) already suggested that *Olympian* 1 and 2 were performed by Pindar himself (cited by Davies 56). See also Harvey's insightful remarks ("Classification" 160) about the problem of the definition of the *epinikion*.

37. See n. 4 above, p. 151. In general, archaic Greek terms for poetry mark the occasions of the song rather than any formal features: see Calame, "Réflexions" 118; West, *Studies* 7, 23; Fowler, *The Nature of Greek Lyric* 90; Gentili, *Poetry and Its Public* 36.

38. E.g., Bowra, *Greek Lyric Poetry* 6; Kirkwood, *Early Greek Monody* 10–11 (who makes an exception for Sappho: 10); Most, "Greek Lyric Poets" 89; Campbell, "Monody" 161. Segal, "The Nature of Early Choral Poetry" 125, is already more cautious. See for the history of the distinction Davies, "Monody" 58–61.

39. Not all of Sappho's wedding songs were assigned to book 9 in the Alexandrian collection of her poems. Most of the other books were arranged by meter and if the epithalamia fitted the meter of one of the other books, they were apparently assigned a place there. Such was the case with frs. 27 and 30, which, together with other poems in the Sapphic stanza, were included in book 1 (Page, *Sappho and Alcaeus* 125). Lasserre, *Sappho* 37–38, 133–35, has argued, on the basis of their meter, that these fragments must be *monodic* wedding songs, but this is highly unlikely. Not only are the two first-person plurals (27.8, 30.9) then very hard to explain (see below), but we know that at least one of the fragments (fr. 30) was a διεγερτικόν, a song

Sappho also used the dactylic hexameter for wedding songs (frs. 105, 106, 143) and for such a song as fragment 142, believed to be the opening line of one of her "amorous" songs.[40] The idea that choral meters are always complex is based in large part on Alcman's first partheneion, which has a fourteen-line stanza. Yet not all dance songs need have been so intricate as this one, which was clearly composed for a solemn occasion.[41] One should note that Alcman composed three-line stanzas as well.[42]

2. Page in his commentary on Sappho and Alcaeus followed Lobel in his assessment that Sappho wrote in her Lesbian vernacular, "uncontaminated by alien or artificial forms and features," with the exception of some "abnormal" poems.[43] However, this distinction, which has recently been disputed,[44] does not correspond to a division between her choral and supposedly monodic songs. Some of the "abnormal" poems appear to be monodic (notably fr. 44), while some wedding songs are as "uncontaminated" as her supposedly monodic songs (frs. 27, 30). Again, we should be aware of other circumstances that can determine the use of, for example, epic diction. Thus it is to be expected that Sappho is able to use more diction familiar to us from epic in poems composed in the hexameter or in a meter close to it (all "abnormal" poems). They are also more appropriate for a song in which she recounts an epic story, like fragment 44, yet no one would argue on this basis that fragment 44 is a choral song.[45]

---

traditionally sung the morning after the wedding night by friends of the bride and groom (Contiades-Tsitsoni, *Hymenaios* 41, 100–101, 128 f.).

40. Campbell, *Greek Lyric* 1:157. We, of course, associate the dactylic hexameter mainly with the *solo* performances of Homer and Hesiod.

41. I would argue the same for Pindar's *epinikia* and the tragic choruses. Dionysius of Halicarnassus (*Comp.* 19 = Stesich. test. 28 Campbell) maintained that "the ancient poets, I mean Sappho and Alcaeus, made their stanzas short, so they did not introduce many variations in their few colons, and they used the epode or shorter line sparingly, but Stesichorus, Pindar, and the like made their periods longer and divided them into many meters and colons *for the sheer love of variety* " (my italics): no mention of monodic versus choral structures.

42. Fr. 3.3 col. iii Page/Davies and, possibly, fr. 14a: see West, "Greek Poetry" 181. This, incidentally, spoils Davies' neat division between "eastern" and "western" poets ("Monody" 63–64).

43. Page, *Sappho and Alcaeus* 327. The so-called abnormal poems are frs. 44, 104a, 105a, 105c, 106–9, 142, and 143.

44. Hooker, *Language and Text*; Bowie, *The Poetic Dialect*; and Nagy, *Pindar's Homer* 94 n. 60. It appears that Sappho's poetry, just like that of Alcaeus, is a complicated mix of old Aeolic, epic, and her local dialect. The same is essentially true for Alcman's (choral) poetry: Calame, *Alcman* xxiv–xxxiv.

45. Rösler, "Ein Gedicht," following Merkelbach ("Sappho und ihr Kreis" 17) and Fränkel (*Early Greek Poetry* 174), has actually argued that fr. 44 was a choral (wedding) song, but on different grounds. For the latest twist in the interpretation of this poem, see Lasserre, *Sappho*

3. This brings us to the contents of Sappho's songs. Many pages have been written about the profoundly personal feelings that Sappho expresses in her lyrics. But can we be sure that these are really her own feelings? Can we be sure that any of the early Greek poems is "personal," for that matter?[46] What is "personality" in such a group-oriented society as archaic Greece? Central to the debate have been poems in which the poet clearly impersonates a character.[47] Some of these we find, interestingly enough, among Sappho's fragments as well.[48] I will not pursue this matter further here. Instead, I will focus on some of the similarities between Alcman's partheneia, Sappho's choral wedding songs, and her so-called love poems.

The discovery of Alcman's partheneia has greatly changed the perception of early Greek choral poetry. Fränkel commented on the first fragment: "the style in the second half of Alcman's maiden song is as simple as that of the monodies of Sappho; in content choral lyric is frequently as personal as monody."[49] Of course, he meant to say that *the chorus,* not Alcman himself, was as "personal" in this song as Sappho in her poems.[50] But if this is true and the same degree of intimacy can be found in Alcman's choral songs as in Sappho's fragments, we must allow at least for the possibility that Sappho's songs were performed by a chorus of young women, just like Alcman's partheneia and her own wedding songs.

Indeed, the same degree of "intimacy" can not only be detected in Alcman's partheneia but in Sappho's wedding songs as well. In fragment 112 Sappho has a choir of girls sing to the bride: "your form is gracious and your eyes / ... / honey-sweet; love streams over your desire-arousing face."[51] One is hard pressed to find another fragment of Sappho that is so "intimate" as this one. The similarity between Alcman's partheneia, Sappho's own

---

81–106, and Contiades-Tsitsoni, *Hymenaios* 102–8, who both argue that it represents a *monodic* wedding song (cf. n. 4 above, p. 151).

46. On this vexed question, see most recently Slings, "The 'I' in Personal Archaic Lyric," and Jarcho, "Das poetische 'Ich.'" For some of the consequences this has for the distinction between choral and monodic poetry, see Russo, "Reading the Greek Lyric Poets" 709–10.

47. Dover, "The Poetry of Archilochus"; West, *Studies* 22 f.; Rösler, review of Tsagarakis, and "Personale reale o persona poetica?"; Slings, "The 'I' in Personal Archaic Lyric" 4 f.

48. Fr. 102 (impersonating a girl speaking to her mother), fr. 137 (dialogue between a man and a woman). For more examples, see Tsagarakis, *Self-Expression* 77–81.

49. Fränkel, *Early Greek Poetry* 170 n. 3.

50. Compare Bowra, *Greek Lyric Poetry* 32, on Alcman fr. 3: "We are left with the impression that the whole company is in love with her [Astymeloisa]."

51. σοὶ χάριεν μὲν εἶδος, ὄππατα δ' ... / μέλλιχ', ἔρος δ' ἐπ' ἰμέρτωι κέχυται προσώπωι; fr. 112.3 4. The context in Choricius makes it clear that these words are addressed to the bride: see Campbell, *Greek Lyric* 1:137, and Contiades-Tsitsoni, *Hymenaios* 101.

wedding songs, and her fragments about the erotic appeal of young women strongly suggests that the latter could have been performed in public and possibly by others than herself.

If we cannot rely on any formal distinction, how then do we judge which fragments qualify for a choral performance, which for a solo one, and which possibly for a mixed mode? I suggest that we study carefully the situation described in the poems, together with any traces of the addressee and possible identification marks of the speaker. In most cases, however, too little of the poems survives to make even an educated guess as to how they were performed, and we had better accept this conundrum instead of touting these fragments as prime examples of personal lyric.

3. "I" AND "WE" IN SAPPHO
AND OTHER EARLY GREEK POETRY

There is one formal feature that can throw some more light on the possible speaker of Sappho's fragments: the use of the first-person singular or plural. It is often assumed that "I" and "we" are interchangeable in archaic Greek poetry, but the situation is in fact not as simple as that. The latest studies of the Homeric language suggest that single characters normally use a first-person singular in referring to themselves, and that instances in which they use a first-person plural are to be explained as indications that they somehow want to include one or more other persons.[52] This is the case both with the individual heroes and with the poet himself.[53]

The same holds true for the archaic Greek poets. Maarit Kaimio, who examined the use of the first person in tragic choruses, mentions three different ways in which a single poet or performer can revert to a first-person plural: to include the person addressed, to include a third person, or to include a larger group (for example the state or the whole of humanity).[54]

---

52. Chantraine, *Grammaire homérique* 2:33–34; Schwyzer and Debrunner, *Griechische Grammatik* 243–44, contra Wackernagel, *Vorlesungen* 1:98 f. Notable exceptions are the possessive pronouns, which I will therefore leave out of consideration. See also Benveniste, "Relationships of Persons in the Verb" 201 f., on the use of the first-person plural in general.

53. E.g., *Il.* 2.486 (all mortals), *Od.* 1.10 (poet and his public); cf. Chantraine, *Grammaire homérique* 2:34.

54. Kaimio, *The Chorus* 30, lists five exceptions, all of which in my opinion can be explained: Solon 7.6 Diehl (= 19.6 West) and Xenophanes 2.12 Diehl (= 2.12 West) are instances of possessive pronouns (see n. 52 above); Anacreon frs. 357 and 395 are indeed troublesome cases, but "us" in fr. 357.6 can be explained as encompassing the poet and Kleoboulos (or even the whole of humanity), while in fr. 395.1 Anacreon may be suggesting that not only his own hair is turning gray but that of his audience as well. The final exception Kaimio mentions is Sappho fr. 121, but this may actually be a choral song. Stobaeus, who cites the fragment, says

Choral poets, on the other hand, use the first-person plural as well as the first-person singular to refer to the group as a whole. A quick glance at the evidence shows that they actually use the first-person singular more often than the first-person plural: Alcman's partheneion fragment 3 has only first-person singulars (nine in total), in fragment 1 in the majority of cases. This is also true for the remains of Pindar's partheneia, paeans, and dithyrambs (*Paean* 6.128 is an exception). In tragedy, according to Kaimio, there is also a preponderance of the use of the first-person singular in self-references of the chorus. This use of the first-person singular by a chorus can be explained in several ways: the chorus is perceived as one body, or each of its members is believed to be speaking for him- or herself, or the first-person singular represents the experiences of another person (e.g., Sappho) with whom the chorus identifies itself.[55]

In other words, where the number of speakers is concerned, the first-person plural is marked and the first-person singular unmarked in archaic Greek poetry.[56] A first-person singular can refer to a soloist or a chorus in virtually all circumstances, but a first-person plural only to a chorus or a soloist who wants to include others. It is therefore possibly revealing to study the use of the first-person plural in Sappho's poems. In fragments 27 and 30 (two wedding songs) and fragment 140a.1 (the hymn for Adonis) the speaker refers to itself with a first-person plural and is therefore, most likely, a chorus. By analogy, fragments 6, 19, and 121 are probably spoken by a chorus as well. Fragments 5, 21, 24a, 38, 147, and 150 are either spoken by a chorus or by a soloist (not necessarily Sappho) who wants to include one or more other persons.

Among the major fragments in Sappho's corpus there are two that make extensive use of first-person plurals: 94 and 96. In fragment 96 (a song for Atthis about a woman in Lydia), the study of the first-person speaker can be combined with an examination of the situation described in the poem. Before taking a closer look at this poem we must determine, however, where exactly it ends. Some scholars have suggested that the poem ends at line 20,[57] but the echo of lines 4–5 in line 21 makes it quite clear that the poem continues.[58] Besides, the strophes 24–26 and 27–29 (and perhaps 21–23, if

---

that it refers to the relative ages of marriage partners and it is possible that the fragment is derived from a wedding song. In any case, it is highly unlikely that Sappho spoke this fragment "in her own voice."

55. Kaimio, *The Chorus* 251; cf. Calame, *Les chœurs* 1:436–39.

56. For the terms "marked" and "unmarked," see Crystal, *Dictionary of Linguistics* 211–12; cf. Nagy, *Pindar's Homer* 5–8, and Martin, *Language of Heroes* 29–30.

57. Theander, "Studia Sapphica II" 67, followed by Schadewaldt, *Sappho* 120, and Kirkwood, *Early Greek Monody* 118. Page, *Sappho and Alcaeus* 95 n. 2, is skeptical of any break.

58. Saake, *Zur Kunst Sapphos* 174; Burnett, *Three Archaic Poets* 311; and Gentili, *Poetry and Its Public* 83.

Ἀδωνίδεον is the correct reading at the end of l. 23: see Voigt ad loc.) all end with the proper name of a god or goddess, following a pattern set by ἀ βροδοδάκτυλος Σελάννα (rosy-fingered Moon) in line 8.[59] We thus seem to be dealing with one fairly long poem (at least forty lines: both beginning and end of the poem are missing).

The first thing to be noticed is the persistent use of the first-person plural by the speaker: .. ώομεν (3), ἀμμ . [. .] (18), ἄμμι (21), and presumably χ' ἄμ[μι in line 27. Of the verb ending in line 3 we cannot say very much, except that the "we" contained in it contrasts itself with the "you" in line 4, who is probably Atthis.[60] ἀμμ- in line 18, probably the subject of the infinitive ἔλθεν, could be an inclusive "we" (speaker or speakers + Atthis), as ἄμ(μι in line 27 seems to be ("and for us ... she [Aphrodite] poured nectar"). But this can hardly be the case with ἄμμι in line 21. Again there is a contrast between the speaker ("we") on the one hand and Atthis on the other: "it is not easy for us to rival goddesses in loveliness of figure, but you have...."[61] Burnett comments about these lines that "the singer praises Atthis with the voice of a group" and "[t]he plurality is undoubted, and more important, the playful self-denigration—so like that of the girls of Alcman's *Partheneion* (or Theocritus's *Helen*)—is a sign that the group here hails Atthis as its leader,"[62] but she does not draw the obvious conclusion that the speaker is therefore most likely a group.

These words are in many ways reminiscent of Alcman's first partheneion, in which the chorus compares its leader, Hagesichora, to goddesses (though falling short of an equation; 96 f.) and her companion, Agido, to the Sun (41), while at the same time playing down their own beauty (64 ff.) and singing talents (85–87; cf. 100–101). To Hallett goes the credit of first having noticed the agonistic quality of Sappho fragment 96 and its resemblance to Alcman's partheneia.[63] Not only is the plural speaker of the poem and the way it contrasts itself to Atthis and the Lydian woman suggestive of a choral performance, but also the actions described in the poem. The woman overseas is thought of as dancing in Lydia right

59. Schubart's emendation of σελάννα for the unmetrical μήνα of the papyrus is supported by Janko, "Sappho Fr. 96.8," who also defends Lobel's suggestion that Selanna represents the personal name of the goddess (contra Page, *Sappho and Alcaeus* 90).

60. Page, *Sappho and Alcaeus* 92; Campbell, *Greek Lyric* 1:123 n. 1; Burnett, *Three Archaic Poets* 302–3; Hague, "Sappho's Consolation for Atthis" 29.

61. ε]ὔμαρ[ες μ]ὲν οὐκ ἄμμι θέαισι μόρ- / φαν ἐπή[ρατ]ον ἐξίσω- / σθαι συ[..]ρος ἔχηισθ'; fr. 96.21–23a. Atthis was indeed said to be comparable to "a goddess for all to see" in ll. 4–5, as was the woman in Lydia whom the speaker likened to the moon goddess (Selanna; ll. 8 f.).

62. Burnett, *Three Archaic Poets* 312.

63. Hallett, "Sappho and Her Social Context" 140.

now,[64] while in the past she enjoyed the singing and dancing (μόλπαι; l. 5) of Atthis. It would be very effective to think of the speakers of this poem as performing a song dance at the same time as the woman in Lydia and like Atthis in the past.[65]

In fragment 94 the use of "we" is more complex. Sappho is probably singing the song herself since her name is mentioned in line 5, although we cannot exclude the possibility of another soloist or a chorus impersonating her (see above). In the first line, Sappho or the girl who left her speaks in the first-person singular (θέλω, 1; με, 2).[66] In lines 4–5 the girl speaks (again) and uses a first-person plural (δεῖνα πεπ[όνθ]αμεν; l. 4). At first it might seem that this first person refers just to herself ("o, how we suffer"), but the echo of these words in line 11 (κάλ' ἐπάσχομεν) makes it clear that she is probably speaking both for Sappho and for herself.[67] The first-person plural in line 8 (πεδήπομεν) is exclusive and probably refers to Sappho and her companions;[68] "we" in line 26 (ἄμ]μες ἀπέσκομεν) refers again to Sappho and the girl, or to Sappho, the girl, and her companions. These companions, together with the girl and Sappho, may have formed the chorus that is mentioned at the end of line 27.[69] Their inclusion in line 8 strongly suggests that they were present at the performance of this song too, either in the audience (as commonly envisioned) or as a chorus supporting Sappho while she was singing.

The whole poem, or at least the preserved part (Sappho's speech to the woman who leaves her), is, I would suggest, concerned with choral performances. Most of the "pleasant things" of which Sappho reminds her, the stringing of flower wreaths (12 f.), putting on garlands (15 f.), wearing

---

64. νῦν δὲ Λύδαισιν ἐμπρέπεται γυναί- / κεσσιν (now she stands out among the Lydian women; 7–8). On ἐμπρέπεται as suggestive of dancing, see Calame, *Les chœurs* 1:91.

65. In l. 20 there appears to be a reference to singing (γαρύει) but it is unclear who the subject is.

66. Gomme ("Interpretations" 255–56), Burnett ("Desire and Memory" and *Three Archaic Poets* 292), Snyder (*The Woman and the Lyre* 26), and Greene ("Apostrophe and Women's Erotics" 239–40) assume that the girl speaks the first line, contra Wilamowitz (*Sappho und Simonides* 50), Page (*Sappho and Alcaeus* 82), Saake (*Zur Kunst Sapphos* 189), and Robbins ("Every Time I Look at You"), who opt for Sappho.

67. Compare Greene, "Apostrophe and Women's Erotics" 240–41. This is a perfect example of an "inclusive" first-person plural (Benveniste, "Relationships of Persons in the Verb" 202), where the speaker includes the addressee together with him- or herself (as opposed to speaker + third person). Speaker and addressee are both referred to in the next line: σ' ἀέκοισ' ἀπυλιμπάνω (I leave you against my will; fr. 94.5).

68. Page, *Sappho and Alcaeus* 78.

69. Even if this reading is uncertain, the word ψόφος (sound) at the end of l. 28 seems to indicate that some musical performance is referred to in these lines (cf. fr. 44.25).

perfumes (18 f.), and going to holy places (25, 27), where there is a "chorus" (? χόρος; 27) and "sound" (ψόφος; 28), agree with the activities of a chorus; and one can even read a linear progression into them, starting with the preparations and leading up to musical performances at temples and other places.[70] In that case Sappho would be reminding a girl of previous performances perhaps at the very moment that she and her choir, of which the girl no longer was part, were performing again a song dance, just as in fragment 96.[71]

4. SOME MAJOR FRAGMENTS:
FRAGMENTS 1, 2, 5, 16, 17, 31, 58, AND 95

So far I have provided positive arguments why certain fragments of Sappho probably were composed for choral presentations. In the following paragraphs, dealing with some of the other major fragments, I will allow myself more latitude. I will reverse Page's "natural supposition" and consider if there is any evidence or indication that these songs may have been performed with the help of choruses.

Fragment 1 was most probably sung by Sappho herself or by someone impersonating her: her name is mentioned in line 20. It is possible, however, that she was accompanied by a group of dancers, just as in fragment 94. West has argued that Sappho deliberately left the name of her beloved unmentioned so the song could be performed on different occasions.[72] This certainly would depersonalize the song. It would also lend special significance to the idea of the repetition of her love feelings in the poem (with every new performance there is the pretense of a new love).[73]

---

70. On the enigmatic ἐξίης πόθο[ν (l. 23), see Burnett, *Three Archaic Poets* 298 n. 56, and Lardinois, "Lesbian Sappho" 18. To Burnett's examples of πόθος expressing sexual desire in Sappho (frs. 36, 48), add frs. 22.11 and 102. ἀπάλαν (either a feminine genitive plural or singular accusative) could refer to a person (cf. frs. 82a, 122, 126); fr. 126 is particularly relevant in this regard: δαύοις ἀπάλας ἐτά(ι)ρας ἐν στήθεσιν (may you sleep on the bosom of your tender companion). On the other hand, already in Homer one can experience desire (ἔρος) or longing (πόθος) for other things besides sex. Since the expression ἐξίημι means "to get rid of a longing by indulging in it" (Page, *Sappho and Alcaeus* 79) and the woman lies in a bed (στρωμνή), the best alternative seems to be that the girl is taking a nap (already suggested by Wilamowitz, *Sappho und Simonides* 50); cf. *Il.* 13.636–37.

71. Fr. 94 has been identified as a "farewell song," which involves memories of previously shared experiences: see most recently Rauk, "Erinna's *Distaff*."

72. West, "Burning Sappho" 310.

73. The poem alludes to at least three different occasions on which Sappho fell in love. She suffers love pains now (25–27) and therefore calls on Aphrodite, who came to her in the past and asked her *then* what she was suffering *this time* (δηὖτε), why she was calling this time,

Fragment 2 is an obvious candidate for a choral performance either by the chorus itself or by Sappho and her chorus. If δεῦρε ... ἐπὶ τόνδε ναῦον (hither ... to this temple) is the correct reading in line 1, and there seems to be no better alternative,[74] we are probably present at a real shrine, however dreamlike this shrine is subsequently represented.[75] Athenaeus quotes the final lines of our fragment: "Come, Cypris, pouring gracefully into golden cups nectar that is mingled with our festivities,"[76] and adds what appears to be an adaptation of Sappho's subsequent line: "for these my companions and yours" (τούτοισι τοῖς ἑταίροις ἐμοῖς γε καὶ σοῖς). If this was still part of Sappho's poem, the *hetairai* associated with the speaker were probably present at the scene as well.[77] We might add that lines 13 f., about Aphrodite pouring nectar for the participants in the festivities, is reminiscent of fragment 96.26 f., where the speaker, whom I identified as a chorus, remembers how Aphrodite poured nectar for them and for Atthis.[78] On the basis of some broad similarities I would argue for a similar interpretation of fragment 17 (the so-called "Hymn to Hera"). Here the singers may be mentioned in line 14 (π]αρθ[εν-).[79] These two fragments together with fragment 140a (the Adonis hymn) suggest that at least some of Sappho's (choral) poetry was composed for ritual occasions, not unlike Alcman's partheneia.

In fragment 5, a poem about her brother Charaxus, Sappho uses, after an initial μοι (? l. 1), the first-person plural (ἄμμι; 7), probably to include

---

and whom she had to persuade this time (15–18). The threefold repetition of δηῦτε in ll. 15–18 emphasizes the recurrence of these feelings.

74. See Page, *Sappho and Alcaeus* 36; see ad loc. Voigt, *Sappho et Alcaeus,* and Campbell, *Greek Lyric* vol. 1.

75. Page, *Sappho and Alcaeus* 42, and Merkelbach, "Sappho und ihr Kreis" 28: contra West, "Burning Sappho" 317; McEvilley, "Sappho Fragment Two"; and Burnett, *Three Archaic Poets* 261 f.

76. ἔλθε (the potsherd reads ἔλοισα) Κύπρι / χρυσίαισιν ἐν κυλίκεσσιν ἄβρως / συμμεμίγμενον (the potsherd reads ὀμ⟨με⟩μείχμενον) θαλίαισι νέκταρ / οἰνοχοοῦσα (here different readings of the potsherd are proposed: Page and Campbell suggest οἰνοχόαισον; Voigt, οἰνοχόεισα); Ath. 11.463e = fr. 2.13–16.

77. In fr. 160, the speaker similarly refers to her companions as ἑταίραι, who, I have argued, may have formed a chorus (see above).

78. Page, *Sappho and Alcaeus* 44. Radt, "Sapphica" 338, adduces as a parallel and a possible echo of this passage Eur. *Tro.* 820, where the *chorus* of Trojan *women* calls on Ganymede, who "walks delicately among golden cups" (ὦ χρυσέαις ἐν οἰνοχόαις ἁβρὰ βαίνων).

79. Compare fr. 30.1 (a wedding song) for a similar self-reference: πάρθενοι. Fränkel, *Early Greek Poetry* 181, already suggested that this poem, which has been variously interpreted as an unspecified hymn to Hera (Page, *Sappho and Alcaeus* 61–62) or a *propemptikon* (Merkelbach, "Sappho und ihr Kreis" 23–25), may have been sung by a chorus.

the other members of her family and/or her friends.[80] If the poem is a *propemptikon* or "send-off" poem, as several scholars have suggested,[81] it is almost certainly performed in public.[82] I believe that this song was sung by Sappho (or someone impersonating her) in public, while her chorus danced. The *philoi* included in ἄμμι in line 7 may refer to these dancers or to members of Sappho's family in the audience.[83]

Fränkel already identified fragment 16 as possibly a choral song.[84] Its opening priamel, followed by a mythical example and praise of the "laudanda," resembles the structure of Pindar's *epinikia*.[85] Hallett added that the isolation of a few distinctive features (Anactoria's step and face in ll. 17, 18) resembles the individual compliments paid to the chorus members in Alcman's first partheneion.[86] Segal, finally, observed that the desire of the

80. Note the use of plural φίλοισι in l. 6, an almost certain supplement in light of ἔχθροισι in l. 7. In another poem about Charaxus (fr. 213 A.b.3) Sappho seems to have used again a first-person plural ("we shall send"? πεμψομε; l. 3).

81. Merkelbach, "Sappho und ihr Kreis" 24 n. 1; Bowra, *Greek Lyric Poetry* 210; and Snyder, *The Woman and the Lyre* 17–18. Governi, "Su alcuni elementi propemptici," has adduced parallels from greetings and farewell scenes both in Homer (*Od.* 6.180, 184–85; 8.461; 15.111–12, 128) and in other Greek poetry (Theog. 691–92) for several lines in the poem (3–4, 6–7).

82. Lasserre, *Sappho* 191, rather speculatively, pictures a performance in front of the whole city, with both Charaxus's friends and potential enemies present. He assumes that Charaxus was present on the basis of a possible imperative ending in l. 15, which he restores to ἐπό]νηχε (Attic: ἐπάνηχε).

83. Fr. 20 appears to derive from a similar song. In fr. 15, Sappho strikes a more critical note about her brother. If this is meant as a satirical poem, as I assume, its delivery is again best pictured in public where it would have effect. The same holds true for those poems in which she vilifies her rivals or girls who went to them: frs. 57, 68a, 71, 131, 133a, 144, 155, 178 (?), 213. I do not exclude the possibility that some of the figures mentioned in this poetry are poetic personae, similar to the stock characters presented in Archilochus's iambics (on which see West, *Studies* 25–28, and Nagy, *Pindar's Homer* 430–31).

84. Fränkel, *Early Greek Poetry* 172.

85. For a detailed comparison, see Howie, "Sappho Fr. 16," esp. 209–14. The similarity was already noted by Fränkel, "Eine Stileigenheit" 90 f., and *Early Greek Poetry* 186; and Bundy, *Studia Pindarica* 5–6. Stern's objection ("Sappho Fr. 16" 349), that the priamel is voiced too personally for choral poetry, is answered by Bundy (6 n. 19), if Pindars *epinikia* are choral (see n. 1 above).

86. Hallett, "Sappho and Her Social Context" 140–42; e.g., ll. 51–55 (about Hagesichora, the chorus leader):

ἀ δὲ χαίτα
τᾶς ἐμᾶς ἀνεψιᾶς
Ἀγησιχόρας ἐπανθεῖ
χρυσὸς [ὤ]ς ἀκήρατος·
τό τ' ἀργύριον πρόσωπον[.]

The streaming hair of my kinswoman Hagesichora blooms like pure gold; her face like silver[.]

speaker in this fragment to make her observations "known to every one" (σύνετον πόησαι / πάντι; ll. 5–6) is suggestive of public discourse.[87]

Fragment 31 can go either way. The poem certainly contains a great number of first-person singular statements, but these could refer to a chorus as well as a soloist. The emotions described can be summarized by what Alcman's chorus says about its chorus leader: με τείρει (she wears me out; fr. 1.77).[88]

Just as in this partheneion or in Sappho fragment 96, a triangle is set up between the speaker, the girl she is in love with, and a third person with whom the girl is involved (in this case a man). Note, for example, the structural opposition between that man, who "appears to be the equal of the gods" (φαίνεταί μοι κῆνος ἴσος θέοισιν / ἔμμεν'; 1–2a), and the speaker, who in lines 15–16 "appears to be little short of dying" (τεθνάκην δ' ὀλίγω 'πιδεύης / φαίνομ' ἔμ' αὔτ[ᾳ). This echo, already noted by Wilamowitz, contradicts Winkler's assertion that the man is "not an actor in the imagined scene."[89] Better Snyder: "[the man is] a foil for the exposition of the speaker's feelings; he is calmly 'godlike' in response to the woman's sweet talk and charming laugh, whereas the speaker, in the same situation, is instantly struck dumb."[90] Both in Alcman fragment 1 and in Sappho fragment 31 the rivals for the affection of the beloved are compared to gods (Alcman fr. 1.41, Sappho fr. 31.1) and they are together with the beloved (Alcman fr. 1.78–79, Sappho fr. 31.3–4), while the speakers are unable to be in her presence. In both poems the speakers are also resigned to this fact. (Sappho fr. 31 continues in l. 17 with the words "but all can be endured," ἀλλὰ πὰν τόλματον.)

As for the occasion on which this song was performed, I would not want to exclude the possibility that it was sung at a wedding, as Wilamowitz

87. Segal, "Eros and Incantation" 64. Burnett, *Three Archaic Poets* 285 n. 19, adduces two parallels for the expression, one from a Pindaric *hyporchema* (fr. 105a.1 Maehler) and one from an *epinikion* of Bacchylides (fr. 3.85).

88. For this reading (instead of με τηρεῖ) and the erotic connotation of the expression, see Page, *Alcman* 91; Merkelbach, "Sappho und ihr Kreis" 3; West, "Alcmanica" 199; Lasserre, "Ornements érotiques" 8; Calame, *Les chœurs* 2:89, and *Alcman* 339–40; and Davies, *Poetarum Melicorum* 26, contra Campbell, *Greek Lyric* 2:366. In Alcman fr. 3.61–62, Astymeloisa is said to cast glances "more meltingly than sleep or death" (τακερώτερα / δ' ὕπνω καὶ σανάτω ποτιδέρκεται).

89. Winkler, "Double Consciousness" 179. See Wilamowitz, *Sappho und Simonides* 57 (cf. Robbins, "Every Time I Look At You" 259).

90. Snyder, "Public Occasion and Private Passion" 13. Both Winkler ("Double Consciousness") and Snyder, following Page, *Sappho and Alcaeus* 20–21, insist on translating κῆνος … ὤνηρ, ὄττις with "that man, *whosoever*" instead of "that man, who" despite the evidence presented by Rydbeck, "Sappho's Φαίνεταί μοι κῆνος."

declared.[91]   The opening line is certainly reminiscent of the traditional *makarismos* of the groom.[92] Most modern interpreters, starting with Page, have discredited this view. Page's main objection is that it would be inappropriate for Sappho (or, presumably, any other speaker) to speak about the intensity of her passions for a bride on her wedding day, but this could be our modern sensitivity.[93]   In fragment 112 of Sappho a chorus describes a bride in very glowing terms, and when it says that "eros streams over her desirable face" (ἔρος δ' ἐπ' ἱμέρτῳ κέχυται προσώπῳ) it is by no means clear that this is supposed to have an effect on her husband only.[94]   Snyder objects that "a wedding song must have chiefly to do with the bride and the groom, not with the speaker's passion for one of them," but as Most remarks: "It is in fact the beauty of the unnamed girl that is the burden of the poem and the justification for its composition and performance: every detail Sappho provides is designed to testify, not to the poet's susceptibility, but to the girl's seductiveness."[95]   In

---

91. Wilamowitz, *Sappho und Simonides* 58. He was followed by Snell, "Sapphos Gedicht" 82; Schadewaldt, *Sappho* 98; Merkelbach, "Sappho und ihr Kreis" 6; Fränkel *Early Greek Poetry* 176; and Lasserre, "Ornements érotiques" 22. Welcker, "Oden" 89–90, already suggested that this poem "veranlasst ist durch die Heirath einer geliebten Schülerin," and "es mag auch eine Huldigung, Preis der Schönheit in dem hohen Ausdruck dieses Entzückens versteckt sehn" ("[this poem] is occasioned by the marriage of a favorite pupil," and "there may also be a celebration, praise of beauty hidden behind the intense expression of her enchantment"). Winkler, "Double Consciousness" 178–80, compares Sappho fr. 31 to *Od.* 6.158–61 (Odysseus's praise of Nausicaa), which in turn has been compared to a wedding song (Hague, "Ancient Greek Wedding Songs" 136–38).

92. Snell, "Sapphos Gedicht" 82–84, who, among other examples, adduces as parallels Sappho frs. 105b, 111.5. See also McEvilley, "Sappho, Fragment Thirty-One," and Latacz, "Realität und Imagination" 86–87, who on the basis of the diction conclude that ὤνηρ, ὄττις ἐνάντιός τοι / ἰσδάνει must refer to a husband. Their own suggestions that the poem refers to the wedding banquet but was performed either before (Latacz; cf. Lasserre, *Sappho* 152) or after it (McEvilley) are unnecessary and unparalleled.

93. Page, *Sappho and Alcaeus* 30 ff. This was also noted by Merkelbach, "Sappho und ihr Kreis" 9, and Segal "Eros and Incantation" 69 n. 19: "we know too little of what conventions on archaic Lesbos would or would not have permitted." There is some evidence to suggest that a bride might be expected to be the object of widespread erotic admiration at ancient Greek weddings: see Seaford, *Reciprocity and Ritual* 36 n. 25.

94. Segal, "Eros and Incantation" 69, already drew the parallel between fr. 112 and fr. 31.

95. Snyder, "Public Occasion and Private Passion" 13; Most, "Greek Lyric Poets" 97. Most continues with an observation, still too often ignored in modern interpretations of archaic Greek poetry: "Sappho's poem bears no trace of the 'egotistical sublime,' of the narcissistic fascination with the private self so characteristic of some modern poetry: if we remember its social frame, we shall be fairer to her—and to the other Greek melic poets as well." Cf. Rydbeck, "Sappho's φαίνεταί μοι κῆνος" 161–62, and Russo, "Reading the Greek Lyric Poets" 707–8.

Alcman's partheneia and in Sappho fragment 112 the women are similarly praised through a declaration of the effect their beauty has on the speaker. Fragment 31, whether performed at a wedding or not, is really an *enkomion*.[96]

Fragment 58 is generally not considered one of the major fragments, but it is significant because, like fragments 21 and 22, it is suggestive of exchanges between Sappho (or another soloist) and the chorus. Line 11 mentions *paides* with beautiful gifts, either of the deep- or violet-bosomed Muses.[97] The speaker (a woman) says that she is overcome by old age and no longer able to do like the young fawns (probably to dance).[98] A similar-looking poem is preserved among Alcman's fragments. Here the speaker (Alcman himself, according to Antigonus, who preserved the fragment) addresses a group of "honey-tongued, holy-voiced girls," telling them that "his limbs no longer can carry" him.[99] I believe that Sappho in this fragment conjures up the same image and that the *paides* of line 11 make up the chorus that is dancing while she (or another performer) is singing.[100]

---

96. Lasserre, "Ornements érotiques" 23, who argues that frs. 47 and 130 were part of similar *enkomia*, and further notes that the "I" person in these poems has more in common with the speaker in choral than in monodic poetry (7 n. 6, 21; cf. Nagy, *Pindar's Homer* 371). Burnett, *Three Archaic Poets* 235, and Race, "'That Man' in Sappho fr. 31" 98–101, compare fr. 31 to Pindar's encomium for Theoxenus (fr. 123 Maehler), where there is also a third person who "meets the liquid glance that gleams from Theoxenus's eye and fails to swell with passion," whereas the speaker, I, "like wax in sun's high heat melt" (Burnett's translation). Compare also Odysseus's words to Nausicaa in *Od.* 6.160–61, which, just as Pindar's, are not intended as a declaration of love but as praise.

97. See Di Benedetto, "Il tema della vecchiaia" 147–48, and Voigt, *Sappho et Alcaeus* ad loc. It is not unlikely that this line constitutes the actual beginning of the poem: Di Benedetto 147; Gallavotti, *Saffo e Alceo* 1:113. Page, *Sappho and Alcaeus* 129, also starts the poem on this line.

98. ὄρχ]ησῃ': Edmonds's conjecture in l. 16, cited by Voigt, *Sappho et Alcaeus*, and Campbell, *Greek Lyric* vol. 1, ad loc.

99. οὔ μ' ἔτι, παρσενικαὶ μελιγάρυες ἰαρόφωνοι / γυῖα φέρην δύναται; Alcman fr. 26.1–2a. Compare Sappho fr. 58.15: γόνα δ' [ο]ὐ φέροισι. Antigonus (cited by Campbell, *Greek Lyric* vol. 2, ad loc.) further specifies that Alcman speaks this poem "being weak from old age and unable to whirl about with the choirs and the girls' dancing" (φησὶν γὰρ ἀσθενὴς ὢν διὰ τὸ γῆρας καὶ τοῖς χοροῖς οὐ δυνάμενος συμπεριφέρεσθαι οὐδὲ τῇ τῶν παρθένων ὀρχήσει). Calame, *Alcman* 474, already noted the parallel with Sappho fr. 58.

100. Sappho fr. 21 describes a similar situation (χρόα γῆρας ἤδη; 21.6b = 58.13b) and here it is clear that we are dealing with some kind of an exchange, for in ll. 11–12 the speaker calls on another woman to "take up" the lyre (λάβοισα, l. 11; cf. fr. 22.9–11) and "sing about the violet-robed one" (Aphrodite, according to Campbell, *Greek Lyric* vol. 1, ad loc.; otherwise perhaps a bride: cf. fr. 30.5). According to Di Benedetto, "Il tema della vecchiaia" 148–49, l. 11 of fr. 58 opened with an invitation to the chorus to sing (e.g., γεραίσετε) and l. 12 contained the instruction to "take up the song-loving, clear-sounding lyre" (... λάβοισαι] φιλάοιδον λιγύραν χελύνναν).

Fragment 95 portrays a conversation Sappho (or another woman) had with a woman in the past (probably Gongyla, whose name is mentioned in l. 4). This situation is reminiscent of fragment 94 and it may have been performed under similar circumstances.[101]

Most of these reconstructions are only suggestions. Ultimately it is impossible to prove that a particular song was sung by a chorus or by Sappho herself, with or without the help of choral dancers, but I hope to have shown that a choral performance of these songs is at least a serious possibility.

5. SAPPHO'S PUBLIC POETRY

I have argued that three modes of performances can be detected in Sappho's poems, all public:

She sang while a chorus of young women danced (e.g., frs. 1, 5, 94, 95, 160?).
The young women did both the singing and the dancing (most epithalamia, frs. 2, 16, 17, 31?, 96).
Exchanges between Sappho or another soloist and the group (frs. 21, 22, 58, 140a).

It is possible that, besides these more or less choral songs, there were genuine monodic songs, performed only by Sappho herself: after all, the *Suda* speaks of Sappho's monodies as well as lyric songs (above). If so, we must ask ourselves where these monodic songs were performed. We really know of only one occasion where more or less monodic poetry was performed in the archaic period: symposia.[102] It could be that Sappho composed some songs for symposia, as did Praxilla (see below), but I can find no trace of them in the remaining fragments, with the exception perhaps of some poems that were composed for the wedding banquet.[103]

---

101. Cf. Page, *Sappho and Alcaeus* 85.

102. Even here the singer could be accompanied by another musician (West, *Studies* 12), and there were group songs as well as exchanges between participants at a symposium (see n. 35 above). Reference is sometimes made to Achilles, who in book 9 of the *Iliad* plays to himself on the lyre and sings about the κλέα ἀνδρῶν (e.g., Kirkwood, *Early Greek Monody* 15), but this is a unique passage that is meant to demonstrate Achilles' isolation from the community in which epic poetry is supposed to be performed. Cf. Hainsworth, *The Iliad*: "An amateur singer . . . who is also a member of the patron class is not really paralleled" (88) and "the verisimilitude of such representations is called into question" (37).

103. On *hymenaioi* performed at the wedding banquet, see n. 4. Parker's comparison of themes in Sappho's poems with those of the other archaic Greek poets, which are intended to show that Sappho's poetry was composed for banquets ("Sappho Schoolmistress" 344–45), are of some interest but they do not reveal how or where Sappho's poems were sung. His inclusion of Alcman among the examples shows that references to feasts, sacrificial meals, garlands, myrrh, and wine are as much at home in choral poetry intended to be performed by young

We may conclude that a monodic performance, by which I mean a single performer accompanying herself on the lyre and singing to a group, is not a likely option for Sappho's poetry. I have argued that Sappho's poems about young women do not fit the monodic mold any more than her wedding songs do or Alcman's partheneia. I have further argued that there are traces of a plural voice in these poems and many parallels with choral poetry (in particular Alcman). The testimonia and Sappho's own poems speak about a variety of performances but not about monodic performances (with the exception of the *Suda*, which mentions monodic songs *in addition to* nine books of other lyric songs). Finally, I disputed the idea that any archaic Greek poet, male or female, would have composed poetry for delivery to a group of young girls in the privacy of her own home, and I suggested that this view of Sappho, which is commonly accepted, first originated in the French salons of the seventeenth and eighteenth century.

By arguing for a more public delivery of Sappho's poems, I do not want to deny the important differences in tone and subject matter between Sappho and most male poets,[104] but instead of seeing this as a difference between a public (male) and a private (female) world (as do Stigers [Stehle], Winkler, and Snyder), I would like to suggest that this reflects a difference between two distinct public voices.[105] Only in this way can we make sense of the many similarities between Alcman's partheneia and Sappho's poetry. I believe that

---

women in public as in so-called sympotic poetry. (I say "so-called" sympotic poetry, because the term is often used for poems whose performance circumstances are really unknown but are assigned to symposia simply for lack of a better suggestion.) It is nevertheless possible to make a distinction between Sappho fr. 2 and the other poems that Parker (344) cites as speaking about a θαλία (feast), without resorting to "special pleading" (345). Only in Sappho does the speaker call upon a god to come "hither ... to this shrine" (δεῦρυ ... ἐπὶ τόνδε ναῦον) in order to share in the festivities. This, of course, does not mean that Sappho's poetry could not have been *later* performed at symposia or banquets: test. 10, Plut. *Quaest. conv.* 622c; cf. Rösler, *Dichter und Gruppe* 101 n. 171.

104. Here recent scholarship that has adopted a feminist perspective has done much to further our understanding of Sappho's poetry: duBois, "Sappho and Helen," and *Sowing the Body* 26–27 (with an important caveat on p. 29); Stigers [Stehle], "Sappho's Private World"; Stehle, "Sappho's Gaze"; Winkler, "Double Consciousness"; Snyder, "Public Occasion and Private Passion"; and Greene, "Apostrophe and Women's Erotics." See also Lasserre, "Ornements érotiques" 30; Hallett, "Sappho and Her Social Context" 138; Burnett, *Three Archaic Poets,* esp. 225–26, 288; Svenbro, "La stratégie de l'amour"; and Race, "Sappho, *Fr.* 16." Skinner, "Woman and Language," in my opinion, goes too far in insisting on the independence of Sappho's poetry.

105. These public voices appear to be gender-specific as far as contents and performance are concerned, but they are not necessarily composed by only men or only women. Alcman composed "maiden songs," as did Pindar (frs. 94a–104d Maehler), Simonides, and Bacchylides (Calame, *Les chœurs* 2:167–74), while Praxilla was credited with writing *skolia* (Snyder, *The Woman and the Lyre* 55–56), a genre that was closely associated with the male domain of the symposium.

in the future it will be fruitful to compare Sappho's poetry more closely with Alcman's partheneia,[106] the poetry of other female poets,[107] and the public voices of Greek women in general. Anthropological studies of women's public or poetic voices in other cultures may be illuminating as well.[108] One of the public speech genres associated with women both in archaic and in rural Greece today was the lament.[109] There are echoes of this speech genre in Sappho's hymns (fr. 140a), in her wedding songs (fr. 114), and in a series of songs that are preserved among her "other" poetry.[110] No matter how one reads Sappho's songs, it is important to realize that most of them probably were intended to be performed in public with the help of choruses.

106. For a beginning, see Calame, *Les chœurs* 1:361 ff., 2:94–97; Hallett, "Sappho and Her Social Context" 139–42; and Cavallini, *Presenza di Saffo* 17–20. The differences between Alcman's partheneia and Sappho's poetry to which Stehle ("Romantic Sensuality, Poetic Sense" 147–49) and Skinner ("Woman and Language" 186–87) have pointed are noteworthy but do not measure up against the many similarities. See Lardinois, "Subject and Circumstance" 73 n. 59.

107. Here Rauk's article, "Erinna's *Distaff*, " deserves special mention. He sees in Sappho fr. 94 and Erinna's *Distaff* a generic type of farewell addresses of women. We may also point out that Praxilla (fr. 747), like Sappho (fr. 140a), composed a hymn for Adonis, a typical women's cult (Burkert, *Greek Religion* 177; Winkler, *Constraints of Desire* 188 f.), and that Telesilla (fr. 717), like Sappho (test. 21, 41; fr. 44a), composed a hymn to Artemis, a goddess presiding over various facets of women's lives including the initiation of young girls (Burkert 151 and Calame, *Les chœurs* 1:174f.).

108. For example, on Crete women can compete with men in witty, poetic responses (*mandinadhes*), mostly of a sexual nature (Herzfeld, *The Poetics of Manhood* 142–46), not unlike the exchange found in Sappho fr. 137. On Madagascar, women are associated with direct, open expressions of anger (Keenan, "Norm-Makers, Norm-Breakers" 137–39); cf. Homer *Il.* 20.252–54 and, perhaps, some of Sappho's satirical poetry. Nagy, *Poetry as Performance* chap. 4, compares Sappho fr. 1 to female initiation songs of the Navajo and Apache.

109. On archaic Greece, see Alexiou, *The Ritual Lament*, esp. 4–14, and Martin, *Language of Heroes* 87; on rural Greece today, see Alexiou, esp. 36–51, and Caraveli, "The Bitter Wounding."

110. Frs. 94, 95, 96. Merkelbach, "Sappho und ihr Kreis" 12 f., refers to these poems as "Trostgedichte" (consolation poems) or "Trostlieder" (consolation songs)—"ähnlich wie wir auch heute noch Leidtragende nach einem Todesfall zu trösten . . . suchen" (similar to the way we try still today to console the afflicted after a death). Stigers [Stehle], "Sappho's Private World" 55–58, describes them as "mourn[ing]" the elusiveness of happiness and taking as their subject "the loss of the beloved by parting," comparing them to fr. 140a (the song for Adonis). Rauk, "Erinna's *Distaff* " 110, actually calls fr. 94 a "lament" and compares it to other laments in Greek literature. In fr. 96, Atthis, the addressee, may be dead, if χάρι σαῖ is the correct reading in l. 17 (cf. *Il.* 22.210–11; *Od.* 4.502; Alc. fr. 38A.7), as is Baucis in Erinna's *Distaff* (n. 107 above).

PART IV

Women's Erotics

ELEVEN

Woman and Language in Archaic Greece, or, Why is Sappho a Woman?

Marilyn B. Skinner

The challenge posed by French theory to received ideas of female consciousness and self-representation has emerged during the past decade as the most urgent intellectual problem confronting feminist literary critics on this side of the Atlantic. Historically, American feminist criticism has been based on an empirical notion of authorship and a concomitant view of literary texts as repositories of gender ideology. During its earliest phases, then, practitioners sought to expose the misogyny of male-authored literature and to posit an alternative female poetics, as contained in a new canon of recovered women writers. Emanating from the Continent, radical attacks on the liberal humanist creed now seem to call that "fundamental feminist gesture" into question.[1] The threat is all the more insidious for being incorporated

An oral version of this essay was delivered at the "Feminist Theory and the Classics" panel presented on 30 December 1990 at the 122nd annual meeting of the American Philological Association in San Francisco, California. I wish to thank the panel co-organizers Nancy Sorkin Rabinowitz and Amy Richlin, my fellow presenters Marilyn A. Katz and Barbara K. Gold, and the two respondents Judith Hallett and Kristina Passman, as well as many members of the audience, for a wealth of stimulating suggestions. Subsequently, in her role as editor, Nancy Rabinowitz carefully assisted me in blocking out a tighter, more linear argument. I also owe a great debt to Eva Stehle and Jane Snyder, who read draft versions of the paper and commented extensively on them. Lastly, my special thanks to David Halperin, whose painstaking efforts to help improve a paper disputing his position manifest an exceptional scholarly generosity, feminist in every sense. This essay was originally published in slightly different form as "Woman and Language in Archaic Greece, or, Why Is Sappho a Woman?" in *Feminist Theory and the Classics*, edited by N. S. Rabinowitz and A. Richlin, 125–44 (New York: Routledge, 1993).

1. Jardine, *Gynesis* 50–64. On the French challenge, see Alcoff, "Cultural Feminism"; Draine, "Refusing the Wisdom"; on traditional American feminist criticism, see Todd, *Feminist Literary History*.

in critiques of patriarchal discourse undertaken by Hélène Cixous, Luce Irigaray, and Julia Kristeva—thinkers who, insofar as they themselves are reckoned as "feminists," might be presumed sympathetic to an engaged feminist enterprise.[2]

Although Cixous, Irigaray, and Kristeva differ considerably with respect to other issues, they jointly insist that woman is excluded from dominant structures of representation.[3] Taking Lacanian psychoanalysis as their methodological point of departure, all three contend that sexual difference is inscribed into Western symbolic systems at the most rudimentary level. Language in a patriarchal culture originates with man, who locates himself as discursive subject and positive reference point of thought; woman is relegated simultaneously to the negative pole of any conceptual antithesis and to a subordinate object position. She can be defined only in terms of her alterity, named in a way that inevitably reduces itself to "not-man." Linguistic transgression, then, must necessarily precede and facilitate her political resistance.

What shape female linguistic transgression might take is, however, a contested matter. Kristeva's formulation is the least oppositional. Rejecting the possibility of a biologically based female identity, she argues instead that subversion of the rational symbolic process occurs only through irruption of a repressed linguistic core, the "semiotic"—affiliated, though not explicitly identified, with the cultural category of the feminine.[4] Cixous, for her part, advocates the active production of *écriture féminine*, a mode of writing informed by sexual difference yet not absolutely restricted to women. Characterized by a lyric openness and a lack of conventional, logical organization—qualities also imputed to the tender utterances of the lost pre-Oedipal mother— the texts of *écriture féminine* are intended to challenge the "phallogocentric" symbolic order directly.[5] Lastly, Irigaray postulates an exclusively female

2. Key passages from the writings of Cixous, Irigaray, and Kristeva were conveniently selected and translated by Marks and de Courtivron, *New French Feminisms*. The difficulties French feminist theory poses for an Anglo-American feminist criticism that regards the text as the representation of an author's personal subjectivity and experience are explored in the classic debate between Kamuf, "Replacing Feminist Criticism," and Miller, "The Text's Heroine." For subsequent elaborations, see, among others, Weedon, *Feminist Practice* 165–66; J. Butler, *Gender Trouble* 1–34; Flax, *Thinking Fragments* 168–78; and Hekman, *Gender and Knowledge* 144–51. Strategies for transcending the ensuing dilemma are put forward by Homans, "Feminist Criticism and Theory"; Alcoff, "Cultural Feminism"; and de Lauretis, *Alice Doesn't*, "The Essence of the Triangle," and "Eccentric Subjects." For further insight into the relevance of French feminist theory to feminist criticism of classical texts, the reader is directed to Gold, "'But Ariadne Was Never There.'"

3. Moi, *Sexual/Textual Politics*.
4. Moi, *Sexual/Textual Politics* 163–67; cf. Hekman, *Gender and Knowledge* 87–90.
5. A. Jones, "Writing the Body."

discourse (*parler femme*) grounded in women's specific libidinal economy. Only by speaking (as) woman, in a language that, like female sexual pleasure itself, is "plural, autoerotic, diffuse, undefinable within the familiar rules of (masculine) logic"[6] can women affirm a bodily desire excluded from standard patriarchal speech.

Of the three positions summarized above, Irigaray's is obviously the most immediately vulnerable to charges of "essentialism," that is, the questionable presupposition of an ontological essence or nature in which all women participate by virtue of their sex.[7] Leading exponents of feminist theory are consequently more and more inclined to treat her assertions nonreferentially, not as factual pronouncements but as rhetorical ploys for displacement of fixed conceptual schemes.[8] Due, however, to her polemic interrogation of Platonic epistemology, which we will examine below, Irigaray has won an unexpected following among feminist students of Greco-Roman culture. With classicists her declarations tend to take on literal force. Adopted as investigative premises, they in turn give rise to tediously homogeneous readings of the Greco-Roman literary tradition, readings whose consequences for the study of women in antiquity are potentially disastrous. In this essay, I attempt both to alert my colleagues to the danger of arriving, via Irigaray, at such a theoretical impasse and to outline a more positive way of conceptualizing the ancient literary record, using Sappho as my exemplary text.

Alone among Continental feminists, Irigaray glances back to the temporal origins of patriarchal discourse, seeking to expose its roots as well as its controlling principles. In *Speculum of the Other Woman*, she grapples with the foundation legend of male linguistic hegemony.[9] Western cultural erasure of woman as speaking subject commences, according to her, in fourth-century B.C.E. Greece, receiving primary metaphysical expression in Plato's "Myth of the Cave" (*Resp.* 7.514a–517a). In that authoritative text the cave is a "metaphor of the inner space, of the den, the womb or *hystera*, sometimes of the earth" (243) and thus linked, by extension, to infancy and prelogical symbiosis with the mother. In Socrates' eyes, it is the prison from which one escapes in order to ascend to the full light of masculine Being and Truth, the abode of the Father. That initiatory pilgrimage once accomplished, return to the dark female abyss is unthinkable: in future, the sole licit relationships will be those between father and son, or philosopher and pupil. "But what becomes of the mother from now on?" asks Irigaray (315). She vanishes

---

6. Burke, "Irigaray" 289.

7. Fuss, *Essentially Speaking* 56–58; Butler, *Gender Trouble* 9–13.

8. Gallop, *Thinking through the Body* 92–99; Fuss, *Essentially Speaking* 71–72; Schor, "This Essentialism."

9. Irigaray, *Speculum* 243–364. Further citations will be given in parentheses in the text.

from sight, for "man has become blind by dint of projecting (himself) into the brilliance of that Good, into the purity of that Being, into that mirage of the Absolute" (362). Obsession with the abstract ideal banishes woman's specificity to the void of the unintelligible.

What results from male abolition of female presence is an underlying "sexual indifference" in the putative representation of gender relations.[10] In a second treatise, *This Sex Which Is Not One*, Irigaray elucidates that notion. Statements purporting to describe an encounter between male and female subjects in fact record the mere interaction of a male subject with externalized and objectified aspects of himself projected onto "woman," a counterfeit token of dissimilarity. Woman's actual subjectivity is ineffable, since in the male "sexual imaginary" she can be no more than "a more or less obliging prop for the enactment of man's fantasies."[11] Later it is stated categorically that *"the feminine occurs only within models and laws devised by male subjects*. Which implies that there are not really two sexes, but only one. A single practice and representation of the sexual" (86; Irigaray's italics). Irigaray's perception of an intrinsic uniformity underlying representations of pseudo-heterosexual congress between man and his manufactured "opposite" is encapsulated in her well-known pun *hom(m)osexualité*. As Gallop concludes: "Irigaray has discovered that phallic sexual theory, male sexual science, is homosexual, a sexuality of sames, of identities, excluding otherness."[12]

Irigaray's portrayal of Platonic idealism, and post-Platonic Greek discourse in general, as a unitary thought system from which the female is summarily excluded resonates powerfully with the misgivings of feminist classical scholars, long accustomed to apologize for the "male-centeredness" of surviving primary sources.[13] It should come as no surprise, then, that recent important work on Greco-Roman gender ideology betrays a deep indebtedness to her ideas. Page duBois, although undertaking what she herself labels "a critique of psychoanalytic theory and its ahistorical, universal claims about gendering," finally revamps Irigaray's contentions into a quasi-historical scenario in which Plato's texts become the instrument whereby woman's distinct metaphorical role in pre-Socratic discourse is usurped by masculinity.[14] Similarly, Georgia Nugent discovers beneath Ovid's facile play with the titillating figure of the hermaphrodite a hom(m)o-sexual "reflection

---

10. Gallop, *The Daughter's Seduction* 58; de Lauretis, "Sexual Indifference."

11. Irigaray, *This Sex* 25. Further citations will be given in parentheses in the text.

12. Gallop, *The Daughter's Seduction* 84.

13. Culham, "Ten Years after Pomeroy" 15–17; cf. Culham, "Decentering the Text," and responses.

14. DuBois, *Sowing the Body* 3, 169–83.

of the (masculine) Same."[15] As the most conspicuous application of Irigaray's ideas by a trained classicist, though, David Halperin's essay "Why Is Diotima a Woman?" merits lengthier consideration.[16]

The Diotima of Plato's *Symposium* is, Halperin argues, a rhetorical trope. Plato puts the Socratic model of philosophical intercourse into the mouth of a prophetess in order to call attention to this model's novel qualities of reciprocity and procreativity. Within the male-structured Greek gender system, those elements had formerly been excluded from masculine eroticism and subsumed wholly under female sexuality. In the *Symposium*, that culturally prescribed feminine "difference" is reappropriated, in an intellectualized and sanitized form, for males. What is true for Diotima, Halperin concludes, also obtains for any other Greek inscription of "woman": in the ancient representational economy the female serves as "an alternate male identity whose constant accessibility to men lends men a fullness and a totality that enables them to dispense (supposedly) with otherness altogether."[17] For Halperin, then, as for anyone else who takes Irigaray's account of Plato's myth literally, it is impossible to find any hint of authentic female reality in the Greek signifier "woman." When an Athenian man speaks to his fellow symposiasts, *Woman*, the universal, does not exist—as Irigaray's mentor Lacan disquietingly asserted.[18]

One dubious effect of this line of reasoning about language is that studies of female literary production are rendered otiose. *Gynocritics*, defined by Elaine Showalter as the investigation of the "history, themes, genres, and structures of literature by women,"[19] was, as I have previously stated, a driving preoccupation of Anglo-American feminist criticism in its earlier developmental stage, during the middle to late 1970s. What energized and justified that sociohistorically based method of inquiry was the assumption that texts composed by women reflect the peculiar conditions of women's lived experience within given cultures, ordinarily the shared experience of a "subculture" marginal to the male public world.[20] According to this hypothesis, female subcultures, especially in preindustrial societies, are wholly occupied with the vital activities customarily assigned to women by a cultural division of labor—the tasks of domesticity, including sexuality, reproduction, and nurturing, and the ceremonies surrounding the human life cycle. On an emotional level, the energies of participants are meanwhile channeled

15. Nugent, "This Sex" 176.
16. Halperin, *One Hundred Years of Homosexuality* 13–51.
17. Ibid., 151.
18. Lacan, "God and the *Jouissance*" 144.
19. Showalter, "Toward a Feminist Poetics" 128.
20. Ibid., 131–32

into female bonding networks, primarily ties among blood and marriage kin, and into attachments, sometimes passionate, between friends.[21] Discourses originating in the female subculture address such concerns, which are separate and distinct from those of males in the same society. Real-life female experience therefore engenders a "female perspective" encapsulated in women's texts. This entire set of commonsense propositions has now been called into question by apostles of French theory.[22] If the Western symbolic system is a male-ordered construct, as they believe, the feminine specificity putatively contained in women's writing must be an illusion.

Let us consider a practical application of that skeptical postulate. Despite its patriarchal bent, Greek society nurtured a lively and continuous tradition of female authorship, extending from the archaic age well into the Hellenistic period.[23] A canonical roster of major women poets, arguably compiled by the learned scholars of Alexandria, was in circulation by Augustan times.[24] Sappho of Lesbos, who flourished approximately 600 B.C.E., headed the list as Homer's counterpart, a complementary model of excellence for her sex (*AP* 7.15). Hellenistic women writers like Erinna and Nossis expressly looked back to Sappho as their exemplar.[25] Applying gynocritic methods to these texts readily illustrates how books by women "continue each other."[26]

Feminist classical scholars have just begun to direct intense critical attention toward Sappho's neglected followers. Continuing that scholarly project would help to validate the creative ventures of contemporary women. It is no secret that texts signed by females are habitually targeted for ideologically motivated suppression. To contemplate the numbers of women thus far silenced is utterly disheartening.[27] But if ancient female poets did sustain a distinct creative tradition, no matter how minor, within such a male-dominated society as that of ancient Greece, patriarchal discourses evidently do not always succeed in drowning women out. Conversely, if the Greek conceptual system is construed as inherently masculine, one must necessarily concede that no Greek woman, not even Sappho, was ever able to transcend androcentric cultural categories.[28] The "female voice" in antiquity would turn out to be a male voice with a slight foreign inflection. Under such circumstances, work on the female literary tradition might well be abandoned as useless, insofar as women's texts could no longer claim

21. Smith-Rosenberg, "The Female World."
22. Jardine, *Gynesis* 40–41; Moi, *Sexual/Textual Politics* 75–80.
23. Snyder, *The Woman and the Lyre.*
24. Antipater of Thessalonica *AP* 9.26; cf. Baale, *Studia in Anytes* 7–9.
25. Rauk, "Erinna's *Distaff*"; Skinner, "Sapphic Nossis."
26. Woolf, *A Room of One's Own* 84.
27. See Russ, *How to Suppress Women's Writing;* Olsen, *Silences.*
28. DuBois, *Sowing the Body,* 29.

to reflect a separate, gender-specific sensibility. This would surely be a discouraging outcome for a feminist scholar seeking to uncover scanty traces of ancient women's subjectivity. For the aspiring woman writer, its corollary implications are even more disturbing.

Before acquiescing in such methodological injunctions, however, we ought to scrutinize French feminist theory more intently. First of all, readers otherwise favorably disposed to a psychoanalytic approach are increasingly troubled by its resolute ahistoricism. Despite her ostensible recourse to origins in setting up Plato as the *ktistēs* of Western metaphysics, Irigaray elsewhere repudiates history as just another hom(m)o-sexual construct (*This Sex* 126, 171–72), a move harshly criticized by Moi.[29] In more sweeping terms, Weedon protests that an investigation of gender confined to the level of textual analysis, "irrespective of the discursive context and the power/knowledge relations of the discursive field within which textual relations are located," is simply inadequate as feminist practice. Similarly, Todd charges that French theory's abstraction of sexual difference from historical flux and change entails a de facto "erasing of the history of women which we have only just begun to glimpse." The argument is taken one step further by Jane Flax, who contends that women's obvious exclusion from public discourse is actually the pragmatic result of a political inequality shaped by material conditions: "culture *is* masculine, not as the effect of language but as the consequence of actual power relations to which men have far more access than women."[30]

Under pressure of these critiques, the denial of history implicit in French feminist theory emerges as both reductionist and perverse. We classical scholars ought to ask ourselves, then, whether adoption of such a timeless model of linguistic gender asymmetry is not so much at odds with our own disciplinary mission as to involve us in embarrassing self-contradiction. For we are students of Greco-Roman civilization, that is, of a given sociotemporal milieu; and we are consequently bound to address the issue of language and gender (or any other issue, for that matter) with proper attention to the conditions of life in particular ancient environments, as far as we are able to ascertain them. History is, by definition, what we are mandated to do.

Second, even within that psychoanalytic model, language itself is not entirely monolithic. Though they place control of logic and normative discourse on the side of the male, Kristeva, Cixous, and Irigaray all make some provision for a disruptive impulse stemming from the female—or from whatever passes for "female" within their respective systems. We have seen that for Kristeva "woman" can be reintroduced into language as that which

29. Moi, *Sexual/Textual Politics* 147–49.
30. Weedon, *Feminist Practice* 166; Todd, *Feminist Literary History* 84; Flax, *Thinking Fragments* 103.

escapes signification, while for Cixous she resurfaces as the pre-Oedipal mother making fond inarticulate noises. For Irigaray, at least in one chapter of *This Sex Which Is Not One*, she materializes in a surprisingly familiar form: as embodied women speaking among themselves.[31] Responding to an interviewer's question about the possibility of evolution within the masculine cultural and political realm, Irigaray cites the new discourses—marginal, to be sure—created by women's liberation movements: "Something is being elaborated there that has to do with the 'feminine,' with what women-among-themselves might be, what a 'women's society' might mean" (*This Sex* 127). At a slightly later point in the interview (135), she expands on that suggestion:

> There may be a speaking-among-women that is still a speaking (as) man but that may also be the place where a speaking (as) woman may dare to express itself. It is certain that with women-among-themselves ... in these places of women-among-themselves, something of a speaking (as) woman is heard. This accounts for the desire or the necessity of sexual nonintegration: the dominant language is so powerful that women do not dare to speak (as) woman outside the context of nonintegration.

Tentative as this formulation may be, Irigaray in my opinion has cleared a space within her own Lacanian cosmos for real-life women interacting as speaking subjects. And though she has contemporary liberation movements in mind, her notion of "places of women-among-themselves" can surely be extended to other communities of women, especially those sheltered to some degree, as a result of unusual cultural circumstances, from patriarchal modes of thought.

I therefore propose to negotiate the restoration of "woman" into the Greek literary tradition as the historical consequence of "women-among-themselves speaking (as) woman," that is, producing woman-specific discourses. In the poetry of Sappho, semiotic analysis has uncovered an elaborate complex of coding strategies differing perceptibly from those of the dominant symbolic order.[32] Open, fluid, and polysemous—and hence conspicuously nonphallic—those strategies are employed to convey the passionate sexual longing felt by a woman—the first-person speaker designated as "Sappho"—for a female companion, who is often but not always physically absent.[33] To me they supply fragmentary but nevertheless arresting evidence

31. For an excellent analysis of the scheme of practical politics outlined in this passage, see Fuss, *Essentially Speaking* 66–70.

32. Stigers [Stehle], "Sappho's Private World"; Burnett, *Three Archaic Poets*; Rissman, *Love as War*; Stehle, "Sappho's Gaze"; Winkler, *The Constraints of Desire* 162–87.

33. Stigers [Stehle], "Sappho's Private World" 47–48; Snyder, "Public Occasion and Private Passion."

that on archaic Lesbos a socially segregated group of girls and women devised its own symbolic system and set of discursive conventions, formally
adapted to the expression of female homoerotic desire and exercised in the
composition and delivery of oral poetry.

That repertory of poetic discourses has been assumed throughout antiquity and down to the present day to be wholly Sappho's own invention,
designed to articulate private feelings; for convenience's sake, it may even
yet be termed a "Sapphic" voice.[34] One need not deny the poetic genius
of the flesh-and-blood singer capable of handling her material with such
artistic economy that it rapidly passed from mouth to mouth throughout the
Greek world and survived intact for many centuries. Yet, given the normal
function of the archaic Greek poet as appointed spokesperson for his or her
community, it is far more likely that Sappho's self-stylization as desiring *ego*,
along with her extensive stock of themes, verse forms and melodies, tropes
and imagery, was largely traditional, a product of many generations of local
creative endeavor. Thus Sappho would have inherited both her social role
and her craft from a long line of female predecessors.[35]

By approaching these songs as social discourses, we avoid the sticky
problems of representation involved in treating a text as the faithful mirror
of an author's unique subjectivity. To redeploy Showalter's concept, then,
Sappho's poetry will here be presumed to distill the shared impressions of a
historically contextualized "subculture," refracting to some degree women's
lived realities, their confrontations with experience, albeit only in synthetic
and highly idealized form. Yet in affording us insights into patterns of
social ideology promulgated among a group of elite Greek women on

34. For an important reading of Sappho as spokesperson for a group, rather than an
individual, consciousness, see Hallett, "Sappho and Her Social Context." In a new study
(Hallett, in progress), subsequent Roman appropriations of Sappho's mode of homoerotic
discourse are surveyed and comprehensively identified as a "Sapphic tradition." While I
am deeply indebted to Hallett for the concept of an ancient gender-specific style of literary
expression capable of articulating female desire, my purpose here is not primarily to defend
her revisionist approach to Sappho nor to trace out the poet's impact on later literature, but
rather to urge my colleagues to forgo constructions of ancient literary history that eradicate
Sappho's achievement and its continuing influence.

35. Plausible arguments for a continuous Greek lyric tradition extending as far back
as the eighth century B.C.E. are supplied by R. L. Fowler, *The Nature of Early Greek Lyric*
9–13. It is worth recalling Virginia Woolf's observation that "if you consider any great
figure of the past, like Sappho, like the Lady Murasaki, like Emily Brontë, you will
find that she is an inheritor as well as an originator, and has come into existence because women have come to have the habit of writing naturally" (*A Room of One's Own*
113). Though I would question the use of the term "writing" in Sappho's case, I believe Woolf's intuitive perception of her as heir to a female poetic tradition is probably
accurate.

sixth-century B.C.E. Lesbos, this body of texts may still prove immeasurably valuable for feminist historical inquiry.[36]

Sappho's friends were able to "speak (as) woman among themselves" precisely because they were not readers. In contemporary postindustrial societies, where males are educationally advantaged, control of electronically based information systems is guarded, and writing is still the primary mode of communication, the ordination of "man" as unmarked subject of discourse is probably inevitable. In predominantly oral societies, on the other hand, women do have readier access to the cultural tradition insofar as it is conveyed by word of mouth. The nucleus of a cultural heritage is, according to Goody and Watt, "the particular range of meanings and attitudes which members of any society attach to their verbal symbols."[37] But that collection of meanings is always open to modification. Within tightly integrated nonliterate societies, then, women can verbally intervene in dominant symbolic systems and append additional "feminine" values to signifiers, provided they have first had occasion to invent their own ways of encoding those values. Given a culture endowed with the custom of female musical performance before same-sex audiences, such occasions do arise: having positioned herself as speaking subject, the singer will tailor her presentation to her listeners' interests, imbuing it, as Showalter has argued, with "women's experience," as that is commonly understood by her society.[38]

Now if, within the oral tradition, a female perspective has thus secured a claim to validity, that perspective could well assume a legitimate, albeit subordinate, place in a subsequent written tradition, so as ultimately to provide readers with an alternative subject position available to either sex. By "subject position" I mean an organized way of seeing the world, constituted through language, that permits the individual to impose a coherent meaning on the circumstances and events of his or her life, simultaneously enjoining practices based on that meaning.[39] Once incorporated into a discursive system, a subject position may be adapted to various ends, long-term or immediate, serious or playful—utilized as a set of practical strategies for

---

36. Here I follow the lead of Homans, "Feminist Criticism and Theory" 173, who holds out to feminist critics a possible route of escape from the liberal humanist/poststructuralist quarrel over individual subjectivity: turning one's attention to collective female discourses.

37. Goody and Watt, "The Consequences of Literacy" 28.

38. In contemporary sex-segregated Middle Eastern cultures, women still create oral poetry and employ it for precisely this purpose: see Joseph, "Poetry as a Strategy of Power"; Abu-Lughod, *Veiled Sentiments* 171–271. The overall effectiveness of female poetic discourse as a power tool depends on its acceptance by men: when memorized and quoted by males, women's songs indirectly provide their composers with a strong voice in the larger community (Joseph 427). As we will see, this modern parallel illuminates the reception of Sappho's songs in antiquity.

39. Weedon, *Feminist Practice* 21–27.

living in the world or, in contrast, appropriated as a vehicle for escapist fantasy. In the ancient literary tradition, the "Sapphic voice" seems to have become just such an alternative subject position.

From the archaic period to the early Hellenistic era, the Greek world experienced a slow transition from orality to literacy.[40] Available evidence, chiefly from Athens, indicates that the capacity to write, with a corollary dependence on written records, spread through the population only gradually, coexisting for a long time with the time-honored mnemonic skills of a nonliterate society.[41] Though women are decoratively shown as readers on fifth-century B.C.E. Athenian vases, in practice they remained disproportionately illiterate, not only in Greece but in all parts of the ancient world and at all historical periods. On the other hand, women storytellers perhaps contributed a great deal to preserving and handing on oral traditions, even after the dissemination of literacy.[42]

Though this societal transformation was already well advanced in his lifetime, Plato in his last treatise still singles out song and dance, rather than books, as the basic medium for transmitting an awareness of cultural values to the young (*Leg.* 2.653c–656c). From time immemorial, oral instruction in the knowledge necessary to survive in Greek society—including an understanding of theology, history, politics, law, and even agriculture, as well as practical training in poetry, music, and rhythmic movement—had been made available to all upper-class youth, girls as well as boys, through their attendance at public festivals and their own parts in cult and ritual. For girls in particular, socialization was achieved by membership in a chorus composed of age-mates, beginning in childhood and continuing until marriage. The anomalous phenomenon of women poets in a rigidly gender-stratified society is plausibly explained by their function as poet-educators for adolescent groups of female initiates.[43] Sappho, it is widely believed, was just such an educator, composing cult songs for the young women enrolled in her sodality or *thiasos* and training them in oral performance.[44]

Responsibility for instructing Greek girls in music and dance was not, however, confined to women. The genre of *partheneia*, or "maiden songs," was extremely popular, and a number of famous male poets—Alcman, Pindar, Simonides, Bacchylides—are credited with producing such works ([Plut.]

40. Havelock, *Preface to Plato*, and "The Preliteracy of the Greeks"; Harris, *Ancient Literacy.*

41. Thomas, *Oral Tradition.*

42. On women's illiteracy, see Cole, "Could Greek Women Read and Write?" and Harris, *Ancient Literacy* 106–8; on women storytellers, see Thomas, *Oral Tradition* 109.

43. Dowden, *Death and the Maiden* 103. On the girls' chorus, see Calame, *Les chœurs.*

44. Merkelbach, "Sappho und ihr Kreis"; Calame, *Les chœurs* 1:385–420; Gentili, *Poetry and Its Public* 72–89.

De mus. 17.1136 f.). Lengthy fragments of two partheneia by Alcman, active in Sparta in the mid-seventh century B.C.E., are frequently compared to Sappho's verses because his speakers, like hers, express a strong homoerotic attraction to the beauty of their companions.[45] This generic resemblance has prompted the suggestion that Sappho was herself a follower of Alcman.[46] At the very least, it proves that her function as socializer of young female initiates could elsewhere be undertaken by men, and thus leads us to wonder about the authenticity of her female perspective. Could Sappho be imposing upon her young charges a cognitive structure derived from, and intended to reinforce, patriarchy? If so, this would be but one more instance of women choosing "to inhabit the space to which they are already assigned" by a male "logic of domination."[47]

I do not believe, though, that that is the case. While Sappho's manipulation of verbal devices like diction, figures of speech, and imagery is clearly indebted to the mainstream tradition,[48] her modes of subjectivity differentiate her to an extraordinary degree from her male counterparts—particularly those working within the same genre, whether partheneion or erotic monody. Specifically, her model of homoerotic relations is bilateral and egalitarian, in marked contrast to the rigid patterns of pursuit and physical mastery inscribed into the role of the adult male *erastēs*, whatever the sex of his love object.[49] The distinction between these two ways of constituting homoerotic passion can be illustrated by juxtaposing Alcman's representations of girls in love with the desiring speakers portrayed in numerous Sapphic texts, most notably her fragment 31.[50] The chorus's admiration of their leaders Hagesichora and Agido in Alcman fragment 1 is permeated with a spirit of eager rivalry, since they are competing with another chorus.[51] Such agonistic tensions emulate the mindset of a male warrior society. Meanwhile, the yearning for Astymeloisa expressed in Alcman fragment 3 betrays an abject dependency quite foreign to Sappho herself.[52] In contrast, Sappho's declarations of passions are a subtle means of awakening the beloved to the

45. Calame, *Les chœurs* 1:420–39; Dover, *Greek Homosexuality* 179–82; Rissman, *Love as War* 119–21.

46. Hallett, "Sappho and Her Social Context" 139–42.

47. DuBois, *Sowing the Body* 29.

48. B. Fowler, "The Archaic Aesthetic."

49. See Foucault, *The History of Sexuality* 2:38–93. On Sappho's model, see Stigers [Stehle], "Sappho's Private World."

50. For the convenience of nonspecialists, the numeration of the fragments of both Sappho's and Alcman's poems is that found in the most recent Loeb editions (Campbell, *Greek Lyric* vols. 1 and 2, respectively).

51. Page, *Alcman* 52–57.

52. Stehle, "Romantic Sensuality, Poetic Sense" 147–49.

mutual pleasures of sexuality. Thus fragment 31 is no anguished confession, but instead a virtuoso display of seductive poetic control: by making her vividly conscious of her own power to captivate others, the speaker draws the addressee into a dense web of sensual self-awareness and so encourages in her a reciprocal erotic response.[53]

There are corresponding differences, too, in each poet's stance toward members of the opposite sex and concomitant portrayal of gender relations. Though Alcman's singing girls are center stage, the gaze fixed upon them is unmistakably male, for in their sweet naïveté and emotional vulnerability they present themselves as unsuspecting objects of heterosexual desire. In Sappho's poetic universe, however, men are hardly a focus of female interest; as Joan DeJean deflatingly remarks, they are "relegated to a peripheral, if not an intrusive, role."[54] Masculine ideology, on the other hand, is present as inescapable background noise, representing both the power of the cultural system to enforce its demands on women[55] and a privileged conceptual framework to which Sappho counterposes her own antithetical outlook. For example, in rebuking the transgressions of her errant brother Charaxus and his mistress Doricha (frs. 5, 7, 15), she seems to be censuring a male economy of desire: erotic obsession, the impulse to possess the object undividedly, has brought public disgrace upon Charaxus himself and provoked unseemly arrogance in his paramour (fr. 15.9–12). Again, the first stanza of fragment 16 confirms the speaker's superior insight into what is "the most beautiful" (*to kalliston*) by opposing her comprehensive and relativistic definition of beauty to a series of overtly male, and patently limited, foils. Lastly, the violence of Sappho's reaction to the sight of her beloved in fragment 31 is enhanced by an indirect contrast with masculine impassivity. While the man sitting opposite the girl must be taken as a hypothetical rather than a concrete figure,[56] his intrusion into this intimate conversation warns of the crass indifference of the great world outside the *thiasos*, less inclined to appreciate the addressee's singular loveliness.

In none of these texts does Sappho close her eyes to the ontological reality of the masculine order. She recognizes it, instead, as a prior and controlling presence, but still avows the ethical superiority of her nonnormative subject position, her radically woman-centered approach to existence. Whenever her texts trope difference by an appeal to gender, then, the female stance affords a posture of resistance to prevailing male attitudes and practices. But the resulting polarity is not inversely "hom(m)o-sexual," in Irigaray's

53. O'Higgins, "Sappho's Splintered Tongue."
54. DeJean, "Fictions of Sappho" 790.
55. Stehle, "Sappho's Gaze" 224–25.
56. Winkler, *The Constraints of Desire* 179.

sense: rather than conjuring up male alterity as the mere negative projection of itself, the speaker's perspective defiantly locates itself against patriarchy, the pre-extant condition. One might state, paradoxically, that Sappho's poetry is literally "heterosexual," for it affirms the availability of distinct, gender-specific modes of subjectivity and directs its audience to choose what is identified as the better, though less advantaged, of two real alternatives.

It appears, then, that the subject position extracted from Sappho's monodies and choral compositions does not replicate patriarchal modes of awareness but rather affords a substitute basis for organizing female experience. Through imaginative identification with the first-person speaker, a girl would have absorbed survival tricks for living within a patriarchal culture: formulas for resisting misogynistic assumptions and so protecting self-esteem, for expressing active female erotic desire, for bonding deeply with other women, and for accepting the underlying ambiguities and absences of full closure inherent in both human discourse and human life. Consequently, she would be, in her adult years, an energetic and wholly socialized participant in female communities—those into which she was born and those she would join upon her marriage. The ultimate purpose of Sapphic song, we may conclude, was to encode strategies for perpetuating women's culture.

But would it really have been possible for a girl who internalized a female subject position to preserve it after leaving the *thiasos* and reentering a patriarchal milieu? Again, let us observe the peculiar epistemic processes of oral cultures. In passing information from one generation to the next, nonliterate societies exhibit "structural amnesia": aspects of the past no longer relevant to present concerns are sloughed off from the record and forgotten.[57] Susan Schibanoff suggests that illiterate women respond to directives from the dominant culture in similar fashion.[58] With no concept of a fixed, unyielding written text to deter them, they can "mishear" utterances in conflict with their own values and thereby resist immasculation. If Schibanoff is right, it follows that adult women in archaic and early classical Greece, segregated from the larger public sphere except on ritual occasions and having little or no exposure to reading or writing, could easily have retained a woman-centered perspective—more easily, no doubt, than their literate great-granddaughters.[59] At separate cult gatherings such as the Adonia and the Thesmophoria, to say nothing of daily private interaction in their own homes, these women had abundant opportunities to speak and joke

57. Ong, *Orality and Literacy* 46–49.
58. Schibanoff, "Taking the Gold" 87–91.
59. On the increased availability of formal education for women from the fourth century B.C.E. onward, see Pomeroy, "TECHNIKAI KAI MOUSIKAI."

among themselves, to chant and dance, to adapt a flexible mythic heritage to their purposes—in short, to propagate their own discourses in relative isolation.[60] We know, for example, that women sang folk songs, because scraps of them have been preserved, including one (*PMG* 869) that may have originated on Lesbos in Sappho's own lifetime: its reference to Pittacus, a ruling tyrant, is suspiciously familiar and quite possibly obscene.[61] It is reasonable to surmise, then, that compositions of Sappho and other women poets also formed part of a widespread female oral tradition handed down from mother to daughter, and that those compositions served, in effect, as a mechanism for opposing patriarchy.

Considered in such a way, Sappho's poetry offers an intriguing parallel to Luce Irigaray's own demonstration of *parler femme*, "speaking (as) woman," in "When Our Lips Speak Together," the essay that concludes *This Sex Which Is Not One* (205–18). There, troping speech as lesbian erotic play, Irigaray gives substance to her conception of a polysemous feminine language enacted through the female body. Communication between her lovers takes place on a timeless, almost wordless plane beyond patriarchal "compartments" and "schemas" (212), where only the body's truths are valid. "You," the addressee, and "I," the speaker, meld into one composite being through simultaneous *jouissance*, and this interchange of inexhaustible orgasmic pleasure constitutes a sharing of consciousness. Because Irigaray's model of female language depends upon corporeal contact, however, the subject is forced to seek a way of embracing across distances and can only appeal, in the end, to a vague notion of mystical somatic fusion (215–16). Yet it seems obvious that a connection with the absent partner cannot be sustained, in practice, without recourse to writing—which poses the danger of reinscription as object within a prefabricated patriarchal account.

Song, Sappho's medium of communication, avoids this pitfall because it is memory based. In oral societies, memory is the repository of all knowledge and the matrix of the collective as well as the individual consciousness. Thus an idealized experience captured in song and committed to memory can surmount the physical limitations of space and time. Meanwhile, song as performance art also provides scope for idiosyncratic self-expression by prescribing that every successive rendition will be unique, produced by one singer at a particular moment in time. The song text is both infinitely repeatable and infinitely varied.[62] Patterns of intimacy forged by erotic

---

60. Winkler, *The Constraints of Desire* 188–209.

61. Campbell, *Greek Lyric Poetry* 448–49.

62. For a theoretical analogy, compare de Lauretis's several arguments for redefining personal subjectivity as an ongoing "process of engagement" with externally formulated social discourses. According to de Lauretis, the agent exercises a considerable degree of

encounters within the Sapphic *thiasos* would consequently have survived a patriarchally enforced separation by marriage, for the searing intensity of the love affair could be rekindled through verses associated with that affair and later performed over and over again during the singer's lifetime.[63] By the same means, the moving lessons learned from her adolescent experience of desire might be imparted to outsiders—women of another community, or her own children and grandchildren.[64] Long after the composer's death and long after the death of her last companion, then, this poetry would have continued to offer generations of women an authentic female subject position. That in turn explains the emergence, century after century, of yet other Greek women poets, for whom their archaic foremother served as enabling prototype and fount of inspiration.

But we should not forget that Sappho's songs would not have gained fame in the wider world, or eventually circulated as written texts, had they not offered something to men as well as to women. Divorced from their primary cultural context, artistic works produced by female communities are subject to marginalization or distortion precisely because they exhibit disturbing deviations from normal social ideology. Thus, to cite an already familiar example, Alcman in his maiden songs is most likely appropriating a Spartan female initiatory discourse akin to the one Sappho herself inherited and making it conform to a masculine symbolic order. Sappho's poetry is, as we have seen, undeniably deviant; yet it was still preserved, transcribed, and ultimately enshrined within the androcentric literary tradition as a special category of discourse. Had men used it solely for voyeuristic gratification, converting its female subjects into erotic objects, they would have drastically modified its content, as we have observed Alcman doing, and excised in the process its woman-oriented elements. Clearly, then, Greek male listeners must have found another, peculiar application for it, one that required its survival intact and unchanged.

Sappho's great poetic achievement, I believe, was to articulate a female desire so compellingly as to make it at once emotionally accessible to men as well as women—although men's responses to it were shaped by far different relations of gender and power. The diffused eroticism that taught female auditors in the sheltered atmosphere of the *thiasos* how to transcend linear symbolic systems was perceived within the masculine sphere

---

self-determination in adapting those discourses to serve her private needs and even combining them into more complex vehicles of consciousness that escape conventional categories (de Lauretis, *Alice Doesn't* 182–86; cf. "Feminist Studies/Critical Studies" 8–10, and "Eccentric Subjects" 144–45).

63. Burnett, *Three Archaic Poets* 277–313.

64. Segal, "Eros and Incantation."

as delightfully idyllic and romantic. Consequently, as we learn from ancient critical pronouncements, anecdotal evidence, and visual representations of the poet as cultural icon, male listeners and readers cherished Sappho's work as a socially permissible escape from the strict constraints of masculinity.[65] In the symposium, singing one of these compositions—songs charged with the comforting presence of benign divinity and flooded with aching but sweet reciprocal desire—would have allowed men momentarily to "play the other," in Zeitlin's phrase, and so to release themselves from the necessity of being at all times publicly competitive and self-controlled.[66]

By logical extension, allusion to Sappho became an obvious tactic for projecting metaphoric "difference" upon one or two antithetical male-structured categories, particularly during the long process of conversion to a writing-based system of literary production. Yet the Sapphic texts still stayed in play as a locus of real differentiation, continually reinscribing into mainstream Greek discourse a set of gender assumptions radically free from male bias. *Pace* Irigaray, woman accordingly maintained a toehold in the Western symbolic order for as long as those texts remained intact. *Pace* Halperin, there is a dash of actual female subjectivity even in Diotima: when he argues persuasively that the Platonic image of reciprocal intellectual eroticism is derived from earlier ideas of female homoerotic relations,[67] Halperin overlooks the fact that Plato's audience would have obtained its artistic impressions of female homoeroticism chiefly from the poetry of Sappho.

65. The psychological spell Sappho exerted over a male listener's imagination is implied at [Longinus] *Subl.* 10.1–3, where the author marvels at her ability to select and combine "the most extreme and intense" (*ta akra . . . kai hypertetamena*) emotions in her descriptions of love. Praise of the charm (*kharis*) and pleasure (*hēdonē*) of her subject matter points to a general perception of her poetry as emotionally enthralling; see Demetr. *Eloc.* 132 and Hermog. *Id.* 2.4 (p. 331 Rabe). Portrayals of Sappho on red-figure pottery (for example, the kalathos by Brygos on which she appears with Alcaeus [Munich 2416, *ARV*² 385/228] and the hydria [Athens 1260, *ARV*² 1060/145] showing her reading in the presence of three female companions, one of whom crowns her with a wreath) hint at widespread use of her songs as entertainment at symposia in fifth-century B.C.E. Athens; cf. the apocryphal tale of Solon's reaction to one such performance (Ael. apud Stob. *Flor.* 3.29.58; Campbell, *Greek Lyric* 1:13, no. 10), which, though admittedly late, nevertheless provides insight into how male listeners responded to Sappho and how her songs were transmitted orally. That cultural image of Sappho explains why the musical theorist Aristoxenus attributed to her the invention of the poignant and affecting mixolydian mode ([Plut.] *De mus.* 16.1136d; for its character, see Plato *Resp.* 3.398e).

66. On Greek mimesis of the female as a theatrical device for affirming elements excluded from ordinary male experience, consult Zeitlin, "Playing the Other." For the pattern of "the Greek male's fascination with and gradual appropriation of the socially suppressed female other," see duBois, *Sowing the Body* 176–77; and, on the symposium as privileged space for the assumption of a "tempered alterity," see Frontisi-Ducroux and Lissarrague, "From Ambiguity to Ambivalence."

67. Halperin, *One Hundred Years* 126–37.

If metanarratives like Irigaray's are to serve as frameworks for profitable scholarly inquiry, they must be pliant enough to admit a blurring of polarities, to incorporate pronounced exceptions to their rules. Confronting a gargantuan heap of male-authored texts, feminist classical scholars have understandably perceived sexual/textual oppression everywhere and so have written off the Greco-Roman literary tradition as a blank page of canonical female silence. But, as Cicero informs us, silenced voices do cry out (*Cat.* 1.21) and, according to Susan Gubar, blank pages can tell tales.[68] While we may accurately describe Western culture as masculine in orientation, we must refrain from subscribing to paradigms of cultural construction that obliterate women's historical contribution to art and learning, for to do so is to do patriarchy's work.

In conclusion, then, I submit that the female-specific discourse known as Sappho's poetry is not so marginal to the Greek, or to the western European, literary tradition as to be readily excluded from consideration as an influential cultural factor, no matter how absolute and totalitarian the grip of the patriarchal symbolic system might appear. As many honorific allusions by later women writers suggest, this discourse did provide generations of ancient women with a (m)other tongue and a basis for constructing a positive account of their own experiences. More important for its perpetuation (and, one might add, for the overall mental health of the culture), Greco-Roman males benefited from the opportunity afforded by Sappho's texts to enact a woman's part, if only in play, and so to enter imaginatively into states of awareness foreign to them. In the innovative Hellenistic period, literary representation itself gained new vitality from incorporating additional elements of the female perspective preserved in Sapphic poetry. Finally, we should not forget that, exactly like their predecessors in antiquity, women taking up the pen at the beginning of the modern era invoked Sappho as a heroic authorizing presence.[69] Thus all contemporary women who write, within the Western tradition at least, may call themselves daughters of Sappho. As we reread her scanty fragments, we consequently do much more than rediscover the woman's voice in ancient literature. We are glimpsing the other shattered surface of what was once a two-sided glass. That no comparable glass has existed until recently for modern man has been his loss, no less than woman's.

68. Gubar, "The Blank Page."
69. Kolodny, "The Influence of Anxiety."

TWELVE

Sappho's Gaze:
Fantasies of a Goddess and Young Man

Eva Stehle

In the fragments of Sappho's poetry and notices about its contents, refer-ences to four myths which belong to a common pattern can be detected. These are the stories of Eos and Tithonos, Selene and Endymion, Aphrodite and Adonis, and Aphrodite and Phaon. The last is complicated by "bio-graphical" descriptions of Sappho's own thwarted love for Phaon. Given that Sappho does not seem to have referred to mythological stories very often, these myths form a significant group.[1] Yet, frustratingly, none of the poems survives well enough to reveal what use Sappho made of any of the myths. It is the purpose of this essay to show why Sappho may have been interested in the pattern to which this set of stories belongs and to suggest the use she made of it. I will begin by describing the four stories as known from elsewhere and the evidence that Sappho used them.

The story of Eos and Tithonos is known from the *Homeric Hymn to Aphrodite* (218–38): Eos (Dawn), enamored of the beautiful Tithonos, snatched him off to her home at the end of the earth. She asked Zeus for immortal life for him, but forgot to ask for immortal youth. Once he had grown old, Eos shut him up in her palace and left him to his fate.[2] In a papyrus fragment

---

This essay was originally published in slightly different form as "Sappho's Gaze: Fantasies of a Goddess and a Young Man," *differences* 2 (1990) 88–125.

1. The exception is the Trojan War, to which Sappho does refer relatively often: 16, 17, 23, 44, and one could add 166 and 105b (Voigt [V.]). Apart from figures connected with the Trojan War, I count eleven references to mythical characters, excluding divinities, whose stories may have been told or at least alluded to. In addition to those discussed here, there are the Tyndaridai, Niobe and Leto, Medea, Theseus, Achelous, and Prometheus.

2. In Homer (*Il.* 9.1, *Od.* 5.1), Eos is said to rise from her bed beside Tithonos to bring light to mortals. Homer may think of him as a god. See Escher in PW under Eos, col. 2658: for other versions of the myth of Tithonos, see P. Smith, *Nursling of Morality* 82–86.

which preserves the right-hand half of a poem of Sappho's (58 V.) appears the two lines: "... rosy-armed Eos ... carrying to the ends of the earth." The name of the person whom she is carrying is lost in the lacuna. But in the five lines directly preceding, the speaker complains about old age, grey hair, and weak limbs. Old age was Tithonos's trouble, and he is the only one of her lovers whom Eos is said to have carried off to her palace at the edge of the world. It seems very probable, then, that the allusion is to the known story.[3]

That Sappho told the second myth, that of Selene (Moon) and Endymion, we know only from a scholium, or marginal comment, on Apollonios's *Argonautica:* "It is said that Selene comes down to the [Latmian] cave to Endymion; Sappho and Nikandros ... tell the story concerning Selene's love."[4] The story has not survived, so we cannot tell whether Selene abducted Endymion in Sappho's version. Sappho's is not the usual tale of Endymion: she may have used a local story of Asia Minor or created this version herself.[5]

The story of Aphrodite and Adonis is known in several variants.[6] According to the best-known version, Adonis was the child of Myrrha's incest with her father: Aphrodite loved the supremely beautiful youth, and they hunted together; Adonis fell, however, gored in the thigh by a wild boar, and died, leaving Aphrodite to mourn him.[7] There are other variants (one is given below). In some it is recorded that Aphrodite laid Adonis down in a lettuce bed as he was dying. What makes the detail interesting is that lettuce was said to cause impotence.[8] Attributed to Sappho is a two-line fragment

---

3. Eos is similar to Aphrodite in some ways: Boedeker, *Aphrodite's Entry*, has argued that Aphrodite is a hypostasis of Eos (10–17).

4. Scholia to Ap. Rhod. 4.57 f. (264 Wendel), partly quoted in Voigt, *Sappho et Alcaeus* 199.

5. See n. 4 and cf. Page, *Sappho and Alcaeus* 273–74, who analyzes the myths into two traditions. The "western" version is that Endymion was king of Elis. Eternal sleep is usually part of his story (but Selene is not): Zeus gave him the right to choose his time of death; or Zeus agreed to grant a wish, and Endymion chose eternal sleep without aging; or Endymion tried to rape Hera, and the sleep was a punishment. The "eastern" version is less well-known: a grave in the Latmian cave is reported by Strabo 14.1.8 and an inscription shows that Endymion was a local hero in that area: cf. Paus. 5.1.5. Cf. also Gebelmann Ackerman and Gisler, *LIMC*, under Endymion, cat. 726–28; Bethe in PW under Endymion, cols. 2557–60, for collected evidence. Sappho could have created her version out of this material, adding the goddess to the story of Endymion's sleep.

6. The best collection of sources for the myth and cult of Adonis, together with extensive discussion, is Atallah, *Adonis*.

7. Ovid *Met.* 10.298–559, 708–59, gives the fullest treatment. Adonis becomes an anemone after death in this telling, on which metamorphosis (into a flower without scent) see Ribichini, *Adonis* 76–78.

8. See Euboulos fr. 13 (Kassel-Austin) and Callim. fr. 478 (Pfuhl) for the statement that Aphrodite laid Adonis in the lettuce: both authors connect the anaphrodisiac nature of lettuce with Adonis's feebleness. Winkler, *Constraints of Desire* 20, attributes this statement to Sappho

(140 V.): "Tender Adonis is dying. Aphrodite, what shall we do? / Beat your breasts, maidens, and tear your garments." Dioskourides calls Sappho a "fellow mourner" to Aphrodite grieving over Adonis, and Pausanias also says that Sappho sang of Adonis.[9] The fragment quoted may be from a cult song, for there was a festival for Adonis celebrated by women, the Adonia: the appearance of reposition in the fragment supports that view of it. But we cannot be sure. Sappho used the hymn form for personal poetry, so she may have used other ritual forms as well. If Aphrodite herself speaks the second line, we may see rather evocation of a mythic scene than a ritual form.

The fourth myth, Aphrodite and Phaon, is much harder to reconstruct. Late sources have it that Phaon was a ferryman of Lesbos who one day ferried Aphrodite, disguised as an old woman, between islands. In gratitude she changed him from an old man into a young and beautiful one. He seduced the women of the island, and met his fate in various ways.[10] Sappho, the Byzantine commentator Palaiphatos tells us, often sang of her love for Phaon.[11] But one of the earliest sources, the comic poet Kratinos, says that *Aphrodite* loved Phaon and hid him in the "lovely lettuce."[12] The best explanation of the evidence is that Sappho sang of Aphrodite's love. The reference to lettuce implies that Phaon was a figure who could be confused with Adonis.[13]

The pattern which the stories have in common is that of a goddess desiring a young, beautiful, mortal man whom she hides away in an enclosed place far from civilization. The young man is or becomes incapacitated sexually

---

by mistake. Cf. also Ath. 2.68f–70a on lettuce. Détienne, *Gardens of Adonis* 67–71, calls attention to the significance of these references.

9. Dioskourides *AP* 7.407 (18.1585 Gow-Page); Paus. 9.29.8 (214 V.). The phrase, "Oh, Adonis," is also quoted from Sappho (117Bb: 168 V.). A suggested restoration of 96.23 V. includes a reference to Adonis: West, "Burning Sappho" 328.

10. Sappho is said to have leaped from the Leucadian rock (an act that cured passion, if one survived it) for love of Phaon. The story probably developed in fourth-century comedy, for it is attested from comic fragments. See Stoessl in PW under Phaon, cols. 1791–93, on its development. See Wilamowitz, *Sappho und Simonides* 25–40, and Nagy, "The Symbols of Greek Lyric," on the complicated question of the relationship between Phaon and the Leucadian rock. Wilamowitz thinks that Phaon was localized at Lesbos only after he became attached to Sappho, Stoessl that Phaon may have been a Lesbian mythic figure of whom Sappho's poetry spread knowledge. The "leap" may originally have been a metaphor for swooning in love.

11. See 211 V. for collected references to the Phaon story, 211a for Palaiphatos.

12. Kratinos was an older contemporary of Aristophanes: *Eq.* 526–36. A scholiast to Lukianos (211c V.) remarks that Aphrodite changed Phaon from old to young because she was in love with him.

13. Cf. Burn, *The Meidias Painter* 40–44, and Beazley, "Some Inscriptions" 320–21, for vase paintings that depict Adonis and Phaon as similar figures. For the two famous vases by the Meidias Painter, one depicting Adonis, one Phaon, see Burn pls. 22–25a, 27–29.

and never leaves his condition of dependence and confinement to return to human society. The moment of impotence seems to be the one chosen by Sappho: the man is sleeping, aged, or breathing his last; the narrator joins Aphrodite in expressing love or grief. How was Sappho using this pattern, what connection did it have with her poetry for and about other women? It is a question that we cannot answer directly, both because Sappho's poetry is so largely missing and because such mythic patterns must be understood in context.

I will therefore approach Sappho's myths through a study of the pattern elsewhere in early Greek literature. The liaison of a goddess with a mortal man (young or not) is a recurring theme in this period. There are numerous other examples besides the ones just given. Why were such stories popular and what possibilities did they offer to Sappho? These will be my preliminary questions, before returning to Sappho's use of them. My investigation has two stages, the first determining what structural and ideological characteristics all such myths have in common, the second how they open space for erotic fantasy.

I

In order to study the pattern as a whole, I must describe some of the other realizations of it known from early Greek literature. To begin with, it lies behind Helen and Paris in the *Iliad*.[14] Aphrodite "snatched" (*ex-herpax'*) Paris from the battlefield and took him to an enclosed place, his bedroom (3.380–82): the verb is the one used of goddesses carrying off beloved youths.[15] There he remains, beautiful, compliant, apparently immobile until she returns to him (with Helen). Aphrodite then goes to find Helen, who is so close to Aphrodite that, as Helen herself implies, she and Aphrodite can replace each other in love relationships.[16] Helen says to Aphrodite, when summoned to the side of Paris: "You go sit by [Paris], leave the way of the gods and no longer tread Olympus with your feet, but always worry over him and guard him until he makes you his wife—or his slave" (3.406–9). In the *Odyssey*, Kirke and Kalypso enact the pattern with Odysseus.[17] Kalypso holds Odysseus captive, desiring him for her

14. Helen was a heroine (i.e., a figure whose grave was worshiped) or a goddess at Sparta: Hdt. 6.61; cf. *Od.* 4.561–69; Theoc. *Id.* 18. Calame, *Les chœurs* 1:334–44; West, "Immortal Helen," and Clader, *Helen,* argue for her being a goddess,

15. The plates in Kahil, *Les enlèvements,* show the increasingly sexualized representation of both Paris and Helen in vase painting in the course of the fifth and fourth centuries B.C.E.

16. Cf. Clader, *Helen,* esp. 58–62, 69–80.

17. *Od.* 10.203–574, 5.55–261. The Kirke and Kalypso episodes are generally thought of as duplicates: cf. *Od.* 9.29–32.

husband, and has offered him immortality. She also mentions two more examples in the course of her protest to Hermes about being forced to let Odysseus go:

> You are harsh, you gods, supremely jealous, you who begrudge goddesses' sleeping openly with men, if one would make him her proper consort. Thus when rosy-fingered Eos chose Orion, the lightly living gods resented it, until chaste, golden-throned Artemis killed him, assailing him with her gentle arrows. Thus when Demeter, yielding to her desire, mingled in love with Iasion in a thrice-plowed field, Zeus was not ignorant but killed him, striking him with a flashing thunderbolt.

The *Theogony,* or rather its pseudo-Hesiodic continuation, offers a list specifically of goddesses who slept with mortal men and of their offspring (965–1020). Included are Demeter and Iasion, Harmonia and Kadmos, Kallirhoe and Chrusaor, Eos and Tithonos, Eos and Kephalos, Aphrodite and Phaethon, Medea and Jason, Psamathe and Aiakos, Thetis and Peleus, Aphrodite and Anchises, Kirke and Odysseus, and Kalypso and Odysseus.[18] Phaethon, whom Aphrodite carried off to be her immortal temple-keeper, is here the son of Eos and Kephalos.[19] In the case of Aphrodite and Phaethon, unlike the others, no issue is mentioned. Finally, the *Homeric Hymn to Aphrodite* tells the story of Aphrodite's seduction of Anchises. Aphrodite appears before Anchises' hut, claiming to be a mortal virgin who was snatched by Hermes from the dance and brought to Mount Ida to be Anchises' wife. Persuaded, Anchises takes her to bed on the spot. Afterward, when Anchises learns who it is that he has just slept with, he cowers and begs not to be made impotent: "Don't let me live strengthless among men, but take pity. For not flourishing of life is the man who sleeps with immortal goddesses" (188–90).[20] In the final conversation between them, Aphrodite reassures him and promises him a son but warns him not to speak of the encounter. To explain why she cannot make him immortal she narrates the story of Eos and Tithonos and, a variation on the pattern, of Zeus and Ganymedes (202–38).[21] If we range down through the fifth century we find the first attested narration

---

18. It is striking that only one of the heroes born to a goddess in this list is central to Greek heroic legend. That is Achilleus, and it has long been noted that Achilleus is a misfit in the Greek genealogical system. Two of the heroes, Aineias and Memnon, are Eastern. Three— Latinos, Agrios, and Geryones—belong to the Far West, and Geryones is more monster than hero. The famous heroes do not come from such unions.

19. Cf. also Eur. *Hipp.* 454–56, who mentions Eos's snatching Kephalos.

20. Cf. Giacomelli [Carson], "Aphrodite and After," for a discussion of the meaning of *amenenos,* "strengthless."

21. Ibycus *PMG* 289 mentioned Tithonos and Ganymedes as young men of great beauty. Tyrtaeus 12.5 (West) referred to Tithonos's supreme beauty.

of Adonis's life in Panyassis's poetry, as Apollodoros records.[22] The reference runs thus:

> Panyasis [sic] says that [Adonis] was a son of Theias, king of Assyria, who had a daughter Smyrna.... [She commits incest with her father, then flees and is changed by the gods into a myrrh tree.] In the tenth month thereafter, the tree having burst, the one called Adonis was born, whom Aphrodite, in secret from the gods, hid in a chest on account of his beauty while he was still an infant and entrusted to Persephone. But when [Persephone] saw him, she refused to give him back. Judgment being in the hands of Zeus, the year was divided into three parts, and [Zeus] ordained that Adonis should remain under his own cognizance for one part of the year, with Persephone for one part, and with Aphrodite for the third part. Adonis assigned to [Aphrodite] his own share also. Later, however, while hunting Adonis was gored by a boar and died. (3.14.4)

While there is no way to know how far the summary draws on Panyassis, it can be argued, on the basis of the coherence of the plot, that the whole summary except the last clause should be attributed to him.[23] Apollodoros may have borrowed the detail of being gored from the better-known version given above.

The Adonis story stands out among the others because it is associated with a festival, the Adonia. Sappho's lines of lament for the dying Adonis may have been meant as a song for the ritual mourning of Adonia. The festival was kept at Athens in the fifth and fourth centuries, and later at Alexandria, as well as elsewhere. The Athenian festival has been reconstructed largely from vase paintings, with help from remarks in Plato and comic writers.[24] It was celebrated by women, who planted seeds of lettuce, fennel, perhaps wheat and barley in pottery vessels or large shards. Once the seeds had sprouted, the pottery pieces were carried to the roofs of the houses, where the sprouts shriveled in the sun and the women lamented. The pots were thrown into the sea or into streams. At some point in the festival incense was burned, fruit was heaped up in baskets, and women danced to flute and tambourine.[25]

22. See, in addition to works cited above, the notes in Frazer's Loeb edition of Apollodorus ad 83–89.

23. This is the solution of Atallah, *Adonis* 53. Ribichini, *Adonis* 133 n. 82, on the other hand, thinks that Panyassis told of Adonis's death after a life of cycling between earth and Hades.

24. In addition to Atallah, *Adonis* chaps. 3–6, see Weill, "Adoniazousai," and Servais-Soyez in *LIMC* under Adonis, nos. 45–49 and cat. 227–28. Ar. *Lys.* 389–96 and Plato *Phdr.* 276b are the most informative contemporary literary sources.

25. At Alexandria, as we learn from Theoc. *Id.* 15, Queen Arsinoe set up a display of Aphrodite and Adonis stretched out together on a banquet couch surrounded by fruit. A singer told Adonis's story. Then with lamenting the image of Adonis was thrown into the sea.

The same mythic pattern of a goddess with a mortal man lies behind Pindar's narrative of Jason and Medea in *Pythian* 4 as well. Euripides' *Hippolytus* and *Phaethon* have links to it. Other examples of the story pattern exist—Kybele and Attis, for instance, Eos and Kleitos, Hylas and the nymphs, the story of Hermaphroditus found in Ovid.[26] The story of Aktaion and Artemis is a negative inversion of the same pattern: she destroys him after he has seen her in the nude.[27] Bacchylides 17 has a deflected example: the young Theseus leaps into the sea and comes to the home of his father Poseidon, where he sees his stepmother Amphitrite: "She put around him a shimmering purple robe and set on his curly hair a faultless wreath that guileful Aphrodite had given her once at her wedding, dark with roses" (112–16): then she sends him back to his ship.[28] A cup by Onesimos shows a youthful Theseus, dressed in a short filmy chiton, standing before Amphitrite. Athena stands between them as if to chaperon Theseus.[29] It is evident that the pattern was popular and generative.

No recent interpretive approach has considered all these stories together, a procedure that may appear too reminiscent of Frazer's.[30] But various strategies have been used on individual myths or subsets of this group.[31]

Cf. Gow, ed., *Theocritus*, esp. 2:262–66. See Weill, "Adoniazousai" 674, for the possibility that it was celebrated at Argos in the mid-fifth century.

26. The narratives of Kybele and Attis are late and divergent, e.g., Ovid *Fasti* 4.223–44 and Paus. 7.17, although his story was known much earlier: it is indirectly attested by Hdt. 1.34–45. Cf. Vermaseren, *The Legend of Atthis*, esp. chaps. 3–4. Eos and Kleitos: *Od.* 15.250–51. Hylas and the nymphs: Theoc. *Id.* 13: this story too was connected with a ritual, a search for the boy (Ap. Rhod. 1.1354). The figure of Hylas is attested by Hellanikos *FGrH* 4 F 131. Hermaphroditus: Ovid *Met.* 4.285–388. Similar is Stesich. *PMG* 279 (placed among the spuria by Page), which sketches the story of the shepherd Daphnis, loved by a nymph, unfaithful to her, and blinded in consequence. On young men as victims of rape and on the fear of sexuality as feminizing, see Zeitlin's excellent discussion, "Configurations of Rape."

27. In the earliest extant version, Eur. *Bacch.* 339, Aktaion is punished because he boasted that he was a better hunter than Artemis. But cf. Stesich. *PMG* 256 (from Paus. 9.2.3), the well-known version, though conflated with one in which Aktaion is killed to prevent his marrying Semele.

28. See Segal, "Myth," for the scene as an erotic initiation of Theseus.

29. For the cup (Paris Louvre G104 and Florence Museo Archeologico PD321), see *LIMC* under Amphitrite no. 75: *ARV* 318.1. It is dated to ca. 300 B.C.E. Cf. also no. 76, where Athena is not present.

30. Frazer, *Adonis*, esp. chaps. 1–3, 9–10, of course, saw in Adonis a paradigmatic case of the vegetation god who yearly dies and is reborn. The pattern is universal, according to his rendition.

31. Boedeker, *Aphrodite's Entry*, argues for an Indo-European background for the myths involving Aphrodite, Eos, Kirke, on the grounds that these goddesses are descendants of Eos, who is cognate with the goddess Ushas of the *Rig Veda:* she distinguishes them from Near Eastern goddesses (chap. 3). Helen as a tree-goddess who withdraws periodically has been claimed for the Indo-Europeans by West, "Immortal Helen." Nagler, "Dread Goddess,"

Of these, the structuralist approach of Marcel Détienne, with its emphasis on the logic of culturally specific symbolism, has been the most productive; consideration of its results will be my starting point. Détienne argues that Adonis represents the extremes of sensuality and sterility, as expressed by his connection with spices and lettuce. In the Adonia (which he claims was celebrated at Athens only by courtesans and their friends) erotic but unfruitful sexuality is negatively contrasted with marriage and reproduction as they were celebrated in the Thesmophoria, a festival of Demeter. The courtesans, on this interpretation, would be enacting their own marginality.

Détienne's work on the Adonis myth and ritual is stimulating because it has shown the way to ideological interpretation of apparently apolitical myth and ritual complexes. A particular myth or ritual can take on meaning from its contrast with other myths and rituals. Narrative details can be read as codes carrying oppositional meaning.[32]   Others have combined structuralist techniques with a historical perspective. Ribichini, for one, undertaking an interpretation that takes the Near Eastern material into account, proposes that Adonis is the Greek conception of the effeminate, ineffectual Near Eastern man, marked by all that the Greek man considers to be antithetical to himself.[33] Adonis is a failed hero. The meaning of the Adonia festival for Athenian men is that by *not* celebrating it they mark their masculine effectiveness.[34] Ribichini assumes an implicit contrast with the normative Greek male self-image as recorded in the figures of the hero and the citizen.

John Winkler criticizes Détienne from a different perspective: in drawing one message from the myth-ritual complex, Détienne assumes a homogeneous social fabric with the citizen males' point of view as the only source

---

using Jungian categories, finds an old pattern of a goddess who lives near the still center of the world and who is maleficent until resisted or overcome, when she becomes a helper, providing information or sending the hero to one who can provide it. Sowa, *Traditional Themes*, treats the patterns in a Jungian framework (esp. chaps. 2–3.5). Segal, "Homeric Hymn," does a structuralist reading of the *Homeric Hymn to Aphrodite* and finds that the child Aineias is a mediation of the contradictions between mortal and immortal, city and wild. P. Smith, *Nursling of Mortality*, follows his method but throws the emphasis on the justification for mortality.

32. Piccaluga, "Adonis e i profumi," criticizes Détienne for his handling of the evidence. Lévêque, "Un nouveau décryptage," wishes a more historical approach had been integrated into the analysis.

33. Ribichini, *Adonis* 13–20, esp. 17 ff. Adonis is consistently identified as an Easterner, from Assyria, Arabia, Syria, or Cyprus. Hesiodic fr. 139 (Merkelbach-West) says his father was Phoenix ("the Phoenician"). He is therefore a fantasy figure of the "effeminized" other in a geographical as well as bodily sense. Sex-role reversal is typical of figures from the Near East in Greek thought: see Ribichini's list, which includes Paris, 69–70.

34. Ribichini, *Adonis* 85–86.

of meaning.[35] The inattention to the question of "meaning for whom?" is especially culpable because Détienne is not using a strict Lévi-Straussian model of contradictions and mediations but positing a contrast of values: one pole is affirmed, the other rejected. Winkler poses the question of the meaning of the Adonia *for the participants*, who, as he correctly points out, are not just courtesans. His reading of the juxtaposition of the Adonia with the Thesmophoria is that the women are enacting the differential involvement in sexual union and reproduction between men and themselves:

> If any contrast is to be drawn between the respective roles of the sexes in cultivating these natural processes, men must be placed squarely on the side of Adonis, Aphrodite's eager but not long enduring lover. What the gardens with their quickly rising and quickly wilting sprouts symbolize is the marginal or subordinate role that men play in both agriculture (vis-à-vis the earth) and human generation (vis-à-vis wives and mothers).[36]

In other words, the gardens are a women's joke about male sexuality. What Winkler has done is to shift the oppositional terms from legitimate and illegitimate sexual union (in Détienne's analysis) to male and female implication in sexual union, as described by the women. Out of the complex of terms used by the ritual, different interpreters have singled out different terms as the significant oppositional ones. Ribichini, concentrating more on the mythic assemblage and less on the ritual, finds the controlling opposition to be the one between the Greek male and the Near Eastern man as constructed in Greek popular culture.

Comparison of Détienne's and Ribichini's readings as if from the hegemonic position of a Greek (especially fifth-/fourth-century Athenian) man and Winkler's as if from that of a Greek (fifth-/fourth-century Athenian) woman exposes the dependence of the analysis on the position assumed by the interpreter, that is, on the social position in whose terms the myth is perceived. Détienne and Ribichini unproblematically adopt the position of the hegemonic male as the place from which to determine the meaning of

---

35. De Lauretis, *Alice Doesn't* 103–6, likewise criticizes the early forms of narratology, which developed under the stimulus of structuralism: "More often than not, however, those efforts all but reaffirm an integrative and ultimately traditional view of narrativity. Paradoxically, in spite of the methodological shift away from the notion of structure and toward a notion of progress, they end up de-historicizing the subject and thus universalizing the narrative process as such" (105–6).

36. Winkler, *Constraints of Desire* 205. In his discussion, Winkler makes use of my interpretation of the myth pattern in Sappho's poetry, which I first put forward in a paper entitled "Sappho and the Enclosing Goddess" at the Berkshire Conference on Women's History in 1981. This paper is a reworked version of that one with different emphases, but its reading of Sappho supports Winkler's very suggestive connection between Sappho's use of the pattern and the women's joking at the Adonia.

the myth and ritual.[37] Winkler constructs the possibility of a different set of shared views among women as the matrix for attributing meaning. The Adonia may indeed have had separate meanings for the female participants and the citizen male observers. The reading strategy of positionality—awareness that interpretation always comes from a specific social, sexual, and intellectual place—allows the modern interpreter to suggest the gist of other discourses besides the hegemonic one.[38] It allows the modern interpreter to escape from the view that myths as ideological formulations work their power to shape thought in undifferentiated fashion within a culture.

I will follow Détienne's lead in seeking an ideological dimension to the set of myths I have singled out, while observing the interpretive position from which the ideology is discerned. However, as soon as one examines this set of myths, including the Adonis myth, for significant codes, it becomes clear that in their emphasis on the sexual code of male and female, Détienne and Ribichini have ignored another code, an equally potent (in symbolic terms) hierarchical opposition, that between divine and human. Adonis's lover is a goddess. Furthermore, in these myths as viewed from the position of a hegemonic male, the two codes produce a contradiction, a point at which cultural logic collapses. The pairing of a goddess and a human man poses, within Greek hegemonic discourse, an irreconcilable conflict between the two established hierarchies, the hierarchy of male and female and that of divine and human. In human relations the female is "tamed" by sexual intercourse, and the subordinate position is identified with the female one. But in divinehuman relations the human is subordinate to divine desire. Sexual intimacy between a human male and a goddess is therefore impossible to think in simple terms because the relative status of the two cannot be determined. The relationship must be adjusted somehow to make it conceivable.[39]

37. I do not mean to imply that the modern interpreter can align her- or himself fully with an ancient figure or social position. Détienne analyzes the myth and ritual from the *modern construction* of the place of an adult citizen man. The idea of positionality is a useful reminder that one is working with a modern construction of a "Greek" social construction.

38. Alcoff, "Cultural Feminism" 428–36, argues the usefulness of an idea of positionality in feminist discussion. It is a valuable interpretive frame in any attempt to move between a work of literature and the society that produced it.

39. Cf. below, n. 65, on hierarchical sexual relations. The practical effect of the two hierarchies on daily life would seem to be quite different. However, the gods were a conceptual form used to think about power relations. Alkman warns the male members of the audience, "Do not attempt to wed Aphrodite" (1.17 *PMG*). The line probably encodes a warning not to seek above one's station, not to seek an enthralling woman as a bride: the thought is cast in terms of divinity and human. Cf. the separation of the two in Pind. *Nem.* 7.1–7. The problematic of the human place vis-à-vis the divine was real.

In the public discourse of early Greece, where these myths are found, the adjustment is the work of narrative. In each telling of each myth the narrative must resolve the conundrum by adjusting the hierarchies and shaping the outcome of the encounter, or, in other words, by assigning a location to the phallus. Given this need for resolution, observation of static codes is not sufficient to discover the ideological working of these myths: we must follow the movement of the narrative. My second source of inspiration, then, is a sentence of Teresa de Lauretis's. Speaking of film, de Lauretis says "the very work of narrativity is the engagement of the subject in certain positionalities of meaning and desire."[40] I must also observe the effect of narrative positioning in creating ideological harmony in these myths.[41]

From the point of view of hegemonic culture, the most conservative move is to ensure that the male/female hierarchy ultimately predominates. There are other possible resolutions that also preserve the male/female hierarchy (without elevating it over the divine/human one), as I will point out below. Not all adjustments, however, would reinforce hegemonic values. If the divine/human hierarchy is emphasized at the expense of the male/female one, an autonomous, sexually active female figure, one who controls the phallus, is created. Thus, cultural logic, through this myth pattern, can potentially offer narratives that subvert male dominance. In fact, public narratives from early Greece avoid this outcome. Using the narratives described above I will show how male/female hierarchy is protected.

The Kalypso episode in the *Odyssey* details the impossible situation that results when neither hierarchy gives way to the other. Odysseus is held captive by Kalypso, who would like to shut Odysseus up forever on her island in a state of emotional and physical dependency. In this condition Odysseus is forced to make love with her: "At night he would lie beside her under compulsion in the hollow cave, an undesiring man beside a desiring [woman]" (5.154–55). The act that defines him as a "man" also defines him as subordinate, for his sexual activity "under compulsion" is the clear sign of his submission to Kalypso.[42] Yet his refusing immortality is his refusal to accept definition as her paramour and the subordinate sexual status implied. Kalypso had no intention of accepting his refusal, as her speech to Hermes makes clear (5.118–36, quoted in part above), while Odysseus's "sweet life was flowing away as he mourned for his homecoming, for the nymph no

40. De Lauretis, *Alice Doesn't* 106.

41. See Suleiman, *Authoritarian Fictions,* on the use of closure in ideological fiction to emphasize the point being made. Closure functions in the myths I will discuss to establish the definite status of the paradigmatic figures.

42. The verb used, *iauein,* does not mean "to make love." It means "to spend the night," but it is used to refer to lovemaking elsewhere in the *Odyssey,* e.g., 11.261, 22.464.

longer pleased him" (5.152–53). According to Athena, Odysseus wants to die (1.59). This impasse in their relationship and in the narrative is dissolved only by displacing the problem upward.[43] Zeus exercises his patriarchal dominion and commands Kalypso (via Hermes) to send Odysseus on his way.

Structurally, then, both hierarchies remain in force. Odysseus's status is preserved, though only because Kalypso lets him go. However, the audience's desire for the narrative to continue means that the audience is positioned to identify Odysseus's autonomy, his sexuality, with narrative movement and to wish for it to prevail over hers. His escape can therefore be read as his triumph. Narrative in this case requires male predominance over the immobilizing goddess.[44]

In the case of Kalypso and Odysseus control of the phallus is contested. Most of the narratives I mentioned resolve the conflict by revising the status of one of the figures. Odysseus's encounter with Kirke points up the contrast. On this occasion Hermes intervenes beforehand to protect Odysseus from Kirke. Not only does Hermes give him the *mold* that inhibits Kirke's magic: he also instructs him to pull his sword on Kirke. When she asks him to her bed, he is not to refuse, "but ask her to swear a great oath of the gods that she will devise no other evil pain for yourself so that she not make you worthless and *unmanned* when you are disarmed/naked" (10.299–301; cf. 336–44). By neutralizing Kirke's power, the gods arrange it so that the male/female hierarchy will predominate from the start and Kirke accommodate herself to Odysseus.[45]

The *Theogony* continuation elevates the male/female hierarchy by other methods. It chooses, apart from the Aphrodite- and Eos-stories, those stories in which the female has been compelled by another god rather than desiring the young man (Thetis), has been at least partly humanized into a mortal woman (Medea, Harmonia), or is a minor nymph. The unions mentioned, except for Aphrodite and Phaethon, are all fertile. Eos and Tithonos have two sons in the *Theogony* (whereas none is mentioned in the *Homeric Hymn to Aphrodite*). Odysseus and Kirke have two children, Agrios and

---

43. Without the gods' intervention Odysseus's story can neither end nor move forward. The narrative signals the impasse by repeating the description of Odysseus's state: 1.11–15, 48–59; 5.11–17.

44. See de Lauretis, *Alice Doesn't* 113–24, on the male as subject, the female as obstacle in myth as analyzed by Lotman. In the complementary fashion, Devereux, *Femme et mythe* 36, citing the myth of Pirithoos—who went to Hades to seduce Persephone, but sat down and found himself immobilized, stuck to his seat—equates immobility with castration and impotence.

45. Kirke too threatened to interrupt Odysseus's journey, although the narrative moves past the threat so rapidly as to neutralize it: after a year Odysseus's men remind him that they should be on their way (10.469–74).

Latinos: Odysseus and Kalypso's son is Nausithoos. The offspring may be metaphorical, for instance, Demeter giving birth to Ploutos (Wealth) and Eos giving birth to Phaethon (the Shining One). This representation minimizes the conflict of hierarchies without acknowledging its existence. From the perspective of the *Theogony* as a whole, these goddesses (except Aphrodite) are hardly powerful, and the production of sons is the only story they are given. For the audience this bareness is satisfying because the lines are attached to a narrative in which Zeus establishes patriarchy by asserting his control over reproduction. These lines link the cosmic order (expressed through the distribution of divinities) with human history and tie the audience, placed in history, into Zeus's plan. Because of their narrative position, the lines can assimilate the sexual power of the female to her reproductive activity and thereby stabilize the location of the phallus, the location of control over the erotic situation, with the man. The goddess is placed within patriarchy and subsumed in the category "mother."

In the one instance of the union of Aphrodite and Phaethon, as told by the author of the *Theogony* continuation, a different resolution is found. The author says of Phaethon, "When he was young, in the tender bloom of glorious youth, a child with light thoughts, laughter-loving Aphrodite darting down snatched him up and made him an enclosed temple-keeper, a shining *daimon,* in her holy shrine" (988–91).[46] The abduction is not said to have been followed by sexual union.[47] Only in Aphrodite's epithet "laughter-loving" is the phallus indirectly and unspecifically signaled via a pun.[48] This vignette settles the status conflict unequivocally in favor of the goddess but deprives Phaethon of all activity, including sexual activity: immortalized and enclosed, he has no further story. As in the case of the *Odyssey,* generation, history, and narrative require male dominance. Phaethon's fate indirectly

---

46. West, *Hesiod: Theogony,* points out ad loc. that *daimōn* is a term used of men who have lived on earth and after death have a limited sort of divine power. The adjective *dios* (shining) is applied to goddesses but not to the higher male gods. (It is also applied to human men.) The text implicitly marks Phaethon's limited and subordinate divinization.

47. In Apollod. 3.14.3 Tithonos is the son of Eos and Kephalos, and his son is Phaethon (by what mother is not said); Adonis is Phaethon's great-great-grandson. The notice indicates both the fluidity of these stories and the fact that the young men were felt to be linked as well as interchangeable. It is remarkable that in Euripides' partly preserved play *Phaethon* the young man is about to marry a goddess on the day that he goes to find Hellos, drives the chariot, and is struck down by Zeus's lightning. Diggle, *Euripides: Phaethon* 10–27, 155–60, thinks that the goddess is a nymph, one of Heliades. He denies any connection between the Phaethon of this myth and the one in Hesiod, but the pattern seems to exert its pull.

48. Hesiod puns on Aphrodite's epithet "laughter-loving," *philomeides,* and a term for genitals, *media,* saying that Aphrodite is laughter-loving because she was born from the severed genitals of Ouranos (*Theog.* 200).

points to the significance of the other couples, whose offspring are part of the audience's "historical" past.

By calling as much attention as it does to Phaethon's youth, the *Theogony* continuation also points to another way to escape from impasse in a re-assertion of male dominance. A narrative may explicitly mark the man as subordinate within the *human* hierarchy: his status may be clarified by making him the object of homosexual love.[49] If a man who is subordinate to a goddess is also subordinate to another man, then his position with re-spect to the goddess does not establish a model of female control that would threaten the male/female hierarchy.[50] Thus in various tellings Dionysos, Apollo, and even Heracles are said to have been Adonis's lovers.[51] Adonis is thereby assimilated to the category of youths who fail to make the transi-tion to adulthood.[52] The fourth-century comic poet Plato emphasizes the humorous results produced by this resolution of the conflict. In four lines quoted from a lost play, *Adonis*, Adonis's father receives a prophecy:

> Oh, Kinyras, king of the Cyprians, hairy-assed men,
> Your child has become most beautiful and most marvelous
> Of all humans, but a pair of deities will destroy him,
> She being rowed with clandestine oars, he by rowing.
>
> (fr. 3 Kock)

The deities are Aphrodite and Dionysos. Adonis, caught between extremes as beloved of a male god and lover of a goddess, will perish of status ambiguity. We cannot tell about narrative positioning in the case of Adonis, but Plato Comicus seems to have presented Adonis as ambiguous and marked for

49. For analysis of the unequal status of the two partners in a male homosexual relationship, see Dover, *Greek Homosexuality* 100–109, and Foucault, *The History of Sexuality* 2: chap. 4, esp. §3. Public norms, not behavior, are in question.

50. One version of the tale of Eos and Kephalos makes explicit Kephalos's submissive character. In a story that may come from Pherekydes, Kephalos's wife Prokris, disguised as a man, came to hunt with him, bringing a javelin that never missed and a dog that always caught its prey. Kephalos wished for these: Prokris set the condition that Kephalos should submit to "him" in sexual intercourse. When they lay down Prokris revealed herself to him and either accused him or was reconciled with him: Ant. Lib. 41.6–7; Hyg. *Fab.* 189. See Fontenrose, *Orion* 91–94. Eos does not occur in this version as the rival of Prokris, but Fontenrose suggests that "Nephele" (Cloud) represents her.

51. In addition to Plato Comicus (below), see Ptolemy Hephaistion in Phot. *Bibl.* 190, 147b.9–12 (Henry) for Herakles; 146b.41–42, 147a.1–3, for Apollo. He calls Adonis "androg-ynous." Atallah, *Adonis* 50–51, calls this a late "deformation" of the myth, adding that the "slender, equivocal ephebe" is an Alexandrian preoccupation. It seems to me rather that the fantasy potential of the myth pattern is increasingly overtly expressed.

52. E.g., Hyakinthos and Narkissos: cf. Ribichini, *Adonis* 128–29. Ribichini stresses that Adonis does not seduce but is seduced, except in one late pastiche found in Servius ad Verg. *Ecl.* 10.18, in which, pressured by Juno, he violates Erinome, beloved of Jupiter.

failure from the beginning, in contrast to his father, king of hairy-assed men. Adonis is also a failed hunter, whose death from the wound inflicted by the boar makes him a victim of male aggression.[53]

From this perspective, it is clear that to mark Adonis as an "effete Easterner" is one more mode of achieving a resolution that preserves (Greek) male sexual control; Ribichini's analysis of Adonis's meaning reveals a strategy for resolving the contradiction in status hierarchies created by the story. The possibility of yielding to a woman is acknowledged, but rejected as non-Greek. And the spices (Adonis's mother Myrrha) and lettuce, whose opposition in the myth Détienne studies, mark the two ends of the narrative (birth and death) and trace Adonis's demasculinization. Adonis is overloaded with markers of his subordinate status, for he is the most prominent mortal lover of Aphrodite.[54] Attis castrates himself, driven mad by Kybele, when he undertakes to marry a nymph (and thus assume adult male status). His sexual subjection is clarified at the moment when he tries to escape from it. Hylas drowns, pulled down into a pool of water by the nymphs—an image of surrender to sensuous passivity. Anchises' statement in the *Homeric Hymn to Aphrodite* that men who sleep with goddesses do not flourish and Hermes' fear that Kirke might unman Odysseus fit in here. In these cases the goddess's control of the phallus is taken literally; it is lost to the man. The man is marked as a non-man: thus there is no question of an otherwise dominant man's yielding sexually to a female.

The *Homeric Hymn to Aphrodite* itself does not make use of the simple resolution suggested by Anchises. Instead it explores at great length the ironies created by the confusion of hierarchies.[55] Zeus shames Aphrodite among the gods by causing her to fall in love with the mortal Anchises. But Aphrodite's desire leads her to exercise her power over the human man, deceiving him while causing him to desire her. Yet her deception is to

53. The boar was sent by Apollo or Ares; in later tellings Apollo himself, Hephaistos, Heracles, Persephone, the Muses, or Artemis kills Adonis: Atallah, *Adonis* chap. 2, esp. 63–74; the earliest extant reference is fourth century B.C.E. (unless it was in Panyassis). Discussion in Ribichini, *Adonis* 108–44, who points out that Adonis is associated with other hunters who are overcome, e.g., Aktaion, Hippolytos, Perdikkas, Kephalos (108). Piccaluga, "Adonis, i cacciatori falliti," concentrates on this aspect of Adonis, believing him to represent a preagricultural life that had been left behind and was therefore coded in myth as inadequate.

54. I do not mean to suggest that my interpretation overrides Ribichini's and Détienne's, that the operation of status hierarchies is the only point of these stories. The need to adjust hierarchies is a constraint, one of various pressures that act on material of diverse origin to produce similar stories.

55. Bergren's excellent discussion of the *Hymn*, "The Homeric Hymn to Aphrodite," takes a different approach—rhetorical analysis—and pays special attention to the distribution of power among the gods. She too emphasizes the ambiguities in the narrative.

cast herself as a mortal woman, an innocent virgin submitting to others' directives. Only so can she be the recipient of Anchises' uninhibited desire. Anchises says to her, "If you are a mortal woman . . . as you say, and come here through the agency of the immortal messenger Hermes and will be called my wife for all time, then no one of the gods or mortal men will restrain me here from mingling in love with you right now" (145–51).[56] Once they have made love she pours sleep over Anchises. Then, dressed again, towering in height to the roof of the hut, and shining with her immortal beauty unveiled, she wakes him. Anchises cowers in the bedclothes, seeing in her swelling figure a portent of his impotence and cries, "Do not let me live strengthless among men"; she now controls the phallus. Yet Aphrodite assures Anchises that she will not only do him no harm but will give him a child, as though she were a mortal woman. In her final statement, however, she explains that she cannot make him divine. Furthermore, he must not mention or boast of the encounter. If he uses it to enhance his male status among humans, Zeus in anger will strike him with a thunderbolt (that is, reduce him to the "strengthlessness" that is his proper lot). Male/female hierarchy has been restored among the gods: Aphrodite is subordinate to the will of Zeus. Between Aphrodite and the human the situation is more ambiguous. Aphrodite, in her desire, provoked Anchises' desire: both desires have been satisfied. Aphrodite's threatening stature at the end is counterbalanced by the fact that she is pregnant.

The *Hymn* closes with Anchises unscathed and a father-to-be but warned of his merely human status: the hierarchies, no longer suspended, are delicately balanced. Yet the *Hymn* also points to a resolved closure, projected beyond its own text. Aphrodite's emphatic warning to Anchises not to speak of the encounter activates the audience's knowledge that Zeus did thereafter strike him with lightning.[57] Anchises must have been unable to keep silent about his encounter with Aphrodite, unable to renounce the glory or resist naming his son's mother. Once the tale exists in public discourse, Anchises must take on the status of a non-man.[58] Narrative positioning here is complex. The

---

56. Anchises' doubt over whether Aphrodite is mortal or goddess in itself sums up the conflict of hierarchies: if she is a goddess he will worship her, if a mortal woman he will take her to his bed. Cf. Bergren, "The Homeric Hymn" 16–17, 20–22, on Anchises' effort to test her with logical alternatives and his *erōs*-induced blindness to flaws in his logic.

57. This statement assumes that the audience for the *Hymn* was already familiar with the tradition: the earliest extant reference is Soph. *Laocoon* fr. 373 (Pearson). P. Smith, *Nursling of Mortality* 142 n. 129, and Rossbach, in PW under Anchises, col. 2107, discuss the evidence; Anchises has an "eldest daughter" in *Il.* 13.428–33, but she may be an invention out of Homer's need for names.

58. I assume that the lightning strike symbolizes unmanning and that the portrayal of Anchises as crippled is both a decorous and an overt representation of his condition. For the

audience notes what Aphrodite wishes to keep hidden and also knows (or guesses) Anchises' fate. But the audience's desire is for Aphrodite's desire to be revealed; it is complicit with Anchises' failure to keep silent, and so replays Aphrodite's shame, but also her desire. We will return to this situation.

These narratives resolve the contradiction in such a way as to preserve the male/female hierarchy. The story pattern calls forth this closure so consistently that the story's potential for subverting the male/female hierarchy must have been felt. The two tales that refuse to reduce the relationship between goddess and man to a simple hierarchy. *Odyssey* 5 and the *Homeric Hymn to Aphrodite* do in fact make use of the contradiction in interested fashion: the contradiction supports a positive evaluation of mortality from the point of view of an adult man. The goddesses Kalypso and Aphrodite consider immortalizing Odysseus and Anchises, but in each case immortality would have as its price subordination and/or confinement. Thus the trade-off for immortality is presented as a loss of sexual autonomy and evaluated as not worth it. Kalypso offers to immortalize Odysseus if he will stay with her even though he does not desire her (5.206–10), so it is conditional on confinement and relinquishing of desire. Aphrodite herself rejects the desirability of immortalizing Anchises because there are only two models for doing so: Ganymedes', with its eternal subordination and passivity (absence of desire), and Tithonos's, which includes (temporary) desire but also aging and confinement as its necessary correlate.[59] So in these two stories the sexual hierarchy of male/female is called on to reconcile the man to his mortal lot.

In a series of instances from the Greek literary canon, we have seen that the self-contradictory notion of a goddess and a man in sexual union is imagined and narrativized in such a way as to protect the adult man's claim to sexual dominance. Narrativity, at work engaging the subject in positionalities of meaning, reproduces the cultural norm for male/female relations. However, other narratives with other resolutions are possible. The story of Demeter and Iasion, of which no early version has survived, may have been told by women (who need not have agreed with Kalypso's interpretation of it) in

---

phallic quality of lightning, cf. the story of Semele: e.g., Eur. *Bacch.* 6–9, and Dodds's notes on the subject in *Euripides.*

59. P. Smith, *Nursling of Mortality* 87–90, and Bergren, "The Homeric Hymn" 33–35, have posed the question why Aphrodite does not ask Zeus for immortality *and* eternal youth for Anchises, as the paradigm of Eos and Tithonos would suggest. Smith argues that Anchises' mortality is taken for granted, or rather, insisted on by the poem, so the thought that it might be otherwise is not entertained. Bergren points out that Zeus's will requires Aphrodite's grief, so the poem does not permit Aphrodite to seek satisfaction. In an article in process I am working out at greater length the argument that the Ganymedes and Tithonos models between them exhaust the possibilities.

connection with the festival for Demeter, the Thesmophoria. Demeter's treatment of Demophon—the baby she started to immortalize, rejected when his mother caught her at it, but continued to favor as he grew up—has affinities with our pattern.[60] In this story and perhaps in the women's version of the Adonis story, whatever it was, divinity is the source of a female power that exposes the imitations of the male. Sappho's narratives may likewise have rewritten the males'—but if so, no hint of it survives in the fragments and notices. If women produced versions that subvert the male/female hierarchy, they have been lost.

By attentiveness to the contradiction and to the requirement that the narrative resolve it somehow, we can see how these narratives are inflected so as to preserve the male/female hierarchy. We can imagine how women might have made a different use of them. Yet I have not answered either of the questions I posed, namely why the pattern is so popular and what its appeal to Sappho was. Male dominance could be asserted directly without the aid of these tales, and for Sappho they appear peripheral to her emotional attachment to other women.

II

Perhaps we should look for the tales' popularity rather than to their (partial) ideological failure. The ideological meaning conferred on these myths by narrative closure cannot always completely contain them. Before closure, the myths may already have suggested images of eroticism whose hold on the imagination the resolution cannot necessarily cancel. As long as the narrative holds the contradiction in suspense, unresolved in favor of either hierarchy, it keeps a space open for fantasies of sexual encounter not controlled by the location of the phallus. So long as the contradiction is unresolved, the phallus is a symbol of domination; the Freudian/Lacanian phallus that imposes definition on the relationship is an indeterminate presence in the envisioned union. The goddess is both desiring and desirable, the man young, pliant, neither clearly possessor nor clearly object of the phallus. Desire and initiation of the affair may belong to the goddess, but the youth may be imagined as a responsive participant. The meeting of these two figures is not pre-scripted: it must be played out according to the dictates of individual fantasy. It can be staged in the imagination according to the script of male dominance, but also from the position of a woman's desire to

---

60. For Iasion cf. scholia to *Od.* 5.125: "he was a farmer, and the earth would give him exceptional harvest, always abounding, and he was rich: therefore they said that he slept with the earth and on this account she gave him good return." For Demophon, see *h. Hom. Cer.* 231–91 and Richardson, *The Homeric Hymn to Demeter* 231–36.

"possess" the man, from a position of narcissism, voyeurism, or fetishism, of refusal of the Oedipus resolution, of a woman's refusal of compulsory heterosexuality. The collapse of cultural logic and the prohibition against condemnation of a divinity emerge as the enabling conditions for imagining women and men in other than their culturally prescribed sexual roles.[61] According to de Lauretis, the work of narrativity is to engage the subject in positionalities of meaning *and desire*. We have asked only about desire for narrative, not yet about how desire is figured into these narratives.

Fantasy works in the visual imagination through the processes of gaze and identification. The idea of analyzing the operation of the gaze was proposed by Laura Mulvey as a way to understand the visual engagement of a viewer with a film narrative. It has been taken up by feminist film critics, including de Lauretis. Mulvey argues that classical Hollywood films reproduce the sexual construction of the man and the woman as described by Freud.[62] The hero is active: he is the one who gazes. The heroine is displayed and aestheticized, the object of the gaze. The man watching the film can identify with the hero as the "bearer of the look" and can gaze possessively at the heroine. The woman *as woman* can only identify masochistically with the heroine's ability to attract the gaze.[63] The possessive gaze, then, is aligned with the phallus: the act of gazing defines the desired sexual object. Through gaze and identification the viewer takes up in fantasy a sexual position in relation to figures presented visually or to the imagination. Though Hollywood films may reinscribe the cultural norms, the processes of gaze and identification can support other positions and other fantasies.[64] This approach, treating

61. The goddess who desires cannot be censured as were, e.g., Phaidra and Stheneboia, mortal women who wished to initiate affairs with young men.

62. Here is a summary of the Freudian basis of Mulvey's analysis (*Visual and Other Pleasures* 14– 26): the processes of scopophilia and of identification with an ego-ideal structure initial pleasure in looking, according to Freud. Within the post-Oedipal order this pleasure is conditioned by differing relations to castration: the man's an active, possessive looking, the woman's a masochistic desire to be looked at. In film, therefore, male pleasure in looking is served by both ego identification and possessive gazing at the female star. The female, however, always threatens to signify castration, so provokes the further mechanisms of fetishism and voyeurism: she is either objectified or examined and exposed. See further Willemen, "Voyeurism," who adjusts some of Mulvey's terms.

63. Mary Ann Doane (personal communication) stresses that Mulvey's analysis applies to a specific historically located and material medium. I make use of the question Mulvey raises about the spectator's relationship to the gaze and the phallus but should emphasize that the differences in economic investment, cultural positioning, level of discourse between Mulvey's material and mine are great and the results of analysis different.

64. Consider this rumination by Barthes: "Death of the Father would deprive literature of many of its pleasures. If there is no longer a Father, why tell stories? Doesn't every narrative lead back to Oedipus? Isn't storytelling always a way of searching for one's origin, speaking

the figures as *visual* images, will permit us to suggest some of the erotic configurations invited by narratives of goddess and mortal man.[65] I will begin with two representations of myths from Athenian vase paintings, since in these cases the visual appeal is explicit and the scene has been detached from the narrative whose closure determines it is ideological shape. In each case the painting is sexually suggestive and permits more than one response—that is, the process of gaze and identification may be variously deployed.

The first is a scene of Eos carrying off a youth, perhaps Kephalos.[66] On a skyphos by the Lewis Painter dated to ca. 450–40, Eos, fully clothed, runs to the right and looks behind her. Her hair is covered by a *sakkos* except for a curl in front of her ear. She wears no jewelry. She carries the youth on her left arm, supporting his legs with her right hand. He has his arm around her neck and seems perfectly acquiescent. His left arm is flung out in a gesture which tilts his nude body slightly outward,

---

one's conflicts with the Law, entering into the dialectic of tenderness and hatred?" (*The Pleasure of the Text* 47).

65. Mulvey grounds her approach in Freudian analysis, which cannot be applied unproblematically to Greek culture. However, the phallus was the central signifier of sexual relations as constructed in social norms and in language in ancient Greece. One was positioned in relation to the phallus: one was penetrator, penetrated, neither, or both. A woman or a boy could only be penetrated or not: a youth might occupy any of the four positions: a hegemonic adult man was (by definition) a penetrator but not penetrated. The difference was enshrined in vocabulary: one was a lover (*erastēs*) or a beloved (*erōmenos/-ē*). The phallus and the act of penetration defined power relations. Cf. Dover, *Greek Homosexuality*, esp. 49–54, 98–99, and Cantarella, *Pandora's Daughters* 24–37; also see Dean-Jones, "The Politics of Pleasure," on the absence of a female erotic gaze in medical writing. Zeitlin, "Configurations" 124, points out that "there is an ideological value to representing the aggressive exercise of phallic power as the physical and concrete sign of male supremacy and potency," but she goes on to discuss the conflicted character of sexuality: it is cultural and natural, tender and violent.

66. Florence, Museo Archeologico 4228: *LIMC* under Eos no. 272: *ARV* 975.35. Two nude youths fleeing are on the back. *Kalos* or *kalē* (beautiful) is written beside each figure. The youth has been variously identified as Kephalos and Tithonos. Eos and a youth is a well-attested subject in ancient art: see *LIMC* catalogue and illustrations 46–288. In one scheme found on Athenian vases, Eos pursues Kephalos, who is in flight. For a scheme similar to the one on this vase, cf. nos. 267–82, esp. 268–70, 274. Cf. also Kaempf-Dimitriadou, *Die Liebe* 16–24, esp. 16, on the popularity of the theme from ca. 490, 20–21 on the schema of our vase. Her no. 198 (pl. 11, 3) is our vase: contrast the youth's resistance in her nos. 193, 194. Eos with Kephalos in her arms appears in earlier art. Paus. 3.18.12 records that Hemera (Day) snatching Kephalos was pictured on the throne of Amyklai, apparently a sixth-century work whose decoration included a great compendium of the major myths. A sixth-century B.C.E. terra-cotta akroterion from Caere in Etruria shows Eos carrying a Kephalos who looks like a child and has his arms around her neck: Andrèn, *Architectural Terra-Cottas* 36–37, pl. 11, no. 40. In the late fifth century the pair formed a terra-cotta akroterion on the Stoa Basileios at Athens: Pausanias 1.3.1; cf. Kaempf-Dimitriadou 63 n. 130.

exposing it to the viewer. In his left hand he holds a lyre. His hair is long and falls in stiff ringlets. Eos has obviously snatched the youth, yet he is complicit. He is a youth, almost equal in size to her, yet the positions are those of mother and child.[67] The vase painting, in fact, seems to suggest simultaneously lovers and mother with child. Gaze and identification can play freely here. The gaze fastens on the youth: Eos is not sexually displayed. The one who gazes with desire sees a youth who is both yielding and "innocent." Omission from the picture of the phallus as the location of power permits the youth's submissiveness to be naturalized as childlike and renders the male status hierarchy irrelevant. At the same time, the parallel placement of the two heads with their similar profiles signals an equality between them. Submissiveness is equated with equality and allows the fantasy of a stabilized homosexual relationship.[68] On the other hand, identification with the youth allows a narcissistic focus on one's own body as the object of the mother's desire. Identification with Eos elicits the fantasy of possessing the child as sexual fulfillment. The pair is eluding unseen pursuers. Escape from society and the son's return to the mother in erotic union are revealed visually as a possible inflection of the myth pattern. Phaidra would find it an engrossing image: so, perhaps, would Aktaion.

A passage from Euripides suggests that the fantasy of return to the mother was recognized, so we can say that a viewer might have identified with Kephalos as a child in its mother's sexually possessive arms. In the *Bacchae*, Dionysos begins to work on Pentheus's suppressed sexual fantasy by offering to take him to the mountains to gaze on the women who are (Pentheus thinks) making love in the thickets. Dionysos's final enticement is that Pentheus will be carried home in his mother's arms:

> D: Follow, I go as a saving guide.
>   Another will lead you back.   P: The one who bore me!
> D: Distinguished in all eyes.   P: It is for that I go.
> D: Carried you will come....   P: You speak my luxuriance.
> D: In the arms of your mother.   P: You will force me to go soft
>   with delight.
>
> (965–69)

67. Devereux, *Femme et mythe,* treats the myth pattern of a goddess and mortal man as a covert allusion to the son's incestuous desire for his mother (chap. 2, esp. 29). The very thought of such union is censured within the myth by representing symbolic castration as the result of even aborted encounters.

68. Plato later theorizes a stabilized and equalized male homosexual relationship based on the conversion of *erōs* into *philia* and the eroticizing of *philia.* See Halperin, "Plato and Erotic Reciprocity."

Pentheus's language in his last two half-lines has overtones both erotic and "effeminate."[69] Dionysos elicits Pentheus's desire to see the women, to be a woman, to be the object of his mother's love. His mother, although not divine, is possessed of more than human power by agency of Dionysos. The same image of luxuriant yielding to a sexual mother-figure is sketched by the vase painting.

Then again, the vase might be viewed from the position of the mother as voyeur, as suggested by the strange version of the Aktaion myth found in Nonnos.[70] As the first stage of his revenge on the house of Kadmos, Dionysus maddens Antonoe, then tells her that her son Aktaion is married to Artemis: the story of his death was a fabrication. The two go out into the wild, where they see Artemis and Aktaion sitting together. The mother spies on her son as he escapes the city to consort with a forbidden woman. Euripides and Nonnos present these respective desires as ones that emerge under Dionysiac dissolving of conscious control: they show us instances of what Greek culture designed as hidden fantasies.

Iconographically, this scene is distinguishable from one version of the scene in which Eos carries her dead son Memnon from the field at Troy only by virtue of the limpness of Memnon's body.[71] In this version Memnon is, like Kephalos, very youthful. Eos was said to have carried off the youthful dead, an appeal to morbid eroticism that assimilates the young man to both Kephalos and Memnon, to child and beautiful hero, as Eos is ambiguously mother and desiring woman.[72]

In sum, the vase painting seizes a moment in the narrative of Eos and the youth when the youth's fate is open and uses it to create an appeal to submerged fantasies. The youth here is both submissive to Eos and an object of the gaze, yet his position in the human hierarchy is not explicit, and the alignment of the heads hints that they are doubles of one another. Furthermore, if the youth is taken as Kephalos, then his depiction here exists in tension with stories of Kephalos as a hunter and husband of

---

69. On the language cf. Dodds, *Euripides*.

70. Nonnos *Dion.* 44.278–54.3; discussed by Fontenrose, *Orion* 34–40, who has other arguments for a close relationship between Artemis and Aktaion. Nonnos is no evidence for early Greek views. But stories such as his illustrate the suggestiveness of the pattern of goddess with young man.

71. See Paris, Louvre 0232 (*LIMC* under Eos no. 332: *ARV* 250.24) by the Syleus Painter, dated to ca. 480. In no. 324 Memnon has a beard. An unbearded Memnon is less common than the bearded type but not rare.

72. Scholia to *Od.* 5.121 and Eust. ad loc. say that the youthful dead were buried before dawn and said to be stolen by Eos. Cf. Vermeule, *Death in Early Greek Art* chap. 5, esp. 162–65. Kaempf-Dimitriadou, *Die Liebe* 62 n. 97, on depictions of a winged female *daimon* who chases a youth.

Prokris.[73] The resulting ambiguity about the youth's status leaves open the painting's "meaning" to the play of fantasy.

The second vase painting is from the end of the fifth century. A fragment of hydria painted by the Meidias Painter shows Aphrodite and Adonis.[74] Aphrodite is seated. Her clinging dress outlines her breasts and nipples. She wears a necklace, and her hair is done up in an elaborate headdress. Adonis, nude, leans back between Aphrodite's knees with his head thrown back in "une attitude d'extase amoureuse."[75] She has her hands on his shoulders. They are surrounded by Erotes and female figures: the woman sitting facing them plays with a bird that perches on her finger. Here the disappearance from history remarked in the case of Phaethon is seen from the inside as immersion in sensuality and ease. Neither figure monopolizes attention as the focus of the scene: the gaze rather takes in the scene as a whole. In this case a dominant figure is absent, excised as unnecessary to the erotic scene. The person positioned as hegemonic male can thus supply the phallus, can gaze on the couple as the embodiment of alternative desires, woman or youth, almost collapsed together in total erotic spectacle. But the scene also invites multiple identifications. The postures and the contact between the figures can suggest to the viewer tactile sensations to be imaginatively reproduced in the viewer's body: the "ecstatic" yet relaxed muscle positions, the implied warmth, the softness of hands and hair. The viewer is both figures, drawn into a fantasy in which desire and sensation are diffused over whole bodies.[76]

Both vase paintings depict the goddess with a young man in such a way as to suggest the attractions of "illegitimate" patterns of sexual intimacy. In the first case, the power granted the female figure led to overlay of the erotic relationships with a mother-child relationship, a doubling that invites fantasies of regression or of reclaiming the child, fantasies formed around Oedipal issues. The second vase painting makes both figures objects of the gaze and/or identification and invites fantasies of loss of gender identity and immersion in sensuality.

---

73. For the confused set of stories about Kephalos, see Fontenrose, *Orion* 86–100.

74. Florence, Museo Archeologico 81948: *LIMC* under Adonis no. 10: *ARV* 1312.1. Aphrodite and Adonis appear on Athenian vases toward the end of the fifth century at the same time as other scenes showing an interest in romance and women's lives: cf. Brendel, "The Scope and Temperament" 37–42; Servais-Soyez in *LIMC* under Adonis, cat. 229.

75. Servais-Soyez in *LIMC* under Adonis, cat. 224.

76. Cf. Silverman's conclusion, "'Suture'" 235, in her analysis of the female role in *Gilda:* "Vidor's film thus poses a temptation ... the temptation to refuse cultural reintegration, to skid off course, out of control, to prefer castration to false plenitude." In the myth of a goddess with a young man castration enables a different kind of plenitude.

The open space of sexual relations thought "otherwise" can be found in narratives of the literary canon as well. The narratives shape configurations in passing that their endings will deny. They can momentarily position the audience so as to gaze in imagination and identify with characters in a noncanonical way. The most overt example is the *Homeric Hymn to Aphrodite* in its complex play with the pattern. The audience hears Anchises' speech of determination to make love to her (quoted above) from Aphrodite's perspective, for this is the effect we have seen her create. Right after Anchises' speech the text continues. "So saying, he took her hand: laughter-loving Aphrodite came slowly, turning her face aside and casting down her lovely eyes. . . ." The sentence anchors the audience's attention on her. "Laughter-loving" (whether or not the pun mentioned above is felt) expresses Aphrodite's subjectivity, her delight in erotic joy. But the delight in her eyes is hidden as she turns her head away. Positioned by knowing her desire and Anchises' ignorance, by sharing her deceit, the audience "sees" Anchises undressing Aphrodite from her perspective. As he proceeds through four lines the audience's anticipation is aroused by the imminence of Aphrodite's fulfillment of her desire. Nor does the text switch to make her the object of the gaze. Although her body is revealed, the text reveals nothing about it. Thus the audience is put in the position of imagining the scene of lovemaking as expression of the woman's subjectivity. When Aphrodite discloses her identity, she reestablishes distance between the scene and the audience. She speaks of her shame from this distance, so it is detached from the preceding scene. The effect of female subjectivity as the audience's position is canceled by the narrative, but remains as an imaginative possibility.

Panyassis's account of the Adonis myth (of which we have only the synopsis) may have resisted its own closure: instead, Adonis cycles between the upper and lower worlds. His extreme, childish youthfulness and his beauty as an object of the gaze are overemphasized by the detail that Aphrodite and Persephone fall for him when he is still a baby. Adonis gives his allotted portion of the year to Aphrodite, a gesture signifying mutual desire, his yielding to her, or both. The final third of the year is allotted to Persephone, to be spent in the underworld. In this segment of the cycle Adonis's beauty condemns him to be in thrall to a female who extinguishes him. Adonis's passivity, the absence of the phallus, means that he cannot survive as a sexual being. Yet Adonis's return undoes the closure and reestablishes sexual intimacy. If the final line of the synopsis referring to Adonis's death from the boar's wound was not in Panyassis's text, then Panyassis left his narrative undecided between rendering Adonis "impotent" (so as to recuperate the male/female hierarchy) and joining him with Aphrodite (so as to imply the irrelevance of the phallus).

The Adonia festival suggests that women may have used the opportunity created by a narrative like Panyassis's to shape their own eroticism in a ritual setting. Winkler's construction of the women's interpretation of the Adonia emphasizes their part in reproduction: they celebrate their female power over life and sexuality. In this way the women give a different emphasis to their established role. Behind that shared focus on nurturance may lie other imagined roles. The Adonia combined dancing and mourning, use of incense, display of fruit, as well as the "gardens" that withered. It was celebrated, at least in part, at night and on the roofs of the houses. Its iconography suggests plentitude as well as loss. The mourning implies identification with Aphrodite. But the celebration was also *for* her. Was it open to women to imagine themselves as substitutes for Adonis? Did the women take both positions in fantasy, Aphrodite and her lover, and collapse the cycle found in Panyassis: Adonis is already gone, already replaced? And was Adonis the child who is lost as well as the lover? This complex set of possibilities—desiring (goddess or youth), mourning, being desired—results in a diffused sexuality, not centered around the phallus, without overtly specified object. The sensuous surroundings (incense, fruit), company of other women, and physical expression in dancing provide multiple gratifications.[77] Vase paintings of the festival show a seated woman lost in contemplation as others carry objects to or from the roof or play the flute and dance, while baskets of fruit and incense burners stand nearby.[78] This is the public face of the festival, the women's activities viewed as spectacle but closed off from the viewer.

In this emotional complex, both normalization of the pattern (Adonis's death) and disguise of the eroticism by mourning protect the festival from suppression: the festival does not confront the hegemonic male with the possibility that women might embrace an eroticism in which he was replaced. The use of fruit and incense and "gardens" further obscures and diffuses the eroticism behind a vegetable code. Détienne's analysis allows us to see how the cult was explained (away) by the dominant culture: by joking about courtesans and their lovers enjoying it, mainstream discourse at once acknowledged curiosity, claimed control (for courtesans live at the mercy of men), and dismissed the cult as marginal.[79]

---

77. Farwell, "Toward a Definition" 212–13, quotes Audre Lorde and Adrienne Rich on the erotic in women as "diffuse and omnipresent energy" created in women's "presence to one another." This description fits the Adonia.

78. *LIMC* under Adonis, nos. 45–49. Cf. also the plates in Atallah, *Adonis.*

79. For association of the Adonia with courtesans, see, e.g., Diphilos fr. 42.38–41.49 (Kassel-Austin); Pherekrates 170 (Kock); Men. *Sam.* 35–50. Later Alkiphron, probably inspired by New Comedy, composed letters purportedly by courtesans to their friends: in two of these, 4.10.1

Diffused eroticism and perhaps the same story of a cycle between the upper and lower worlds are indicated by Praxilla's lines on Adonis (*PMG* 747). According to her *Hymn to Adonis*, Adonis, when asked by those below what the loveliest thing that he has left behind was, said, "Loveliest [of all the things] I leave are the light of the sun, next the shining stars and the face of the moon and also ripe cucumbers and apples and pears." This list, judged inane by the world at large, gave rise to the saying, "Sillier than Praxilla's Adonis." One might guess at a connection with the Adonia and perhaps Adonis's parting from the upper world during the festival. In that case the disguise mentioned in the previous paragraph is at work. Praxilla's lines have an interesting resonance with two lines of Sappho's: "I love luxuriance . . . this light of the sun and beauty eros assigned as share to me also."[80] These are the last two lines of the fragment in which she mentions Tithonos.

As we have seen, the pattern produces images of the desiring woman, the sexual mother with her son, the submissive but responsive man—all figures censored by the dominant culture. These emerge as the phallus is displaced *within the text* from its centrality as the signifier of desire. How the gazer views these figures created within but against the narrative depends on how she or he positions her- or himself in relationship to the phallus. The viewer may supply the phallus. Or the one gazing from the position of hegemonic male may disavow the phallus in order to identify with both figures, or with one of the figures, with the woman as lover of the beautiful boy or the reverse, in fantasies of passivity, transvestism, youthfulness.[81] From the position of the female, gaze and identification with the goddess are not disjunctive: that is, from this position one can both look at and "be" the goddess. Notice the difference from the woman's gaze in the description of film theory: this is not the woman's constituting herself as the *object* of mother's gaze, but identification with the one who controls the relationship.[82] The masochistic

---

and 4.14.8, the Adonia is mentioned: in the latter a woman is invited to bring her "Adonis" (her lover) and a garden for the celebration. Adonis is called Aphrodite's beloved (*erōmenos*).

80. Voigt, *Sappho et Alcaeus* 58.

81. Willemen, "Voyeurism" 212–13, points out that male scopophilia should have the man as its object since its origin is in autoeroticism. But scopophilia would be directed at the mother as well, to determine her status. It is perhaps worth noting that the two most important objects of the boy's initial scopophiliac interest, the mother and the child himself, can be reproduced in the pair goddess and young man.

82. Modern film theorists have had trouble theorizing a woman's gaze. De Lauretis, *Alice Doesn't*, extends Mulvey's original notion, that the woman shifts between identification with the (male) gaze and with the screen image, to the idea of a double identification with both simultaneously, as well as with the mythic subject and the narrative image, with movement and closure (134–56, esp. 141–44). Mulvey, *Visual and Other Pleasures* 29–38, later suggests that the woman regresses to a never-fully-represented active phallic stage. Doane, *The Desire to Desire* 6–13, discusses the difficulty that various discourses have in providing an account of

narcissism of the female spectator is not called out because the story does not construct a possessive male gaze. A woman is free in fantasy of the male figure whose look identifies her to herself. The male is available on the contrary as an object of her gaze, a man younger (if she will), not older, compliant, not "superior." The evidence for women's inflection of this pattern is of course almost impossible to come by. That women were engaged with it is shown by the fact that they celebrated the Adonia festival and that a young man figures in Demeter myths.

III

If one reason for the popularity of the mythic pattern of goddess with young man is that it opened space for fantasies of uncodified erotic relationships, then Sappho's interest in the pattern may begin to appear more intriguing. The discussion so far also suggests that the way to approach Sappho's use of the myths is by examining the processes of gaze and identification in her poetry.

Sappho often describes a woman gazing. A notice tells us, "Sappho says she saw 'a child too tender picking flowers'" (122 V.). A line reads, "[When] I look at you [it seems to me] that you [are not] Hermione, but to compare you to light-haired Helen [is not out of place]" (23 V.).[83] In the scrappy end of 96 V. we can read, "It isn't easy to look like a goddess. [but] you ..." Furthermore, Sappho describes the gaze as having a powerful, even physiological effect on the gazer. In 22 V. the narrator observes that the dress of another woman caused the addressee to "quail" when she saw it.[84] In 31 V. the narrator describes the violent effects of the sight of another woman on her: "When I look at you briefly, then I can no longer speak, but my tongue is broken, at once light fire has run under my skin ..." (7–10).

In describing the effect of the gaze on the gazer as overwhelming, Sappho does not differ from other Greek writers.[85] However, Sappho does part company from them in her articulation of the experience: she avoids or breaks down the opposition between viewer and viewed that is created by the gaze. At the end of 31 V. (partially quoted above), the narrator says:

woman's subjectivity. She suggests that the projected female spectator is divided unbridgeably between "masculinity" and narcissism.

83. This translation is based on the supplements printed by Campbell, *Greek Lyric* vol. 1: Voigt's text, *Sappho et Alcaeus,* is more conservative, but the idea is clear enough.

84. The narrator of Sappho's fragmentary poems is often not demonstrably female. I assume, in the absence of evidence to the contrary, that it is a female voice.

85. Examples are legion. See, e.g., *Il.* 14.294; Plato *Chrm.* 155d–e, *Phdr.* 251a–e. On seeing and being seen in the *Hippolytus* of Euripides, see Luschnig, *Time Holds the Mirror* 3–15; on tragedy generally Durup, "L'espressione tragica" 144–50.

"I am greener than grass and I seem to myself to be little short of death" (14–16). The narrator's gaze has shifted from the other woman to herself. With her new focus she observes herself both from within and from without. The audience too must shift from the simple position of "looking" at another to the ambiguous position of both sharing the narrator's experience and watching her. By contrast, the gaze that remains focused on the object is correlated with lack of erotic effect; the poem sharply distinguishes the narrator's unmoved gaze at the man in the opening two lines ("That man seems to me to be the equal of the gods") from the disruptive gaze at the woman.[86] Similarly, in 1 V. "Sappho" describes Aphrodite's smile and repeats Aphrodite's speech from "Sappho's" own point of view, then takes on Aphrodite's voice. The switch is sudden, and the audience must simply shift perspective to suit. The narrator of 96 V. describes the beauty of the absent woman and the woman's desire for the addressee: the narrator's relationship to the absent woman is characterized by both gaze and identification. In 95 V. the narrator's desire to see the lotus-filled dewy banks of Acheron may be a displacement from her desire for a woman, but the poem is too fragmentary to tell for sure.

Sappho has other techniques for blurring gaze and identification. Description in her poetry is often both very sensuous and very unspecific.[87] A woman's beauty is displaced onto the surroundings: song, scents, flowers, rich cloth, enclosed places all reflect the woman's erotic attractiveness. 94 V. is full of flowers and scent, and in 96 V. the woman's beauty is deflected onto the landscape.[88] Dika is asked in 81 V. to weave garlands so that the graces will look on them. The very fragmentary 92 V. seems to be a list of different colored robes, plus garlands. Aphrodite is invited to come to a shrine in a seductive landscape in 2 V. Sappho often refers to singing and music. Replacing the "look" at a woman by atmosphere, hearing, smell means that the distinction of self and other inherent in gazing is dissolved. Sometimes Sappho offers the addressee/audience a mirror for self-reflection. In 94 V. the narrator describes to the addressee, who is leaving, the addressee's own sensuous ways of adorning herself. In 22 V. the narrator tells the addressee of her (the addressee's) own desire for

---

86. Likewise, the man's gaze at the woman is unmoved. Race argues that "godlike" must mean "strong" (rather than, e.g., "happy") and refer to his self-possession in looking on her: he compares Pind. fr. 123 (Snell-Mähler). Robbins, "'Every Time I Look at You,'" likewise contrasts the man's gaze with Sappho's. Hierarchy is operative between man and woman—his is a phallic gaze—and Sappho invokes the divine/human hierarchy to emphasize it. The two hierarchies are additive here.

87. Cf. Winkler, "Gardens of Nymphs," on Sappho's metaphoric language for the body.

88. Cf. McEvilley, "Sappho, Fragment 94," who calls the scene in 94 V. a dream landscape, an idealized past.

another.[89] The adjective "lovely," which opens the second stanza, could refer either to the addressee or to the woman she desires.[90]

In all of these instances the audience's gaze is given no object of desire to focus on except a self-reflective one, an image of the addressee's own desirability. Both within the poetry and for the audience the two processes of visual fantasy, gaze and identification, are blurred. This practice means that the gaze cannot be aligned with the phallus. Sappho would have reinstated the operation of the male/female hierarchy by analogy had she used the gaze to objectify the one desired. Instead she constructs poetry in and through which the gaze opens the self to disintegration, shifting position, identification with the other, or mirroring of the viewer's desiring self.[91] Through her use of the gaze to dissolve hierarchy, Sappho creates the same kind of open space for imagining unscripted sexual relations that the mythic pattern of goddess with young man makes possible. By this means Sappho can represent an alternative for women to the cultural norms.[92]

The long fragment (or possibly a complete poem) 16 V. is important because it shows clearly the connection between Sappho's treatment of the gaze and her depiction of women's erotic life as separate from the dominant culture. A translation follows:

Some say a host of horsemen, some of men on foot.   1
Some say of ships, among sights on the black earth
Is the most beautiful. I say that it is that thing
    Which one desires.

Very easy it is to make this understandable   5
To all, for she who surpassed by far
All humans in beauty, Helen, that man
    Who was the best

Abandoned and sailed off to Troy;   9
Nor to her child or her own parents
Did she give any thought: rather there led her astray
    [. . . . .]

89. See Di Benedetto, "Il tema della vecchiaia" 146, for a suggested thematic contrast between this fragment and 21 V.

90. This statement is tentative since it is not clear where the poem began and the preserved part is too fragmentary to be sure that the reference of the adjective was not unambiguous.

91. Doane, *The Desire to Desire*, points out that she analyzes the merger of identification and desire in the "woman's film" of the 1940s as problematic for women (esp. 22–33) and remarks that what is missing in the Greek period is commodification of the woman. I would add that Sappho's poetry presumes the possibility of sexual desire between women, so that blurring (it is not merger in the case of Sappho) of gaze and identification does not replace but rather permits a relationship with another.

92. Cf. Stigers [Stehle], "Sappho's Private World," on Sappho's depiction of mutual (rather than dominant and subordinate) love relations among women.

[Aphrodite?], for easily turned (?) . . .   13
[. . . . . lightly [. . . . .]
Who (?) recalls to me Anaktoria,
    Who is not here.

I would wish rather to see her lovely step   17
and the bright sparkle of her face
Than the chariots of the Lydians and those in armor
    Fighting on foot.[93]

(The tortuous translation of the second and third stanzas preserves approximately the original word order, for I wish to make a point about it.) The poem works out a contrast between conventional assessments, those supporting the social construction, or what one might call the public gaze, and the narrator's view of the location of women's emotional lives. Helen is by conventional agreement the "most beautiful." For Helen, to accept this social role would be to remain narcissistically focused on herself as the object of the gaze. Instead, as a subject, possessor of a desire that she has defined for herself, she finds the "most beautiful" elsewhere.[94] Yet Paris, the object of her gaze, is not named or even mentioned in the poem. Helen's name is juxtaposed in the second stanza with the words, "the man / who was the best." The juxtaposition suggests Paris, but the very meaning of the words "man" (husband) and "best" depends on whether Paris or Menelaos is meant. The momentary ambiguity reveals the arbitrary character of the epithet "best." The man's identity is not revealed until the beginning of the following stanza: there the verb "abandoned" establishes that Menelaos is the man referred to. The adjective "best" is therefore another conventional epithet, but its public character eclipses Helen's individual choice of Paris. That is, the narrator can "see" Menelaos, who has a fixed public status, but not Paris, whose quality is conferred by Helen's love and is therefore invisible to others. On the other hand, Menelaos appears in the poem as a consequence of Helen's abandoning him: his only role is to be *not* "what one loves." Again in line 11, the audience will be reminded of Paris by the verb "led her astray," but again he is not named. The subject is lost in the

93. There is a large bibliography on this poem. See the annotated bibliography through 1985 in Gerber, *Studies in Greek Lyric Poetry.*
94. Some have been disturbed that Helen, who is introduced as a judge of beauty, is herself described as exceeding all humans in beauty. On Helen's significance for the logic of the primal, see esp. duBois, "Sappho and Helen"; Most, "Sappho Fr. 16"; Thorsen, "The Interpretation of Sappho's Fragment 16"; Wills, "The Sapphic 'Umwertung.'" Wills notes the opposition between conventional and personal evaluations in the poem (440–41). DuBois, unlike the others, considers that Sappho meant to oppose male and female stories. Thorsen has a good discussion of the logic of the poem as a whole. Burnett, *Three Archaic Poets* 277–90, takes a different approach and focuses on memory.

lacuna of line 12 or 13: the most likely possibility is that it was an epithet of Aphrodite.[95] The object of the woman's gaze is invisible, unnamed, not objectified. The result of eliding mention of Paris is that the relationship between Helen and Paris remains unspecified, the phallus unlocated, hierarchy suspended. Helen's gaze does not create a distinct object for the audience, nor does Helen slip back into her old role by becoming the object of Paris's gaze or guidance. The concretized male figure is left behind in the world of armies and conventional assessments.

If the subject of the verb "led astray" was Aphrodite, then she replaces Paris in desiring and conferring beauty on Helen. By virtue of naming Aphrodite, the poem transforms the relationship into one between women, one in which Helen is both the subject who desires and also responsive to Aphrodite. This complex paradigm (Helen/unnamed Paris, Helen/Aphrodite) allows the narrator to find loveliest—not Helen—but a woman unknown to epic, Anaktoria. Like Helen, who left her parents and daughter, the narrator rejects conventional expectations linked with epic on the one hand and marriage and family on the other for a love of her own choosing. The logic of the poem illustrates the relationship of female desire to the public world of prescribed social relations. Aphrodite both represents the woman who chooses her love and offers divine affirmation of love that contravenes the cultural norm.

But because Anaktoria is absent, the narrator's gaze must reconstruct her in fantasy. The separation of the narrator from Anaktoria produces the straightforward gaze that is not attributed to Helen. Helen sailed off to Troy rather than suffer separation, but the narrator must construct an imaginative image through the gaze of fantasy. Yet even in imagination the narrator does not offer simply an objectified Anaktoria to the audience. By referring to Anaktoria's way of walking and the sparkle of her face, she creates rather an image of light and movement.[96]

Helen and Paris in 16 V. adumbrate the pattern of a goddess with a young man: the poem shows how Sappho could inflect the pattern to create open space for fantasy. Since Aphrodite doubles both Helen and Paris, the interplay of relations among them permits multiple configurations of gaze and desire. In a more complex way than on the Adonis vase discussed earlier,

95. Scansion is against the possibility that "Paris" stood in the lacuna of either line. A god or quality is more likely to be the subject of the verb "lead astray" than a human: "love" is a possibility. See Voigt's critical apparatus ad loc.

96. Both Rissman, *Love as War* chap. 2, and Wills, "The Sapphic 'Umwertung,' " think that Anaktoria's "light" and "movement" imply a comparison with the armies, that Sappho assimilates love and war rather than opposing them. Rissman argues that this poem is a *recusatio* of epic (48–54).

eroticism blurs gender identity. Sappho could have used the four myths in question to the same effect, treating the young man's gender as irrelevant (since he is not a dominating figure). In fact, in two of the myths the narrator is (apparently) associated or identified with the goddess. The maidens in 140 V. lament with or as Aphrodite for the loss of Adonis. The confusion over whether Sappho or Aphrodite loved Phaon implies that Sappho adopted Aphrodite's voice, singing of Aphrodite's love for Phaon, perhaps as an analogy to a love of her own. The story of Selene and Endymion may have been similarly used. The pattern also provided an image of a separate emotional space where female desire might express itself, for in the myths the young man is hidden in the wild or at the end of the earth.

However, what most forcibly strikes one about the fragments and notices is that the young man is portrayed at the point of impotence. Endymion is sleeping, Adonis dying.[97] By portraying the man's "strengthlessness," Sappho reinstates hierarchy: the young man is demoted to passivity, and the goddess prevails. The goddess can gaze at the young man with a possessive look. Selene's gaze on Endymion must have been straightforward, the gaze that Sappho's poetry usually avoids constructing. The maidens perhaps watch Adonis as he fades. But the goddess and youth cannot be a couple because he is succumbing or has succumbed to the fate that destroys him in the canonical narrative. Sappho invokes narrative closure as it enervates the mortal, assimilates him to a non-man, in order to preserve the male/female hierarchy.

These figures are parallel to Paris in 16 V. Conversely, his absence from the text becomes even more significant when aligned with these stories. As argued above, not naming him means that the poem avoids reinstating hierarchy and conventional assessment, while indicating the invisibility of an object's loveliness to those who do not love it. But ultimately Paris becomes an absence for Helen herself. He was killed in battle toward the end of the Trojan War, and she returned to live with Menelaos. The hierarchy-scrambling relationship based on desire is lost, and the relationships prescribed by the social structure triumph. 16 V. can be seen as both imitating Helen's choice and pointing to its evanescence. In that case, the military forces that some find loveliest become more significant: they are the means by which the dominant

---

97. In 58 V., the only case where the narrator seems to have compared herself to the human member of the mythic pair (Tithonos), she seems to be lamenting her age and feebleness. In this case the point may be rather the goddess's care for a human despite her mortality. It may also be the survival of song, for Tithonos's voice runs on unquenchably, and a reference to a lyre appears just above the lines on Tithonos in Sappho's text. Cf. Di Benedetto, "Il tema della vecchiaia" 152–63, who conjectures, on the basis of the last two lines (quoted in connection with the Adonia), that Sappho is claiming love of life in spite of age, in contrast to Tithonos.

culture is enforced against individual desire, so are rightly aligned with the conventional assessments. The narrator's desire for the absent Anaktoria is perhaps also longing for one who has been reclaimed by her family and her role in the social structure.

Sappho seems to have used the mythic pattern of goddess and young man not to picture nonhierarchical sexual intimacy but rather to reflect the fragility of her ideal of mutual desire under the pressure of the dominant culture. We can guess that she chooses the moment of closure in order to represent the closure that social demands forced on women's love lives. Many of Sappho's poems are about departure and absence: the women she knew seem to have been obliged to marry and leave or follow families elsewhere. However, the resolution in these particular myths in favor of the divine/human hierarchy (over the male/female one), in favor of the goddess, means that Sappho could at least use them to support women's claim to subjectivity in the face of objectification by others. A woman's subjectivity, like the goddess's, is represented as surviving the destruction of her love life.[98] The pattern of a goddess with a young man is thus a model for women's loves: it validates the location of love and desire apart from the established social structures, analogizes the woman to a goddess to support her claim to subjectivity and active desire, and acknowledges the impossibility of retaining the relationships formed there in the face of social demands on the woman. The young man of the myth, then, may have represented both the fantasy of escape from cultural definition and the power of cultural demands to reclaim the individual.

In these myths, in sum, Sappho perhaps saw a reflection of the working of the dominant ideology: through its own internal contradictions it opened space briefly for mutual erotic relationships, which it then closed down in its insistence that a woman's life follow the canonical narrative. Yet in Sappho's subversive logic, the straightforward gaze, the narrator's gaze in imagination at Anaktoria in 16 V., Selene's gaze at Endymion, is what is left to the woman when the desired other is lost. The absence of the other that transforms the gaze into projection also transforms the woman into a subject and possessor of the gaze.

98. Compare 96 V., in which the woman who has departed now shines like the moon when it causes the stars to fade. Though separated from Lesbos and/or Atthis, the woman continues to stand out from her surroundings. Hague, "Sappho's Consolation for Atthis," thinks that the simile is left hanging because it is an art image of the woman's loneliness: this too is an aspect of it.

THIRTEEN

The Justice of Aphrodite in Sappho 1

Anne Carson

Dionysius of Halicarnassus, the earliest recorded critic of Sappho's first poem, praised it for its cohesion and smoothness of construction.[1] Since that time the poetic quality of the poem has not, I think, been doubted but controversy has arisen about the meaning of the poem. Much of the controversy has focused upon the penultimate stanza, lines 21–24. Recent scholarship provides us with several decades of debate about this stanza—particularly about its tone.[2] There has been no debate about the actual events to which the stanza alludes. It is assumed that the events are obvious. I think that this assumption is untrustworthy, and that debate about the tone of the stanza could be eliminated, or at least radically simplified, if we were to clarify our notion of what is going on in these verses.

Lines 21–24 present the words of Aphrodite to Sappho. Sappho has suffered an injustice at the hands of her beloved, and has called upon Aphrodite to alleviate the pain of this injustice. The girl with whom Sappho is in love has apparently fled from Sappho's advances, rejected her gifts, and refused her love. Aphrodite therefore makes three promises or predictions to Sappho concerning the fate which lies in store for the unresponsive girl. Aphrodite says: "For in fact if she is fleeing, soon she will pursue. And if she is rejecting gifts, instead she will give them. And if she does not love, soon she will love, even if she does not want to."

This essay was originally published in slightly different form as "The Justice of Aphrodite in Sappho Fr. 1," *Transactions of the American Philological Association* 110 (1980) 135–42.
1. Dion. Hal. *Comp.* 173–79.
2. Bibliography can be found in Saake, *Zur Kunst Sapphos* and *Sapphostudien*; Stanley, "The Role of Aphrodite." To these may be added Gentili, "Il 'letto insaziato' di Medea"; Bonnano, "Osservazioni"; Bonaria, "Note critiche al testo di Saffo"; Lasso de la Vega, "La oda primera de Safo"; Marry, "Sappho and the Heroic Ideal."

Although interpreters have differed about the tone of these words of
Aphrodite, they have universally agreed about the situation being described.
Aphrodite is promising, it is generally held, an ideal erotic revenge in the
form of a mutual reversal of the roles of lover and beloved. She is promising
to reverse the situation that exists between Sappho and her beloved, to turn
the tables, so that the girl who is now indifferent to Sappho will experience a
change of heart and will pursue Sappho with gifts and love. This standard
view is recently expressed, for example, by Sir Kenneth Dover in his book
Greek Homosexuality. Dover says: "The other person, who now refuses gifts
and flees, will not merely yield and 'grant favours' but will pursue Sappho
and will herself offer gifts."[3]

This is a plausible interpretation, but it is not what the Greek words say.
Aphrodite's statements contain no direct object. She does not say that the
girl will pursue Sappho, she does not say that the girl will give gifts to Sappho,
she does not say that the girl will love Sappho. She merely says that the girl
will pursue, give gifts, and love.[4] There is an interpretation of these words
available to us which imposes no assumptions on the grammar and which,
furthermore, is in better agreement with the traditions of Greek erotic poetry.
For it is not the case generally in Greek poetry that scorned lovers pin their
hopes on a mutual reversal of erotic roles. In general, forlorn lovers console
themselves with a much less fantastic thought: namely, that the unresponsive
beloved will one day grow up and become a lover himself, or herself, and in
the role of lover will pursue an unresponsive beloved and will come to "know
what it feels like" to be rejected. Within the strict conventions of Greek
homosexual Eros such a revenge is fairly certain. There are clearly defined
ages of life appropriate to the roles of lover and beloved.[5] In the course of
time the beloved will naturally and inevitably become a lover, and will almost

3. Dover, *Greek Homosexuality* 177. Ll. 18–19 in particular are generally understood to
support such an interpretation since, despite the uncertainty of the text, it is clear that these
verses contain a reference to someone coming into someone's *philotata*. The various readings
which have been suggested are cited and discussed by Bonaria, "Osservazione." Most plausibly,
these verses refer to Sappho's beloved and the fact that she is not reciprocating Sappho's love.
Whether the girl once reciprocated and now refuses, or never reciprocated at all, depends
on the reading of 18–19. But even if reconciliation of some kind is involved here, this need
not affect the explanation of ll. 21–24, for Aphrodite appears to begin a new line of thought
with her question "Who is wronging you?" With this question Aphrodite passes from the
specific injustice at hand to the general principle of justice that governs such cases.

4. Schadewaldt, *Sappho* 89, and Privitera, "La rete di Afrodite" 47 n. 44, remark on the
absence of a direct object. Both assume that, if it were expressed, the object would be "you."

5. Plato *Symp.* 183d–e, 190d–e; Alexis fr. 70 Kock; Theoc. *Id.* 7.120 and Gow ad loc.; *AP*
12.22, 31, 32, 33, 46, 176, 186, 195, 224, 228, 229; Theopompus Comicus fr. 29 Kock and Dover's
comments in *Greek Homosexuality* 87 n. 48; Plut. *Mor.* 770b–c; Licht [Brandt], *Sexual Life in Ancient
Greece* 416 f.; Flacelière, *L'amour en Grèce* 43–70; Devereux, "Greek Pseudo-Homosexuality" 82.

inevitably experience rejection at least once. This idea recurs repeatedly in Greek poetry and surely reflects a common human experience.[6] A vivid example of it is furnished by a graffito from Stabiae:[7]

εἴ τις καλὸς γενόμενος
οὐκ ἔδωκε πυγίσαι· ἐκῖνος καλῆς
ἐρασθεὶς μὴ τύχοι βεινήματος.

The poet Theognis expresses the same thought. Theognis says to his beloved:

αἴδεό μ᾽, ὦ παῖ ⟨ ⟩, διδοὺς χάριν, εἴ ποτε καὶ σὺ
  ἕξεις Κυπρογενοῦς δῶρον ἰοστεφάνου
χρηΐζων καὶ ἐπ᾽ ἄλλον ἐλεύσεαι, ἀλλά σε δαίμων
  δοίη τῶν αὐτῶν ἀντιτυχεῖν ἐπέων.

(1331–34)

Respect me, oh lad, and grant me favor, if ever in your turn you will come to another to crave the gift of the violet-crowned Cyprus-born. May the divinity grant that you meet with the same words that I meet now.

This theme becomes a topos in Hellenistic poetry. We meet it, for instance, in the seventh *Idyll* of Theocritus, in an epigram attributed to Callimachus and in many poems of the *Anthology*,[8] from which I have drawn the following two examples:

Ἄρτι γενειάζων ὁ καλὸς καὶ στερρὸς ἐρασταῖς
  παιδὸς ἐρᾷ Λάδων· σύντομος ἡ Νέμεσις.

(*AP* 12.12)

Just as he is getting his beard, Lado, the fair youth, cruel to lovers, is in love with a boy. Nemesis is swift.

Ἀλλ᾽ ἱλαροῦ μετάδος τι φιλήματος ἔσθ᾽ ὅτε καὶ σὺ
  αἰτήσεις τοιάνδ᾽ ἐξ ἑτέρων χάριτα.

(*AP* 12.16.3–4)

6. See Gow ad Theoc. *Id.* 7.118; Dover, *Greek Homosexuality* 58; Jones, "Tange Chloen semel Arrogantem" 81–84; Fraenkel, *Horace* 414.
7. This obscene graffito is published by D'Orsi, "Un graffito di Stabia," and cited by Jones, "Tange Chloen semel Arrogantem" 82.
8. Theoc. *Id.* 7.118; [Callim.] *Epigr.* 63 Pfeiffer; *AP* 5.21, 27, 92, 164, 273, 280, 298; 11.73, 374; 12.35, 109, 160, 186, 193; Nonnus *Dion.* 16.297. Professor E. Robbins has drawn my attention to a parallel in Ovid *Met.* 3.405. Hor. *Carm.* 3.26, properly interpreted, presents a scenario similar to that of Sappho fr. 1. C. P. Jones, "Tange Chloen semel Arrogantem," has rightly proposed that Horace here prays for Chloe to fall (unhappily) in love with some third person. Jones draws upon the Hellenistic tradition to demonstrate that the typical rejected lover, having resigned his own suit, trusts the course of time to impose upon his beloved the nemesis of an unrequited passion. Cf. Hor. *Carm.* 1.25, with the parallels collected by Nisbet and Hubbard, *A Commentary on Horace* 289–301, esp. *AP* 5.298, in which *Dikē* is asked to punish the beloved's haughtiness with grey hair and wrinkles.

But give me a taste of a happy kiss. The time will come when you will beg such favor from others.

If this line of interpretation can be applied to Sappho's poem, it considerably deepens the impact of her words, for she is not daydreaming about imaginary reversals but looking forward to a concrete and inevitable revenge. This interpretation also gives more point to the phase κωὖκ ἐθέλοισα, (even against her will) in line 24. This phrase has provoked much comment and some emendation of the manuscripts' reading.[9] The interpretation which I am proposing confirms the reading of the manuscripts on grounds of sense, for, if the beloved is to become a lover, she will naturally take on a lover's state of mind. To find oneself doing things against one's will is the perennial condition of the lover. It is an axiom of Greek love poetry that Eros is ἀνάγκη (necessity) for the lover but not for the beloved.[10] Greek lovers describe their experience as that of being coerced by a force outside oneself. In Archilochus, love is a force which "subdues" the lover (δάμναται; fr. 196 West [W.]). Ibycus sees himself as an old horse compelled (ἀέκων) by Eros to line up for another race with love (PMG 287). Theognis speaks of the "compulsions" imposed on him by a boy's love, using the phrase ἀεκούσια πολλὰ βίαια, "many violent things that go against my will" (1343), and echoes Sappho's κωὖκ ἐθέλοισα with κοὖκ ἐθέλοντος (1342). A typical lover in the Anthology complains:

ἀγρεύσας ἕλκει τῇδ' ὁ βίαιος Ἔρως
ἐνθάδ' ὅπου τὸν παῖδα διαστείχοντ' ἐνόησα·
αὐτομάτοις δ' ἄκων ποσσὶ ταχὺς φέρομαι.
(AP 12.85.4–6)

Violent love caught me and drags me here, here where I saw the boy go through the gate; and I am borne swiftly by my feet moving of their own will.

The beloved, traditionally, does not participate in the emotions that move the lover and hence has no occasion to experience love as a coercion.[11] Xenophon compares the paidika confronting his lover's desire with a sober man watching a drunk (Symp. 8.21) The beloved is the cool and indifferent fulcrum of a magnetic attraction which draws the lover to itself by force.[12]

---

9. A survey of the controversy concerning κωὖκ ἐθέλοισα may be found in Bonaria, "Note critiche al testo di Saffo" 159.

10. On anankē in erotic contexts see Dover, Greek Homosexuality 60–62; Schreckenburg, Ananke 59–60; Loraux, "Sur la race des femmes" 84 n. 157; Gerber, "Varia Semonidea" 20–21.

11. "In a homosexual relationship ... the eromenos is not expected to reciprocate the eros of the erastes" (Dover, Greek Homosexuality 52).

12. Sappho's fr. 31 is perhaps the clearest evocation in literature of this situation. Ibycus takes for granted that his beloved is unaware of and indifferent to the effect he is having (PMG 360). Plato gives us several images of a beautiful young man as the cool center of a

So, if the beloved girl in Sappho's poem is to leave behind the role of beloved
and take on, properly and completely, the role of lover, this will necessarily
involve a coercion of her will. As lover, she will, by definition, find herself
acting κωὖκ ἐθέλοισα.

The interpretation I am proposing also mitigates a certain harshness of
transition between the fifth and sixth stanzas, which has been criticized
by commentators on the poem.[13] The fifth stanza ends with an emphatic
request from Aphrodite for the identity of the unjust beloved. "Who is it
who is wronging you?" Aphrodite asks Sappho. This question is never
answered. Instead we pass immediately to the sixth stanza and its series
of predictions about the future of the beloved. The connective is καὶ γάρ,
which permits a translation "for in fact if she is fleeing, soon she will pursue,"
and so on.[14] This transition becomes easier if we understand Aphrodite as
putting forward not a specific program of revenge tailored to Sappho, but
a general theory of lover's justice. For, in the latter case, Aphrodite's line
of thought may be seen to be something like "Who is it who is wronging
you? Well, whoever it is, you are absurd to worry about it, for in fact if
she is now fleeing, soon she will pursue," and so on. In other words, the
ellipse of an answer to Aphrodite's question τίς σ' ἀδικήει· is deliberate:
a deliberate dramatization of the universal law of justice on which lovers
can rely as surely as they can rely on the passage of time. Aphrodite's words
imply that, from the point of view of justice, it does not matter who the unjust
girl is: in time everybody grows too old to be pursued. "Brigitte Bardot will
never be sixty," said Brigitte Bardot in an interview with *Time* magazine in
1974. In making this statement Mlle Bardot was referring not, I think, to the
likelihood of a tragedy in her fifty-ninth year but rather to the fact that the
persona or role called "Brigitte Bardot" would not be compatible with sixty
years of life. Similarly in the Greek context, no one can play the beloved
forever. That is part of the justice of Aphrodite.

Aphrodite's tone, then, is one of brisk and reassuring dismissal, as the
goddess of love disclaims the possibility that Sappho's beloved, no matter
who she is, will remain an object of desire forever. Controversy about the
tone of the poem was stirred in 1955 with Sir Denys Page's imputation of
irony to this passage.[15] Aphrodite speaks in tones of amused reproof, Page

---

magnetic field of attention in a room of men, e.g., *Chrm.* 154c–155e; *Euth.* 274c. Sophocles
may be comparing the beloved to a lodestone in fr. 886 Pearson (cf. *AP* 12.152). See also
Dover, *Greek Homosexuality* 55–56, and the comments of Fränkel, *Early Greek Poetry* 524, on the
"force-field of love."

13. Cameron, "Sappho and Aphrodite" 238.
14. Denniston, *The Greek Particles* 108–9.
15. Page, *Sappho and Alcaeus* 12–18.

felt, smiling at Sappho "as a mother with a troublesome child," while Sappho reports the words and smile of the goddess "not without amusement at her own expense." Page further insisted that in Greek it is impossible διώκειν (to pursue) an object which does not φεύγειν (to flee).[16] He therefore took line 21 to predict that the beloved girl would pursue Sappho whereupon Sappho would run away. Since Sappho herself is the narrator of Aphrodite's words, this puts the poet in the position of praying passionately for an object which, at the same time, she declares she will reject. The nimble psychology of such an attitude is, in Page's view, an example of the "remarkable detachment" with which Sappho manages her own emotions, a detachment which dictates the amused irony of Aphrodite's tone and the unserious mood of the whole poem. This interpretation of the poem's tone, and the controversy aroused by it, have been based on a misunderstanding of the events of stanza 6. Once we have adjusted our notion of who is chasing whom in lines 21–24, the possibility of irony becomes irrelevant.

If the interpretation of these verses which I have put forward is tenable, it adds a dimension to Sappho's conception of erotic justice. The dimension is time. Sappho imagines that time itself, given the nature of things, will enact the justice of Aphrodite upon the unjust beloved ταχέως ... ταχέως (quickly). The idea that time is the enactor of justice is not an unfamiliar one in archaic and early classical thought. It is implied in the Aeschylean notion of a family curse, as well as in Hesiod's belief that justice and injustice are rewarded by natural occurrences like plague, famine, or the birth of children. Pindar tells us that βία δὲ καὶ μεγάλαυχον ἔσφαλεν ἐν χρόνῳ (force and arrogance stumble in time; *Pyth.* 8.15). Solon summons the Earth to witness his justice ἐν δίκῃ χρόνου (in the justice of time; 36.3 W.). Anaximander speaks of the order of the universe in terms of *dikē* which is judged κατὰ τὴν τοῦ χρόνου τάξιν (according to the order of time; DK B 1). Sappho's assumption, that justice is an enactment of time in erotic contexts, fits in with the belief of other archaic poets that justice is in general so enacted. Her language emphasizes, especially by repetition of the adverbs δηὖτε (15, 16, 18) and ταχέως (21, 23), the rhythm of time which orders erotic experience, creating and recreating the same impasse (δηὖτε) and ever proposing the same consolation (ταχέως).

The question remains, what difference does this interpretation make to the sense of Sappho's poem as a whole? The poem begins and ends with a request that Aphrodite release Sappho from the pain, grief, and anxiety that

---

16. There has been nearly universal objection to Page's restriction of the meaning of διώκειν. See, e.g., Koniaris, "On Sappho I"; Krischer, "Sapphos Ode an Aphrodite"; Stanley, "The Role of Aphrodite" 316 f.

she feels as a rejected lover. Aphrodite's words in lines 21–24 presumably address themselves in some way to this request. How do they do so?

Aphrodite is reassuring Sappho that her anguish over this particular girl is almost at an end. It is a commonplace of homosexual relations between men in the Greek tradition that the lover's desire fades sharply as soon as the boy's beard begins to grow. Plutarch cites a dictum of Bion the sophist to the effect that the beard making its appearance on the face of the beloved "liberates the lover from the tyranny of Eros."[17]   It is plausible that there were parallel sentiments among Greek women who engaged in homosexual relationships, and that Sappho could expect to be liberated from her desire for this particular girl as soon as the girl became obviously too old to play the role of beloved. Aphrodite's words in lines 21–24, then, are a promise to Sappho of release from erotic tyranny. Her promise is based on the principle of her justice. If we have interpreted it correctly, this is an eternal principle which can be relied on as confidently as can the fact that time passes and young people grow old and lovers love without return, δηὖτε … δηὖτε … δηὖτε.

The reinterpretation here proposed for the sixth stanza of Sappho's first poem permits clarification of the text, grammar, syntax, choice of words, tone, and overall sense, as well as integrating the stanza much more satisfactorily with the rest of the poem, and integrating the poem more satisfactorily with the traditions of Greek erotic verse and with archaic currents of thought on the subject of justice. The poem is seen to unfold unironically on one plane of sentiment and expression in a way which vindicates the assessment of Dionysius of Halicarnassus and undercuts modern controversies about irony. Sappho is saying exactly what she means—no less, no more. She is not praying to Aphrodite for a reconciliation with her beloved. She is praying for justice.

17. Plut. *Mor.* 770b–c. See also Pind. *Ol.* 1.67–71; Theog. 1327–28; Plato *Symp.* 183d–e, *Prot.* 309a; *AP* 11.36, 51; 12.22, 26, 27, 30, 39, 41, 174, 191, 215; Dover, *Greek Homosexuality* 86.

FOURTEEN

Apostrophe and Women's Erotics in the Poetry of Sappho

Ellen Greene

I

One of the most compelling issues in Sappho criticism during the last two decades has been the question about how Sappho's gender has shaped or determined the nature of her poetic discourse. Recent scholars have provided powerful arguments for showing how Sappho's poetry is not merely the spontaneous effusion of a passionate woman. These scholars have pointed up the many formulaic and conventional aspects of Sappho's poems that link Sappho to rather than separate her from the poetry of her male counterparts.[1] As Jack Winkler argues, however, Sappho redefines the cultural norms expressed in the social and literary formulas of archaic poetry from the perspective of her "private" woman-centered world. Winkler does not deny the public, performative character of Sappho's poetry and her use of the emblems of male, public culture, but he defines, aptly, how Sappho's poetry may be regarded as "private":

> And yet, maintaining this thesis of the public character of lyric, we can still propose three senses in which such song may be "private": first, composed in the person of a woman (whose consciousness was socially defined as outside the public world of men); second, shared only with women (that is, other "private" persons ... ;

I wish to thank Yopie Prins, Eva Stehle, Paul Allen Miller, Charles Platter, and David H.J. Larmour for constructive criticism on earlier versions of this paper. I am also grateful to Sander Goldberg for his astute editing of the version of this essay that was published in *TAPA* 124 (1994) 41–56. Finally, this essay owes much to ongoing conversations with James Hawthorne, who helped me sharpen my arguments and make my ideas more readable.
    1. For exponents of this view, see Calame, *Les chœurs*; Carson, "The Justice of Aphrodite"; Lasserre, "Ornements érotiques"; Nagy, "The Symbols of Greek Lyric," and *Pindar's Homer*; Svenbro, "Death by Writing," in *Phrasikleia*.

and third, sung on informal occasions, what we would simply call poetry readings, rather than on specific ceremonial occasions such as sacrifice, festival, leave-taking, or initiation.[2]

Although Winkler argues for the gender-specificity of Sappho's poetic discourse and cultural attitudes, he nonetheless attributes to her a "double consciousness"—an ability to speak bilingually, that is, in the languages of both the male public arena and the excluded female minority. I believe, however, that Winkler does not take his views far enough about how Sappho's marginal status as a woman produced a version of desire significantly different from male archaic poets. Recent feminist scholars, while acknowledging Sappho's indebtedness to Homer and to the traditions of archaic poetry, contend that Sappho's poetry presents what Marilyn Skinner calls a "woman-specific discourse[,] ... an elaborate complex of coding strategies differing perceptibly from those of the dominant symbolic order." Skinner describes those strategies as "open, fluid, and polysemous—and hence conspicuously nonphallic."[3] Similarly, Eva Stehle compares Sappho's erotic poems with those of Archilochus, Ibycus, and Anacreon and argues that a pattern of mutuality emerges in Sappho's poetry in sharp contrast to an hierarchical mode of eroticism that is prevalent in male patterns of erotic discourse. Like Skinner, Stehle maintains that by creating an "open space for imagining unscripted sexual relations ... Sappho can represent an alternative for women to the cultural norms."[4]

My own argument in this paper will attempt to further the views put forth by Stehle and Skinner by providing a theoretical framework for understanding Sappho's fragments as offering an erotic practice and discourse outside of patriarchal modes of thought. I hope to show how Sappho constructs erotic experience outside male assumptions about dominance and submission through a close reading of fragment 94. I will pay particular attention to the apostrophic structure of the poem and show how it dramatizes an experience of desire as mutual recognition. I will also discuss the last two stanzas of fragment 1—a poem that is thought by some critics to deviate from patterns of mutuality in Sappho and contradict the view that Sappho's mode of discourse represents female homoerotic desire with its own symbolic systems and conventions.

In her book *The Bonds of Love*, Jessica Benjamin's analysis of gender and domination and her concept of "intersubjectivity" offer a theoretical perspective that, I believe, helps clarify a women's erotics in Sappho. Benjamin offers

2. Winkler, "Double Consciousness" 165.
3. Skinner, "Woman and Language" 182.
4. Stehle, "Sappho's Private World" 108.

an illuminating, feminist analysis of the psychological underpinnings of erotic domination; her discussion of the relation between gender and domination demonstrates the complex intertwining of sexual and social domination. In her analysis, Benjamin identifies the unequal complementarity in which "one is always up and the other down" not only as the basic pattern of erotic domination, but also as a specifically *masculine* mode of thought and practice that permeates all social organization. It is masculine because, as Jane Flax observes, "culture *is* masculine, not as the effect of language but as the consequence of actual power relations to which men have far more access to women."[5] Benjamin's concept of intersubjectivity—"that space in which the mutual recognition of subjects can compete with the reversible relationship of domination"—describes a mutuality between lover and beloved based on a subject position for women that defies cultural norms and furnishes an alternate basis for categorizing female experience.[6]

As Skinner suggests, it is from Sappho's position of marginality that she is able to construct an alternative to the phallic representation of desire. In the segregated female world of the *hetairia*,[7] Sappho could express active female erotic desire and claim an authentic subject position—what Teresa de Lauretis calls an "eccentric discursive position outside the male ... monopoly of power," a "form of female subjectivity that exceeds the phallic definition" of woman as *object* or Other.[8] Furthermore, de Lauretis maintains the premise that women's *difference* is a consequence not of biology but of their specific condition of exploitation and gender oppression, which affords them a position of knowledge and struggle that gives rise to possible alternative modes of structuring erotic discourse and practice. Thus, the Sapphic subject, because it speaks from a place of discourse located outside patriarchy, can construct a model of erotic relations that is as Marilyn Skinner puts it "bilateral and egalitarian, in marked contrast to the rigid patterns of pursuit and physical mastery inscribed into the role of the adult male *erastēs*, whatever the sex of his love object."[9] The model to which Skinner refers is undeniably homoerotic. De Lauretis, as well, posits the "eccentric" female

5. Flax, *Thinking Fragments* 103.
6. Skinner, "Woman and Language" 184–85.
7. See Parker, "Sappho Schoolmistress," for his compelling argument against the modern construction of a *thiasos*—with Sappho as a sort of cult leader. I agree with Parker that there is no evidence of a ritual or cultic function for Sappho's poems or that Sappho's social role was anything other than that of poet. Thus, Parker argues that Sappho "should be seen, not in a *thiasos* (whatever that might be) but, like Alcaeus, in a *hetairia*, an association of friends[,] ... a group of women tied by family, class, politics, and erotic love." I concur with Parker's view that a *hetairia* rather than a *thiasos* is a more appropriate construction of Sappho's "society."
8. De Lauretis, "Eccentric Subjects" 126–27.
9. Skinner, "Woman and Language" 186.

subject as one that refuses the terms of the heterosexual contract. Indeed, in a society as male dominated as Sappho's most likely was, one can easily see that the expression of active female desire was most accessible in the context of an autonomous and homoerotic woman's culture. I believe, however, that it is possible for contemporary readers of Sappho—both men and women—to discover in Sappho's articulation of female desire an alternative to the competitive and hierarchical models of eroticism that have dominated Western culture.

II

One of the most striking features of Sappho's poetry is her use of apostrophe to play out the conflicts of her erotic drama. In his essay on poetic apostrophe, Jonathan Culler points out that literary critics have largely considered apostrophe a meaningless convention that is taken for granted as an inherited, accidental characteristic of the genre.[10] But indeed studying the role of apostrophe is crucial to an understanding of poetic discourse itself. As Culler argues, "Apostrophe is different in that it makes its point by troping, not on the meaning of a word, but on the circuit or situation of communication itself."[11] In other words, what Culler calls "the vocative of apostrophe" is a device that the poetic voice uses to dramatize its own calling, its ability to summon images of its own power so as to establish, with an object, a relationship that helps to constitute an image of self.

Thus, apostrophe poses the problem of the poetic subject as a problem of the addressee's *relation* to it. The addressee becomes a live presence only when poetic voice constitutes itself. The "figure of voice" dramatizes both its own speaking and its power to give life to inanimate objects or to make present an absent addressee. As Barbara Johnson puts it, "Apostrophe is a form of ventriloquism through which the speaker throws voice, life, and human form into the addressee, turning its silence into mute responsiveness."[12] Apostrophe raises the question of whether the sheer act of utterance can animate lifeless objects and heal the pain of separation and loss. By conferring presence on an absent addressee, the lover transforms the beloved from an object into a subject, effecting in the process a discourse between two subjects. The idea that the vocative posits a relationship between two subjects is greatly intensified in the context of erotic

10. Culler, *The Pursuit of Signs* 136–54. This chapter, "Apostrophe," is one of the most influential studies of the use of poetic apostrophe and has drawn attention to its importance as a literary device.

11. Ibid., 43.

12. B. Johnson, "Apostrophe" 185.

poetry. The erotic subject is faced with the beloved's absence *and* with self-dissolution.[13] Not only does the act of apostrophe make present the absent object of desire, but it also is the mechanism through which the erotic subject constitutes itself.

Sappho's dramatic use of address and invocation in her erotic fragments shows the paradoxical relationship between the debilitating and fragmenting effects of eros on the self and the reconstruction of the self in the poetic act. In Sappho's poems, the speaker often associates the diminishing of verbal power—attendant on separation from the beloved—with a kind of death. Apostrophe—the recuperation of voice through memory—reanimates the "I" through a reinscription of an individual poetic voice into a communal discourse. I shall argue that fragment 94 shows a progression from third-person narrative to second-person address to the emergence of first-person "we" and that this progression is inextricably bound up in the performative and communal context of Sappho's poems. That Sappho's narrator reconstitutes her fragmented self by establishing a relationship with her addressee *in the time of the apostrophe* refers us to the transforming and animating activity of the poetic voice. However, the inclusion of an audience (the "we") in the grammar of the poem—in the present moment of discourse—moves the speaker outside a radical interiorization and narcissism whereby the other is merely a projection of self.[14]

Fragment 94 illustrates how Sappho's apostrophizing voice affirms the eroticism of her narrator by erasing the distinction between self and other, speaker and addressee, and creates an intimacy based, in Luce Irigaray's words, on a "nearness so pronounced that it makes all discrimination of identity, and thus all forms of property, impossible."[15] Sappho doesn't fantasize about the beloved as separate from herself, as an object either to gaze at or describe.[16] Irigaray's assertion that "the predominance of the visual ... is particularly foreign to female eroticism"[17] seems consistent with the way Sappho pictures love relations in 94 as an environment of mutual enclosure and reciprocity. The speaker's erotic fulfillment comes not from making the beloved a beautiful object of contemplation, but by drawing the

13. From Homer through the early Greek lyric poets, erotic experience is closely associated with a loss of vital self, and even death. For an insightful discussion of this, see Carson, *Eros the Bittersweet*.

14. Culler, *The Pursuit of Signs* 146.

15. Irigaray, *This Sex* 31. Irigaray's work has been extremely influential in articulating ideas about the question of woman's *essence* and of a female sexuality. Irigaray's view of feminine sexuality, which supplants the logic of the gaze with the logic of touch (22–33), seems especially relevant to a discussion of the mutuality of desire in Sappho's poetry.

16. Stehle, "Sappho's Gaze."

17. Irigaray, *This Sex* 25–26.

beloved to her by making the beloved a part of the lover's interior world of memory and imagination.

τεθνάκην δ'ἀδόλως θέλω.
ἄ με ψισδομένα κατελίμπανεν   2
πόλλα καὶ τόδ' ἔειπ [
ὤιμ' ὡς δεῖνα πεπ[όνθ]αμεν
Ψάπφ', ἦ μάν σ'ἀέκοισ' ἀπυλιμπάνω.   5
τὰν δ' ἔγω τάδ' ἀμειβόμαν
χαίροισ' ἔρχεο κἄμεθεν
μέμναισ'. οἶσθα γὰρ ὥς σε πεδήπομεν.   8
αἰ δὲ μή, ἀλλά σ' ἔγω θέλω
ὄμναισαι[. . . (.)] [. . (.)] . . αι
. . [   ] καὶ κάλ' ἐπάσχομεν.   11
πό[λλοις γὰρ στεφάν]οις ἴων
καὶ βρ[όδων   ]κίων τ' ὔμοι
κα . . [   ] πὰρ ἔμοι περεθήκαο,   14
καὶ πόλλαις ὑπαθύμιδας
πλέκταις ἀμφ' ἀπάλαι δέραι
ἀνθέων . [   ] πεποημμέναις,   17
καὶ π . . . . . [   ] . μύρωι
βρενθείωι . [   ]ρυ[. .]ν
ἐξαλείψαο καὶ βασιληίωι,   20
καὶ στρών[αν ἐ]πὶ μολθάκαν
ἀπάλαν πα . [   ] . . . ων
ἐξίης πόθο[ν   ] νιδων,
κωὔτε τις [   ] . . τι
ἶρον οὐδυ[   ]
ἔπλετ' ὄππ[οθεν ἄμ]μες ἀπέσχομεν,   26
οὐκ ἄλσος .[   ] . ρος
                ]ψοφος
              ] . . . οιδιαι   29

Honestly, I wish I were dead.
Weeping she left with many tears,

And said; "Oh what terrible things
we endured. Sappho, truly,
against my will I leave you."

And I answered: "Go, be
happy, and remember me;
For you know how we cared for you.

And if not, then I want
to remind you . . . of the wonderful
things we shared.

For many wreaths of violets and
roses . . .
you put on by my side,

And many woven garlands
fashioned of flowers,
you tied round your soft neck,

And with rich myrrh,
fit for a queen,
you anointed . . .

And on a soft bed,
tenderly,
you satisfied [your] desire.[18]

And there was
no sacred place
from which we were absent,

no grove,
no dance,
no sound. . . ."[19]

The fragment opens with the expression of a wish to die. Since the beginning of the poem is missing, the poem does not tell us who speaks the first extant line—the speaker or the other woman. Scholars who attribute the line to the speaker interpret the poem as "a complex picture of longing and pain" and view the speaker as a woman overcome by frenzy and grief. Burnett argues persuasively that the other woman rather than the speaker utters the wish to die in the fragment's opening line. As Burnett shows, "The disconsolate girl thinks that parting is the end of life and love, but her wiser mistress commands her to go her way rejoicing."[20] In accord with Burnett's view, Snyder argues that "[t]he poem, then, is hardly a 'confession,' but rather a recapturing of past pleasures through memory, by which the 'dreadful things' mentioned by the girl—that is, the impending separation—are transformed into Sappho's 'beautiful things' beginning in stanza 4."[21] I concur that it is the other woman who speaks the first line of the fragment—a line that plunges the poem into the realities of separation and loss. Moreover, attributing the opening line to the other woman heightens the

18. L. 23 is usually translated with *your desire*. But the verb in the line is active rather than middle, so it may refer to someone else's desire. The ambiguity may well be intentional since, in the context of mutual desire, it does not matter who is satisfying whom.

19. The Greek text of fr. 94 comes from Campbell, *Greek Lyric Poetry*. The English translation of the poem is my own.

20. Burnett, "Desire and Memory" 23.

21. Snyder, *The Woman and the Lyre* 26.

tension in the poem between the two speakers—whose different approaches toward the separation are reflected in their correspondingly different modes of discourse.

Indeed, the stark wish to die is expressed baldly, without the embellishment of poetic images. The use of the word ἀδόλως initiates a conversational diction and tone that accentuate the contingencies of circumstance. The time-bound world of circumstance evoked here is reinforced by the speaker's use of third-person narrative to describe a past event that is irreversible—the painful departure and loss of her beloved. The vocative Ψάπφ' in line 5, although framed within a narrative in the past tense in which the beloved addresses "Sappho," introduces an apostrophic element into the narrative. This apostrophe in the narrative creates a sense of dramatic immediacy that begins to bridge the gap between the past of narration and the now of discourse.

The drama of separation unfolds as we hear the distinct voices of the speaker and her departing lover shift back and forth in nearly ritualized responsion to one another.[22] The speaker's direct recollection of the time of departure locates both the narrator and the woman who is leaving in a temporal sequence of events in which they are each distinct characters within the narrative reported by the speaker. The predominantly descriptive mode of discourse here preserves the sense of separateness between the two lovers. This separateness is reinforced by the parallel structure of the first four stanzas, which all end in verbs that function in responsion to one another.

The speaker's request in line 8 that the woman remember (χαίροισ' ἔρχεο κἄμεθεν μέμναισ') draws the poem away from the dramatic portrayal of the woman leaving to the more inward situation of remembering. And although we are still in the narrative frame, the speaker's verbal imperatives to the woman (go and remember) are spoken as second-person address. The speaker has moved from reporting a past event in the third person to reporting the reciprocal apostrophes spoken by the two lovers. These two modes of discourse—third-person narrative and the reporting of second-person address—both remain within a temporal frame. It is not until the "we" emerges at line 8 that the speaker begins to turn away from narrative altogether. The "we" of πεδήπομεν initiates a shift from reported speech to a detemporalized mode of discourse in which the individual voices of the two lovers are no longer clearly differentiated. Furthermore, "we" in πεδήπομεν (we cared) connects the "I" and the "you" of the poem to a communal context. There is much debate and speculation in Sappho criticism about how and under what conditions Sappho's poems were performed. But many

---

22. See McEvilley, "Sappho, Fragment 94," for an insightful discussion of the way responsion between the two lovers works in the poem.

scholars believe that her fragments were performed either by Sappho herself or by a chorus of women to an audience comprising a community of other women.[23] Thus, the audience becomes implicated in the poetic enactment of eros as the speaker includes the group in a communal discourse that both proclaims and provokes desire.

In stanza 4, the pattern of shifting voices changes as the speaker's own point of view and poetic voice take over. The speaker's assertion at line 9 that she will remind her beloved if she doesn't remember focuses attention on the poetic voice and its ability to activate the past and make it come alive in the present. The word θέλω (I wish) at the end of line 9, expressing the speaker's wish to remind her departing lover about their past happiness, echoes the earlier wish to die in the opening line of the fragment. The repetition of θέλω in the parallel contexts of death and memory suggests the active transformative power of the poetic voice as it replaces the will to die with the will to create.

In fact, it doesn't seem to matter whether the woman remembers or not. Αἰ δὲ μή (and if not), at the beginning of the fourth stanza, conjoined to the emphatic ἔγω θέλω (I wish), suggests a negation of narrative temporality, by making the evocativeness of the speaker's own apostrophizing voice the central issue. The speaker turns away from narrative and addresses the beloved as a presence in a "time of discourse rather than story."[24] The speaker's clearly delineated voice offering her beloved an abstract consolation about how great the past was gives way to the dissolution of both their voices—voices that become subsumed within a detemporalized, intersubjective space inclusive of speaker, addressee, and an audience of women. As Culler points out, apostrophes displace the temporal sequences of narration by "removing the opposition between presence and absence from empirical time and locating it in a discursive time."[25] The move from empirical to discursive time is heightened in stanza 4, which brings about a transition to a more remote time and introduces a use of language that abounds in poetic images.

The picture in stanzas 5 through 10 is one of idyllic beauty and blissful satisfaction. As against the clearly delineated voices and personalities at the beginning, here the "I," "you," and "we" of the poem are all linked in the aura of sensations and erotic stimulation. Boundaries of person, object, and place seem to break down as everything in the environment dissolves into a totality of sensation. The speaker's erotic vocabulary—images of

23. See Calame, *Les chœurs*; Nagy, *Pindar's Homer*; and Lardinois, "Subject and Circumstance," for arguments that support a view of Sappho's poetry as choral.

24. Culler, *The Pursuit of Signs* 149.

25. Ibid., 150.

violets, roses, woven garlands, perfume, and soft beds—creates a song of seduction that enacts both the mesmerizing spell of desire and the power of the poet's voice to suspend time and draw the poem's audiences into what Dolores O'Higgins calls "the dangerous felicity of listening."[26] This atmosphere of sensual stimulation, however, does not seem to be placed in any actual environment; rather, the images of flowers, soft couches, perfumes, the shrine, and the grove all have a generalizing force that suggests remoteness from the world. Even the long series of flower images seems to function in isolation from nature and does not seem to refer to any specific ritual function or purpose except for the sensual enjoyment of the lovers and its poetic enactment.[27] What is emphasized about the flowers is the way they are artfully fashioned into beautiful garlands for the lovers to wear.

In spite of the speaker's rapt absorption in the woman whose presence she invokes, there is no emphasis on describing the woman *independent* of the effect she has on the narrator herself, or separate from the atmosphere their shared erotic experience generates. In the last two stanzas of the fragment, the sense of fullness, expressed in the repetition of negatives that negate the lovers' absence at the shrine, the grove, and the dance, contrasts with the emptiness implicit in the earlier verbs of abandonment and departure. The negation of place to denote presence suggests that it is the mutual experience of the two lovers that gives form to the world. The implication is that place comes alive only in the presence of the other.

Jessica Benjamin sees woman's sexual grounding in intersubjective space as her solution to the problem that woman's desire is not localized in space—not linked to phallic activity and its representations: "When the sexual self is represented by the sensual capacities of the whole body, when the totality of space between, outside, and within our bodies becomes the site of pleasure, then desire escapes the borders of the imperial phallus and resides on the shores of endless worlds."[28] Indeed, in Sappho's fragment the space inhabited by the two lovers expands outward to the seemingly endless spaces of streams, temples, and groves. The movement from the interior space connoted by the "soft bed" to the exterior space of the temple, the grove, and the dance reinforces the earlier link between the speaker, her addressee, and the circle of listening, perhaps singing, women. The effortless motion from interior to exterior space that suggests the dissolving of spatial boundaries correlates with the breakdown in clearly distinct positions of self and other, subject and object. Moreover, the connections in the poem between the

26. O'Higgins, "Sappho's Splintered Tongue" 162.
27. See Stehle, "Retreat from the Male," for a discussion of Sappho's use of flower imagery in an erotic context.
28. Benjamin, *The Bonds of Love* 130.

personal and collective discourses of women suggests an intersubjectivity that embraces a cultural system significantly different from male models of competitive and hierarchical self–other relationships.

III

It may be argued that fragment 1 departs from a pattern of mutuality in Sappho's poems. Anne Carson, for example, holds that in fragment 1 Sappho portrays erotic relations as an endless game of flight and pursuit, thus presenting a model of erotic relations that involves the dominance of one over the other.[29] This view is based largely on the famous lines in the next-to-last stanza spoken by Aphrodite to console the rejected or abandoned "Sappho": "For if she flees, soon she will pursue; and if she does not receive gifts, soon she will give them. And if she loves not, soon she will love even against her will" (21–24).

Carson sums up what she takes to be the usual interpretation of these lines: "Aphrodite is promising . . . an ideal erotic revenge in the form of a mutual reversal of the roles of lover and beloved." Carson, however, argues that Aphrodite is offering not a "specific program of revenge tailored to Sappho, but a general theory of lover's justice."[30] Carson believes that Aphrodite is not reassuring Sappho that she will eventually be reconciled with her beloved; rather, Aphrodite suggests to Sappho that her beloved will outgrow her position as beloved, become a lover herself (of some younger beloved, not Sappho), and experience the state of mind of the pursuer, the one taken by eros against her will. Moreover, Carson argues that Aphrodite's consoling words to Sappho dramatize the universal law of justice which guarantees, through the passage of time, that the beloved will grow too old to be pursued as an object of desire.

Carson's argument hinges on her observation that Aphrodite's statements to Sappho contain no direct object. In other words, Carson contends that Aphrodite does not say that *Sappho* will be the object of the girl's pursuit or the recipient of her gifts, only that the girl will someday pursue, give gifts, and love. Thus, from the "observation" that Aphrodite is *not* offering Sappho reconciliation with her beloved, Carson infers that Sappho is *not* asking Aphrodite to turn the affections of the girl toward Sappho—rather Sappho is merely asking Aphrodite for justice or revenge.

Carson's observation of the importance of the lack of a direct object in Aphrodite's consolation of Sappho is, I believe, quite astute. But I think she has misunderstood its significance. The mere fact that Aphrodite does

29. Carson, "The Justice of Aphrodite."
30. Ibid., 230.

not *explicitly* mention a direct object does not exclude the possibility that Aphrodite is reassuring Sappho that her beloved will eventually desire her, Sappho, in particular. Indeed, Aphrodite's question to Sappho in lines 18–19 (τίνα δηὖτε πείθω ... σαγην ἐς σὰν φιλότατα; "Whom, again, am I to persuade to come back into friendship with you?") seems to imply that Sappho wants Aphrodite's help in turning the girl's love in Sappho's direction (ἐς σὰν φιλότατα). The σὰν in line 19 suggests this specificity.

I think that the real significance of the lack of direct objects (of fleeing, pursuing, and loving) in these lines is that Sappho is suggesting that neither she nor her beloved are *objects* of each other's love. The speaker does not imagine that the consummation of (her) love involves *either* domination or submission. The beloved is figured as a *subject* whether she is fleeing or pursuing, giving or receiving. Indeed, it may be argued that the subject "she" in these lines can be either the speaker or her beloved. The speaker is describing, in general terms, the reciprocal movements of desire in which she and her beloved both participate in the process of giving and receiving, loving and being loved—a process that, according to the grammar of the poem, involves *only* subjects. Moreover, the incantatory quality of the lines evokes what Charles Segal calls the "hypnotic effect of love's *thelxis*." Segal argues that "the rhythmical echo between the first and third lines ... almost seems to assure the success of this spell-like promise."[31] If it is true, as Segal argues, that the fulfillment of love means *thelxis*, then surely both lover and beloved must both fall under the same spell for love to be fully realized. By definition, it seems, the "magic of eros" implicates both lovers in a circularity of desire that requires reciprocity.

Moreover, in the context of the whole poem it seems much more likely that Sappho seeks reconciliation rather than revenge. The initial and final stanzas frame the poem with Sappho's invocation of Aphrodite *in the present*. But the body of the poem is in the past tense. Sappho is remembering an earlier occasion when she called to Aphrodite and Aphrodite came to her. The body of the poem narrates that past encounter. We learn through Sappho's narration of the encounter that Sappho has called on Aphrodite before for the same purpose: to ask Aphrodite's help in persuading Sappho's beloved to turn her affections back in Sappho's direction. If it is merely erotic justice Sappho wants, then once Sappho recalls Aphrodite's "words of justice" from that earlier encounter she would have no reason to continue to call on Aphrodite again to enact the same revenge, the same universal law of justice; there would be no reason for Sappho to continue the invocation of Aphrodite in the last stanza. If, however, Sappho is asking for Aphrodite's

31. Segal, "Eros and Incantation" 67.

aid in turning her beloved's affections toward her, then it makes perfect sense that Sappho should invoke Aphrodite once again. The present invocation differs from past invocations in that it involves a different woman whom Sappho wants Aphrodite to persuade.

The language of the last stanza of the poem reinforces this reading. It returns to the present moment of discourse and reminds us of Sappho's original prayer to Aphrodite in the first and second stanzas. Although the imperative ἔλθε (come) in line 25 recalls the ἔλθε in line 5, the fact that the qualifying ἀλλά is absent here, that the verb is in the emphatic first position, and that there is a repetition of imperatives (λῦσον, τέλεσσαι, ἔσσο) suggests a far more powerful voice than the voice of helpless supplication we hear at the beginning of the poem. The narrator speaks with a confidence in the fulfillment of her desires; λῦσον (release) along with τέλεσσαι (to fulfill) and τέλεσον (fulfill) stresses this sense of release and fulfillment. There are no negative verbs here, as in the previous stanza, to suggest the possibility of defeat.

Sappho's use of military terminology in her request to Aphrodite to be her ally (σύμμαχος) in the last line of the poem may seem to identify Sappho with masculine values of conquest and militarism.[32] I believe, however, that Sappho appropriates aspects of dominant cultural values for purposes that establish her resistance to such values. In asking Aphrodite to be her cofighter or fellow soldier in the "battle" of love, Sappho asks Aphrodite to come into an alliance of mutuality with her. Although as allies they are not equals, "Sappho" becomes capable of imagining herself eliciting desire in her beloved through her contact with Aphrodite. Thus, Aphrodite's descent in the third stanza of the poem may be regarded as a description of the speaker's ascent. The swiftness and rapid movement of Aphrodite's descent and its empowering effect on "Sappho" suggest that, through the power of her voice (her invocation), the speaker herself is taking flight and bringing heaven down to earth.

As Winkler notes, Aphrodite's descent in fragment 1 recalls the scene in the *Iliad* where Aphrodite enters the battlefield and ends up retreating to Olympus to heal the stab wound inflicted on her by Diomedes. It may seem that by referring to Aphrodite as the speaker's potential σύμμαχος, Sappho transfers masculine values of conquest to the sphere of love. But in light of Aphrodite's (Homeric) reputation for ineffectual, obstructive conduct in martial affairs and her clearly inappropriate presence in the exclusively male world of the battlefield, it would seem that Aphrodite's role as "Sappho"'s ally would not follow the male model for σύμμαχοι. Thus, we cannot assume

32. See Rissman's analysis of military imagery in Sappho's poetry, *Love as War*.

that an alliance between the speaker and Aphrodite involves the attempt to conquer an adversary. In addition, it is interesting to note that sparrows, instead of horses, drive Aphrodite's chariot as it makes its descent. This deviation from the Iliadic model reinforces the poem's resistance to values of militance and conquest.

Moreover, in line 3 "Sappho" asks Aphrodite *not* to subdue her with cares. Sappho uses the word δάμνα (subdue)—a word often associated with conquest and domination—to express what she does *not* want from Aphrodite. It seems that Sappho negates the values associated with δάμνα and substitutes in its place an alliance with Aphrodite that turns the domination of one over the other into persuasion—the power to seduce another into a relationship of mutual desire.[33] The identification with Aphrodite implied by the speaker's ability to imagine herself as Aphrodite's "ally" shows a change in the way the speaker sees herself. Here, as in fragment 94, the operations of memory—recalling a past experience in which the speaker's desires were fulfilled—bridge the gap between speaker and goddess and between the lover and her beloved. In lines 21–24, the voices of Aphrodite and the speaker "Sappho" are no longer clearly differentiated. That Sappho does not clearly identify the speaker in these lines suggests a dissolving of the boundaries between the speaker and the goddess—and an incorporation within the speaker of Aphrodite's persuasive powers.

The speaker's assertive tone in the last stanza expresses a confidence in her own ability to conjure longing in the beloved. The ability to imagine herself in an alliance with Aphrodite elevates the speaker to a position of greater empowerment. The speaker asks Aphrodite to be her σύμμαχοος not in order to conquer or dominate the beloved, and certainly *not* to make the beloved passively accept "Sappho's" affections. Rather, "Sappho" calls on Aphrodite to help stir the beloved from passive indifference into *active* affection. The speaker imagines a situation where her beloved actively pursues. And we should not assume that "Sappho" has to become passive if her beloved is to become active. That would be simply to *assume* the male model of dominance and submission. The poem itself in no way suggests this. On the contrary, the purpose of "Sappho's" alliance with Aphrodite is to rouse her beloved, so that *each* is to be both lover and beloved, active participants in a reciprocity of desire—both of them active, desiring subjects.

In her study of the historical and cultural context of homosexuality in ancient Greece, Eva Cantarella points to a sharp contrast between the social roles of male and female homosexual bonds. The male pederastic model, with its distinct roles of dominance and submission, served as an instrument

---

33. I wish to thank Paul Allen Miller for suggesting to me the importance of δάμνα in the context of reciprocal, nonhierarchical desire.

in the educational and political development of young men. Sex between man and boy symbolized the transfusion of political power from the superior older man to his younger beloved.[34] By contrast, although homosexual erotic relations among women may also have had an educational and social role, those relations were not linked to the institutional structures of power as male pederastic relations were. As Cantarella puts it: "But what symbolic and social significance could be attached to love between women? Sex between women takes place on an equal basis, it does not involve submission, it cannot symbolize the transmission of power (not even the power of generation, the only power held by women)."[35]

Constructing the love between women expressed in the circumscribed context of an *hetairia* on the model of pederasty assumes an access to institutional power women did not have, and more importantly, assimilates female homoeroticism to male power relations. Thus, the discursive position of even the most educated and cultured of women (e.g., Sappho) in the context of the male-dominated public sphere must surely have been *outside the center,* as de Lauretis puts it.[36] Perhaps it is the position of eccentricity that allows the Sapphic subject to resist the eroticization of woman as "Other"[37] and thus to construct a language of desire beyond the binaries of self and other, a language that reinterprets categories of gender and reinscribes a place for women in cultural discourse.

34. See Dover, *Greek Homosexuality,* and Foucault's highly influential analysis of sexuality and power relations in ancient Greece, *The History of Sexuality* vol. 2.

35. Cantarella, *Bisexuality* 83.

36. See de Lauretis, "Eccentric Subjects."

37. See MacKinnon, *Feminism Unmodified*. MacKinnon responds to de Beauvoir's assertion that "[h]umanity is male and man defines woman not in herself but as relative to him; she is not regarded as an autonomous being. . . . He is the Subject, he is the Absolute—she is the Other" (*The Second Sex* xviii). MacKinnon argues that gender is less a matter of sexual difference than an instance of male dominance and the appeal to biology as the determining "fact" of women's sexual specificity is an ideological consequence of the male epistemological stance of objectivity that reflects not only control through objectification, but also its eroticization of the act of control itself. Thus, "the eroticization of dominance and submission creates gender. . . . The erotic is what defines sex as inequality, hence as a meaningful difference. . . . Sexualized objectification is what defines women as sexual and as women under male supremacy" (50).

FIFTEEN

Sappho and the Other Woman

Margaret Williamson

Reading Sappho is a seductive project for a feminist. Although not the only woman poet known from antiquity, she is certainly the most significant.[1] Her poetic achievement was so legendary that a poem attributed to Plato calls her the tenth Muse[2] —an indication also of how transgressive was the role of woman poet. Another aspect of her fascination is her position in history—around the turn of the seventh and sixth centuries B.C.E., in a world still dominated by aristocratic power, contested though that power already was: she thus escapes the radical exclusion of women from public life that was a by-product of fully developed democracy in city-states like Athens. She also precedes by two centuries the discourse of fourth-century philosophy, to which many recent theorists have allotted a privileged role in the genealogy of Western ideas of sexual difference.[3]

Another version of this essay appears in *Language and Gender: Interdisciplinary Perspectives,* edited by Sara Mills (London: Longman, 1995).

Quotations from Sappho and Alcaeus are from the plain prose translation in the Loeb Classical Library edition (Campbell, *Greek Lyric*), which like all other current texts of Sappho depends to some extent on editorial reconstruction. See Campbell's notes on the most disputed passages: for more detail, see Page, *Sappho and Alcaeus.* The fullest recent scholarly edition is Voigt, *Sappho et Alcaeus.*

1. Other ancient women poets are now receiving increasing attention: for an overview, see Snyder, *The Woman and the Lyre,* with references.

2. *AP* 9.506. Despite its traditional attribution this is probably among the many epigrams written in the Hellenistic period and passed off under the names of classical authors: see Page, *Further Greek Epigrams* 125–27. The "tenth Muse" label rapidly became a cliché in allusions to Sappho.

3. Two particularly relevant to this essay are Foucault (see *The History of Sexuality*), whose genealogy of modern sexuality goes back only to the fourth century B.C.E., and Irigaray (especially *Speculum*), on whom see further below, nn. 16, 27.

This essay attempts to address what must be the fundamental question about Sappho: in what ways, if any, can she be said to be writing as a woman, even though she shares many aspects of poetic tradition with male writers? I shall approach it through a comparison of some of her poems with those of a male author of love poetry, Anacreon, who wrote a few generations later than Sappho. It must be said at the outset, though, that the difficulties entailed in reading her are formidable. The tantalizing fragments of her poems reach us through over two and a half thousand years of neglect, random selection, and censorship, and through the reconstructions of scribes, textual critics, and papyrologists. And some of the accidents that have befallen her text seem simply too bad to be true. What accident was it, for example, that garbled the one word in the ode to Aphrodite, Sappho's only complete surviving poem, that tells us whether the singer is in love with a man or a woman—and that in a poem where Sappho herself is, unusually, named as the singer?[4] At this point, as at many others, the would-be critic of Sappho cannot avoid the sense of peering through a series of fragmented and distorting prisms at a fragile and ever-receding text.

Two further factors adding to this sensation are, at one end of the process, our ignorance of the social circumstances in which Sappho wrote and sang and, at the other, the iconic status she has acquired for many twentieth-century readers. If the weight of previous centuries bears heavily on her texts so, in the twentieth century, do the desires of many of their women readers today: to discover the originary voice of female poetic consciousness and, perhaps, of lesbian sexuality.

Even if many of them must now be put on one side,[5] these questions are worth mentioning for positive as well as negative reasons. One of the effects of the last twenty years or so of critical theory is liberation from some versions of empiricism: an acceptance of the desires motivating all reading. I make no apology, therefore, for subjecting the iconic figure of Sappho to an explicitly motivated reading that takes up one of the central questions of feminist theory: the relationship between language and gender.

---

4. Only one word in poem 1 indicates the gender of the beloved. The manuscripts on which modern texts are based give three variant readings of the text at this point, none of which can be correct because none both makes sense and fits the meter and dialect. The currently accepted reading, which makes the beloved female, depends on an emendation that was proposed only in the nineteenth century. It is defended in his edition by the German philologist Bergk (*Poetae Lyrici* ad loc.) with the simple statement that "we are dealing with the love of a *girl* (de *puellae* amore agitur)": he reaches this conclusion mainly on the basis of Sappho's other poems.

5. I address the textual transmission of Sappho's poems and the question of whether she can be described as lesbian in the modern sense in chaps. 2 and 4 of *Sappho's Immortal Daughters*.

Within classical studies Sappho has increasingly been identified as a crucial (though not the only) figure in debates about gender in the ancient world. I single out three treatments in particular. For Jack Winkler, Sappho's exclusion from mainstream, masculine culture gives her a privileged, and paradoxically more inclusive, perspective on its dominant paradigms.[6] Thus, in the ode to Aphrodite, Sappho can write in counterpoint to Homer's epic epiphanies, embracing them from an ironic vantage point. Eva Stehle, on the other hand, following Simone de Beauvoir, seems to indicate female biology as the basis in Sappho of an erotic reciprocity which evades the structures of phallic domination that elsewhere pervade archaic poetry. In a more recent piece, she draws on film theory to analyze the gaze in Sappho as a means of dissolving hierarchy.[7]

My reading of Sappho, though in some measure influenced by both these writers, attempts to consider the question from a slightly different, and explicitly linguistic, angle. It involves looking at a feature of her writing that, though touched on by both Winkler and Stehle,[8] merits further exploration: the subject positions mapped out in her poetry. I shall be considering the different voices in her poetry, and the way in which they seem to construct the positions of subject and object, self and other, the "I," "you," sometimes "she," and occasionally "he" positions. My concentration will be mainly on love poetry and the configurations of individual desire: this is, therefore, a partial sampling of her corpus.

The background to my discussion is provided through a challenge issued by Plutarch. In the introduction to his essay on the virtues of women, Plutarch both opens and forecloses the question under consideration when he puts forward the proposition that "the art of poetry or of prophecy is not one art when practiced by men and another when practiced by women, but one and the same" (*De mul. vir.* 243b). The truth of this statement can, he suggests, be tested by setting alongside each other the poems of Sappho and of Anacreon. Although Anacreon was not an exact contemporary of Sappho, the accidents of survival mean that we have more of his love poetry than of any other archaic lyric writer, making him an especially rewarding subject for comparison with Sappho. Following Plutarch's suggestion I begin, therefore, with an analysis of self–other relationships in Anacreon, even though many of the

6. Winkler, "Double Consciousness."

7. Stigers [Stehle], "Sappho's Private World"; Stehle, "Sappho's Gaze."

8. See, e.g., Winkler, "Double Consciousness" 167: "Sappho's poem ... contains several personal perspectives, whose multiple relations to each other set up a field of *voices* [my emphasis] and evaluations."

erotic structures identifiable in his work are paralleled in other male love poets.[9]

SELF AND OTHER IN ANACREON

The relationship between self and other where desire is concerned in Anacreon can often be seen to follow one of two distinct patterns. In the first, Love is personified as an adversary who either subdues the speaker or seeks to do so. One boxes with Love, as in 396, flees him (400), or gives thanks for having escaped his bonds (346). The mildest version of his effect seems to be his summons to the speaker in 358 to dally with a girl from Lesbos ("golden-haired Love strikes me with his purple ball and summons me to play with the girl in the fancy sandals"): other accounts of his impact represent it as violent, as in the image of Eros as a smith (413) who strikes the speaker with a bronze hammer and dips him in freezing water. Occasionally, as in the poem about the girl from Lesbos, the object of the speaker's passion is alluded to (see also 378), but the primary relationship is one between Eros and the lover, who experiences himself as either the victim or the adversary of a powerful external force.

In another equally common pattern, the speaker addresses the object of his passion: the relationship is between the speaker and an addressee, an "I" and a "you." What is noticeable here too is the tendency for the imagery to reflect an adversarial relationship; but this time it is the speaker who takes the dominant role. A good example is a well-known poem addressed to a sexually inexperienced girl, in which, by a common erotic metaphor, she is compared to an untamed foal whom the speaker imagines himself bridling and riding (417). This scenario of erotic domination is clearly also present in 346, which is again addressed to a youthful love object, a beautiful but fearful boy (or possibly girl); the poem goes on to allude to the hyacinth meadows in which Aphrodite tied her horses. It reappears, in wittily inverted form, in 360, in which the boy with girlish looks holds, says Anacreon, the reins of his soul. Here, therefore, Love's domination of the speaker has been replaced by the speaker's wished-for mastery of the addressee: even when, as in 360, the relationship is humorously inverted, the basic pattern is one in which one side or the other must end up in control, and the integrity of the "I" position is either completely secure or completely at risk.

---

9. See Stigers [Stehle], "Sappho's Private World," who gives examples also from Archilochus and Ibycus and comments, "The man is helpless, stricken by the power of Eros or Aphrodite, but toward the particular boy or girl who attracts him the man is confident and prepared to seduce" (46). She attributes these patterns to "male sexual psychology" (50).

We have, therefore, two main patterns, one involving Eros and the speaker, the other the speaker and a beloved. Both, however, are structured in essentially the same way: the self–other relationship is essentially one of domination. The frequent repetition of this pattern suggests an overriding concern with establishing the boundaries between subject and object, and then with establishing the subject's control, in a kind of zero-sum competition of the erotic.[10] A few brief observations about this structure are called for. First, this concern with maintaining the boundaries and the supremacy of the "I" makes particular sense when related to the likely context of performance of these poems. The symposia, drinking parties attended by aristocratic males for which this poetry was almost certainly destined, had a markedly political function: that of consolidating bonds between members of the group and of asserting their political dominance over those outside it. Recent work, inspired by Foucault, on male homosexual roles in classical Athens has demonstrated that the articulation of sexual roles in a public context has a political dimension: a male citizen's assumption of an active, dominant role in his sexual life is an index of his capacity as a citizen.[11]

The situation of aristocratic symposiasts in the archaic period resembles in some ways that of citizens in classical Athens. They too were members of an elite whose privileges distinguished them sharply from other members of the community and were jealously guarded. Studies of symposiastic groupings have emphasized their importance as a defensive formation against the threat to aristocratic power and privilege posed by hoplite warfare and the wider distribution of wealth.[12]

It has long been accepted by critics of archaic lyric that at least some symposiastic poetry is directly related to the political aspirations of its audiences: that exhortations to military virtue and patriotism, for example, express a collective ideal. Love poetry, though, has traditionally been interpreted as belonging to a more individual, confessional mode.[13] The patterns sketched above, however, suggest that its rhetoric of exclusivity and supremacy is employed in the interests of a collective, rather than an individual, identity. It is the aristocratic group as a whole whose identity in relation

10. There is another group of poems suggesting a more equal, negotiated relationship between *erastēs* and *erōmenos*: see, e.g, 359, 378, 402c, 467. I discuss the relationship between this and the other two groups in "Eros the Blacksmith."

11. See in particular Halperin, *One Hundred Years,* and Winkler, "Double Consciousness." Both draw on Foucault's work on sexuality, especially on *The History of Sexuality.* See also Dover, *Greek Homosexuality.*

12. On symposia, see Murray, "The Greek Symposium," "The Symposium as Social Organisation," *Early Greece,* and *Sympotica*; Rossi, "Il simposio"; Vetta, ed., *Poesia e simposio.*

13. For an overview of current critical positions, see Slings, "The 'I' in Personal Archaic Lyric," with references.

to an other is figured in the structures of love poetry. The performer of a song ostensibly addressed to his beloved sings *about* his erotic mastery of another, but necessarily *to* that other; and sometimes the youthful object of his passion appears to be fictional. In these cases in particular, it is clear that his audience consists of those occupying the same subject position as himself, and his gesture of mastery is one in which all of this audience are implicated.

Second, this analysis of the ways in which social context informs love poetry also helps make sense of the other pattern of subject-object relations in Anacreon: that between the speaker and Eros. The shattering effect of Eros on the "I" is tolerable only if the agent, rather than being an individual other, is a personification or deity. To regard this threat as the effect of another human individual would be unacceptable for the community of aristocratic subjects to which singer and audience both belong. We shall return to this question of singer and audience in relation to Sappho.

The last point to note before embarking on a comparison with Sappho is that in the pattern involving two human individuals, subject and object positions are gendered, but their relation to biological sex is a mediated one. Thus, though the "I" is always an adult male, the other is always younger but can be either male or female. The subject-object polarity is articulated both with gender and with relations of power, so that to occupy the position of love object is also to occupy the weaker, feminine position, regardless of one's sex.

SAPPHIC VOICES AND THE OTHER

To turn to Sappho at this point is to enter a completely different world, in which the range of voices, positions, and self–other relationships in the expression of desire is far wider and far more subtly modulated. To illustrate this I shall look first at a very damaged poem, fragment 22. The parts of this text that are legible, including editorial supplements, are, in translation, as follows:[14]

> ... task ... lovely face ... unpleasant ... otherwise winter ... pain(less?) ... I bid you, Abanthis, take (your lyre?) and sing of Gongyla, while desire once again flies around you, the lovely one—for her dress excited you when you saw it; and I rejoice: for the holy Cyprian herself once blamed me for praying ... this (word?) ... I wish ...

At the point at which these fragments begin to be intelligible, the speaker commands a second woman, Abanthis, to celebrate in song her desire for

---

14. This poem survives only in a badly damaged version on papyrus, and some of the readings translated here depend on editorial supplements which are controversial. The main trend of my argument can, however, be defended even without conjectural supplements.

a third. This is evidently not the first time Abanthis has felt such desire, as the adverb "once again," traditionally used of the renewed onset of love, suggests: this is confirmed in the next strophe by the description of Gongyla as "the lovely one," and an account of the way in which her appearance excited Abanthis's longing. The speaker then, with the explicit statement "and I rejoice," takes up for the first time her own stance in relation to this scenario.

But is it really the first time? A closer look at the poem suggests that "once again" haunts this entire scene in a way that has from the beginning drawn in the speaker too, and that begins to open up some of the differences between this and the erotics of Anacreon. In this poem there is a subtle process of association between different subject positions in operation throughout, which has the effect of eliding them, blurring without removing their boundaries. The person I have so far called a speaker is in fact, of course, a singer (this is, after all, *literally* lyric poetry): it is in song that she bids Abanthis sing. The process of elision between the "I" and "you" positions is compounded further when the speaker proceeds herself to name Abanthis's desire: she is doing, in that second strophe, what she has commanded Abanthis to do in the preceding one. It is significant too that, just as desire is distributed among different speakers, so too it is distributed through different moments in time: the desire which was excited (repeatedly, apparently) in the past is to be spoken in the future as well as the present. The positions from which desire is articulated and the moments of its articulation, therefore, constantly shift and merge into one another: what is constant is the movement of desire itself through the poem.

In fragment 96, of which we have much more, a similar process can be traced. The least damaged part of the text translates as follows:

> ... Sardis ... often turning her thoughts in this direction ... (she honoured) you as being like a goddess for all to see and took most delight in your song. Now she stands out among the Lydian women like the rosy-fingered moon after sunset, surpassing all the stars, and its light spreads alike over the salt sea and the flowery fields; the dew is shed in beauty, and roses bloom and tender chervil and flowery melilot. Often as she goes to and fro she remembers gentle Atthis and doubtless her tender heart is consumed because of your fate ...

Once again the singer, the "I" of the poem, speaks to "you" and "she," both female, of their desire. A distant "she," a woman now (probably) in Sardis, the capital of Lydia, is described as turning her thoughts in this direction. Then the poem modulates into the past in order to describe her desire for the speaker's interlocutor, the "you" of the second strophe. The focus now shifts back through both time and space to the woman in Lydia, who in her present surroundings is likened, in an extended simile, to the rosy-fingered moon; and finally her desire for Atthis (who I am assuming to be the "you" of strophe 2) is recapitulated through her memory.

Here we can see an even more subtle and elusive play of desire at work, which once again works partly through an elision of the speaking positions. The singer is again associated through her song with the "you" of the second strophe: the woman now in Lydia, she says (or rather sings), "took most delight in your song." This time, though, the effect of the speaker's implication in the other woman's desire is even more complex than in fragment 22. The singer sings of a song that aroused desire, thereby performing through her poem an act designated within it as erotic, and thus constructing herself as a potential object of desire. She also, though, enacts desire from the subject, speaking point of view when she turns to the lengthy simile that names in song the woman's beauty. As in fragment 22, this effect simultaneously represents the gaps between subjects and bridges, without erasing, them. It is this effect that I am trying to capture by the term "elision," with the distances between the three speaking positions of the poem figured through, on this occasion, space as well as time. When finally she returns to the Lydian woman's desire for Atthis, in the sixth strophe, it is in a way marked by distances of both space and time: her longing for Atthis is possible only through the memory that bridges those distances.

It is evident from these two poems, and others besides, that there is a constant process of subtle and multifarious shifts going on between the speaking voices, and the subject positions, in Sappho's poetry. "I," "you," and "she" (and in fr. 96 we should also add "we") are never clearly differentiated, securely demarcated positions, but are constantly linked in a polyphonic, shifting erotic discourse, a kind of circulation of desire in which the gaps between subjects, figured through time and space, are at the same time constantly bridged by the operations of love and memory.[15] How different from the monologic erotic discourse of Anacreon, in which the only form self–other relationships seem to take is that of struggle that will end in the mastery of one over the other.

There are several major points of contrast here with Anacreon. The fact that this is a female voice speaking, astonishing though that is when one thinks of the silences that surround it, is only the beginning. Much more important is the way in which this female voice has been able to avoid

---

15. I prefer to speak of the elision of subject positions, and of a circulation of desire, rather than, with Stigers [Stehle], "Sappho's Private World" (followed now by Skinner, "Woman and Language"), of reciprocity and mutuality: the latter description seems to me to take insufficient account of the transaction's embeddedness in social and linguistic practice. Another way of putting this, on a linguistic level, would be to say that it overlooks the effects of *différance* (Derrida, *Speech and Phenomena*).

speaking from the feminine position occupied by the addressees of Anacreon and of other male love poets. Instead we have a polyphony of voices whose neither-one-nor-two,[16] neither-subject-nor-object, relationship successfully both evades and contests the polarities found in Anacreon, and inscribed in the tradition in which he writes.

It is important to note, though, that although the boundaries between subjects are elided, they are not dissolved: there is a constant spacing effect between speaking positions. The most obvious way of achieving this is through the gaps of space and time found throughout Sappho's poetry. A second way, which we may note in passing, in which this spacing effect is achieved in Sappho is through the use of reported speech. This too is highly characteristic of her, and the ode to Aphrodite (fr. 1), combining reported speech with a set of complex temporal shifts, is an obvious example. Both resources are lacking in Anacreon, whose much sharper subject-object division does not require them: his poetry takes place for the most part in an undifferentiated present and makes little use of reported speech.

One of the most important contrasts with Anacreon, however, takes us back to the relationship between singer and audience. I suggested for Anacreon an isomorphism between the self–other relationship within the poetry and that of its sympotic audience with the world outside the symposium. For Sappho we are, of course, lacking historical information about who listened to her songs. But the analysis offered so far of her poetry offers a way of reading relationships with and between the members of her audiences within the poems themselves.

In the two fragments of Sappho considered so far, 22 and 96, the singing voice itself is an important way of achieving the effect of elision between speaking positions. In this circulation of desire, the singing voice plays a crucial role in that it both arouses and expresses desire, linking all the female figures who speak and are spoken of in the poem and making them both subjects and objects of desire. Not only this: the self-referential allusions to song also, I have suggested, return upon the subject of enunciation, the poet, and draw her in too. There is thus a second kind of elision: between the enunciating and enunciated subjects.[17] Conversely, the addressee, the desired and desiring other, is not limited to the ostensible addressee of each poem, but ultimately includes the entire circle of women. If song itself both arouses and expresses desire, then to sing at all is to enter into an

---

16. As the terminology shows, this analysis is influenced by the work of Luce Irigaray: see particularly *This Sex*. On the use of Irigaray by classicists, see now Skinner, "Woman and Language," and below, n. 27.

17. Calame, *Le récit*, applies this distinction to the analysis of Greek poetry, though he has very little to say about Sappho.

open-ended, unbounded erotic dialogue with the entire group: the erotics of Sappho's poetry implies, therefore, a community of singing, desiring women. The contrast with poems of Anacreon in which a beloved other is addressed lies in the fact that in them the speaking positions within and outside the poem are often insulated from each other by the gap between ostensible and actual addressee.

My analysis has so far depended, however, on poems that evoke an all-female world. But there are others. If, in the poems so far considered, Sappho successfully evades the gendered polarities found in Anacreon and other male love poets, what of those poems in which the masculine intrudes upon this secluded world? Can her implication with a community of singing, desiring female subjects always provide a position from which to contest the position of feminine, object, other?

I shall address this question by looking at two more poems, each of which involves explicit opposition to the masculine. Perhaps Sappho's best-known poem is fragment 31, which famously charts the speaker's distress as she looks at a beloved woman in the company of a man:

> He seems as fortunate as the gods to me, the man who sits opposite you and listens nearby to your sweet voice and lovely laughter. Truly that sets my heart trembling in my breast. For when I look at you for a moment, then it is no longer possible for me to speak; my tongue has snapped, at once a subtle fire has stolen beneath my flesh, I see nothing with my eyes, my ears hum, sweat pours from me, a trembling seizes me all over, I am greener than grass, and it seems to me that I am little short of dying. But all can be endured, since . . . even a poor man . . .

What the poem says on a surface level is obvious enough, even if it has given rise to a good deal of discussion as to the man's identity: what is important for present purposes is only that he is male.[18] As the speaker looks at him, he in turn, like the female lovers in the poems discussed before, is listening to a beloved woman's desire-arousing voice. The spectacle of her rival's relation to this woman then, on the level of surface meaning, causes the speaker such pain that she has the sensation of bodily disintegration. The final, damaged fragments suggest some kind of recovery, but cannot be interpreted with confidence.

What is of interest here is the way in which the poet's disintegration is represented in terms of speaking positions. As in previous poems, the addressee of this poem is herself speaking: but to her male companion, not to the singer of the poem. One of the consequences is, within the poem, the

18. Many scenarios have been proposed: see Page, *Sappho and Alcaeus*. The tendency in more recent criticism is to read the opening as a rhetorical trope ("whoever sits opposite you . . .") rather than a real figure: see Winkler, "Double Consciousness" 74.

cessation of the singer's own voice. But the breaking of the erotic dialogue between female speakers is not the only cause of the disintegration. The other, I suggest, within the rhetoric of the poem, is the introduction of an objectifying gaze, whose direction is represented grammatically. The quoted section of the poem is framed by a very significant verb: "to seem." At the opening, the single (in Greek) word translated as "he seems" constructs the male lover as the object of the speaker's gaze. But the direction of that gaze is reversed within the poem, when the speaker herself becomes the object of a gaze: the last phrase reads literally "I seem to myself."

There are two ways of interpreting this reversal, both of which can be taken to be in play simultaneously. The repetition of the verb has, to begin with, the effect of suggesting a simple reversal of the gaze with which the poem opened: as she looked then at her male rival, he now looks at her. The physical disintegration of the speaker can be understood therefore as the consequence of her becoming the object of male gaze. But more important than the gender of the gazer is the way in which the gaze itself reintroduces what was absent from the previous two poems, namely a polarized division between subject and object positions.[19]

Linked with the introduction of this division is the fact that the fragmenting of the female speaker's self, and body, occurs not only on the literal level of description but also linguistically, as can be seen first from the description of herself as "greener than grass," and then from her use of the word "I seem." With this verb the subject's position itself becomes a divided one, since it involves the speaker in representing herself to herself from another's perspective, and therefore in splitting.[20]   One can, then, read this disintegration of the female subject as the consequence of her move from being the subject of the gaze to being its object: a move that itself depends on the fact that the gaze demarcates these positions far more sharply than Sappho's more customary mode of engagement with others, the voice. Subject and object positions, in the phrase "I seem to myself," then collide or conflict rather than, as in the previous poems, being elided.[21] It is worth

19. For a fuller treatment of the gaze in Sappho, see Stehle, "Sappho's Gaze," whose subtle and powerful analysis attributes to it some of the blurring and de-hierarchizing effects linked in this essay with the voice.

20. It is significant that the use of the verb "appeared" is identified by Barthes as a sure indication of the move from personal to impersonal narration: a move that also, according to his categories, occurs in this poem. See Barthes, "Structural Analysis of Narratives" 112; see also, on nondialectical self–other relations, Jefferson, "Bodymatters."

21. The context of this poem in Longinus's account provides a fascinating sideline on this discussion. Longinus, to whom we owe the survival of most of this poem, famously celebrates it as an example of poetic unity: he marvels at Sappho's "selection of the most important details and her combination of them into a single poem" (*Subl.* 10.3). This in itself seems surprising,

noting too that the spacing effects which made that elision possible in the earlier poems are missing here: the tense of this poem, unlike many others of Sappho's, is a continuous present. It seems, therefore, that engagement with a masculine world is reflected in the range of techniques used as well as in terms of content.

It is of course possible to align the movement of this poem with the scenario of domination envisaged in Anacreon and to see this as, so to speak, the beloved's-eye view of things: a brief attempt by the object to speak. No doubt there is no accident in the fact that we have a female speaker describing the disintegration brought about by a male gaze. But it is important to separate the idea of gendered subject positions from that of gender in a simple sense, even if, as here, they happen to coincide. What has changed between this and the earlier poems is not just the introduction of a male figure: it is, more importantly, the introduction of a gendered subject-object polarity, in which the speaker appears momentarily to be in the subject position (subject of the gaze) but is then forced also into that of its object. It is the resulting contradiction that causes her disintegration into a mute, fragmented body. The example of this poem suggests, then, that it is not the mere assumption of a speaking position by a woman that counts, but the negotiation of the subject-object polarity: in other words the successful negotiation of the feminine, rather than the female, position.

In my final example, the speaker once again engages with the masculine. Fragment 16, the Anactoria poem, with its apparently self-conscious allusion to both dominant cultural values and poetic tradition, presents us quite explicitly with a woman challenging her marginal position in the culture. This time the speaker emerges from her encounter on a very different note; and once again the key to understanding why is the way in which the speaker is positioned within the poem:

> Some say a host of cavalry, others of infantry, and others of ships, is the most beautiful thing on the black earth, but I say it is whatsoever a person loves. It is perfectly easy to make this understood by everyone: for she who far surpassed mankind in beauty, Helen, left her most noble husband and went sailing off to Troy with no thought at all for her child or dear parents, but (love) led her astray ...

---

given the poem's stress on *dis*-unity. And yet one detail of the text he quotes raises at least the possibility that he was more alive to the text's disintegration than his argument allows. The phrase "to myself," occurring immediately after "I seem," can be construed as an attempt to heal the division between subject and object, even though in so doing it also serves to highlight it. Longinus, however, in the text transmitted to us, omits it altogether, though he continues his quotation with a few words that apparently come after it. The missing words have been restored only through the insertion of a further papyrus scrap (fr. 213): Longinus's version of the line reads simply "I seem," omitting the telltale recuperative phrase. On the context of this omission in Longinus, see Hertz, "A Reading of Longinus."

lightly ... (and she?) has reminded me now of Anactoria who is not here; I would rather see her lovely walk and the bright sparkle of her face than the Lydians' chariots and armed infantry.

The categories with which the poem plays are easily identified. The culturally prestigious, and masculine, values of militarism and heroism are evident at the beginning and (what I take to be)[22] the end of the poem, as well as in the allusion to Troy and the account of Helen's abandoned husband as "her most noble husband"—a description with strong connotations of military prowess. However, there are also reminders of the ways in which women are valued within the culture—in terms of their beauty, and of their role within marriage and the family. It is not difficult to see how, even on first reading, the poem challenges these values. In the first strophe the emphatic "but I say" announces a strong and explicit challenge to a society that, collectively, values militarism above anything else, and claims the right to substitute an individual's desire—"whatsoever a person loves"—for that collectively sanctioned one. The markedly general phrasing of the opening then gives way to an example that defines the substituted desire as sexual, and a woman's: that of Helen, who left "her most noble husband" and went to Troy. A comparison with the treatment of Helen by Alcaeus, a male contemporary of Sappho's, also from Lesbos, exposes the rehabilitation that is going on here: far from suppressing the consequences of her action, one of Alcaeus's two treatments of Helen (42) singles her out as the cause of Troy's destruction and contrasts her with the virtuous and fertile Thetis; the other (283) stresses her limited responsibility for her actions. She was, according to Alcaeus, "crazed" by Paris when she followed him over the sea, and it is his transgression, not hers, against the laws of hospitality and exchange that is stressed. In Sappho's version, as Page duBois has pointed out, Helen is not the object of exchange (or theft) between men, but celebrated as "an 'actant' in her own life, the subject of a choice, exemplary in her desiring."[23] The poem suggests, therefore, a double reversal of established values: love is to be valued above war, and women are to take on an active, desiring subjectivity.

But this concentration on the strategy of substitution expressed in the opening strophe is vulnerable. Deconstructive criticism has taught us to read utterances as threatened by the repression on which they are founded, and the poem's attempt at mastering the values and paradigms of Greek culture seems to lay itself open to being read in this way. From such a

22. The papyrus on which this poem was found continues with damaged sections of three more lines. Most editors think they are the beginning of another poem: some think they continue this one. I should make clear my assumption that the speaker is, as in almost all Sappho's poems, female.

23. DuBois, "Sappho and Helen" 86–87.

perspective, the insistent repetitions ("perfectly," "everyone," expressed in Greek by variants of the same word: *panchu, panti*), like the emphatic "but I say," suggest the fragility of the opening proposition rather than its strength. The claim to revalue militarism by means of language, to set in motion and then to control a process of linguistic substitution, sets up a structure that is open to reversal—and that is, within the poem, reversed. The presentation of Helen's desire makes the substitution she performs an ambiguous and unstable one: its object, Paris, is indicated only metonymically by a phrase— "to Troy"—which also connotes war and the destruction catalogued by Alcaeus. The values repressed by the speaker in the first strophe seem to return here, then, as well as in the final strophe, where the Lydian army is the measure of Anactoria's value to the speaker. According to this account, Sappho's revaluation is only the obverse of Alcaeus's in his poem 42, which was also announced as structured within language by the opening phrase "as the story goes"; and the movement of the poem as a whole is that of a desire for linguistic mastery that is threatened and dispersed by the otherness it seeks to control.

I began my argument with an attempt to examine Plutarch's assertion that the art of poetry was undifferentiated by gender. If my earlier analyses of Sappho have tended to prove him wrong, fragment 16 seems thus far to bring us up against an uncomfortable relativism vis-à-vis Sappho and Alcaeus. Once again, however, it is the relationship between the subject positions in fragment 16 that is the key to Sappho's distinctiveness. In this poem they are linked with another crucial element: the quintessentially female figure of Helen.

The dualities that Helen embodies have been persuasively outlined by Ann Bergren.[24] In Herodotus's account of the origins of the long-standing hostility between Greeks and Persians—which includes the Trojan War—the women who move from one side to another, as marriage or love partners, have an ambiguous status: they are both subjects and objects of the exchange (or theft). Helen, who is also part of this self-renewing sequence of exchange, theft, and reparation, partakes of this ambiguity in a way we can glean from the poems of Sappho and Alcaeus just considered. That is, she both chooses Paris and is chosen by him, both abandons and is stolen from her husband, exchanges and is exchanged. This pattern conforms, of course, to Lévi-Strauss's analysis of the position of women in both kinship and linguistic structures as that of both signs and generators of signs.[25] The duality can be found on a linguistic level too in the *Iliad*, where Helen is first encountered weaving in a tapestry the narrative of the war (3.125–28). She is, thus, both

24. Bergren, "Language and the Female."
25. Lévi-Strauss, *Structural Anthropology* 60–62.

subject and author of the narrative, its weaver and herself woven into it by the rhapsode, the "song stitcher." Like the Sapphic singing voice, therefore, she elides the positions of enunciating and enunciated subject.

This duality is, no doubt, part of what motivates Sappho's interception of Helen in her long wandering through Greek literature. But the way in which she is drawn into the chain connecting the three female figures of the poem—the speaker, Helen, and Anactoria—is also important, and it draws on the fluidity of subject positions that we have traced elsewhere. The link between the three female figures of this poem, once again formed partly by verbal repetition, is one that has eluded some of the poem's critics. The author of a standard commentary on Sappho, for example, says apropos of Helen's first appearance: "It seems inelegant ... to begin this parable, the point of which is that Helen found [the most beautiful thing] in her lover, by stating that she herself surpassed all mortals in this quality."[26] But what he is objecting to is the poem's most crucial move, and it is signaled precisely by the way in which the description of Helen, "who far surpassed mankind in beauty," echoes the opening reference to "the most beautiful thing," once again using variants of the same Greek word (*kalliston, kallos*). The effect of this repetition is to hint that Helen is the object of the speaker's desire, announced in the first strophe. Helen then, in the next strophe, becomes herself a desiring subject, who goes away to Troy. But her oscillation does not end there. Another verbal echo links her with the absent Anactoria: the word translated as "walk," *bama*, is formed from the same verb as that for "went" in the account of Helen's journey to Troy, *eba*. The speaker, thus, is a desiring subject; Anactoria, at the end, is a desired object: but Helen, in between, by means of the now familiar elision, is both.

It is this elision that slides out from under the tyranny of the opening propositions, implicating both the speaker and Helen in an endless chain of substitution in which each is both subject and object, speaker and spoken. This, more than the opening challenge, is the move by which the poem really subverts the discourse in which it is framed, and we can see this in the resulting disruption and instability of gender categories. In sailing to Troy, leaving behind her family, for example, she imitates the action of the Homeric heroes; but this assumption of a male role at the same time enacts the female speaker's erotic impulse. In leaving "her most noble husband," to go to Troy, she rejects but also embraces each of the competing values in the first strophe—the object of individual desire and the values of heroism and militarism. We could multiply these antitheses indefinitely, and yet they could hardly mimic the text's resistance to them. The elision of subject and

---

26. Page, *Sappho and Alcaeus* 53.

object results, then, in the confounding of mythical categories of gender: and it is here that the elision in Sappho of what is elsewhere a gendered polarity has its most radical effect.

CONCLUSIONS

The rejoinder to Plutarch that emerges from this reading of Sappho is, therefore, a fundamentally and fruitfully ambiguous one. Sappho writes, we can say, as a woman precisely to the extent that she writes as not-a-woman: from a position, that is to say, that undercuts and contests the "hommosexual" structures defining femininity. We may wish to ask further what defines this position: is it to be located in linguistic or psychic structures or, indeed, the female body?

This study hints at a further possibility. For Sappho's time and place we can hardly talk of her social situation as the background to her poetry: the sparsity of our information renders the distinction between fore- and background untenable. What I have done is, *faute de mieux,* to read a social context within, rather than behind, the poetry. The exercise suggests that the gendering of Sappho's poetic discourse takes place through that of her audience; and, furthermore, that gender is a matter of relations of power at least as much as of biological sex. It is the fact that she addresses an audience of equals, of singing, desiring women whose song and desire endlessly refract her own, that makes possible her characteristic mode of address: to the other woman of my title.[27]

Since this is explicitly a motivated reading, I may perhaps be allowed to end by introducing another woman into my account of the Anactoria poem. You may think she is already there: the reader. The disruption of gendered positions that I have traced in relation to the figures of the poem has as its correlate that of the reader's position. The opening "some say" of the poem bears ambivalently on the gender of the reader. Gendered in Greek to the extent that, say, the word "mankind" is in English, it apparently contains

27. As implied in Irigaray's pun *parler-femme/par les femmes.* This is an important qualifier of her other famous punning term, *hommosexualité*: taken together, they suggest that women can escape the constraints of patriarchal discourse, but that this is possible only on the basis of social practice. Analyses of ancient culture in terms only of *hommosexualité* lead to the distortions that are contested, rightly, by Skinner, "Woman and Language." On the complexities of *parler-femme,* see especially Whitford, *Luce Irigaray* chap. 2. Irigaray's later work, such as her essay "Divine Women" (in *Sexes and Genealogies* 57–72), suggests that divine paradigms may also be a basis for it: the importance in Sappho of Aphrodite offers some confirmation of this. See also Cantarella, *Bisexuality,* on the different relationship to power structures for women, which (she argues) meant that homosexual love did not symbolize the transmission of power as it did for men.

the male reader only to assimilate his desire to that of the female speaker and of Helen: but a female reader is from the beginning both uneasily contained and excluded by it. It is from this fragmented position that reader and poem conduct their negotiation with gender, a negotiation that when it pauses in the last strophe has at least won a place for Anactoria alongside those massed and glorious armies. The place and the moment that Anactoria inhabits may be distant, conditional, and fleeting: but I think we can claim this as a kind of victory.

BIBLIOGRAPHY

Abbott, G. F. *Macedonian Folklore*. Cambridge: Cambridge University Press, 1903
Abu-Lughod, Lila. *Veiled Sentiments: Honor and Poetry in a Bedouin Society*. Berkeley: University of California Press, 1986.
Ackerman, Hans Christoph, and Gisler, Jean-Robert. *Lexicon Iconographicum Mythologiae Graecae*. 4 vols. to date. Amsterdam: Artemis, 1981–.
Alcoff, Linda. "Cultural Feminism versus Post-structuralism: The Identity Crisis in Feminist Theory." *Signs* 13 (1988) 405–36.
Alexiou, Margaret. *The Ritual Lament in Greek Tradition*. Cambridge: Cambridge University Press, 1974.
Andrèn, Arvid. *Architectural Terra-Cottas from Etrusco-Italic Temples*. 2 vols. Lund: C. W. K. Gleerup, 1939–40.
Aristotle. *The Nicomachean Ethics*, translated by H. Rackham. Cambridge: Harvard University Press, 1962.
Arthur, Marilyn B. "Early Greece: The Origins of the Western Attitude toward Women." *Arethusa* 6 (1973) 7–58.
Atallah, Wahib. *Adonis dans la littérature el l'art grecs*. Paris: Klincksiek, 1966.
Austin, Norman. *Archery at the Dark of the Moon*. Berkeley: University of California Press, 1975.
———. "The Function of Digressions in the *Iliad*." *Greek, Roman, and Byzantine Studies* 7 (1966) 295–312.
Baale, Maria Joanna. *Studia in Anytes poetriae vitam et carminum reliquias*. Harlem: J. L. E. I. Kleynenberg, 1903.
Bagg, Robert. "Love, Ceremony, and Daydream in Sappho's Lyrics." *Arion* 3 (1964) 44–82.
Ballentine, F. G. "Some Phases of the Cult of the Nymphs." *Harvard Studies in Classical Philology* 15 (1904) 97–110.
Balmer, Josephine, trans. *Sappho: Poems and Fragments*. Newcastle: Bloodaxe Books, 1992.
Barilier, E. "La figure d'Aphrodite dans quelques fragments de Sappho." *Études de Lettres* III.5 (1972) 20–61.

Barker, Andrew. *Greek Musical Writings.* Vol. 1, *The Musician and His Art.* Cambridge: Cambridge University Press, 1984.

Barnard, Mary. "Static." In *Woman Poet.* Vol. 1, *The West*, 34. Reno, Nev.: Regional Editions, 1980.

Barrett, W. S., ed. *Euripides Hippolytos.* Oxford: Oxford University Press, 1964.

Barthes, Roland. *The Pleasure of the Text*, translated by Richard Miller. New York: Hill, 1975.

———. "Structural Analysis of Narratives." In *Image Music Text*, edited by S. Heath, 79–124. London: Noonday, 1977.

Bartky, Sandra Lee. *Femininity and Domination.* New York: Routledge, 1990.

Beazley, J. D. *Attic Red-figure Vase-painters.* 2nd ed. 3 vols. Oxford: Oxford University Press, 1963.

———. "Some Inscriptions on Vases: V." *American Journal of Archaeology* 54 (1950) 310–22.

Benjamin, Jessica. *The Bonds of Love: Psychoanalysis, Feminism, and the Problem of Domination.* New York: Pantheon, 1988.

Bennett, C. "Concerning 'Sappho Schoolmistress.'" *Transactions of the American Philological Association* 124 (1994) 345–47.

Benveniste, Emile. "Relationships of Persons in the Verb." In *Problems in General Linguistics,* translated by M. E. Meek, 195–204. Miami: University of Miami Press, 1971. [The article was first published in French in *BSL* 43 (1946) 1–12.]

Bergk, Theodor. *Poetae Lyrici Graeci.* 3 vols. Leipzig: Teubner, 1882.

Bergren, Ann. "*The Homeric Hymn to Aphrodite*: Tradition and Rhetoric, Praise and Blame." *Classical Antiquity* 8 (1989) 1–41.

———. "Language and the Female in Early Greek Thought." *Arethusa* 16 (1983) 69–95.

———. "Sacred Apostrophe: Re-Presentation and Imitation in the Homeric Hymns." *Arethusa* 15 (1982) 83–108.

Bernikow, Louise, ed. *The World Split Open: Four Centuries of Women Poets in England and America.* New York: Vintage, 1974.

Bethe, Erich. "Die dorische Knabenliebe, ihre Ethik und ihre Idee." *Rheinisches Museum für Philologie* 62 (1907) 438–75.

Boardman, John. *Athenian Red Figure Vases: The Archaic Period.* London: Thames and Hudson, 1975.

Boardman, John, and E. La Rocca. *Eros in Greece.* London: John Murray, 1978.

Boas, Franz. *Kwakiutl Tales.* New York: Columbia University Press; Leiden: Brill, 1910.

———. *The Mythology of the Bella Coola Indians.* New York: n.p., 1898.

Boedeker, Deborah Dickmann. *Aphrodite's Entry into Greek Epic.* Leiden: Brill, 1974.

———. *Descent from Heaven: Images of Dew in Greek Poetry and Religion.* Chico, Calif.: Scholars Press, 1984.

———. "Sappho and Acheron." In *Arktouros: Hellenic Studies presented to Bernard W. M. Knox on the Occasion of His 65th Birthday,* edited by Glen W. Bowersock, W. Burkert, and M. Putnam, 40–52. New York: W. de Gruyter, 1979.

Bolling, G. "POIKILOS and THRONIA." *American Journal of Philology* 79 (1958) 275–82.

———. "Restoration of Sappho, 98a 1–7." *American Journal of Philology* 80 (1959) 276–87.

Bonaria, M. "Note critiche al testo di Saffo." *Humanitas* 25–26 (1973–74) 155–83.

Bonnano, M. G. "Osservazioni sul tema della 'giusta' reciprocità amorosa da Saffo ai comici." *Quaderni urbinati di cultura classica,* no. 16 (1973) 110–23.

Bonner, C. "KESTOS IMAS and the Satire of Aphrodite." *American Journal of Philology* 70 (1949) 1–6.

Bourdieu, Pierre. *Algeria 1960: The Disenchantment of the World*. Cambridge: Cambridge University Press, 1979.

————. "The Sentiment of Honour in Kabyle Society." In *Honour and Shame: The Values of Mediterranean Society*, edited by J. G. Perisiany, 191–241. London: Weidenfeld and Nicolson, 1966.

Bowie, Angus M. *The Poetic Dialect of Sappho and Alcaeus*. New York: Arno Press, 1981.

Bowra, Cecil Maurice. *Greek Lyric Poetry from Alcman to Simonides*. Oxford: Oxford University Press, 1961.

————. *Pindar*. Oxford: Clarendon Press, 1964.

Brashear, W. "Ein Berliner Zauberpapyrus." *Zeitschrift für Papyrologie und Epigraphik* 33 (1979) 261–78.

Bremer, Jan M. "Pindar's Paradoxical ἐγώ and a Recent Controversy about the Performance of His Epinicia." In *The Poet's 'I' in Archaic Greek Lyric*, edited by S. R. Slings, 40–58. Amsterdam: VU University Press, 1990.

Bremmer, Jan N. "Adolescents, *Symposion*, and Pederasty." In *Sympotica: A Symposium on the Symposion*, edited by Oswyn Murray, 135–48. Oxford: Oxford University Press, 1990.

Brendel, Otto. "The Scope and Temperament of Erotic Art in the Greco-Roman World." In *Studies in Erotic Art*, edited by T. Bowie and C. Christenson, 3–108. New York: Basic Books, 1970.

Broccia, Giuseppe. "Per l'esegesi di Sapph. 31 LP." *Annali del Liceo Classico Dettori di Cagliari* 1 (1962–63) 16 p.

————. Πόθος ε ψόγος : *Il frammento 6 D. e l'opera di Archiloco*. Rome: Bonacci, 1959.

Bundy, Elroy L. *Studia Pindarica*. Berkeley: University of California Press, 1986. [First published in 1962 as vol. 18, nos. 1 and 2, of the *University of California Publications in Classical Philology*.]

Burke, Carolyn. "Irigaray through the Looking Glass." *Feminist Studies* 7 (1981) 288–306.

Burkert, Walter. *Greek Religion: Archaic and Classical*, translated by John Raffan. Cambridge, Mass.: Basil Blackwell, 1985. [Original title: *Griechische Religion der archaischen und klassischen Epoche* (Stuttgart: Verlag W. Kohlhammer, 1977).]

Burn, Lucilla. *The Meidias Painter*. Oxford: Oxford University Press, 1987.

Burnett, Anne. "Desire and Memory (Sappho Frag. 94)." *Classical Philology* 74 (1979) 16–27.

————. "Performing Pindar's Odes." *Classical Philology* 84 (1989) 283–93.

————. *Three Archaic Poets: Archilochus, Alcaeus, Sappho*. Cambridge: Harvard University Press, 1983.

Bury, J. B., S. A. Cook, and F. E. Adcock, eds. *Greek Literature from the Eighth Century to the Persian Wars*. Vol. 4 of *Cambridge Ancient History*. Cambridge: Cambridge University Press, 1926.

Butler, Judith. *Gender Trouble: Feminism and the Subversion of Identity*. New York: Routledge, 1990.

Butler, Samuel. *The Authoress of the Odyssey*. London: A. C. Fifield, 1897.

Buxton, R. *Imaginary Greece: The Context of Mythology*. Cambridge: Cambridge University Press, 1994.

Calame, Claude. *Les chœurs de jeunes filles en Grèce archaïque.* 2 vols. Rome: Edizioni dell'Ateneo e Bizzarri, 1977.

――――. *Choruses of Young Women in Ancient Greece,* translated by Janice Orion and Derek Collins. Lanham, Md.: Rowman and Littlefield, 1994.

――――. *I Greci e l'eros: Simboli, pratiche e luoghi.* Rome: Laterza, 1992.

――――. *Le récit en Grèce ancienne: énonciations et représentations des poètes.* Paris: Meridiens/Klincksieck, 1986.

――――. "Réflexions sur les genres littéraires en Grèce archaïque." *Quaderni urbinati di cultura classica,* no. 17 (1974) 113–28.

――――, ed. *Alcman Fragmenta.* Rome: Edizioni dell' ateneo, 1983.

Calder, William M., III. "F. G. Welcker's *Sapphobild* and Its Reception in Wilamowitz." In *Friedrich Gottlieb Welcker, Werk und Wirkung,* edited by William M. Calder, 131–56. Hermes Einzelschrift 49. Stuttgart: Franz Steiner Verlag Wiesbaden, 1986.

Cameron, A. "Sappho and Aphrodite." *Harvard Theological Review* 57 (1964) 237–39.

――――. "Sappho's Prayer to Aphrodite." *Harvard Theological Review* 32 (1949) 1–17.

Campbell, David A. *Greek Lyric Poetry.* London: Macmillan, 1967.

――――. "Monody." In *Cambridge History of Classical Literature,* edited by P. E. Easterling and B. M. W. Knox, 1.1:161. Rev. ed. Cambridge: Cambridge University Press, 1989.

――――. "Sappho." In *Cambridge History of Classical Literature,* edited by P. E. Easterling and B. M. W. Knox, 1.1:162–68. Rev. ed. Cambridge: Cambridge University Press, 1989.

――――, ed. and trans. *Greek Lyric.* 5 vols. Loeb Classical Library. Cambridge: Harvard University Press, 1982–93.

Cantarella, Eva. *Bisexuality in the Ancient World.* New Haven: Yale University Press, 1992.

――――. *Pandora's Daughters: The Role and Status of Women in Greek and Roman Antiquity,* translated by Maureen B. Fant. Baltimore: Johns Hopkins University Press, 1987.

――――. *Secondo natura: La bissessualità nel mondo antico.* Rome: Editori riuniti, 1988.

Caraveli, Anna. "The Bitter Wounding: The Lament as Social Protest in Rural Greece." In *Gender and Power in Rural Greece,* edited by J. Dubisch, 169–94. Princeton: Princeton University Press, 1986.

Carey, C. "The Performance of the Victory Ode." *American Journal of Philology* 110 (1989) 545–65.

――――. "Sappho Fr. 96 LP." *Classical Quarterly,* n.s. 28 (1978) 366–71.

――――. "The Victory Ode in Performance." *Classical Philology* 86 (1991) 192–200.

Carson [Giacomelli], Anne. "Aphrodite and After." *Phoenix* 34 (1980) 13–19.

――――. *Eros the Bittersweet.* Princeton: Princeton University Press, 1986.

――――. "The Justice of Aphrodite in Sappho Fr. 1." *Transactions of the American Philological Association* 110 (1980) 135–42. [Citations above are to the version published in this volume.]

Cavallini, Eleonora. "Erinna." In *Rose di Pieria,* edited by F. De Martino, 97–135. Bari: Levante, 1991.

――――. *Presenza di Saffo e Alceo nella poesia greca fino ad Aristofane.* Ferrara: [Giornale filologica ferrarese?], 1986.

Chantraine, P. *Grammaire Homérique.* Vol. 2, *Syntaxe.* Paris: Éditions Klincksieck, 1953.

Cherniss, Harold F. "The Biographical Fashion in Literary Criticism." *Classical Philology* 12 (1943) 279–92.

Chicago, Judy. *The Dinner Party.* Garden City, N.Y.: Doubleday, 1979.

————. *Through the Flower.* Garden City, N.Y.: Doubleday, 1975.

Clader, Linda. *Helen: The Evolution from Divine to Human in Greek Epic Tradition.* Leiden: Brill, 1974.

Clay, J. S. "Sappho's Hesperus and Hesiod's Dawn." *Philologus* 124 (1980) 302–5.

Cody, John. *After Great Pain: The Inner Life of Emily Dickinson.* Cambridge: Harvard University Press, 1971.

Cole, Susan Guettel. "Could Greek Women Read and Write?" In *Reflections of Women in Antiquity,* edited by Helene P. Foley, 219–45. New York: Gordon and Breach, 1981.

Contiades-Tsitsoni, E. *Hymenaios und Epithalamion: Das Hochzeitslied in der frühgriechischen Lyrik.* Beiträge zur Altertumskunde Bd. 16. Stuttgart: Teubner, 1990.

Cook, Albert, ed. *The Odyssey.* New York: Norton, 1974.

Cook, Blanche Wiesen. "'Women Alone Stir My Imagination': Lesbianism and the Cultural Tradition." *Signs* 4 (1979) 718–39.

Crane, G. *Backgrounds and Conventions of the Odyssey.* Frankfurt am Main: Athenäum, 1988.

Crystal, David. *A Dictionary of Linguistics and Phonetics.* 3rd ed. Cambridge, Mass.: Basil Blackwell, 1991.

Culham, Phyllis. "Decentering the Text: The Case of Ovid." *Helios* 17 (1990) 161–70.

————. "Ten Years after Pomeroy: Studies of the Image and Reality of Women in Antiquity." *Helios* 13 (1986) 9–30.

Culler, Jonathan. *The Pursuit of Signs: Semiotics, Literature, Deconstruction.* Ithaca: Cornell University Press, 1981.

Damon, P. "Modes of Analogy in Ancient and Medieval Verse." *University of California Publications in Classical Philolology* 15 (1961) 272–80.

Dane, J. A. "Sappho Fr. 16: An Analysis." *Eos* 79 (1981) 185–92.

Danielewicz, J. "Experience in Its Artistic Aspect in Sappho's Subjective Lyrics." *Eos* 58 (1969–70) 163–69.

Davidson, Olga M. "Aspects of Dioscurism in Iranian Kingship: The Case of Lohrasp and Goshtasp in the *Shāhnāme* of Ferdowsi." *Edebiyāt* 1 (1987) 103–15. [Rewritten as chapter 8 of O. M. Davidson, *Poet and Hero in the Persian Book of Kings* (Ithaca: Cornell University Press, 1994).]

Davies, Malcolm. "Alcman fr. 59a P." *Hermes* 111 (1983) 496–97.

————. "Monody, Choral Lyric, and the Tyranny of the Hand-Book." *Classical Quarterly* 38 (1988) 52–64.

————. Review of C. Calame, *Alcman Fragmenta. Gnomon* 58 (1986) 358–89.

————, ed. *Poetarum Melicorum Graecorum Fragmenta.* Vol. 1, *Alcman, Stesichorus, Ibycus.* Oxford: Oxford University Press, 1991.

Davison, John A. *From Archilochus to Pindar.* London: Macmillan, 1968.

Dean-Jones, L. "The Politics of Pleasure: Female Sexual Appetite in the Hippocratic Corpus." *Helios* 19 (1992) 72–91.

de Beauvoir, Simone. *The Second Sex,* translated by H. M. Parshley. New York: Vintage, 1974.

DeJean, Joan. "Fictions of Sappho." *Critical Inquiry* 13 (1987) 787–805.

————. *Fictions of Sappho,* 1546–1937. Chicago: University of Chicago Press, 1989.

de Lauretis, Teresa. *Alice Doesn't: Feminism, Semiotics, Cinema.* Bloomington: Indiana University Press, 1984.

————. "Eccentric Subjects: Feminist Theory and Historical Consciousness." *Feminist Studies* 16 (1990) 115–50.

————. "The Essence of the Triangle, or Taking the Risk of Essentialism Seriously: Feminist Theory in Italy, the U.S., and Britain." *differences* 1 (1989) 3–37.

————. "Feminist Studies/Critical Studies: Issues, Terms, and Contexts." In *Feminist Studies/Critical Studies,* edited by de Lauretis, 1–19. Bloomington: Indiana University Press, 1986.

————. "Sexual Indifference and Lesbian Representation." *Theatre Journal* 40 (1988) 155–77.

————. *Technologies of Gender.* Bloomington: Indiana University Press, 1987.

Del Grande, C. "Saffo, Ode *phainetai moi kenos isos.*" *Euphrosyne* 2 (1959) 181–88.

De Martino, F. "Appunti sulla scrittura al femminile nel mondo antico." In *Rose de Pieria,* edited by De Martino, 17–77. Bari: Levante, 1991.

Denniston, J. D. *The Greek Particles.* Oxford: Oxford University Press, 1954.

Derrida, Jacques. *Speech and Phenomena, and Other Essays on Husserl's "Phenomenology of Signs,"* translated by D. M. Allison. Evanston, Ill.: Northwestern University Press, 1973.

Détienne, Marcel. *The Gardens of Adonis,* translated by Janet Lloyd. Atlantic Highlands, N.J.: Humanities, 1972.

————. *Les maitres de vérité dans la Grèce archaïque.* Paris: F. Maspero, 1967.

Devereux, George. *Femme et mythe.* Paris: Champs-Flammarion, 1982.

————. "Greek Pseudo-Homosexuality and the 'Greek Miracle.' " *Symbolae Osloenses* 42 (1967) 69–92.

————. "The Nature of Sappho's Seizure in fr. 31 LP as Evidence of Her Inversion." *Classical Quarterly,* n.s. 20 (1970) 17–31.

Di Benedetto, Vincenzo. "Intorno al linguaggio erotico di Saffo." *Hermes* 113 (1985) 145–56.

————. "Il tema della vecchiaia e il fr. 58 di Saffo." *Quaderni urbinati di cultura classica,* no. 48 (1985) 145–63.

————. "Il volo di Afrodite in Omero e in Saffo." *Quaderni urbinati di cultura classica,* no. 16 (1973) 121–23.

Dieterich, Albrecht. *Nekyia: Beitrage zur Erklarung der neuendeckten Petrusapokalypse.* Leipzig: Teubner, 1913.

Diggle, James, ed. with commentary. *Euripides: Phaethon.* Cambridge: Cambridge University Press, 1970.

Dimock, G. E., Jr. "The Name of Odysseus." In *Homer,* edited by George Steiner and Robert Fagles, 106–21. Englewood Cliffs, N.J.: Prentice Hall, 1962.

Doane, Mary Ann. *The Desire to Desire: The Woman's Film of the 1940s.* Bloomington: Indiana University Press, 1987.

Dodds, E. R. *Euripides: The Bacchae.* 2nd ed. Oxford: Oxford University Press, 1960.

Dodson, Betty. *Liberating Masturbation.* New York: Dodson, 1975.

Domingo, M. "The Role of the Female in Ancient Epic." Ph.D. diss., Princeton University, 1980.

Donado, J. V. "Cronologia de Erinna." *Emerita* 41 (1973) 349–76.

D'Orsi, L. "Un graffito greco di Stabia." *La Parola del Passato* 23 (1968) 228–30.

Dover, K. J. "Classical Greek Attitudes to Sexual Behaviour." *Arethusa* 6 (1973) 59–73.

————. "Eros and Nomos (Plato *Symposium* 182a–185c)." *Bulletin of the Institute of Classical Studies* 11 (1964) 31–42.

————. *Greek Homosexuality.* Cambridge: Harvard University Press, 1978.

————. "The Poetry of Archilochus." In *Archiloque*, 81–122. Entretiens Hardt 10. Geneva: Fondation Hardt, 1964.

Dowden, Ken. *Death and the Maiden: Girls' Initiation Rites in Greek Mythology*. London: Routledge, 1989.

Draine, Betsy. "Refusing the Wisdom of Solomon: Some Recent Feminist Literary Theory." *Signs* 15 (1989) 144–70.

duBois, Page. "Sappho and Helen." *Arethusa* 11 (1978) 89–99. [Citations above are to the version published in this volume.]

————. *Sappho Is Burning*. Chicago: University of Chicago Press, 1995.

————. *Sowing the Body: Psychoanalysis and Ancient Representations of Women*. Chicago: University of Chicago Press, 1988.

Durup, Sylvie. "L'espressione tragica del desiderio amoroso." In *L'amore in Grecia*, edited by Claude Calame, 143–57. Rome: Laterza, 1984.

Eisenhut, W. *Antike Lyrik*. Darmstadt: Wissenschaftliche Buchges, 1970.

Eitrem, S. "La magie comme motif littéraire chez les Grecs et les Romains." *Symbolae Osloenses* 21 (1941) 39–83.

Eliade, Mircea. *The Forge and the Crucible*, translated by S. Corrin. New York: Harper, 1963.

Ellmann, Mary. *Thinking about Women*. New York: Harcourt Brace, 1968.

Fairweather, Janet A. "Fiction in the Biographies of Ancient Writers." *Ancient Society* 5 (1974) 231–75.

Färber, H. *Die Lyrik in der Kunsttheorie der Antike*. Munich: Neuer Filser Verlag, 1936.

Farnell, L. R. *Greek Hero Cults and Ideas of Immortality*. Oxford: Oxford University Press, 1921.

Farwell, M. "Toward a Definition of Lesbian Literary Imagination." In *Feminist Theory in Practice and Process*, edited by M. Malson, J. O'Barr, S. Westphal-Wihl, and M. Wyer, 210–19. Chicago: University of Chicago Press, 1989.

Flacelière, Robert. *L'amour en Grèce*. 1960. Reprint, Paris: Hachette, 1971.

————. *Love in Ancient Greece*, translated by James Cleugh. London: F. Muller, 1962.

Flax, Jane. *Thinking Fragments: Psychoanalysis, Feminism, and Postmodernism in the Contemporary West*. Berkeley: University of California Press, 1990.

Foley, Helene P. " 'Reverse Similes' and Sex Roles in the *Odyssey*." *Arethusa* 11 (1978) 7–26.

————, ed. *Reflections of Women in Antiquity*. New York: Gordon and Beach, 1981.

Fontenrose, Joseph. *Orion: The Myth of the Hunter and the Huntress*. Berkeley: University of California Press, 1981.

Foster, B. O. "Notes on the Symbolism of the Apple in Classical Antiquity." *Harvard Studies in Classical Philology* 10 (1899) 39–55.

Foucault, Michel. *The History of Sexuality*. Vol. 1. New York: Vintage, 1980.

————. *The History of Sexuality*. Vol. 2, *The Use of Pleasure*. New York: Vintage, 1985.

————. *The History of Sexuality*. Vol. 3, *The Care of the Self*, translated by Robert Hurley. New York: Vintage, 1986.

Fowler, Barbara Hughes. "The Archaic Aesthetic." *American Journal of Philology* 105 (1984) 119–49.

Fowler, R. L. *The Nature of Greek Lyric: Three Preliminary Studies*. Toronto: University of Toronto Press, 1987.

Fraenkel, Eduard. *Horace*. Oxford: Oxford University Press, 1957.

Frame, D. *The Myth of Return in Early Greek Epic*. New Haven: Yale University Press, 1978.

Fränkel, Hermann. *Dichtung und Philosophie des frühen Griechentums.* Munich: Beck, 1962.

———. *Early Greek Poetry and Philosophy,* translated by Moses Hadas and James Willis. New York: Harcourt Brace Jovanovich, 1973.

———. "Eine Stileigenheit der frühgriechischen Literatur" (1924). In *Wege und Forme frühgriechischen Denkens,* 40–96. 3rd ed. Munich: C. H. Beck, 1968.

Frazer, Sir James George. *Adonis, Attis, Osiris.* Part 4 of *The Golden Bough.* London: Macmillan, 1966.

———. *Apollodorus.* 2 vols. Cambridge, Mass.: Harvard University Press, 1921.

Frisk, H. *Griechisches etymologisches Wörterbuch.* Heidelberg: C. Winter, 1954.

Frontisi-Ducroux, François, and François Lissarrague. "From Ambiguity to Ambivalence: A Dionysiac Excursion through the 'Anakreontic' Vases," translated by Robert Lamberton. In *Before Sexuality: The Construction of Erotic Experience in the Ancient Greek World,* edited by David M. Halperin, John J. Winkler, and Froma I. Zeitlin, 211–56. Princeton: Princeton University Press, 1990.

Fuss, Diana. *Essentially Speaking: Feminism, Nature, and Difference.* New York: Routledge, 1989.

Gallavotti, C. *Saffo e Alceo: Testimonianze e frammenti.* Vol. 1, *Saffo.* 3rd rev. ed. Naples: Libreria Scientifica Editrice, 1957.

Gallop, Jane. *The Daughter's Seduction: Feminism and Psychoanalysis.* Ithaca: Cornell University Press, 1982.

———. *Thinking through the Body.* New York: Columbia University Press, 1988.

Gentili, Bruno. "Aspetti del rapporto poeta, committenti, uditorio nella lirica corale greca." *Studi urbinati di storia, filosofia e letteratura* 39 (1965) 10–88.

———. "L'interpretazione dei lirici greci arcaici nella dimensione del nostro tempo." *Quaderni urbinati di cultura classica,* no. 8 (1969) 7–21.

———. "Il 'letto insaziato' di Medea e il tema dell' *Adikia* a livello amoroso nei lirici (Saffo, Teognide) e nelle *Medea* di Euripide." *Studi classici e orientali* 21 (1972) 60–72.

———. "Lirica greca arcaica e tardo arcaica." In *Introduzione allo studio della cultura classica,* 57–105. Milan: Marzorati, 1972.

———. "Il Partenio de Alcmane e l'amore omerotico femminile nei tiasi spartant." *Quaderni urbinati di cultura classica,* no. 22 (1976) 59–67.

———. *Poesia e pubblico nella Grecia antica da Omero al V secolo.* Rome: Laterza, 1985.

———. *Poetry and Its Public in Ancient Greece: From Homer to the Fifth Century,* translated by A. Thomas Cole. Baltimore: Johns Hopkins University Press, 1988.

———. "Aspetti del rapporto poeta, committente, uditorio nella lirica orale greca." *Studi urbinati di storia, filosofia e letteratura* 39 (1965) 70–88.

———. "La veneranda Saffo." *Quaderni urbinati di cultura classica,* no. 2 (1966) 37–62.

———, ed. *Anacreon.* Rome: Ateneo, 1958.

Gerber, Douglas E. *Euterpe: An Anthology of Early Greek Lyric, Elegiac, and Iambic Poetry.* Amsterdam: Hakkert, 1970.

———. "Studies in Greek Lyric Poetry: 1967–1973." *Classical World* 70 (1976) 65–157.

———. "Studies in Greek Lyric Poetry: 1975–1985; Part I." *Classical World* 81 (1987) 73–144.

———. "Varia Semonidea." *Phoenix* 33 (1979) 19–24.

Gernet, Louis. *Anthropology of Ancient Greece,* translated by John Hamilton and Blaise Nagy. Baltimore: Johns Hopkins University Press, 1981.

Giacomelli, Anne. *See* Carson, Anne.

Gold, Barbara. " 'But Ariadne Was Never There in the First Place': Finding the Female in Roman Poetry." In *Feminist Theory and the Classics,* edited by Nancy Sorkin Rabinowitz and Amy Richlin, 75–101. New York: Routledge, 1993.

Gomme, A. W. "Interpretations of Some Poems of Alkaios and Sappho." *Journal of Hellenic Studies* 77 (1957) 255–66.

Goody, Jack, and Ian Watt. "The Consequences of Literacy." In *Literacy in Traditional Societies,* edited by Goody, 27–68. Cambridge: Cambridge University Press, 1968.

Gouldner, A. *Enter Plato: Classical Greece and the Origins of Social Theory.* New York: Basic Books, 1965.

Governi, A. "Su alcuni elementi propemptici in Saffo e in Omero." *Studi italiani di filologia classica* 53 (1981) 270–71.

Gow, A. S. F., ed. *Theocritus.* 2 vols. Cambridge: Cambridge University Press, 1950.

Gow, A. S. F., and D. L. Page, eds. *The Greek Anthology: Hellenistic Epigrams.* 2 vols. Cambridge: Cambridge University Press, 1965.

Greene, Ellen. "Apostrophe and Women's Erotics in the Poetry of Sappho." *Transactions of the American Philological Association* 124 (1994) 41–56. [Citations above are to the version published in this volume.]

Greimas, A. J. *Sémantique structurale, rechreche de methode.* Paris: Larousse, 1966.

——— . *Structural Semantics,* translated by Daniele McDowell, Ronald Schleifer, and Alan Velie. Lincoln: University of Nebraska Press, 1983.

Griffiths, Alan. "Alcman's Partheniaion: The Morning after the Night Before." *Quaderni urbinati di cultura classica,* no. 22 (1976) 7–30.

Gronewald, M. "Fragmente aus einem Sappho-Kommentar: Pap. Colon. inv. 5860." *Zeitschrift für Papyrologie und Epigraphik* 14 (1974) 114–18.

Grube, G. M. A. *Plato's Thought.* Boston: Beacon Press, 1935.

Gruppe, O. "Die eherne Schwelle und der Thorikische Stein." *Archiv für Religionswissenschaft* 15 (1912) 359–79.

——— . *Griechische Mythologie und Religionsgeschichte.* Vol 1. Munich: Beck, 1906.

Gubar, Susan. " 'The Blank Page' and the Issues of Female Creativity." In *The New Feminist Criticism: Essays on Women, Literature, and Theory,* edited by Elaine Showalter, 292–313. New York: Pantheon, 1985.

Guntert, Hermann. *Der arische Weltkönig und Heiland: Bedeutungsgeschichtliche Untersuchungen zur indo-iranischen Religionsgeschichte und Altertumskunde.* Halle am Salle: M. Niemeyer, 1923.

——— . *Kalypso: Bedeutungsgeschichtliche Untersuchungen auf dem Gebiet der indogermanischen Sprachen.* Halle am Salle: M. Niemeyer, 1909.

Hague, Rebecca. "Ancient Greek Wedding Songs: The Tradition of Praise." *Journal of Folklore Research* 20 (1983) 131–43.

——— . "Sappho's Consolation for Atthis, Fr. 96 LP." *American Journal of Philology* 105 (1984) 29–36.

Hainsworth, B. *The Iliad: A Commentary.* Vol. 3, *Books 9–12.* Cambridge: Cambridge University Press, 1993.

Hallett, Judith P. "Sappho and Her Social Context: Sense and Sensuality." *Signs* 4 (1979) 447–64. [Citations above are to the version published in this volume.]

——— . In progress. *Breathing Beneath the Images: Latin Literary Texts and the Recovery of Elite Roman Women.*

Halperin, David M. *One Hundred Years of Homosexuality and Other Essays on Greek Love.* New York: Routledge, 1990.

———. "Plato and Erotic Reciprocity." *Classical Antiquity* 5 (1986) 60–80.

Halperin, David, John Winkler, and Froma Zeitlin, eds. *Before Sexuality, The Construction of Erotic Experience in the Ancient Greek World.* Princeton: Princeton University Press, 1990.

Hamm, Eva.-Marie. *Grammatik zu Sappho und Alkaios.* Berlin: Akademie-Verlag, 1957.

Harvey, A. E. "The Classification of Greek Lyric Poetry." *Classical Quarterly* 5 (1955) 157–74.

———. "Homeric Epithets in Greek Lyric Poetry." *Classical Quarterly* 7 (1957) 206–23.

Havelock, Eric A. *Preface to Plato.* Cambridge: Harvard University Press, 1963.

———. "The Preliteracy of the Greeks." *New Literary History* 8 (1979) 369–91.

Heath, M. "Receiving the κῶμος: The Context and Performance of Epinician." *American Journal of Philology* 109 (1988) 180–95.

Heath, M., and M. R. Lefkowitz. "Epinician Performance." *Classical Philology* 86 (1991) 173–91.

Hekman, Susan J. *Gender and Knowledge: Elements of a Postmodern Feminism.* Boston: Northeastern University Press, 1990.

Henderson, Jeffrey. *The Maculate Muse: Obscene Language in Attic Comedy.* New Haven: Yale University Press, 1975.

Hertz, N. "A Reading of Longinus." In *The End of the Line: Essays on Psychoanalysis and the Sublime,* 1–20. New York: Columbia University Press, 1985.

Herzfeld, Michael. *The Poetics of Manhood: Contest and Identity in a Cretan Mountain Village.* Princeton: Princeton University Press, 1985.

Herzog, R. "Auf den Spuren der Telesilla." *Philologus* 91 (1912) 1–21.

Homans, Margaret. "Feminist Criticism and Theory: The Ghost of Creusa." *Yale Journal of Criticism* 1 (1987) 153–82.

Hooker, J. T. *The Language and Text of the Lesbian Poets.* Innsbrucker Beiträge zur Sprachwissenschaft Bd. 26. Innsbruck: Rauchdruck, 1977.

Horkheimer, Max, and Theodor Adorno. *Dialectic of Enlightenment,* translated by John Cumming. New York: Seabury, 1972.

Householder, Fred W., and Gregory Nagy. *Greek: A Survey of Recent Work.* The Hague: Mouton, 1972.

Howie, J. G. "Sappho Fr. 16 (LP): Self-Consolation and Encomium." In *Papers of the Liverpool Latin Seminar.* Vol. 1, 1976: *Classical Latin Poetry, Medieval Latin Poetry, Greek Poetry,* edited by F. Cairns, 207–35. Liverpool: Cairns, 1977.

Hubbard, T. K. "The Subject/Object-Relation in Pindar's Second *Pythian* and Seventh *Nemean.*" *Quaderni urbinati di cultura classica,* no. 51 (1986) 53–72.

Istituto papirologico G. Vitelli. *Dai papiri della Società Italiano.* Omaggio all'XI Congresso Internazionale. Florence: F. LeMonnier, 1965.

Irigaray, Luce. *Sexes and Genealogies,* translated by Gillian C. Gill. New York: Columbia University Press, 1993.

———. *Speculum of the Other Woman,* translated by Gillian C. Gill. Ithaca: Cornell University Press, 1985.

———. *This Sex Which Is Not One,* translated by Catherine Porter, with Carolyn Burke. Ithaca: Cornell University Press, 1985.

Jacoby, F. *Die Fragmente der griechischen Historiker.* Berlin: Weidmann, 1923.

Jaeger, Werner. *Paideia: The Ideals of Greek Culture*, translated by Gilbert Highet. Oxford: Oxford University Press, 1965.

Janko, R. "Berlin Magical Papyrus 21243: A Conjecture." *Zeitschrift für Papyrologie und Epigraphik* 72 (1988) 293.

————. "Sappho Fr. 96.8 L-P: A Textual Note." *Mnemosyne*, ser. 4, 35 (1982) 322–24.

Janni, Pietro. "Due note omeriche." *Quaderni urbinati di cultura classica*, no. 3 (1967) 7–30.

Jarcho, V. N. "Das poetische 'Ich' als gesellschaftlich-kommunikatives Symbol in der frühgriechischen Lyrik." In *The Poet's 'I' in Archaic Greek Lyric*, edited by S. R. Slings, 31–39. Amsterdam: VU University Press, 1990.

Jardine, Alice. *Gynesis: Configurations of Woman and Modernity*. Ithaca: Cornell University Press, 1985.

Jeanmaire, Henri. *Couroï et Courètes: Essai sur l'éducation spartiate et sur les rites d'adolescence dans l'antiquité hellénique*. Lille: Bibliothèque universitaire, 1939.

Jefferson, A. "Bodymatters." In *Bakhtin and Cultural Theory*, edited by Ken Hirschkop and David Shepherd, 152–77. Manchester: Manchester University Press, 1989.

Johnson, Barbara. "Apostrophe, Animation, and Abortion." In *A World of Difference*, 184–99. Baltimore: Johns Hopkins University Press, 1987.

Johnson, Thomas H. *Emily Dickinson: An Interpretive Biography*. Cambridge: Harvard University Press, 1955.

Jones, Ann Rosalind. "Writing the Body: Toward an Understanding of *l'écriture féminine*." *Feminist Studies* 7 (1981) 247–63.

Jones, C. P. "Tange Chloen semel Arrogantem." *Harvard Studies in Classical Philology* 75 (1971) 81–83.

Joseph, Terri Brint. "Poetry as a Strategy of Power: The Case of Riffian Berber Women." *Signs* 5 (1980) 418–34.

Kaempf-Dimitriadou, S. *Die Liebe der Götter in der attischen Kunst des 3. Jahrhunderts, v. chr.* Antike Kunst Beiheft 11, 1979.

Kahil, Lily. *Les enlèvements et le retour d'Hélène*. 2 vols. Paris: Boccard, 1953.

Kaimio, Maarit. *The Chorus of Greek Drama within the Light of the Person and Number Used*. Commentationes Humanarum Litterarum 46. Helsinki: Societas scientarum Fennica, 1970.

Kakridis, P. I. "Une Pomme mordue." *Hellenica* 25 (1972) 189–92.

Kamuf, Peggy. "Replacing Feminist Criticism." *Diacritics* 12 (1982) 42–47.

KazikZawadzka, Irena. *De Sapphicae Alcaicaeque elocutionis colore epico* [Archiwum Filologiczne IV]. Wroclaw: Wydawnicto Polskeiej Akademii Nauk, 1958.

Keenan, E. "Norm-Makers, Norm-Breakers: Uses of Speech by Men and Women in a Malagasy Community." In *Explorations in the Ethnography of Speaking*, edited by Richard Bauman and Joel Scherzer, 125–43. Cambridge: Cambridge University Press, 1974.

Killeen, J. F. "Sappho Fr. 111." *Classical Quarterly* 23 (1973) 197.

Kirk, Geoffrey S. "A Fragment of Sappho Reinterpreted." *Classical Quarterly* 13 (1963) 51–52.

Kirkwood, G. M. *Early Greek Monody: The History of a Poetic Type*. Ithaca: Cornell University Press, 1974.

Klein, E. *Comprehensive Etymological Dictionary of the English Language*. Amsterdam: Elsevier, 1971.

Koerte, Alfred. *Meandri quae supersunt*. Leipzig: Teubner, 1957.

Kolodny, Annette. "The Influence of Anxiety: Prolegomena to a Study of the Production of Poetry by Women." In *A Gift of Tongues: Critical Challenges in Contemporary American Poetry,* edited by Marie Harris and Kathleen Aguero, 112–41. Athens: University of Georgia Press, 1987.

Koniaris, G. L. "On Sappho I." *Philologus* 109 (1965) 30–38.

———. "On Sappho fr. 31 (L-P)." *Philologus* 112 (1968) 173–86.

Kostis, N. "Albertine: Characterization through Image and Symbol." *PMLA* 84 (1969) 125–35.

Kranz, W. *Geschichte der griechischen Literatur.* 3rd rev. ed. Bremen: Schünemann, 1958.

Kretschmer, P. *Die griechischen Vaseninschriften, ihrer Sprache nach untersucht.* Gütersloh: C. Bertelsmann, 1894.

Krischer, T. "Sappho's Ode on Aphrodite." *Hermes* 96 (1968) 1–14.

Lacan, Jacques. "God and the *Jouissance* of Woman." In *Feminine Sexuality: Jacques Lacan and the "école freudienne,"* edited by Juliet Mitchell and Jacqueline Rose, translated by Jacqueline Rose, 137–48. New York: Norton, 1982.

Lacey, W. K. *The Family in Classical Greece.* London: Thames and Hudson, 1968.

Lanata, Giuliana. "L'ostracon fiorentino con versi di Saffo." *Studi italiani di filologia classica* 32 (1960) 64–90.

———. *Poetica pre-platonica: testimonianze e frammenti.* Florence: La nuova Italia, 1963.

———. "Sul linguaggio amoroso di Saffo." *Quaderni urbinati di cultura classica,* no. 2 (1966) 63–79. [Translated in this volume.]

Lardinois, André. "Lesbian Sappho and Sappho of Lesbos." In *From Sappho to de Sade: Moments in the History of Sexuality,* edited by J. N. Bremmer, 15–35. London: Routledge, 1989. [The second edition (1991) contains some slight revisions and updates.]

———. "Subject and Circumstance in Sappho's Poetry." *Transactions of the American Philological Association* 124 (1994) 57–84.

Lasserre, François. "Ornements érotiques dans la poésie lyrique archaïque." In *Serta Turyniana: Studies in Greek Literature and Palaeography in Honor of Alexander Turyn,* edited by John L. Heller and J. K. Newman, 1–33. Urbana: University of Illinois Press, 1974

———. *Sappho, une autre lecture.* Padua: Editrice Antenore, 1989.

Lasso de la Vega, J. S. "La oda primera de Safo." *Cuadernos de Filologia Clásica* 6 (1974) 9–93; 7 (1974) 9–80.

Latacz, J. "Realität und Imagination: Eine neue Lyrik-Theorie und Sapphos φαίνεταί μοι χῆνος-Lied." *Museum Helveticum* 42 (1985) 67–94.

Latte, Kurt. Review of Hermann Fränkel, *Dichtung und Philosophie. Göttingische gelehrte Anzeigen* 207 (1953) 30–42.

Lattimore, R. *Greek Lyrics.* Chicago: University of Chicago Press, 1960.

Lawler, L. B. "On Certain Homeric Epithets." *Philological Quarterly* 27 (1948) 80–84.

Lefkowitz, M. R. "Critical Stereotypes and the Poetry of Sappho." *Greek, Roman, and Byzantine Studies* 14 (1974) 113–23.

———. "Cultural Conventions and the Persistence of Mistranslation." *Classical Journal* 68 (1972) 31–38.

———. "Who Sang Pindar's Victory Odes?" In *First Person Fictions: Pindar's Poetic 'I,'* 191–201. Oxford: Oxford University Press, 1991. [The article was first published in *American Journal of Philology* 109 (1988) 1–11.]

————. "ΤΩ ΚΑΙ ΓΩ: The First Person in Pindar." In *First Person Fictions: Pindar's Poetic 'I,'* 1–71. Oxford: Oxford University Press, 1991. [The article was first published in *Harvard Studies in Classical Philology* 67 (1963) 177–253.]

Leumann, Manu. *Homerische Wörter.* Basel: Reinhardt, 1950.

Lévêque, Pierre. "Un nouveau décryptage des mythes d'Adonis." *Revue des Études Anciennes* 74 (1972) 180–85.

Lévi-Strauss, C. *The Elementary Structures of Kinship,* translated by J. H. Bell, J. R. von Sturmer, and R. Needham. Boston: Beacon Press, 1969.

————. *Structural Anthropology,* translated by Claire Jacobson and Brooke Grundfest Schoepf. New York: Basic Books, 1968.

Liberman, G. "A propos de Sappho" [review of F. Lasserre, *Sappho: Une autre lecture*]. *Revue de Philologie* 63 (1989) 229–37.

Licht, Hans [Paul Brandt]. *Sexual Life in Ancient Greece,* translated by J. H. Freese. London: Routledge, 1932.

Lippard, Lucy. "Quite Contrary: Body, Nature, Ritual in Women's Art." *Chrysalis* 2 (1977) 30–47.

Littlewood, A. R. "The Symbolism of the Apple in Greek and Roman Literature." *Harvard Studies in Classical Philology* 72 (1968) 147–81.

Lloyd-Jones, Hugh. *The Justice of Zeus.* Berkeley: University of California Press, 1971.

Lobel, Edgar, and Denys Page, eds. *Poetarum Lesbiorum Fragmenta.* Oxford: Oxford University Press, 1955.

Loraux, N. "Sur la Race des Femmes et Quelque-Unes de ses Tribus." *Arethusa* 11 (1978).

Lord, A. B. "Homer and Other Epic Poetry." In *A Companion to Homer,* edited by A. J. B. Wace and F. H. Stubbings, 179–214. New York: Macmillan, 1963.

Lorde, Audre. "Love Poem." In *Amazon Poetry,* edited by Joan Larkin and Elly Bulkin. Brooklyn, N.Y.: Out and Out Books, 1975.

Lugauer, M. "Untersuchungen zur Symbolik des Apfels in der Antike." Diss., Erlangen-Nürnberg, 1967.

Luschnig, C. A. *Time Holds the Mirror: A Study of Knowledge in Euripides' Hippolytus.* Mnemosyne suppl. 102. Leiden: Brill, 1988.

Maas, Martha, and Jane McIntosh Snyder. *Stringed Instruments of Ancient Greece.* New Haven: Yale University Press, 1989.

MacKinnon, Catherine. *Feminism Unmodified: Discourses on Life and Law.* Cambridge: Harvard University Press, 1987.

Macleod, C. W. "Two Comparisons in Sappho." *Zeitschrift für Papyrologie und Epigraphik* 15 (1974) 217–20.

Maehler, H., ed. *Pindari carmina cum fragmentis.* Part 2, *Fragmenta. Indices.* Leipzig: Teubner, 1989.

Maltomini, F. "P. Berol 21243 (Formulario Magico): Due Nuove Letture." *Zeitschrift für Papyrologie und Epigraphik* 74 (1988) 247–48.

Manieri, F. "Saffo: appunti di metodologia generale per un approcio psichiatrico." *Quaderni urbinati di cultura classica,* no. 14 (1972) 44–64.

Marcovich, M. "Sappho Fr. 31: Anxiety Attack or Love Declaration?" *Classical Quarterly,* n.s. 22 (1972) 19–32.

Marks, Elaine, and Isabelle de Courtivron, eds. *New French Feminisms.* Amherst: University of Massachusetts Press, 1980.

Marrou, H. I. *Histoire de l'éducation dans l'Antiquité.* Paris: Éditions du Seuil, 1965.

Marry, J. D. "Sappho and the Heroic Ideal." *Arethusa* 12 (1979) 71–92.

Martin, R. P. *The Language of Heroes: Speech and Performance in the "Iliad."* Ithaca: Cornell University Press, 1989.

Marzullo, Benedetto. *Studi di poesia eolica.* Florence: Le Monnier, 1958.

Mazzarino, Santo. "Per la storia del Lesbo nel VIo secolo A.C." *Athenaeum* 20 (1942) 38–78.

McCartney, E. S. "How the Apple Became the Token of Love." *Transactions of the American Philological Association* 56 (1925) 70–81.

McEvilley, Thomas. "Imagination and Reality in Sappho." Ph.D. diss., University of Cincinnati, 1968.

———. "Sappho, Fragment 94." *Phoenix* 25 (1971) 1–11.

———. "Sappho, Fragment Two." *Phoenix* 26 (1972) 323–33.

———. "Sappho, Fragment Thirty-One: The Face behind the Mask." *Phoenix* 32 (1978) 1–18.

Meerwaldt, J. D. "Epithalamia I: De Himerio Sapphus imitatore." *Mnemosyne,* ser. 4, 7 (1954) 19–38.

Merkelbach, Reinhold. "Sappho und ihr Kreis." *Philologus* 101 (1957) 1–29.

Miller, Nancy K. "The Text's Heroine: A Feminist Critic and Her Fictions." *Diacritics* 12 (1982) 48–53.

Moi, Toril. *Sexual/Textual Politics: Feminist Literary Theory.* London: Methuen, 1985.

Morgan, K. A. "Pindar the Professional and the Rhetoric of the κῶμος." *Classical Philology* 88 (1993) 1–15.

Mossé, C. *La tyrannie dans la Grèce antique.* Paris: Pressos universitaires de France, 1969.

Most, Glenn. "Greek Lyric Poets." In *Ancient Writers: Greece and Rome.* Vol. 1, *Homer to Caesar,* edited by T. J. Luce, 75–98. New York: Scribner's, 1982.

———. "Sappho Fr. 16.6–7 L-P." *Classical Quarterly* 31 (1981) 11–17.

Mulvey, Laura. *Visual and Other Pleasures.* Bloomington: Indiana University Press, 1989.

Murr, Josef. *Die Pflanzenwelt in der griechischen Mythologie.* Innsbruck: Wagner'schen Universitats-Buchhandlung, 1890.

Murray, Oswyn M. *Early Greece.* Cambridge: Harvard University Press, 1993.

———. "The Greek Symposium in History." In *Tria Corda: Studies in Honour of A. Momigliano,* ed. E. Gabbi, 257–72. Como: Edizioni New Press, 1983.

———. "The Symposium as Social Organisation." In *The Greek Renaissance of the Eighth Century BC,* edited by R. Hägg, 195–99. Stockholm: Svenska institutet i Athen, 1983.

———, ed. *Sympotica: A Symposium on the Symposion.* Oxford: Oxford University Press, 1990.

Muth, R. " 'Hymenaios' und 'Epithalamion.' " *Wiener Studien* 67 (1954) 5–45.

———. Review of E. Contiades-Tsitsoni, *Hymenaios und Epithalamion. Gnomon* 65 (1993) 585–88.

Nagler, Michael. "Dread Goddess Endowed with Speech." *Archaeological News* 6 (1977) 77–85.

Nagy, Gregory. *The Best of the Achaeans: Concepts of the Hero in Archaic Greek Poetry.* Baltimore: Johns Hopkins University Press, 1979.

———. *Comparative Studies in Greek and Indic Meter.* Cambridge: Harvard University Press, 1974.

———. "Copies and Models in Horace *Odes* 4.1 and 4.2." *Classical World* 87 (1994) 415–26.

———. *Greek Mythology and Poetics*. Ithaca: Cornell University Press, 1990.

———. "Phaethon, Sappho's Phaon, and the White Rock of Leukas." *Harvard Studies in Classical Philology* 77 (1973) 137–77. [Citations above are to the version published in this volume.]

———. *Pindar's Homer: The Lyric Possession of an Epic Past*. Baltimore: Johns Hopkins University Press, 1990.

———. "Pindar's Olympian 1 and the Aetiology of the Olympic Games." *Transactions of the American Philological Association* 116 (1986) 71–88.

———. *Poetry as Performance: Homer and Beyond*. Cambridge: Cambridge University Press, 1995.

———. "Theognis and Megara: A Poet's Vision of His City." In *Theognis of Megara: Poetry and the Polis*, edited by T.J. Figueira and G. Nagy, 22–81. Baltimore: Johns Hopkins University Press, 1985.

Newton, R. M. "The Rebirth of Odysseus." *Greek, Roman, and Byzantine Studies* 25 (1984) 5–20.

Nilsson, Martin P. *Griechische Feste*. Leipzig: Teubner, 1906.

Nisbet, R. G. M., and Margaret Hubbard. *A Commentary on Horace: Odes* 1. Oxford: Oxford University Press, 1970.

Nugent, Georgia. "This Sex Which Is Not One: De-Constructing Ovid's Hermaphrodite." *differences* 2 (1990) 160–85.

O'Higgins, Dolores. "Sappho's Splintered Tongue: Silence in Sappho 31 and Catullus 51." *American Journal of Philology* 111 (1990) 156–67.

Olsen, Tillie. *Silences*. 1978. Reprint, New York: Delta/Seymour Lawrence, 1989.

Ong, Walter J. *Orality and Literacy: The Technologizing of the Word*. London: Methuen, 1982.

Onians, Richard Broxton. *The Origins of European Thought about the Body, the Mind, the Soul, the World, Time, and Fate*. Cambridge: Cambridge University Press, 1954.

Page, Denys L. *The Homeric Odyssey*. Oxford: Oxford University Press, 1955.

———, ed. *Alcman: The Partheneion*. Oxford: Oxford University Press, 1951.

———, ed. *Further Greek Epigrams*. Rev. R. D. Dawe and J. Diggle. Cambridge: Cambridge University Press, 1981.

———, ed. *Poetae Melici Graeci*. Oxford: Oxford University Press, 1962.

———, ed. *Sappho and Alcaeus: An Introduction to the Study of Ancient Lesbian Poetry*. Oxford: Oxford University Press, 1955.

Paradiso, A. "Saffo, la poetessa." In *Grecia al femminile*, edited by N. Loraux, 39–72. Rome: Laterza, 1993.

Parker, Holt N. "Sappho Schoolmistress." *Transactions of the American Philological Association* 123 (1993) 309–51.

Parry, A., ed. *The Making of Homeric Verse*. Oxford: Oxford University Press, 1971.

Parry, Milman. "The Traces of the Digamma in Ionic and Lesbian Greek." In *The Making of Homeric Verse*, edited by Adam Parry, 319–403. Oxford: Oxford University Press, 1971.

———. "The Traditional Metaphor in Homer." *Classical Philology* 28 (1933) 30–43.

Pauly, August Friedrich. *Paulys Realencyclopaedie der classischen Altertumswissenschaft*, edited by Georg Wissowa, Wilhelm Kross, and Karl Mittelhaus. 34 vols. Stuttgart: Metzer, 1894–1972.

Peradotto, John, and J P. Sullivan, eds. *Women in the Ancient World*. Albany: SUNY Press, 1984.

Peterson, D. L. "A Probable Source for Shakespeare's Sonnet CXXXIX." *Shakespeare Quarterly* 5 (1954) 381–84.

Pfeiffer, Rudolf. *History of Classical Scholarship—From the Beginnings to the End of the Hellenistic Age.* Oxford: Oxford University Press, 1968.

Pfuhl, Ernst. *Malerei und Zeichnung der Griechen.* Munich: Buckmann, 1923.

Piccaluga, Giulia. "Adonis e i profumi di un certo strutturalismo." *Maia* 26 (1974) 33–51.

———. "Adonis, i cacciatori falliti e l'avvento dell'agricoltura." In *It Mito Greco: Atti del Convegno Internazionale, Urbino 7–12 maggio 1973,* edited by B. Gentilli and G. Paioni, 33–48. Rome: Ateneo, n.d.

Poland, Franz. *Geschichte des griechischen Vereinswesens.* Leipzig: Teubner, 1909.

Pomeroy, S. *Goddesses, Whores, Wives, and Slaves: Women in Classical Antiquity.* New York: Schocken Books, 1975.

———. "TECHNIKAI KAI MOUSIKAI: The Education of Women in the Fourth Century and in the Hellenistic Period." *American Journal of Ancient History* 2 (1977) 51–68.

Privitera, G. A. "Ambiguità antitesi analogia nel fr. 31 L.P. di Saffo." *Quaderni urbinati di cultura classica,* no. 8 (1969) 37–80.

———. "La Rete di Afrodite." *Quaderni urbinati di cultura classica,* no. 4 (1967) 47–58.

Propp, V. *Morphology of the Folktale,* translated by Laurence Scott. Austin: University of Texas Press, 1968.

Putnam, Michael. "*Thronia* and Sappho 1.1." *Classical Journal* 56 (1960–61) 79–83.

Race, W. H. "Sappho, *Fr.* 16 L.-P. and Alkaios, *Fr.* 42 L.-P.: Romantic and Classical Strains in Lesbian Poetry." *Classical Journal* 85 (1989–90) 16–23.

———. " 'That Man' in fr. 31 L.-P." *Classical Antiquity* 2 (1983) 92–101.

Radt, S. L. "Sapphica." *Mnemosyne,* ser. 4, 13 (1970) 337–47.

Rauk, John. "Erinna's *Distaff* and Sappho Fr. 94." *Greek, Roman, and Byzantine Studies* 30 (1989) 101–16.

Redfield, J. "The Women of Sparta." *Classical Journal* 73 (1977–78) 148–49.

Ribichini, S. *Adonis: aspetti 'orientali' di un mito greco.* Rome: Consiglio Naz. delle Richerche, 1981.

Richardson, N. J. *The Homeric Hymn to Demeter.* Oxford: Oxford University Press, 1974.

Richlin, Amy, ed. *Pornography and Representation in Greece and Rome.* Oxford: Oxford University Press, 1992.

Richter, Gisela M. A. *Kourai.* London: Phaidon, 1968.

———. "Sculpture, Greek." In *The Oxford Classical Dictionary.* Oxford: Oxford University Press, 1970.

Rissman, Leah. *Love as War: Homeric Allusion in the Poetry of Sappho.* Beitrage zur klassischen Wissenschaft 157. Konigstein: Hain, 1983.

Rivier, A. "Observations sur Sappho, 1, 19 sq." *Revue des Études Grecques* 80 (1967) 84–92. [Reprinted in *Études de littérature grecque,* 235–42 (Geneva: Droz, 1975).]

Robbins, Emmet. " 'Every Time I Look at You ...': Sappho Thirty-One." *Transactions of the American Philological Association* 110 (1980) 255–61.

———. "Who's Dying in Sappho Fr. 94?" *Phoenix* 44 (1990) 111–21.

Robert, C. "Athena Skiras und die Skirophorien." *Hermes* 20 (1885) 349–79.

———. "Die Phaethonsage bei Hesiod." *Hermes* 18 (1883) 434–41.

Robinson, David M. *Sappho and Her Influence.* Boston: Marshall Jones, 1924.

Robinson, David M., and Edward J. Fluck. *A Study of the Greek Love-Names, Including a Discussion of Pederasy and a Prosopographicia.* Baltimore: Johns Hopkins Press, 1937.

Rohde, Erwin. *Psyche: Seelencult und Unsterblichkeitsglaube der Griechen.* Freiburg: Mohr, 1898.

Roscher, W. *Ausführliches Lexicon der griechischen und römischen Mythologie,* 6 vols. Leipzig: Teubner, 1884–1937.

Rosen, Phillip, ed. *Narrative, Apparatus, Ideology: A Film Theory Reader.* New York: Columbia University Press, 1986.

Rosenmeyer, T. "Alcman's Partheneion I Reconsidered." *Greek, Roman, and Byzantine Studies* 7 (1966) 321–59.

Rösler, W. *Dichter und Gruppe: eine Untersuchung zu den Bedingungen und zur historischen Funktion früher griechischer Lyriker am Beispiel Alkaios.* Munich: Wilhelm Fink Verlag, 1980.

———. "Ein Gedicht und sein Publikum: Überlegungen zu Sappho fr. 44 Lobel Page." *Hermes* 103 (1975) 275–85.

———. "Persona reale o persona poetica? L'interpretazione dell' 'io' nella lirica greca arcaica." *Quaderni urbinati di cultura classica,* 48 (1985) 131–44.

———. Review of François Lasserre, *Sappho: une autre lecture. Anzeiger für die Altertumswissenschaft* 45 (1992) 197–99.

———. Review of O. Tsagarakis, *Self-Expression in Early Greek Lyric: Elegiac and Iambic Poetry. Gnomon* 52 (1980) 609–16.

Rossi, L. "Il simposio greco arcaico come spectacolo a se stesso." In *Atti del VII convegno di studi: Spettacoli Conviviali,* 41–50. Viterbo Maggio: Il Centro, 1983.

Rudhardt, J. *Notions fondamentales de la pensée religieuse et actes constitutifs du culte dans la Grèce classique.* Geneva: Fondation Hardt, 1958.

Russ, Joanna. *How to Suppress Women's Writing.* Austin: University of Texas Press, 1983.

Russo, Joseph. "The Meaning of Oral Poetry: *The Collected Papers of Milman Parry* : A Critical Re-assessment." *Quaderni urbinati di cultura classica,* no. 12 (1971) 27–39.

———. "Reading the Greek Lyric Poets (Monodists)." *Arion* 1 (1973–74) 707–30.

Russo, Joseph, and B. Simon. "Homeric Psychology and the Oral Epic Tradition." *Journal of the History of Ideas* 29 (1968) 483–98.

Rydbeck, L. "Sappho's φαίνεταί μοι κῆνος, ὅττις [V. 2]: A Clue to the Understanding of the Poem." *Hermes* 97 (1969) 161–66.

Saake, H. *Sapphostudien: Forschungsgeschichtliche, biographische und literarästhetische Untersuchungen.* Munich: Ferdinand Schöningh Verlag, 1972.

———. *Zur Kunst Sapphos: Motiv-analytische und kompositionstechnische Interpretationen.* Munich: Ferdinand Schöningh Verlag, 1971.

Sandbach, F. H., ed. *Menandri Reliquiae Selectae.* Rev. ed. Oxford: Oxford University Press, 1990.

Schadewaldt, W. *Sappho: Welt und Dichtung, Dasein in der Liebe.* Potsdam: Eduard Stichnote, 1950.

———. "Zu Sappho." *Hermes* 71 (1936) 363–73.

Schaps, David. "The Women of Greece in Wartime." *Classical Philology* 77 (1982) 193–213.

Scherer, A. *Gestirnnamen bei den indogermanischen Völkern.* Heidelberg: Winter, 1953.

Schibanoff, Susan. "Taking the Gold out of Egypt: The Art of Reading as a Woman." In *Gender and Reading: Essays on Readers, Texts, and Contexts,* edited by Elizabeth A. Flynn and Patrocinio P. Schweickart, 83–106. Baltimore: Johns Hopkins University Press, 1986.

Schmitt, R. *Dichtung und Dichtersprache in indogermanischer Zeit.* Wiesbaden: Harrassowitz, 1967.

Schor, Naomi. "This Essentialism Which Is Not One: Coming to Grips with Irigaray." *differences* 1 (1989) 38–58.

Schreckenburg, H. *Ananke: Untersuchungen zur Geschichte des Wortegebrauchs.* Munich: Beck, 1964.

Schwyzer, E., and A. Debrunner. *Griechische Grammatik.* Vol. 2, *Syntax und syntaktische Stilistik.* Munich: C. H. Beck, 1950.

Scott, William C. *The Oral Nature of the Homeric Simile.* Leiden: Brill, 1974.

Seaford, Richard. *Reciprocity and Ritual: Homer and Tragedy in the Developing City State.* Oxford: Oxford University Press, 1994.

Segal, Charles. "Alcman." In *Cambridge History of Classical Literature,* edited by P. E. Easterling and B. M. W. Knox, 1.1:127–45. Rev. ed. Cambridge: Cambridge University Press, 1989.

——— . "Circean Temptations: Homer, Virgil, Ovid." *Transactions of the American Philological Association* 99 (1968) 419–42.

——— . "Eros and Incantation: Sappho and Oral Poetry." *Arethusa* 7 (1974) 139–60. [Citations above are to the version published in this volume.]

——— . "The Homeric Hymn to Aphrodite: A Structuralist Approach." *Classical World* 67 (1973–74) 205–12.

——— . "The Myth of Bacchylides 17: Heroic Quest and Heroic Identity." *Eranos* 77 (1979) 23–37.

——— . "The Nature of Early Choral Poetry." In *Cambridge History of Classical Literature,* edited by P. E. Easterling and B. M. W. Knox, 1.1:124–27. Rev. ed. Cambridge: Cambridge University Press, 1989.

——— . "The Phaeacians and the Symbolism of Odysseus' Return." *Arion* 1 (1962) 17–64.

——— . "Transition and Ritual in Odysseus' Return." *La Parola del Passato* 22 (1967) 321–42. [Reprinted in *The Odyssey,* edited by Albert Cook, 165–86 (New York: Norton, 1974).]

Setti, Alessandro. "Nota a un nuovo frammento di Alceo." *Studi italiani di filologia classica* 27–28 (1956) 519–35.

Showalter, Elaine. "Toward a Feminist Poetics." In *The New Feminist Criticism: Essays on Women, Literature, and Theory,* edited by Showalter, 125–43. New York: Pantheon, 1985.

——— , ed. *The New Feminist Criticism: Essays on Women, Literature, and Theory.* New York: Pantheon, 1985.

Silverman, Kaja. " 'Suture' (excerpts)." In *Narrative, Apparatus, Ideology: A Film Theory Reader,* edited by Phillip Rosen, 219–35. New York: Columbia University Press, 1986.

Skinner, Marilyn B. "Sapphic Nossis." *Arethusa* 22 (1989) 5–18.

——— . "Woman and Language in Archaic Greece, or, Why Is Sappho a Woman?" In *Feminist Theory and the Classics,* edited by N. S. Rabinowitz and A. Richlin, 125–44. New York: Routledge, 1993. [Citations above are to the version published in this volume.]

Slater, Philip. *The Glory of Hera.* Boston: Beacon Press, 1968.

Slings, S. R. "The 'I' in Personal Archaic Lyric: An Introduction." In *The Poet's 'I' in Archaic Greek Lyric,* edited by Slings, 1–30. Amsterdam: VU University Press, 1990.

Smith, H. R. W. *Der Lewismahler (Polygnotos II).* 1939. Reprint, Mainz: Zabern, 1974.

Smith, Peter. *Nursling of Mortality: A Study of the Homeric Hymn to Aphrodite.* Frankfurt: Lang, 1981.

Smith-Rosenberg, Carroll. "The Female World of Love and Ritual: Relations between Women in Nineteenth-Century America." *Signs* 1 (1975) 1–29.

Snell, Bruno. *The Discovery of the Mind,* translated by T. G. Rosenmeyer. Cambridge: Harvard University Press, 1953.

———. "Sapphos Gedicht *phainetai moi kenos.*" *Hermes* 66 (1931) 71–90.

———. "Zur Soziologie des archaischen Griechentums: Der Einzelne und die Gruppe." *Gymnasium* 65 (1968) 48–58.

Snyder, Jane McIntosh. "Public Occasion and Private Passion in the Lyrics of Sappho of Lesbos." In *Women's History and Ancient History,* edited by Sarah B. Pomeroy, 1–19. Chapel Hill: University of North Carolina Press, 1991.

———. "Sappho in Attic Vase Painting." Forthcoming. [A one-page summary of the oral version of this paper can be found in *APA Abstracts* (1993) 171.]

———. *The Woman and the Lyre: Women Writers in Classical Greece and Rome.* Carbondale: Southern Illinois University Press, 1989.

Sowa, Cora. *Traditional Themes and the Homeric Hymns.* Chicago: Bolchazy, 1984.

Stanley, Keith. "The Role of Aphrodite in Sappho Fr. 1." *Greek, Roman, and Byzantine Studies* 17 (1976) 305–21.

Stehle [Stigers], Eva. "Retreat from the Male: Catullus 62 and Sappho's Erotic Flowers." *Ramus* 6 (1977) 83–102.

———. "Romantic Sensuality, Poetic Sense: A Response to Hallett on Sappho." *Signs* 4 (1979) 464–71. [Citations above are to the version published in this volume.]

———. "Sappho's Gaze: Fantasies of a Goddess and a Young Man." *differences* 2 (1990) 88–125. [Citations above are to the version published in this volume.]

———. "Sappho's Private World." In *Reflections of Women in Antiquity,* edited by Helene P. Foley, 45–61. New York: Gordon and Breach, 1981.

Stella, L. A. "Strumenti musicali della lirica greca arcaica." In *Lirica greca da Archiloco a Elitis: Studi in onore di Filippo Maria Pontani,* 17–32. Padua: Liviana, 1984.

Stern, E. M. "Sappho Fr. 16 L.P.: Zur strukturellen Einheit ihrer Lyrik." *Mnemosyne,* ser. 4, 13 (1970) 348–61.

Stigers, Eva. *See* Stehle, Eva.

Suleiman, Susan. *Authoritarian Fictions: The Ideological Novel as a Literary Genre.* New York: Columbia University Press, 1983.

Svenbro, Jesper. *Phrasikleia: An Anthropology of Reading in Ancient Greece.* Ithaca: Cornell University Press, 1993.

———. "Sappho and Diomedes." *Museum Philologum Londiniense* 1 (1975) 37–49.

———. "La stratégie de l'amour: Modèle de guerre et théorie de l'amour dans la poésie de Sappho." *Quaderni storia* 19 (1984) 57–79.

Theander, C. "Studia Sapphica II." *Eranos* 34 (1937) 49–77.

Thomas, Rosalind. *Oral Tradition and Written Record in Classical Athens.* Cambridge: Cambridge University Press, 1989.

Thorsen, Synnoeve des Bouvrie. "The Interpretation of Sappho's Fragment 16 L. P." *Symbolae Osloenses* 53 (1978) 5–23.

Todd, Janet. *Feminist Literary History.* New York: Routledge, 1988.

Treu, Max. "Neues über Sappho und Alkaios." *Quaderni urbinati di cultura classica,* no. 2 (1966) 9–36.

————. *Sappho, griechisch und deutsch.* Munich: Beck, 1968.

————. *Von Homer zur Lyrik.* Munich: Beck, 1955.

————, ed. *Sappho.* 3rd ed. Munich: E. Heimeran, 1963.

Trumpf, J. "Kydonische Apfel." *Hermes* 88 (1960) 14–22.

————. "Über das Trinken in der Poesie des Alkaios." *Zeitschrift für Papyrologie und Epigraphik* 12 (1973) 139–60.

Tsagarakis, Odysseus. *Self-Expression in Early Greek Lyric: Elegiac and Iambic Poetry.* Palingenesia 11. Wiesbaden: Franz Steiner Verlag, 1977.

Turyn, A. "The Sapphic Ostracon." *Transactions of the American Philological Association* 73 (1942) 308–18.

————. *Studia Sapphica.* Eos suppl. 6. Paris: Leopoli, 1929.

van Erp Taalman Kip, A. M. "Enige interpretatie-problemen in Sappho." *Lampas* 13 (1980) 336–54 [with a brief summary in English].

Vermaseren, Maarten. *The Legend of Attis in Greek and Roman Art.* Leiden: Brill, 1966.

Vermeule, Emily. *Death in Early Greek Art and Poetry.* Berkeley: University of California Press, 1979.

Vernant, J.-P. "Le Mariage." In *Mythe et société en Grèce ancienne,* 62–63. Paris: F. Maspero, 1974.

————. *Myth and Society in Ancient Greece,* translated by Janet Lloyd. New York: Zone Books, 1974.

Vetta, M., ed. *Poesia e simposio nella Grecia antica: guida storica e critica.* Rome: Laterza, 1983.

Voigt, Eva.-Marie, ed. *Sappho et Alcaeus: Fragmenta.* Amsterdam: Athenaeum-Polak and Van Gennep, 1971.

Wackernagel, J. *Vorlesungen über Syntax.* 2 vols. Basel: Emil Birkhäuser, 1926.

Walsh, George. *The Varieties of Enchantment.* Chapel Hill: University of North Carolina Press, 1984.

Ward, Donald. *The Divine Twins: An Indo-European Myth in Germanic Tradition.* Berkeley: University of California Press, 1968.

Weedon, Chris. *Feminist Practice and Poststructuralist Theory.* Oxford: Basil Blackwell, 1987.

Wehrli, F. *Die Schuler des Aristoteles: Texte und Kommentar.* Vol. 1, *Dikaiarchos.* 2nd rev. ed. Basel-Stuttgart: Schwabe, 1967.

Weill, Nicole. "Adoniazousai ou les femmes sur le toit." *Bulletin de Correspondence Hellénique* 90 (1966) 664–98.

Welcker, F. G. *Sappho von einem herrschenden Vorurteil befreyt.* In *Kleine Schriften zur Griechischen Litteraturgeschichte,* 2:80–144. Bonn: Eduard Weber, 1845. [First published as a monograph in Göttingen (1816).]

————. "Über die beiden Oden der Sappho." In *Kleine Schriften,* 4:68–99. Bonn: Eduard Weber, 1861. [First published in *RhM* 11 (1857) 226–59.]

Wender, D. "Plato, Misogynist, Paedophile, and Feminist." *Arethusa* 6 (1973) 75–90.

West, M. L. "Alcmanica." *Classical Quarterly* 15 (1965) 188–202.

————. "Burning Sappho." *Maia* 22 (1970) 307–30.

————. *Greek Lyric Poetry.* Oxford: Oxford University Press, 1993.

————. "Greek Poetry 2000–700 B.C." *Classical Quarterly* 23 (1973) 179–92.

————. "Immortal Helen: An Inaugural Lecture Delivered 30 April 1975." Bedford College, University of London.

————. "Melica." *Classical Quarterly* 20 (1970) 205–15.

————. *Studies in Greek Elegy and Iambus.* Berlin: Walter de Gruyter, 1974.

————, ed. *Hesiod: Theogony.* Oxford: Oxford University Press, 1966.

————, ed. *Iambi et Elegi Graeci ante Alexandrum Cantati.* 2 vols. 2nd rev. ed. Oxford: Oxford University Press, 1989–92.

Westermann, Anton, ed. ΜΥΘΟΓΡΑΦΟΙ: *Scriptores Poeticae Historiae Graeci.* Braunschweig: G. Westermann, 1843.

White, J. W. *The Scholia on the "Aves" of Aristophanes.* Boston: Ginn, 1914.

Whitford, Margaret. *Luce Irigaray: Philosophy in the Feminine.* London: Routledge, 1991.

Whitman, C. H. *Homer and the Heroic Tradition.* Cambridge: Harvard University Press, 1958.

Wigodsky, M. "Anacreon and the Girl from Lesbos." *Classical Philology* 57 (1962) 109.

Wikander, S. *Der arische Männerbund: Studien zur indo-iranischen Sprach- und Religionsgeschichte.* Lund: Ohlsson, 1938.

————. "Nakula et Sahadeva." *Orientalia Suecana* 6 (1957) 66–96.

Wilamowitz-Moellendorf, Ulrich von. "Der Chor der Hagesichora." *Hermes* 32 (1897) 251–63. [Reprinted in his *Kleine Schriften,* 1:209–20 (Berlin: Weidmann, 1935).]

————. "Die griechische Literatur des Altertums." In *Die Kultur der Gegenwart,* vol. 1.8 of U. von Wilamowitz-Moellendorff et al., *Die griechische und lateinische Literatur und Sprache,* edited by P. Hinnenberg. Berlin: Teubner, 1905.

————. *Pindaros.* Berlin: Weidmann, 1922.

————. *Sappho und Simonides: Untersuchungen über griechische Lyriker.* Berlin: Weidmann, 1913.

Will, E. "De l'aspect éthique des origines grecques de la monnaie." *Revue historique* 212 (1954) 209–31.

Will, F. "Sappho and Poetic Motion." *Classical Journal* 61 (1966) 259–62.

Willemen, Paul. "Voyeurism, the Look, and Dworkin." In *Narrative, Apparatus, Ideology: A Film Theory Reader,* edited by Phillip Rosen, 210–18. New York: Columbia University Press, 1986.

Williamson, Margaret. "Eros the Blacksmith." In *Thinking Men: Masculinity and Its Self-Representation in the Classical Tradition,* edited by L. Foxhall and J. Salmon. New York: Routledge, forthcoming.

————. *Sappho's Immortal Daughters.* Cambridge: Harvard University Press, 1995.

Wills, Garry. "The Sapphic 'Umwertung aller Werte.'" *American Journal of Philology* 88 (1967) 434–42.

————. "Sappho 31 and Catullus 51." *Greek, Roman, and Byzantine Studies* 8 (1967) 167–97.

Winkler, John J. *The Constraints of Desire: The Anthropology of Sex in Ancient Greece.* New York: Routledge, 1990.

————. "Double Consciousness in Sappho's Lyrics." In *The Constraints of Desire: The Anthropology of Sex in Ancient Greece,* 162–87. New York: Routledge, 1990.

————. "Gardens of Nymphs: Public and Private in Sappho's Lyrics." In *Reflections of Women in Antiquity,* edited by Helene P. Foley, 63–90. New York: Gordon and Breach, 1981. [Citations above are to the version published in this volume.]

Wirth, P. "Neue Spuren eines Sapphobruchstücks." *Hermes* 91 (1963) 115–17.

Wittig, Monique. "Paradigm." In *Homosexualities and French Literature: Cultural Contexts, Critical Texts,* edited by George Stambolian and Elaine Marks, 114–21. Ithaca: Cornell University Press, 1979.

Wittig, Monique, and Sande Zeig. *Lesbian Peoples: Material for a Dictionary.* New York: Avon, 1979.

Woolf, Virginia. *A Room of One's Own.* 1929. Reprint, San Diego: Harcourt Brace Jovanovich, 1957.

Zeitlin, Froma I. "Configurations of Rape in Greek Myth." In *Rape,* edited by S. Tomaselli and R. Porter, 122–51. Oxford: Blackwell, 1986.

———. "Playing the Other: Theater, Theatricality, and the Feminine in Greek Drama." *Representations,* no. 11 (1985) 63–94.

Zuntz, Günther. "De Sapphus carminibus e3, e4, e5." *Mnemosyne,* ser. 3, 7 (1939) 81–114.

CONTRIBUTORS

Claude Calame is professor of Greek at the University of Lausanne. His interest in modes of poetic enunciation and his curiosity about social and cultural anthropology led him to the study of ritual and symbolic aspects of ancient Greek literature. Among his publications are *Les chœurs de jeunes filles en Grèce archaïque*, 2 vols. (Rome, 1977), translated as *Choruses of Young Women in Ancient Greece* (Lanham, Md., 1995); *Le récit en Grèce ancienne* (Paris, 1986); *Thésée et l'imaginaire athénien* (Lausanne, 1990); *I Greci e l'eros* (Rome, 1992). He has also edited several collected volumes, including *L'amore in Grecia* (Rome/Bari, 1984); *Métamorphoses du mythe en Grèce antique* (Geneva, 1988; and *Figures grecques de l'intermédiaire* (Lausanne/Paris, 1992).

Anne Carson is professor of classics at McGill University. She is the author of *Eros the Bittersweet* (Princeton, 1986), numerous articles on ancient Greek literature, and poetry of her own.

Page duBois is professor of classics at the University of Southern California. Her many publications include *Centaurs and Amazons: Women and the Pre-History of the Great Chain of Being* (Ann Arbor, 1982); *Sowing the Body: Psychoanalysis and Ancient Representation of Women* (Chicago, 1988); *Torture and Truth* (New York, 1990); and *Sappho is Burning* (Chicago, 1995).

Ellen Greene, the editor of this volume, is assistant professor of classics at the University of Oklahoma. She has published articles on gender and sexuality in the poetry of Sappho, Catullus, Propertius, and Ovid. Her book, *Gender, Power, and the Poetics of Desire: Studies in Latin Love Poetry* (forthcoming, Chapel Hill), examines representations of women and the construction of gender in Catullus, Propertius, and Ovid.

Judith P. Hallett, professor of classics at the University of Maryland, College Park, has published widely on Latin language and literature; women, sexuality and the family in classical antiquity; and the classical tradition. In the summer of 1994, she codirected a summer institute for college faculty on "Sappho and Lady Mary Wroth: Major Writers of Classical Antiquity and the English Renaissance," which was funded by the National Endowment for the Humanities.

Giuliana Lanata is a professor at the University of Genoa. In addition to numerous articles, her books include *Poetica preplatonica: testimonianze e frammenti* (Florence, 1963); *Medicina magica e religione popolare* (Rome, 1967); *Gli atti dei martiri come documenti processuali* (Milan, 1973); *Legislazione e natura nelle novelle giustinianee* (Naples, 1984; *Esercizi di memoria* (Bari, 1989); *Processi contro i cristiani negli atti dei martiri* (Turin, 1989); and *Società e diritto nel mondo tardo antico: sei saggi sulle novelle giustinianee* (Turin, 1994).

André Lardinois is assistant professor of classics at the University of Minnesota. His main area of study is early Greek poetry. He coauthored a book, with T. C. W. Oudemans, entitled *Tragic Ambiguity: Anthropology, Philosophy and Sophocles' Antigone* (Leiden, 1987), and he has published several articles on Sappho and Greek tragedy.

Mary R. Lefkowitz is the Andrew W. Mellon Professor in the Humanities at Wellesley College. Her books include *Heroines and Hysterics* (London, 1981); *Women's Life in Greece and Rome,* with Maureen B. Fant (Baltimore, 1982); *Women in Greek Myth* (London, 1986); and most recently *Not Out of Africa* (New York, 1996), and *Black Athena Revisited,* with Guy MacLean Rogers (Chapel Hill, 1996).

Gregory Nagy is the Francis Jones Professor of Classical Greek Literature and professor of comparative literature at Harvard University. He is the author of *The Best of the Achaeans: Concepts of the Hero in Archaic Greek Poetry* (Baltimore, 1979), which won the Goodwin Award of Merit, American Philological Association, in 1982. His most recent book is *Poetry as Performance: Homer and Beyond* (Cambridge, 1996). Earlier publications include *Comparative Studies in Greek and Indic Meter* (Cambridge, Mass., 1974); *Greek Mythology and Poetics* (Ithaca, 1990); and *Pindar's Homer: The Lyric Possession of an Epic Past* (Baltimore, 1990). In July 1994, he became chair of Harvard's classics department.

William Robins is assistant professor of English at the University of Toronto.

Charles Segal is professor of Greek and Latin at Harvard University. He is a fellow of the American Academy of Arts and Sciences and served as president of the American Philological Association for 1993–94. His most recent books are *Euripides and the Poetics of Sorrow* (Durham, N.C., 1993); *Oedipus Tyrannus:*

Tragic Heroism and the Limits of Knowledge (New York, 1993); *Singers, Heroes, and Gods in the Odyssey* (Ithaca, 1994); and *Sophocles' Tragic World: Divinity, Nature, Society* (Cambridge, Mass., 1995).

Marilyn B. Skinner is professor of classics at the University of Arizona. She has published numerous articles on the female poetic tradition in ancient Greece, focusing on Sappho and her successors Corinna, Erinna, and Nossis. She has also published widely on Roman constructions of gender and sexuality, especially in the poetry of Catullus, and is coeditor of the forthcoming essay collection *Roman Sexualities*.

Eva Stehle is associate professor of classics at the University of Maryland. Her interests center on ancient religions, poetry and performance, and women's roles in these areas. Her book, *Performance and Gender in Ancient Greece* (Princeton, 1996), concludes with a chapter on Sappho.

Margaret Williamson is senior lecturer in classical studies at St. Mary's University College, University of Surrey. She has written on various aspects of Greek literature and has assisted with translations of Greek tragedy for the stage. She is the author of *Sappho's Immortal Daughters* (Cambridge, Mass., 1995).

Jack Winkler was professor of classics at Stanford University until his death in 1990. He is the author of *Auctor and Actor: A Narratological Reading of Apuleius' Golden Ass* (Berkeley, 1985) and *Constraints of Desire: The Anthropology of Sex and Gender in Ancient Greece* (New York, 1989). He is coeditor, with David Halperin and Froma Zeitlin, of *Before Sexuality* (Princeton, 1990) and, with Froma Zeitlin, of *Nothing to Do with Dionysos?* (Princeton, 1990).

INDEX

Homer, *Iliad (continued)*
goddesses, 71, 245–46, 250; goddesses' snatching of men, 196; Helen in, 84, 91n10, 196, 261–62; Meleager story, 83; Teichoskopia, 97–98
Odyssey: enchantment of hearers, 74; goddesses, 71, 85–86, 196–97, (*see also* Kalypso; Kirke); Helen in, 84–85; Nausicaa episode, 98–101, 168n91, 169n96; passage of suitors to land of dead, 35–36, 36–38, 45, 53; as solar metaphor, 37; women's role, 85–86, 91
Homeric Hymns, *see under individual hymns by name*
hom(m)osexualité, 178, 263n27
homosexuality
FEMALE: Anacreon on, 128; anxiety, 31–32, 122, 123, 128; attitudes to, 126–29, 143, 146; *hetairai* associated with, 121n30; initiatory function, 120–24; mutuality and reciprocity, 149, 186–87, 242, 244, 246–47, 252–53, 263n27; pedagogic role, 12, 247; practice, evidence in Sappho for, 13, 60, 107, 108–9, 131–32, 142, 144–45, 146–47; in Sappho's circle, 17–18, 60, 120–24; Sappho's feelings of, 122, 123, 132, 142
MALE: age of lovers, 7, 135, 226–32; agonistic model, 186–87, 213n68, 246–47, 251–53, 263n27; ephebic poetry on, 13; initiatory function, 122, 123–24; passive, 127n10, 206n49; pedagogic function, 12; Pindar on, 123, 136; poets', 123, 127; treatment of young men, 123–24, 144, 145–46
Horace, 153, 154; scholiast to, 126
horses, 35, 43, 44–45, 147–48, 251
human/divine hierarchy, 202–10
Hylas and nymphs, 199, 207
hymenaioi, 119, 151, 157
Hymn to Aphrodite, 15, 47, 200n31; Anchises and Aphrodite, 197, 207–9, 216; Eos and Tithonos, 193–94
Hymn to Apollo, 63, 155
Hymn to Pan, 24

hymns, 67–68, 74, 152
Hyperion, 46

Iasion, 197, 209–10
Ibycus, 21, 54, 123, 147; on force of Eros, 15, 229
illiteracy and resistance to patriarchal culture, 188
illusion, 32–33, 73
imagery, male and female, 147, 148, 186
immediacy, dramatic, 240
impersonation of character in poem, 159
impotence of human consorts of goddesses, 195–96, 197, 204n44, 205, 208, 216, 224; lettuce and, 194, 200, 207
incantatory language, 3–4, 58–75; epic poetry and, 61; examples in Sappho, 64–70, 244; juncture of ritual and private, 73–75; language, 58–63; oral performance, 70–73, 75; techniques, (alliteration), 65–66, 67–68, 68–69, (assonance), 65–66, 67, (polysyndeton) 66, 69, (repetition) 66, 67–68, 68–69, 69–70, (rhythm) 64, 66, 67, 68–69, 70n20, 74, 75; see also *thelxis* (enchantment) *and under* Sappho, WORKS
Incert. 16 (Lesbian fragment), 106
incest, 48, 49, 88
Indo-European mythology, 48, 49, 53, 199n31
initiatory function, 120–24, 172n108
institutional force, Sappho's poetry as, 5, 134–35, 136–39, 144, 147
intersubjectivity, 234–35, 242–43
Iragaray, Luce, 176–78, 182, 189, 237; see also *hom(m)osexualité*; *parler femme*
irony, 230–31, 232, 250
isos theoisin (equal to the gods), 31, 32–33, 100–101, 167
Ištar, 54

Jason, 197, 199
jealousy, 30, 31, 33
Jerome, St., 133n31
Joyce, James, 130n20
justice, erotic, 7, 226–32, 243–44

Kaimio, Maarit, 160, 161
kalos inscriptions, 136n46
Kalypso, 47, 85, 196–97, 203–4, 205, 209
Kephalos and Eos, 49, 197, 206n50, 212–15